PRAISE FOR *AMERICAN*

"For the first time a former KGB employe[...] scribe Donald Trump's historic relationship with the Kremlin. It's a bombshell that must be looked into."

—Robert Baer, former CIA operative and author of *See No Evil*

"A must-read. The barrel's plenty hot, and there are Russian shell casings all around."   —*Kirkus Reviews* (starred review)

"I said in 2017 that Trump had more Russian connections than Aeroflot, and *American Kompromat* documents every flight. Trump's loyalty to Russian dictator Vladimir Putin was deeper and more insidious than merely envying his wealth and power. America has removed Putin's puppet from the White House, but the KGB man who controlled him is still in the Kremlin, eager to repeat the success of his greatest operation: President Trump. Read Craig Unger to understand why the danger to American democracy is far from over."

—Garry Kasparov, chairman of the Renew Democracy Initiative and author of *Winter Is Coming: Why Vladimir Putin and the Enemies of the Free World Must Be Stopped*

"By compiling decades of Trump's seedy ties, disturbing and consistent patterns of behavior, and unexplained contacts with Russian officials and criminals, Unger makes a strong case that Trump is probably a compromised, trusted contact of Kremlin interests."

—John Sipher, *The Washington Post*

"Craig Unger has just published a wonderful, well-written book. The jewel in the crown is how the KGB cultivated Donald Trump. With assistance of the eminent former KGB officer Yuri Shvets, *American Kompromat* establishes how it really took place."

—Anders Åslund, senior fellow, Atlantic Council

"Make[s] the unassailable case that Donald J. Trump has been cultivated by Soviet and Russian leaders." —*CounterPunch*

"Craig Unger, who gave us the important books *House of Bush, House of Saud* and *The Fall of the House of Bush*, once again delivers. Unger probes the matter deeply. Indeed, the entire book is meant to serve as the counter-intelligence investigation that was promised by the Mueller Report, but which failed to materialize. Among many useful aspects of this book, *American Kompromat* provides a detailed retelling of that particular disappointment and highlights the role that Attorney General William Barr played in lying to the American public about Mueller's work." —*Journal of Cyber Policy*

"Unger has compiled a mountain of fascinating information, revealing how dark forces, working behind the scenes, attempted to use potentially compromising acts that threatened to drag potential targets down the rabbit hole of betrayal, all in an effort to control our politics. [A] fascinating book." —*Global Geneva*

AMERICAN KOMPROMAT

How the KGB Cultivated
Donald Trump, and Related Tales of
Sex, Greed, Power, and Treachery

CRAIG UNGER

DUTTON

DUTTON

An imprint of Penguin Random House LLC
penguinrandomhouse.com

Previously published as a Dutton hardcover in January 2021
First Dutton trade paperback printing: January 2022

THE LIBRARY OF CONGRESS HAS CATALOGED THE HARDCOVER EDITION OF THIS AS FOLLOWS:

Names: Unger, Craig, author.
Title: American kompromat : how the KGB cultivated Donald Trump, and related
tales of sex, greed, power, and treachery / Craig Unger.
Description: New York : Dutton, 2021. | Includes index.
Identifiers: LCCN 2020042304 (print) | LCCN 2020042305 (ebook) |
ISBN 9780593182536 (hardcover) | ISBN 9780593182550 (ebook)
Subjects: LCSH: Trump, Donald, 1946– Friends and associates. | Trump,
Donald, 1946– Relations with Russians. | Political corruption. | Rich
people—Political activity. | Intelligence service—Russia (Federation) |
United States—Foreign relations—Russia (Federation) |
Russia (Federation)—Foreign relations—United States.
Classification: LCC E913.3 .U53 2021 (print) | LCC E913.3 (ebook) | DDC 973.933092—dc23
LC record available at https://lccn.loc.gov/2020042304
LC ebook record available at https://lccn.loc.gov/2020042305

Dutton trade paperback ISBN: 9780593182543

Printed in the United States of America
1st Printing

CONTENTS

PART ONE

CHAPTER ONE

THE MONSTER PLOT

November 2020

I t had been the worst of times—like in Dickens's *A Tale of Two Cities*, but without the hope and light. It was the age of foolishness, the season of darkness, the winter of despair. America had been on the road to authoritarianism, and the pace had been relentless. There was disorder, chaos, and uncertainty throughout the United States. Democracy had been hanging in the balance, and it was dangling by a thread. The entire country was on tenterhooks, still waiting for the final results.

The nation was polarized in a way that it had not been since the Civil War. A line had been drawn. You were on one side or the other. It was us versus them.

To most of the country, he was vulgar and vile, a misogynistic, racist firebrand, a buffoon who knew only his own pecuniary interests and prejudices and would stop at nothing to satiate them. He was clownish and repellent. But well before the election, it had become clear that he was far more dangerous than that suggested, that his buffoonery masked real demagoguery, that he was a tyrant who had mesmerized tens of millions of people, and that it didn't matter to them what he said or did. He spoke for them. To them, he was a great leader. Even though he had implemented anti-science-based policies that had led to the deaths of hundreds of thousands of Americans, he could do no wrong—thanks to a cult of personality created and aroused by his Trumpian spectacles and amplified by a sycophantic right-wing media. He was America's own autocrat.

Everyone was exhausted. There was widespread unemployment. He had put federal troops in the streets—American soldiers fighting American citizens on American soil. He installed foxes in every bureaucratic henhouse in government. The Russians had undermined the US elections in 2016 and Trump had collaborated with them. Now, everyone was waiting to see what he would do next.

These were the signposts of a new era. Police killed George Floyd, Breonna Taylor, and other unarmed black men and women. White supremacists killed protesters—and were celebrated for it in some quarters. Far-right militias bearing automatic weapons rode in caravans up the West Coast and planted their Confederate flags in front of protesters. In Portland, Oregon, the shooting had begun—teenagers, assault weapons—with the promise of more to come. The Justice Department had designated New York, Portland, and Seattle as "anarchist jurisdictions," as if it were a precursor to declaring martial law. Paranoid conspiracy theories were promoted by QAnon and other right-wing groups. Trump urged his followers to vote twice—once by mail, once in person. He repeatedly refused to promise that he would cede the presidency if Joe Biden won. In the first presidential debate, Trump called on white supremacists—the Proud Boys—to go on standby. It was as if he knew in advance that he would lose the election and was doing everything he could to discredit the results and stay in office. Everything.

He even said as much at a White House press conference in September: "We'll want to have—get rid of the ballots and you'll have a very—we'll have a very peaceful—there won't be a transfer, frankly. There'll be a continuation."[1]

There won't be a transfer.

Fascism was in the air.

Now that the election had taken place, it was more evident than ever. All the votes had not yet been counted, and Joe Biden clearly appeared to be winning, but Donald Trump falsely claimed victory. With so much undecided and the nation in limbo, one thing had become horrifyingly clear: This really *was* America, and it wasn't pretty. One way or another, the nightmare we were living through would likely go on and on.

For months, much of the country had been self-isolated, quarantined, and/or curfewed during the COVID pandemic, the days blending together *Groundhog Day*–style, "a recurring horror show" as Fintan O'Toole wrote in the *Irish Times* in April 2020, "in which all the neuroses that haunt the American subconscious dance naked on live TV."[2]

Time had collapsed. It had no meaning to tens of millions of Americans who stayed home day after day, locked down in semi-isolation. And truth had collapsed as well. News cycles could be measured in nanoseconds, huge parts of them so tainted with disinformation that many viewers were unsure what to believe.

Born with the original sin of slavery, the United States, thanks to a virus, was pulling back the curtain to reveal its dark, dark secrets for all to see—an impossibly decadent shadow world of *kompromat* (the Russian term for compromising material), treachery, sex trafficking, racism, and greed.

Even after the election, a malevolent narcissist was still at the helm, a man who had deliberately infected the nation with a murderous stupidity that was followed blindly by millions of supporters who lived in a cultlike world of paranoid fantasies and magical thinking, blithely spreading the dual virus of Trumpian hate and lethal disease. All this was promoted and amplified by Fox News, Breitbart News, and other right-wing outlets, weaponized by Russian intelligence via social media, and incorporated into paranoid conspiracies by QAnon and other extremist cults.

Under Trump, the entire country had devolved into an authoritarian state in which Trump brazenly used the power of the state to help his electoral chances. Deceit was the new norm. The count of Trump's lies from the *Washington Post*'s "Fact Checker" had passed twenty thousand.[3] And now it was not just any kind of deceit, but lies that were anti-science and free of reason. Lies that killed hundreds of thousands of Americans.

One after another, the institutions and practices Americans had taken for granted—honoring the rule of law, having free and fair elections, the United States Postal Service, congressional oversight, reliable health care information in the face of a deathly pandemic—had been defunded, politicized, weaponized, and compromised so thoroughly that they scarcely existed anymore.

And in the Department of Justice, Attorney General William P. Barr held sway as Trump's chief enabler, granting Trump imperial powers, emasculating Congress, eliminating inspectors general (the guardians of checks and balances) right and left, granting clemency to criminals who played key roles in subverting the 2016 election, and, through phony investigations of Ukraine and Joe Biden, rewriting history so as to exculpate both Donald Trump and Russian president Vladimir Putin.

In effect, as attorney general, Barr, a leading figure in the newly emergent Catholic right—with its ties to Opus Dei, a mysterious fringe sect with roots in fascist Spain—was bringing in a new strain of religious authoritarianism and theocratic nationalism to join forces with Trumpism on their way to collision after collision with the US Constitution. All this in a world of decadence and depravity tied to figures like Jeffrey Epstein and Ghislaine Maxwell, whose pedophile operation trafficked in underage girls as young as eleven, and also had links to Russian intelligence.

This was a war for the soul of America. And at the heart of it all were seemingly simple questions that had never been answered. Indeed, almost absent from the presidential campaign was any discussion of what put Trump in the White House in the first place: Russia.

Even Trump's most stalwart Republican supporters had been stunned at the Helsinki summit in July 2018 when, during a press conference, he kowtowed to Putin and accepted at face value Putin's denial that Russia had interfered in the 2016 US presidential election. Why had Trump thrown American intelligence agencies, all seventeen of them, under the bus and sided with Putin instead? Why did he pull US troops out of Syria—as Putin wished? Why did he cut back on American troops in Germany—as Putin wished? Why did Trump do and say nothing when it was widely reported that Russia was offering bounties to be paid to Afghan troops who killed American soldiers?

How did it come to this? What did the Russians have on him? Could Donald Trump really be a Russian asset?

————

In a *New York Times* op-ed written three months before the 2016 election, the former Central Intelligence Agency director Michael Morell answered that last question in the affirmative, writing, "In the intelligence business, we would say that Mr. Putin had recruited Mr. Trump as an unwitting agent of the Russian Federation."[4] In January 2017, shortly before Donald Trump's inauguration, Michael Hayden, the former head of both the CIA and the National Security Agency, called Mr. Trump "a clear and present danger" to America's national security and "a useful idiot," a term often attributed to Vladimir Lenin that refers to naive Westerners who were especially susceptible to manipulation for propaganda and other purposes.[5] (He later added, "That is actually the most benign explanation I can come up with.")[6]

In December 2017, the former national intelligence director James Clapper asserted that Trump was, in effect, an intelligence "asset"* serving Russian president Vladimir Putin.[7] And in 2019, the former CIA director John Brennan declared Trump to be "wholly in the pocket of Putin" and went further on *Meet the Press*, where he added that he had called Trump's behavior "treasonous, which is to betray one's trust and aid and abet the enemy, and I stand very much by that claim." Far from being partisan left-wing Democrats, these men are intelligence professionals whose analyses are based on factual reality rather than on their political interests.

There are boundaries in America's political discourse—or at least there were until Trump's presidency. There still were taboos. One

———

* Clapper later clarified his remark on CNN: "I am saying this figuratively. I think you have to remember Putin's background. He's a KGB officer. That's what they do. They recruit assets. And I think some of that experience and instinct of Putin has come into play here, and he's managing a pretty important 'account,' if I could use that term, with our president."

simply didn't say that the president of the United States is a Russian asset. And yet, in one form or another, Brennan, Clapper, Hayden, and Morell did precisely that.

Yet somehow these extraordinary allegations—that the president of the United States was an operative for a hostile foreign power—have not been taken seriously enough to become part of the national conversation. It's as if the entire country was in denial—even after Donald Trump's impeachment. Even after the election.

What really happened?

———

The mere suggestion of a Russian asset in the Oval Office calls to mind *The Manchurian Candidate*, the classic 1962 movie depicting brainwashing and mind control as a means for communists to seize power—in other words, the kind of paranoia that is often dismissed as the stuff of wild-eyed conspiracy theorists.

But what if a version of *The Manchurian Candidate*'s nightmarish scenario really did take place, not in the same way, of course, but with Donald Trump? What if the Soviets *had* groomed Trump as an asset who eventually found his way into the White House? What if they had approached Trump long ago—not as someone destined to be president but as one of many assets they carefully cultivated—and somehow or other they had hit the jackpot? What if they had installed an operative in the Oval Office without firing a single shot, executing the most devastatingly effective attack on American sovereignty in plain sight?

Those questions were posed by Glenn Carle, a former CIA national intelligence officer, sometime around January 2016, ten months *before* the presidential election. By that time, Carle was deeply alarmed by the various connections he saw between Trump's team and the Russians, but he wasn't quite sure who to talk to. He had served twenty-three years in the clandestine service, in European, Balkan, and political-military affairs, but now that he was retired and growing organic tomatoes in New England, he no longer had standing in Langley, the headquarters of the Central Intelligence Agency.

"I was really hopping up and down about this," he told me. "I couldn't sit here without telling someone that we're about to have *The Manchurian Candidate* story realized!"

For all the mystique of the CIA, Carle lived in a world very much based on empirical reality, and it was jarring to be thrust into such a shadowy, paranoid universe. Part of the problem was that the question itself was so horrifying, so dire, that no one wanted to take it seriously. The natural response was that this can't be so. That it can't happen here.

Anxious to alert authorities, he reached out to a former ambassador, someone from an oversight committee, and a colleague or two in the agency. Those who were no longer serving in the government shared his alarm when he described his assessment. But no one on the inside responded to him.

Finally, Carle talked to another retired CIA official, someone who was considerably older and who'd had ample experience with Soviet operations. "And he said, 'At end of the 1960s, we were concerned about what we called the Monster Plot.'"

The Monster Plot was a theory propagated by James Jesus Angleton, the famed Cold Warrior and chief of counterintelligence for the CIA from 1954 to 1975, who had become notorious for his obsessive Ahab-like pursuit of the notion that the Soviets had placed an asset at the very top of the CIA or the US intelligence community, and that they would put someone in place at the highest levels of the executive branch.

In the course of his quest, Angleton came to personify a powerful, dark component of American culture, the deranged and paranoid Cold War mole hunter fanatically searching for real or imagined spies planted in the heart of the CIA and deception plots aimed at the American government.

In a country where elemental questions remain unanswered about what the government does behind closed doors, Angleton's dark pursuits suggested a cosmic hole at the center of the American psyche and helped define the genre of spy books and movies including Norman Mailer's *Harlot's Ghost* and Jefferson Morley's biography *The Ghost: The Secret Life of CIA Spymaster James Jesus Angleton* as well as movies such as *The Good Shepherd*.

Few people questioned Angleton's brilliance, but according to a 2011 article in *Studies in Intelligence*, the paranoia that was such an elemental part of his theories paralyzed CIA operations against the Soviets for almost two decades because he "became convinced that the KGB had penetrated CIA at high levels. . . . Angleton took the position that virtually every major Soviet defector or volunteer was a KGB provocation."[8] His studies of a single Soviet defector sometimes went on for ages. In the intelligence academies of the Soviet Union, trainees delighted in studying Angleton because he had paralyzed the CIA for so long.[9]

Though the CIA devoted enormous resources to get to the bottom of it, in the end, Angleton, who died in 1987, came up empty-handed. After decades of analyzing his data, the CIA concluded that his theories were not feasible. He had been wrong.

The Monster Plot was still a sore point with the agency even fifty years later, and as a result, Carle's friend warned him that it had torn apart the agency. Nevertheless, when the call was over, Carle had persuaded him to poke around a bit. After all, it would be surprising if the Russians didn't try to place an asset as high as possible in the American government. There was already plenty of evidence that Russian intelligence had focused enormous amounts of attention on Trump, his family members, and people who had access to him.

Carle's friend made a few calls and finally got back to him.[10] "Times have changed," the old hand said. "It *is* conceivable now."

———

So is Donald Trump a Russian asset?

Yes.

But the way in which it happened is significantly different from the scenario in the Monster Plot postulated by Angleton. Even though Trump's liaison with the KGB (Komitet Gosudarstvennoy Bezopasnosti, or Committee for State Security) started more than forty years ago, what has happened since—namely, the installation of a Russian asset in the White House—is *not* simply the carefully calculated result of one extraordinarily cunning, long-term counterintelligence operation.

It's more complicated than that. "When people start talking about Trump's ties to the KGB or Russian intelligence, some are looking for this super-sophisticated master plan, which was designed decades ago and finally climaxed with Trump's election as president of the United States," said Yuri Shvets, a former major in the KGB who came to the United States and now lives outside Washington, DC.

But what happened with Trump can best be seen as a series of sequential and sometimes unrelated operations that played into one another over more than four decades. According to Shvets, with the Soviets and their Russian successors, standard tradecraft has been to develop assets and data that might not have an immediate payoff but that could offer far more value years or even decades in the future. "That's a big difference between the KGB and some Western HUMINT [human intelligence] agencies," Shvets told me during my first interview in what became an extended series of conversations that began in fall 2019. "The KGB is very patient. It can work a case for years. Americans want results yesterday or maximum today; as a result, they have none. They don't get it—that if you round up nine pregnant women, the baby would not be born within a month. Each process must ripen."

———

The ascent of Donald Trump to the presidency of the United States in 2016 did not take place in a vacuum, nor did his grab for unprecedented executive power that far transcend democratic norms.

Starting back in the Soviet era, the KGB and its successors methodically studied various components of the American body politic and the economic forces behind it—campaign finance, the US legal system, social media, the tech sector, K Street lobbyists, corporate lawyers, and the real estate industry—and exploited every loophole they could find. In the end, they began subverting one institution after another that was designed to provide checks and balances to safeguard our democracy, including our elections, our executive branch, the Department of Justice, and the intelligence sector.

For the most part, the American media covered the Trump–Russia scandal as if it were a series of major criminal inquiries—following the investigations, prosecutions, and trials of Paul Manafort, Roger Stone, Michael Cohen, and other Trump associates; the Mueller Report; Trump's impeachment and no-witness acquittal in the Senate; and all the rest.

But the investigation began as a counterintelligence investigation, not a criminal probe, and therein lies the problem. Successful intelligence operations often have far higher stakes than ordinary crimes. After all, paying hush money to a porn star out of campaign finances is illegal and can result in jail time, as it did for former Trump lawyer Michael Cohen. But it pales in significance to installing a Russian asset in the Oval Office. And, believe it or not, that may be perfectly legal.

That's because, as the KGB and its successor agencies know all too well, intelligence operations are designed to operate *within* the law, which, thanks to lax regulations, lax enforcement, and the very nature of counterintelligence, has given the Russians plenty of latitude. After all, this is a country in which laundering massive amounts of money through anonymously purchased real estate can be done with virtually no risk. It is a country in which it's possible to take money from Russian intelligence, to establish communications with Russian intelligence, and, in effect, to be a Russian asset without breaking the law. It is a country in which the Russians can hire highly paid attorneys as lobbyists, who just happen to have access to loads of important secrets, and use them to get what they want.

When one thinks about it like that—as an intelligence operation rather than as individual crimes—suddenly the interactions of Trump surrogates and Trump himself with dozens of Soviet émigrés, Russian mafiosi, businessmen, and the like over forty years can be seen in an entirely different light, not so much as crimes but as part of standardized intelligence operations that served to bring Trump into the KGB's fold, that tested him to see if he was worth cultivating, that compromised him through lucrative money-laundering schemes, sycophantic flattery, pie-in-the-sky Trump Tower Moscow projects, extravagantly well-paid franchising projects, and more. Hundreds of articles have been written about Trump's ties to oligarchs like Aras Agalarov and his son, Emin, who promoted the Trump-owned Miss Universe pageant in Moscow in 2013; about campaign manager Paul Manafort, who had received $75 million from pro-Putin oligarchs and whose chief assistant, Konstantin Kilimnik, was an operative for Russian military intelligence; about Trump's highly lucrative deals with the Bayrock Group, a real estate development firm run by Soviet émigrés; and about so much more.

And many, if not all of those transactions, must be viewed not just as dubious financial deals with formerly Soviet entities, but as part of a long, ongoing Russian intelligence operation.

Indeed, during the 2016 election cycle, the Russian Federation's Federal Security Service, or FSB, the Russian successor to the Soviet KGB, found plenty of ways to subvert America's elections without breaking the law. There was nothing illegal, for example, about naturalized American citizens like the Odessa-born billionaire oligarch Len Blavatnik and his businesses contributing millions to Mitch McConnell's GOP Senate Leadership Fund and to the Republican Senatorial Campaign Committee, as he did in 2016.

In addition, vitally important contacts between Russian intelligence and the Trump campaign took place in plain sight without attracting undue attention—as happened in April 2016 at a major foreign policy event for the Trump campaign at Washington's Mayflower Hotel, hosted by the Center for the National Interest (CNI), a conservative foreign policy think tank led by Dimitri Simes, who served as an informal foreign policy adviser to the Trump operation.

The Russian-born Simes himself is curious figure who served as a foreign policy adviser to Richard Nixon and whose career includes prestigious posts at various universities and think tanks—Columbia University, the Paul S. Nitze School of Advanced International Studies at Johns Hopkins, the University of California at Berkeley, and the Carnegie Endowment for International Peace—as well as being head of CNI and publisher of its foreign policy bimonthly magazine, the *National Interest*.

The Mueller Report concluded that Simes was not working for the Kremlin, but it noted that Simes and CNI had "many contacts with current and former Russian government officials." Michael Carpenter, the managing director of the Penn Biden Center for Diplomacy and Global Engagement and a foreign policy adviser on Russia to Vice President Joe Biden, told me, "It's very transparent what [Simes's] agenda is. He is completely pro-Kremlin and always has been."[11]

Others went further and described Simes as "an agent of the Kremlin embedded into the American political elite," as Yuri Felshtinsky did in a 2018 article on Gordon, a Russian-language site in Ukraine.[12]

To make his case, Felshtinsky reported that Simes, through CNI, organized meetings between high-level officials at the Federal Reserve and the US Department of the Treasury with Maria Butina, who was later arrested on espionage charges and pleaded guilty to a felony charge of conspiring to influence US politics. Felshtinsky is the coauthor—with Alexander Litvinenko, the FSB lieutenant colonel who died of polonium poisoning—of *Blowing Up Russia*, about how the state security apparatus seized power in Russia.

Simes's ties to his motherland go back to Soviet days, and when Putin won power, he took the bit and became a wholehearted supporter. But in *Politico*, Ben Smith wrote that by 2011, Simes had embarrassed the Richard Nixon Family Foundation–funded CNI because he had become an apologist for Putin and attacked Senator John McCain for denouncing Russia's invasion of Georgia.[13]

Along similar lines, Yuri Shvets told me that when he was still in the KGB, he crossed paths with Simes at the press center of the Ministry of Foreign Affairs (MFA) in Moscow and wanted to recruit him on the spot. "I saw Simes, and he was always lonely," said Shvets. "Americans didn't talk to him. Soviets didn't talk to him."

Shvets discussed the matter with his superior, who wanted to check it out with headquarters. "And the next day, he calls me saying, 'Stand down. He's being taken care of,'" Shvets told me. Translation: There was no need to recruit Simes because he was already a contact of the KGB. Similarly, in an interview for this book with researcher Olga Lautman, General Oleg Kalugin, the former head of counterintelligence for the KGB, recalled running into Simes at an event in Washington after Kalugin had defected to the United States in 1995.

As Kalugin saw it, Simes had been avoiding him most of the evening, so he finally went up to Simes and was shocked by what he heard.

"You're a traitor," Simes told Kalugin.

"I was no longer connected with the KGB," Kalugin said. "That's why he called me 'traitor.'"

When Donald Trump appeared at the Mayflower Hotel under Simes's auspices to put forth his first formal presentation of his foreign policy, the media portrayed the event as precisely that: a Republican Party presidential candidate putting forth his foreign policy objectives. But in fact the event had been orchestrated by Simes, who, according to Shvets, Kalugin, and Felshtinsky's report, was working for Russian intelligence. According to documents released by the Senate Intelligence Committee in August 2020, Simes testified before the Senate that this was where he introduced Donald Trump to Russian ambassador to the United States Sergey Kislyak for the first time.

Trump may not have been doing anything illegal at the Mayflower, but the Russians were there and in a position to expose him.

That was kompromat.

That was how it worked. The press covered the event as something that was completely normal. In fact, nothing illegal was taking place. Nevertheless, Russian intelligence had essentially hijacked Trump's foreign policy in plain sight and nobody noticed.

Neither Simes, who has subsequently relocated to Moscow, nor the Center for the National Interest returned my phone calls.

In a similar vein, there was nothing unlawful about the president's son Donald Trump Jr. accepting an honorarium of $50,000 plus, as the *Wall Street Journal* reported, to give a speech at the Ritz Hotel in Paris on October 11, 2016, just one month before the election, sponsored by the Center of Political and Foreign Affairs (CPFA), a French think tank.[14]

But Don Jr.'s appearance takes on a different hue when one considers that the CPFA "was assessed by French intelligence to be a front organization and influence operation for Russian intelligence services to promote Russian policies in the Middle East," as former CIA officer Glenn Carle told me.

The couple in charge consisted of the CPFA cofounder Fabien Baussart, who had nominated Vladimir Putin for the Nobel Peace Prize, and his wife, Randa Kassis, a former model from Syria who has supported Russian intervention in Syria and cooperation with Bashar al-Assad's regime.

Both Baussart and Kassis "are openly linked with the Russians," Renaud Girard, a French journalist who served as the moderator, told ABC News. "They don't hide it at all."[15] ABC cited French news reports describing Kassis as a Syrian-born activist who had met regularly with senior Kremlin officials seeking Russian support for her position.

According to the *Wall Street Journal*, Kassis said she told Donald Trump Jr. that it was essential to cooperate with Russia in the Middle East. "We have to be realistic. Who's on the ground in Syria? Not the U.S., not France," she explained. "Without Russia, we can't have any solution in Syria."[16]

Immediately after talking with him, she flew to Moscow, where she met with Foreign Minister Sergei Lavrov, with whom, *The Guardian* reported, she is good friends.[17] Shortly afterward, the Ministry of Foreign Affairs issued statements about Don Jr.'s speech. As Kassis explained in a Facebook post, "I succeeded to pass [to] Trump, through the talks with his son, the idea of how we can cooperate together to reach the agreement between Russia and the United States on Syria."

"The Russian MFA echoing a political line that the Russian intelligence service is planting in ostensibly aboveboard events like the Paris dinner fits the classic pattern of Russian disinformation and intelligence-driven propaganda," Glenn Carle told me. "The participants are tools or dupes of Russian intelligence."

He added that in terms of national security, the Paris meeting alone "would suffice to make Don Jr. someone you could never trust or touch for an intelligence service.

"That does not make Donald Trump Jr. a spy," he said. "But to an intelligence officer, if such exploitation is repeated over and over, it *does* make them a de facto asset of Russian intelligence, whatever the individual may believe."

After all, Don Jr. was being paid by operatives close to Russian intelligence who wanted his father, as president, to implement policies favorable to Russia.

In terms of criminal prosecution, it is highly probable that there would be no criminal case to make against Don Jr. "It's not illegal," said Carle. "You can't get a conviction in a court, so that is taken by the journalists and the public as proof of their innocence. You're innocent unless you're guilty. But that's not true in intelligence."

Understanding that, as well as exploiting those loopholes, was a key tenet of KGB tradecraft and, later, of its successors in Russian intelligence. So when it came to laundering billions of dollars through real estate, lax regulations allowed buyers to keep their anonymity. That, in turn, gave developers like Donald Trump license to say that he had no clue who the buyers *really* were or how they'd made their money. And if he had no knowledge that the money in question was illicit, he was not culpable. It was as simple as that.

Discovering how and why all that happened means investigating a cut-rate electronics store in Manhattan that was really controlled by the KGB in the 1980s, and reporting, for the first time, that the owner, Semyon Kislin, was allegedly a "spotter agent" for the legendary Soviet spy agency who had opened the door to cultivating Donald Trump as a Soviet asset. It means examining a huge Soviet spy nest at the United Nations during the so-called spy wars of that period, and revealing that another one of the Soviets who first reached out to Trump was also an alleged KGB operative who, more than twenty years later, went to extraordinary lengths to camouflage the real "origin story" of how the KGB developed Donald Trump as a Soviet asset.

It means exploring what happened at KGB counterintelligence headquarters in Yasenevo, outside Moscow, in 1987, where the Active Measures directorate distributed a memo celebrating the first successful active measure—a disinformation operation in which a freshly groomed asset broadcast KGB talking points in major American newspapers—seeing that the asset in question was none other than Donald Trump.

My book will show how kompromat works by examining Jeffrey Epstein's pedophile sex-trafficking operation, where he got his money from, his links to Israeli intelligence and to Robert Maxwell, Ghislaine Maxwell's father, who worked so closely with the KGB. Similarly, it will look into how Russian intelligence penetrated Epstein's operation and placed within it Russian nationals who infiltrated the highest level of Silicon Valley and America's tech sector as part of Vladimir Putin's assault on America.

It will delve into Epstein's fifteen-year friendship with Donald Trump, the women with whom they consorted, and how their friendship ended, Epstein's ties to the super pimps whose modeling agencies supplied girls for Russian oligarchs—and kompromat for Russian intelligence.

It will show how William Barr, during his first term as attorney general, under George H. W. Bush, opened the door, inadvertently perhaps, to Russian espionage activities in 1991. And it will show how nearly thirty years later, Barr and his associates in the new Catholic right, some of whom have ties to Opus Dei, came to play such a huge role in both the Department of Justice and the Supreme Court, and how Barr, as Trump's attorney general, helped undermine the rule of law.

———

One might think questions of Trump's ties to Russia would have been fully addressed by now. After all, the Trump–Russia scandal began to unravel almost immediately after his inauguration. Indeed, less than a month after Trump became president, on February 13, 2017, he got rid of National Security Advisor Michael Flynn for lying about his ties to the Russians. The very next day, Trump urged FBI director James Comey *not* to investigate Flynn. "I hope you can see your way clear to letting this go, to letting Flynn go. He is a good guy. I hope you can let this go," said Trump.[18]

According to the Mueller Report, "The circumstances of the conversation show that the President was asking Comey to close the FBI's investigation into Flynn."

But Comey refused to do the president's bidding—which would have breached the invisible firewall between the executive branch and the FBI—so on May 9, 2017, Trump fired him, too, and then told the world that the entire Trump–Russia thing was a hoax. As he explained to Lester Holt on NBC just two days later, "I said to myself, I said, 'You know this Russia thing with Trump and Russia is a made-up story.'" He insisted that there was no special relationship between himself and the Russians.

However, on May 10, the day after he fired Comey, Trump had already set about to make sure his Russian friends were happy and met privately in the Oval Office with Russia's foreign minister Sergei Lavrov and US ambassador Sergey Kislyak. As the *Washington Post* noted, even though this unusual meeting with two top Russian officials took place at the seat of American power, no American reporters or photographers were invited.[19] The only journalist present was the photographer for TASS, the official Russian news agency. President Trump had decided to keep out the American media because he said they reported "fake news," and instead invited *Russian* state news—in fact, the very same outlet whose reporters, such as Yuri Shvets, often did double duty as intelligence officers spying on America.

The presence of Ambassador Kislyak was also unusual in that he was a key figure in the Trump–Russia investigation and had been present in the secret meetings with former national security advisor Flynn, who pleaded guilty to lying to the FBI. "I just fired the head of the F.B.I.," Trump told Lavrov and Kislyak.[20] "He was crazy, a real nut job. I faced great pressure because of Russia. That's taken off."

Then, according to current and former US officials, the president proceeded to reveal highly classified intelligence to Lavrov and Kislyak that reportedly jeopardized an important source of information on the Islamic State. The information came from an intelligence-sharing partner that had not given the US permission to share it with Russia. A knowledgeable US official told the *Washington Post* that the intelligence was classified at one of the highest levels used by American spy agencies as "code-word information." Trump, he said, "revealed more information to the Russian ambassador than we have shared with our own allies."[21]

And when Trump insisted that the pressure from the Russian probe had been "taken off," he was being a bit too optimistic. Firing Comey had not ended the investigation; it merely triggered the appointment of Robert Mueller as the special counsel who was mandated to take over the Comey probe. Specifically, the one-page document signed by Deputy Attorney General Rod Rosenstein said, "The Special Counsel is authorized to conduct the investigation confirmed by then-FBI Director James B. Comey in testimony before the House Permanent Select Committee on Intelligence on March 20, 2017."

Comey had been reasonably clear in articulating the nature of the investigation when he testified before the House Intelligence Committee in March. "The FBI," he told the committee, "as part of our counterintelligence mission, is investigating the Russian government's efforts to interfere in the 2016 presidential election, and that includes investigating the nature of any links between individuals associated with the Trump campaign and the Russian government and whether there was any coordination between the campaign and Russia's efforts."

And if that is not clear enough, acting FBI director Andrew McCabe was more specific. "We opened this case in May 2017 because we had information that indicated a national security threat might exist, specifically a counterintelligence threat involving the president and Russia," McCabe told the *New York Times*.[22]

———

The difference between counterintelligence and criminal investigations is not some minor legal distinction. It's fundamental. Criminal investigations are intended to lead toward prosecution; counterintelligence are not. Instead, they are undertaken to thwart an adversary's spying, espionage, or sabotage—the adversary in this case, of course, being Russia.

Even though they are not about breaking the law per se, counterintelligence investigations may well involve issues that are far more serious than criminal probes. In this case, the point of a counterintelligence investigation was to protect the United States from Russian interference in America's elections. From cyberwarfare. From disinformation. From Russian assets who had been groomed for years, perhaps decades, and were finally in place to do real damage to vital American institutions.

And yet when the Mueller Report was published, the only part of it dealing with counterintelligence was one solitary paragraph, saying that the FBI "embedded personnel at the Office who did not work on the Special Counsel's investigation, but whose purpose was to review the results of the investigation and to send—in writing—summaries of foreign intelligence and counterintelligence information to FBIHQ and FBI Field Offices. Those communications and other correspondence between the Office and the FBI contain information derived from the investigation, not all of which is contained in this Volume."

And that was it.

When Mueller was first appointed and the Republicans held both houses of Congress, tens of millions of Americans had put their faith in him, with his anvil jaw and his Boy Scout–like reputation for rectitude, as a new American hero, ready to ride in on his steed and restore the rule of law. Who better than Mueller to finally rein in an increasingly sociopathic president who was acting more and more like Putin's puppet?

But now that Mueller had delivered, there was no counterintelligence investigation. People at the highest levels of law enforcement were stunned. "I expected that issue [the counterintelligence threat involving President Trump and Russia] and issues related to it would be fully examined by the special counsel team," Andrew McCabe told the *Times*. "If a decision was made not to investigate those issues, I am surprised and disappointed. I was not aware of that."

Countless hats and T-shirts had trumpeted, "It's Mueller Time!," only to wind up in the remainder bin.[23] What America got instead was Mueller Lite.

In the end, of course, the Mueller probe produced enormous amounts of evidence regarding *criminal* activities that led to the indictment of thirty-four individuals and three companies. Ten men pleaded guilty or were convicted of crimes, including seven Trump associates— namely, Trump campaign manager Paul Manafort, campaign aide Rick Gates, National Security Advisor Michael Flynn, campaign aide George Nader, confidant Roger Stone, adviser George Papadopoulos, and Trump attorney/fixer Michael Cohen.

But as damning as such convictions were, the Stormy Daniels charges and other Mueller indictments were nothing compared with the grave national security threat presented by Trump's close relationship to Putin and Russian intelligence. So the Mueller Report simply omitted—or perhaps buried—the counterintelligence investigation it had been mandated to do.

The investigation into Trump's well-documented four-decade relationship with the Russian Mafia, a de facto state actor, and Russian intelligence, and all the financial transactions between them, was nowhere to be found. As Adam Schiff (D-CA), chairman of the House Intelligence Committee, told the *Washington Post*, "Just as a reminder, this all began as an FBI counterintelligence investigation into whether people around then-candidate Trump were acting as witting or unwitting agents of a foreign power. So it began as a counterintelligence investigation, not as a criminal investigation.[24]

"It may not be a crime for a candidate for president to seek to make money from a hostile foreign power during an election and mislead the country about it," he added. "But the counterintelligence concerns go beyond mere violation of criminal law. They're at one time not necessarily a criminal activity and at the same time potentially far more serious than criminal activity because you have the capacity to warp U.S. policy owing to some form of compromise."

All of which calls to mind journalist Michael Kinsley's long-held maxim: The real scandal isn't what's illegal; it's what *is* legal. Sometimes the most egregious and corrupt wrongdoings are perfectly lawful. And that is particularly true when it comes to intelligence operations.

A serious counterintelligence investigation, then, would presumably have asked how the KGB began its relationship with Trump and whether Trump had been compromised first by the Soviets and later by Russia. It would have asked how deeply Trump was indebted to the Russian Mafia, because he had made a fortune laundering millions of dollars from former Soviets through his real estate. How much business had he done with operatives of Russian intelligence and/or the Russian Mafia? Did Russia have kompromat on Trump? Was he a Russian asset? How far back did his relationship go? How much did he make laundering money for them? What about other members of his family, the Trump administration and campaign, other politicians?

What follows is an attempt to answer some of those questions, based on interviews with more than a dozen former officers from the KGB, the CIA, and the FBI; several friends and associates of Jeffrey Epstein and Ghislaine Maxwell; officers, priests, and members of Opus Dei; former officials at the Department of Justice; lawyers at white-shoe Washington law firms; and thousands of pages of FBI investigations, police investigations, and articles on the Internet in English, Russian, and Ukrainian.

My book will answer some of those questions by telling how a relatively insignificant targeting operation by the KGB's New York *rezidentura* (New York station) long ago—an attempt to cultivate an influential businessman as a new asset—triggered a sequence of intelligence protocols that morphed into the greatest intelligence bonanza in history. It will tell how, more than four decades ago, Trump made contact with a suspected KGB operative when he bought hundreds of TV sets from a Soviet electronics store in Manhattan that was a KGB front. It will tell how, in 1987, Trump was named by the KGB's Service A, the Active Measures directorate, as an operational asset carrying out a so-called active measure by spouting KGB talking points as propaganda in the American press. ("Active measures" is a term used by Soviet and Russian security services for conducting political warfare via disinformation, propaganda, the fabrication of counterfeit official documents, and the establishment of front organizations, assassinations, and political repression, among other means.)

And it will show that Natalia Dubinina, daughter of the late Soviet ambassador to the United Nations and United States, Yuri Dubinin, allegedly worked for the KGB when she was employed at the UN's Dag Hammerskjöld Library and first met Donald Trump. It will show that on November 9, 2016, the day after Trump's election, the Russian newspaper *Moskovsky Komsomolets* published a strange interview with Natalia Dubinina about her contacts with Trump in 1986 that, upon closer examination, appears to be an active measure intended to disguise the origins of Trump's ties to the KGB. And it will show that, in September 1987, Donald Trump, allegedly a newly cultivated asset, took out full-page ads in the *Washington Post, New York Times,* and *Boston Globe* that had disseminated KGB talking points, an event that called for a celebratory memo to be circulated at First Chief Directorate's headquarters on the perimeter of Moscow.

It will also tell the story of how William Barr helped cover up Trump's alliance with Russia and facilitated the ongoing Trump-Russia operation by inflating the powers of the presidency, with the aid of his fellow law firm partners, many of whom had represented Russian interests and some of whom, like Barr himself, are tied to Opus Dei. It will examine how the Jeffrey Epstein–Ghislaine Maxwell sex-trafficking operation provided a source and marketplace for the dirty little secrets of the richest and most powerful men in the world, and how Russian intelligence may have penetrated the Epstein-Maxwell ring and used it to infiltrate the highest levels of Silicon Valley and the worlds of artificial intelligence, supercomputers, and the Internet.

And finally, my book will examine how, before, during, and after the 2020 presidential campaign, with the COVID-19 pandemic ravaging America, killing more than 250,000 people and infecting more than 12 million, Trump began shutting down oversight of the corruption throughout his administration as he fired one inspector general after another; spreading false information about the pandemic that led to more COVID deaths in the United States than anywhere else in the world; destabilizing the United States Postal Service to make the vote-by-mail operation seem unreliable at a time when in-person voting was likely to be dangerous; and having Attorney General Barr put forth the most autocratic interpretation of the doctrine of the "unitary executive" imaginable, thereby clearing the way for Trump and his cronies to ignore subpoenas, seize Congress's power of the purse, destroy congressional oversight, end the rule of law, and take on powers that threatened to end American democracy.

CHAPTER TWO

THE SPOTTER

According to Yuri Shvets, the former high-ranking officer in the KGB, the Soviet spy agency first got its foot in the door more than forty years ago and began cultivating Donald Trump as a prospective asset. Shvets described to me in great detail elements of a long-term series of intelligence tasks and procedures that comprised what was arguably the most successful intelligence operation in history—ending up with a Russian asset in the White House as president of the United States. Of course, many important questions remain unanswered. But in the end, what is now known strongly suggests that Donald Trump was first approached by the Soviet Union's KGB by 1980, was compromised by its agents repeatedly over the ensuing decades, and has behaved as a Russian asset since, most obviously after he became president.

The exact date is unclear, but the operation began after Trump, about thirty years old at the time, launched plans to take over the enormous and decrepit Commodore Hotel adjacent to New York City's Grand Central Terminal in 1976 and convert it into the Grand Hyatt New York.

The Grand Hyatt, which opened in 1980, was the first big score for Trump, then a brash real estate developer from Queens determined to make his mark across the river in Manhattan. How Trump, under the tutelage of attorney Roy Cohn, the Mafia lawyer and dark satanic prince of the McCarthy era, cashed in countless political favors has been widely reported, including how he got the inside fix on insanely generous tax abatements and the like. Trump, who had paid only one dollar for the option to buy the dilapidated monstrosity, made an immense fortune with the project and was put on the path to becoming a national figure.[1]

For all that, one rather banal, obscure, and incidental detail in the development of the Grand Hyatt may be the key to unraveling the mystery of Donald Trump's ties to Russian intelligence. That detail is the reported purchase by Trump of hundreds of television sets for the new hotel from Semyon "Sam" Kislin, a Ukrainian Jew who emigrated from Odessa in 1972 and co-owned a small electronics store in New York.

Kislin's store, Joy-Lud Electronics, was located at 200 Fifth Avenue at Twenty-Third Street, an intersection best known for its proximity to the iconic Flatiron Building and Madison Square Park. Today, the sixteen-story building, which was once the site of the luxurious Fifth Avenue Hotel, is best known as the location for Eataly, the massive marketplace for *risotto al tartuffo* and various other Italian delicacies. Not a trace remains of Joy-Lud Electronics, which was located there in the eighties, when the building was known as the International Toy Center and provided a home for dozens of businesses in the toy industry.

Manhattan at the time was awash with cut-rate electronics stores such as 47th Street Photo and Crazy Eddie ("His prices are IN-SA-A-A-A-A-ANE!" went the late-night-TV pitch) selling every electronic gadget imaginable. But Joy-Lud proclaimed its distinctiveness with a sign on its front door proudly asserting, "We speak Russian." Consequently, Kislin's store, which he co-owned with Tamir Sapir, another Soviet émigré, carved out a unique niche among the only people allowed to travel abroad under the Soviet system: diplomats, KGB officers, and Politburo members, all of whom bought their electronic equipment there before returning to the Soviet Union.

The reason for Joy-Lud's popularity among the Soviets wasn't solely that they were Russophones. It also had to do with technical specifications. Unlike American television, Soviet TV employed the PAL and SECAM technical standards, which were widely used in Europe and Russia. (The US standard is known as NTSC.) That meant conventional American sets were worthless in the Soviet Union. At the same time, when Soviet diplomats, businessmen, and spies—and there were hundreds of them—returned to the USSR, no one wanted to be empty-handed when it came to having the latest videocassette recorder—be it VHS or Betamax.

Kislin's Joy-Lud filled that niche. "For every espionage agent in the United States who had spent four or five years in this country and was returning back to Moscow, it was a must to bring back a TV set," said Yuri Shvets, who was familiar with the store when he served in the KGB's Washington station in the mid-eighties. "But you couldn't buy a TV set in a regular American store which would work in Moscow. The only place was Kislin's."

As a result, their largely Soviet clientele was known as "vacuum cleaners," a moniker bestowed on officials, émigrés, and tourists who hoovered up vast quantities of electronic equipment and consumer goods to take back to the Soviet Union. As soon as their planes from Moscow landed at John F. Kennedy International Airport, throngs of Soviets asked to be taken to the store, and not merely because its walls were covered with autographed pictures of celebrated Soviet singers, writers, athletes, and cosmonauts who had been customers; Kislin and his partner had learned how to curry favor with the powers that be.[2] "They had special refund policies for the elite," said a Soviet émigré who was familiar with the store. "They would accept the unwanted equipment even without its packaging and give them something else—no questions asked."

For Soviet customers, it also wasn't just techno lust for the latest new gadgets, which, of course, wouldn't be available in the Soviet Union for eons. There was also their resale value. As the New York Times reported, a video camera that cost $1,000 at Kislin's store could be resold in the Soviet Union for forty times the average monthly Soviet salary. "They could buy a videotape recorder here, sell it in Russia, and buy a house," said Kislin's partner, Sapir, who died in 2014.[3] Sony Trinitron TVs, VHS and Betamax videotape players, and Nikon cameras flew off the shelves, ready for resale on the Soviet black market.

At the store, Kislin and Sapir had brilliantly positioned themselves to win over Soviet bigwigs as clients, running into, as Sapir did, a boyhood friend from the old country who surfaced as bodyguard to Soviet foreign minister Eduard Shevardnadze, once the longtime KGB chief in the Soviet Republic of Georgia. Others who came by included Foreign Minister Andrei Gromyko; future KGB counterintelligence chief and, subsequently, prime minister, Yevgeny Primakov; and Georgy Arbatov, the Kremlin's American-based media spokesman.[4]

But one such client didn't quite fit in with the rest—Donald J. Trump.

Many details about Trump's transaction with Kislin are not known. In fact, Kislin himself seems to be the only source of it, having told *Bloomberg Businessweek* in 2017 that he "had sold Trump about 200 televisions on credit."

According to *Bloomberg Businessweek*, Trump, who later developed a reputation for stiffing his vendors, made sure he paid Kislin on time. "I gave [Trump] 30 days, and in exactly 30 days he paid me back," Kislin said. "He never gave me any trouble."[5]

But there was more to it than that.

————

Semyon Kislin was born in 1935 in Odessa, the Ukrainian seaport on the shore of the Black Sea, which had been notorious as a haven for Jewish gangsters and thugs, as depicted by the great Russian writer Isaac Babel a generation earlier in *The Odessa Tales*. There, Kislin became well known for running what Ukrainians called "popular deli number one . . . the best in Odessa."[6]

Situated on Odessa's renowned Deribasovskaya Street near the Passage, an elegant and baroque market adjacent to the Gorodskoy Sad (City Garden), the store was so celebrated and the family did so well, according to Kislin's wife, Ludmila, that they were able to afford a car with a full-time personal driver,[7] an extraordinary luxury in the impoverished Soviet Union.*

————

* Deribasovskaya Street appeared once again in the world of Trump, thanks to *Weather Is Good on Deribasovskaya, It Rains Again on Brighton Beach,* a 1993 Russian screwball comedy about the Russian Mafia in which art prefigures life. The movie is about diplomatic meetings between the president of the United States and the general

Under Soviet communism, of course, there was no private owner-ship of businesses, but running a food store was a highly favored posi-tion nonetheless. Thanks to chronic food shortages throughout the Soviet Union, up to 40 percent of all foodstuff passed through the black market, providing plenty of opportunity for corruption.[8]

In that context, former KGB officer Yuri Shvets told me, it was im-possible to successfully navigate such corrupt precincts without being wired in with the powers that be—and in the end, that meant working with the KGB. "For a Jewish guy to run a fresh produce store back then was like walking on a minefield," said Shvets.[9] "This was a time when the KGB was going after people to get information. It would be inevi-table that the director of a large grocery story in Odessa would be re-cruited by the KGB."

Shvets should know. When I first met him, in October 2019 at a steak house in Tysons Corner, Virginia, about ten miles outside Wash-ington, DC, he was wearing a sport jacket and jeans, no tie, and looked younger than his sixty-seven years.

In the mid-eighties, Shvets identified himself as a Washington cor-respondent for the Soviet news agency TASS. But that job was merely a cover. Shvets's real career was working in counterintelligence for the KGB, a position that afforded him access to highly sensitive materials. He was there to recruit American spies.

Shvets's tenure with the KGB in Washington in the mid-eighties happened to coincide with the period during which the KGB had be-gun to keep an increasingly close eye on Donald Trump through the New York *rezidentura* (station), the sister outpost to Shvets's home of-fice in Washington. As a result, Shvets had decades of hands-on expe-rience with KGB tradecraft and the protocols it used to recruit new spies, personal acquaintance with the KGB's top brass, and an under-standing of disinformation, the use of compromising materials, and various other ruses employed by Russian intelligence to throw West-ern observers off the trail. Thanks to his experience there, he was able

---

secretary of the Soviet Union being put at risk, thanks to various crimes by the Russian Mafia. The movie features casino scenes shot at Trump's Taj Mahal in Atlantic City.

to state confidently that Donald Trump had been cultivated as an asset for the KGB.

According to Shvets, Kislin was recruited on the eve of his emigration from the Soviet Union in 1972 by the Odessa field office of the KGB, which had a special "Jewish department" to oversee the recruitment of Jews from Odessa who wanted to emigrate from the Soviet Union. "I spoke to a two-star general who had worked there at the time," Shvets told me, "and he said many of the Jews who were immigrating signed papers saying they would cooperate with the KGB. It was almost an ultimatum. If you want to immigrate, you agree to cooperate. You sign the pledge to cooperate with the KGB. And Kislin was one of those recruited."

In an email to me, Kislin denied that he had any such relationship. "My family and I emigrated as Jewish refugees," he wrote. "There was no agreement with any entity tied to the USSR."

But Shvets was not alone in asserting that the Soviets had introduced subterfuge into the way they sometimes allowed oppressed Soviet Jews to immigrate to Israel and the United States. The strategy was brilliantly designed to exploit legislation sponsored by Senator Henry M. "Scoop" Jackson (D-WA) and Representative Charles A. Vanik (D-OH), who were concerned about the plight of Soviet Jews who weren't being allowed to leave the country.

In a nutshell, the Jackson–Vanik Amendment to the Trade Act of 1974 allowed the Soviet Union to enjoy normal trade relations with the United States, but *only* if Jewish refugees were allowed to emigrate. Which turned out to be exactly what the Soviets wanted. General Oleg Kalugin explained how then–KGB chief Yuri Andropov, who later led the USSR as general secretary of the Communist Party of the Soviet Union, reached out to him for advice about Jackson–Vanik. "I was summoned to Andropov's office and asked if I had any ideas of what to do about this," Kalugin recalled.[10]

While many saw the amendment as a move to force the Soviets to recognize human rights—and that was its intention—Kalugin saw it as a great opportunity for the KGB. "First, I said, we should choose a substantial number of the Jews who want to immigrate. That would relax the increasing tensions and help shut up the Voice of America and BBC programs that blame Russia for anti-Semitism."

All well and good, but Kalugin also included a Trojan-horse-like component to what appeared to be the newly benevolent Soviet emigration policy. "We told [the émigrés], you can go, but you will provide us with information. And they pledged their services to us," Kalugin said.[11]

For many émigrés, it was an offer that was hard to refuse, because the KGB had leverage on any family left behind. And in the United States, the operation had insulated itself from criticism because anyone who tried to discuss the dangers of letting in so many Soviet Jews risked being labeled anti-Semitic.

Later, perhaps several years later, the KGB would follow up by sending an officer to talk to the émigrés, according to Kalugin. "He would tell them, 'Hi. Best regards from . . . ,' and he would mention some name and then some key words, which would suggest that the émigré knows who is he dealing with."

And what was their task after that? "To penetrate all Western institutions. Government, primarily, and business, particularly high technology," said Kalugin. "That's something Russia was always behind. But also the government organizations. And some did succeed in that sense."

So in the aftermath of Jackson–Vanik, the Soviet Union magnanimously allowed hundreds of thousands of Soviet Jews to immigrate to the United States. By any measure, it was an extraordinary achievement in human rights. Jewish dissident Alexander Lerner declared that fulfillment of these promises meant "a profound improvement of the emigration policy and that it should be responded to positively by the world."

But the amendment also had the effect of creating a hole in America's defenses so massive that huge numbers of Russian criminals and KGB spies could and did inundate the United States. In the last half of the seventies, Kalugin himself sometimes went to Soviet night spots like Rasputin in Brooklyn's Brighton Beach in hope of recruiting new talent—that is, Russian mobsters who would work in tandem with the KGB. "I'd look around, pick up some people, and check their backgrounds with Moscow to see if they were good enough to promote a relationship with."

In the United States, of course, the Italian Mafia would have been at war with the feds, but the Soviets and the Russians were different. They coopted the Russian Mafia. They weaponized organized crime. As Kalugin told me, "The Mafia is one of the branches of the Russian government today."

So, under cover of this new, more humanitarian emigration policy, the Soviets opened the floodgates. Hence, legislation with the goal of allowing Jewish refugees to immigrate to America had the unintended consequence of fueling the growth of the Russian Mafia and a new generation of KGB assets in America—one of whom was Donald Trump.

————

It was under these circumstances that Kislin left Odessa for good in 1972, departing first for Israel and later the United States. His first stop in the United States was Boston, where he worked as a grocery clerk and cabdriver, among other jobs, before moving to New York just as the first wave of Soviet émigrés had begun to flood into Brooklyn's Brighton Beach. Among his first jobs, according to a post on WikiReading in Russian and translated by Google Translate, Kislin "unloaded fish at night, and during the day he sold vegetables at the market to feed his . . . wife and two children. . . . How much sweat, and even blood, he shed on Brighton pavements, running around the entire Russian quarter in search of work."[12]

Of course, many émigrés who agreed to work with the KGB forgot about their promises as soon as they got to the United States. But Kislin was different. Before long, he and his partner, Tamir Sapir (né Temur Sepiashvili), had set up the small electronics store on lower Fifth Avenue that sold goods to fellow Soviets. According to Shvets, Kislin stayed loyal to the KGB and turned Joy-Lud Electronics into an outpost that played a unique role for Soviet intelligence.

That was Kislin's way of cooperating: Joy-Lud Electronics was ultimately controlled by the KGB.

Shvets believes that Kislin's motive in starting the store was part of "a deliberate decision" to cooperate with the KGB.[13] "Because he is recruited by the KGB and establishes himself in New York, this is already a big operation," Shvets told me.

As soon as Joy-Lud opened, Shvets said, standard KGB modus operandi had it that the case was moved to the KGB's First Chief Directorate (FCD), which was in charge of all foreign intelligence operations for the Soviet Union, and was handled by the FCD New York *rezidentura*.* As for Kislin, after his immigration to the United States, Shvets said, his case file was forwarded to the Moscow KGB headquarters.

Joy-Lud became an important outpost for the KGB. It was Crazy Eddie with a Russian accent, always filled with KGB agents and high-level Soviet dignitaries. A key to its existence had to do with the KGB's sensitivity about electronic eavesdropping. "The KGB was always paranoid about the CIA or FBI planting some kind of sophisticated bugging device into electronic equipment, because that was exactly what they were doing with respect to American diplomats, CIA officers, buildings in Moscow," said Shvets.

As a result, the KGB wanted to guarantee that various diplomats, consular officials, and intelligence operatives who returned to their homeland with the latest Sony Walkman weren't unwittingly broadcasting their secrets into the listening posts at Langley or Quantico, Virginia, the respective homes to the CIA and FBI facilities. But since Kislin was co-owner and he was with the KGB, Soviet dignitaries had no such concerns. "They were absolutely confident that the FBI or CIA couldn't use Kislin's store for their purposes," said Shvets. "The KGB must have had profound trust in Kislin to allow him selling equipment to his unique Russian clients, many of whom were bearers of the country's top secrets. There was no other store in the world that had access to so many secrets."

Kislin wasn't the only one in the store who was connected to the KGB. His partner and co-owner, Tamir Sapir, had also fled the Soviet Union to go to Israel and then the United States in the early seventies, and was on a similar path. Starting out in Kentucky, he took a succession of jobs—caring for the elderly, selling tools, working as a janitor—before moving to New York, where he, too, drove a cab. "I worked day

---

* After the demise of the USSR, the Russian Federation's Foreign Intelligence Service (SVR) became the successor to the FCD.

and night, because I wanted to buy out the car. I slept at the airport, waiting for the first flight to arrive," said Sapir, according to the *Georgian Journal*.[14] "In six months, the taxi became mine."

In the former Soviet Union, both Sapir and Kislin were veritable poster boys for up-by-their-bootstraps Soviet émigrés, who, having arrived in the United States with the proverbial three dollars in their pockets, held menial jobs for a few years, and then somehow or other became incredibly wealthy.

Of course, that was the giveaway. That was the tell. They were not oligarchs, but they were just one rung lower on the ladder—wealthy Soviet émigrés who got rich through their ties to the new powers that came to be when Russia began developing into a real Mafia state after the collapse of the Soviet Union.

In Sapir's case, clues revealing his ties to the intelligence services surfaced in his home country. According to the *Georgian Journal*, he returned to the Soviet Union in 1984 to attend the Academy of the Ministry of the Interior, which was closely tied to Soviet intelligence.

But at the time, Shvets notes, that would have been an extremely odd choice for a Jewish émigré who had already fled the Soviet Union. It was hard enough for Jews to emigrate from the Soviet Union in the seventies, as Sapir did, but to return to the USSR later and study at a university so closely tied to the KGB made no sense. "So it is either a mistake, a hoax, or an awkward 'legend' to cover Sapir's training as an intelligence officer," Shvets said. He added that the article in the *Georgian Journal* was "a typical story of infiltrating a KGB intel agent into the US."[15]

According to Shvets, the awkward legend was often a tell that revealed how the KGB disguised and falsified the personal histories of its operatives. As a result, he looked for how Jews and other beleaguered ethnic minorities were given perks by the KGB if they played along; how some jobs at the United Nations and in the USSR were reserved for those in the KGB; which institutions were really KGB fronts; and how disinformation was disseminated to hide the truth. When tradecraft was poorly done, he said, it was a dead giveaway.

Meanwhile, for Soviet diplomats and spies, Joy-Lud was the place to see and be seen. A story titled "Breakfast in Winter at Five in the

Morning," by Shtemler Ilya Petrovich, published on WikiReading, tells how the Soviet ambassador to the United Nations ran into his Israeli counterpart at the Joy-Lud checkout counter and had a fortuitous unplanned discourse—at a time when the two nations did not even have diplomatic relations.[16] And, of course, KGB operatives were always dropping by to sample the latest hardware.

The KGB had bugged tourist hotels in Moscow to listen in on Americans and other Westerners for years, so, through Joy-Lud, they could make sure they were not being victimized by similar American practices. Considering how risk-averse the KGB was, its giving Kislin this responsibility was a measure of how deeply it trusted him. "Every big Soviet official coming to the United States went there," said Shvets, "because the local KGB station had taken full responsibility to make sure that this place is safe and the electronic equipment was safe."

And those customers happened to be the very same Soviet diplomats and high-level officials who were overseeing spectacularly lucrative black markets in Western goods in the Soviet Union. That made it easy for Joy-Lud to sell thousands of VCRs, microwaves, TVs, and other electronic equipment to Soviet customers. In return, Sapir told *Forbes* magazine, his customers included the former Soviet minister of petrochemicals, who granted Sapir rights to distribute tens of thousands of tons of fertilizer and tens of millions of barrels of oil, while pocketing fees that made him rich.[17]

Given that all commodities—oil, gas, and the like—were under the control of the KGB, and it was up to the KGB to give out licenses to sell commodities, the mere fact that Sapir sold commodities, in effect, confirmed his ties to the KGB, because selling oil was impossible without KGB approval.

Meanwhile, the FBI had become suspicious and had put Joy-Lud under surveillance.[18] But few people really knew that Kislin's store had the KGB seal of approval, and in addition to selling "clean," bug-free electronics to Soviet operatives, it could also be used by the KGB to initiate overtures to prospective assets.

More specifically, it appeared to Shvets that Kislin himself had finally become operational and that all signs pointed to Kislin being "a spotter agent," which meant that "his task was to look around for potential targets for KGB recruitment and report on a regular basis." Once he had spotted someone and reported, it was then up to his handler to initiate cultivation and recruitment.

For the most part, the KGB's approach to categorizing agents was very different from the CIA's. "The CIA approach was either what we call developmental—that is, someone we are working on—or it was a recruited agent," said Rolf Mowatt-Larssen, a senior fellow at the Harvard Kennedy School's Belfer Center for Science and International Affairs and a former CIA station chief in Moscow.[19] "There was really no other category. But the Russians had many different categories."

For the KGB and its successors, under the broad category of assets, there were both agents and contacts. According to Shvets, the agent is someone who clearly understands that he works for Russian intelligence and is knowingly tasked to complete specific assignments.

Within that context, there were agents who could be tasked to perform specific operations, and they could be categorized as handlers, recruiters, penetration agents, keepers, "useful idiots," and the like. "One agent may provide information, bringing documents from the CIA," Shvets said. "But Kislin was not an agent informant. I believe he was a spotter agent."

As for contacts, unlike agents, a trusted contact is someone who does favors for his Russian handler, but because of a personal relationship, not because he is tasked. In most cases, Shvets notes, trusted contacts understand that they are dealing with Russian intelligence, but they are usually not told that. "Trusted contacts, they are not recruited," said Shvets. "Relations with them are cultivated over time. You just build relations over time with a trusted contact."

And, according to Shvets, Kislin had spotted Donald Trump, who, under the KGB classification, eventually became a special unofficial contact—a rare variation of trusted contact that was applied to high-level KGB intelligence assets, like the late industrialist Armand Hammer and the late British media mogul Robert Maxwell.

CHAPTER THREE

THE ASSET

Serious observers of the Trump–Russia saga know the backstory. It began in the seventies when New York City was on the brink of bankruptcy, when the mere thought of investing in the city was considered reckless, and a young, vain, narcissistic, and ruthlessly ambitious real estate developer named Donald Trump was just starting out. It was a time when Soviet émigrés had just begun to trickle into Brooklyn's Brighton Beach and nearby Coney Island, bringing with them Soviet bakers, meat markets, pushcarts, and stores selling blintzes, borscht, herring, and knishes—plus enormous gaudy supper clubs and cabarets.

The Soviets also brought with them other less desirable commodities—most notably numerous mafiosi who had black belts in corruption and later engaged in money laundering, pump-and-dump stock manipulations, and scams that were specially devised to exploit loopholes in tax laws and manipulate markets.

In the end, of course, their various lucrative enterprises would create the need to launder untold billions of dollars, a need that could best be filled by a wealthy real estate developer who had loads of luxury condos to sell and was willing to look the other way when it came to the source of the money.

To a large extent, Trump's involvement with the Russian Mafia and his subsequent financial dealings with the Russians is a matter of public record—even though it was strikingly absent from the Mueller Report. For more than three decades, at least thirteen people with known or alleged links to the Russian Mafia held the deeds to, lived in, or ran criminal operations out of Trump Tower in New York or other Trump properties. Many of them used Trump-branded real estate to launder vast amounts of money by buying multimillion-dollar condos through anonymous shell companies. And the Bayrock Group, the real estate development company that was based in Trump Tower and had ties to the Kremlin, came up with a new business model to franchise Trump condos after he'd lost billions of dollars in his Atlantic City casino developments—all of which made the perpetually bankrupt Donald Trump rich again and would lead to a new post-Soviet age of kleptocracy, in which America was injected with the virus of oligarchy and ended up with Donald Trump in the White House.

In fact, the KGB had initiated surveillance of Trump even before Kislin came into the picture. It began in 1977, after Trump married Ivana Zelníčková, a Czech national from a town in Moravia called Zlín in the Gottwaldov district, where the Czechoslovakian secret service (StB) had a plainclothes secret police force that was very much in league with the KGB. That meant Zlín was sort of the Czech equivalent to Langley or Quantico.

According to a joint report by the UK's *Guardian* and the Czech Republic's *Respekt*, in the late seventies the StB started keeping a close eye on Ivana and her wealthy husband, in part by surveillance of Ivana's father. "We knew Trump was influential," former StB Gottwaldov district boss Vlastimil Daněk told *Respekt*. "He announced that he wanted to become president one day, we were interested in knowing more about him. And not only us, the intelligence part of the StB also showed interest in him. But I don't want to say details, I don't want to have any problems."[1]

The *Respekt* article concluded that the StB received information about Trump and his wife that was "of a private nature (about their children and their illnesses, about the private journeys of the influential couple)." It added that the StB also showed interest in Trump's political ambitions and the high circles in Washington to which he had access.

Shvets says the report is accurate, but he questioned whether the information had any real value, given the distance between Trump and his Czech in-laws. "Once people married a foreigner in the West and got out of the country, the possibility of using the entire KGB against their spouse was really very, very limited," Shvets said. "And what kind of intelligence could [Trump's] father-in-law provide? They were living separately. There was an ocean separating them."

Moreover, even though the StB reported directly to the KGB, Shvets says it is not clear the Czechs would have shared their files on Trump. "There was a system of cooperation between the intelligence services," he said. "Both countries had databases of individuals and subjects, and they would share information if asked to."

That meant if the KGB's New York *rezidentura* wanted information from the Czechs on Trump, they could reach out to the StB— theoretically.

But in practice, the system did not work as well as it was meant to. "The whole system was unreliable," said Shvets. "When you reveal your interest to another intelligence service, it's not confidential anymore." As he saw it, if he shared information with a rival intelligence service, they might well turn around and try to recruit the same man.

In any case, the StB continued to keep an eye on Trump for many years to come. According to *The Guardian*, after the 1988 election of George H. W. Bush, it became increasingly aware of Trump's political ambitions and its interest in him intensified—enough to send an operative to meet with Trump.[2]

Less than a year later, in September 1989, a small delegation from Czechoslovakia, led by František Čuba, the chairman of Czechoslovakia's showcase model farm, went to New York and met with Trump in Trump Tower, a meeting that was closely monitored by the StB. According to the reports, the essence of the meeting was relatively anodyne—Trump advised Čuba to buy a Sikorsky helicopter, and Čuba invited Trump to visit his agricultural cooperative, Slušovice. He hoped to initiate relationships with large capitalist companies. More significant than the content of the meeting, however, was the fact that it was monitored closely by Jaroslav Jansa, an StB collaborator.

What may have been an ambitious long-term operation suffered a major setback, however, two months later when the Velvet Revolution led to the end of communism in Czechoslovakia. As for Trump, he eventually did visit Čuba in Slušovice when he went to Czechoslovakia for the funeral of Ivana's father. Though the occasion was a sad one, it was not without intrigue. According to *The Guardian*, one of the mourners was the StB's Jansa, who was stationed about a hundred yards away from the Trumps.[3]

There's no reason to believe Kislin's opening to Trump was in any way related to the Czech operation. They may have been simply two independent operations that eventually zeroed in on the same target.

On its face, the sale of television sets between Kislin and Trump had a few anomalies that were more than a bit puzzling. The Hyatt Corporation has been a blue-chip outfit in the world of franchises for decades. Why was it getting television sets from a small Soviet shop like Joy-Lud instead of a reliable wholesaler? And those kinds of small electronic stores rarely if ever extended credit. Why was Kislin doing such favors for Trump? And why would the Grand Hyatt New York need TVs that had dual systems that could receive broadcasts from the Soviet Union? The answers may be lost to the ravages of time.

Barbara Res later worked for Trump for forty years as the most highly placed female executive in his company, but at that time she was working for the general contractor HOH Construction as superintendent and project manager developing the Grand Hyatt. In a text message to me, Res said she was unfamiliar with Kislin or the transaction.

But from Trump's point of view, the purchase made no sense, unless, perhaps, he was getting the TVs at a spectacularly low price. According to Yuri Shvets, the KGB modus operandi would have been to have Kislin offer the TV sets to Trump at low, low prices. Once the deal was made, he said, the KGB may have discreetly installed bugging devices in them—but that is merely speculation. However, this was the way the KGB got its foot in the door and got close enough to prospective assets to see whether they were worth the effort to cultivate.

At the time, however, Trump was not yet a particularly well-known name outside New York—especially to the KGB. Remember, this was *before* the eighties, with its greed-is-good ethos, the big swinging dicks of Wall Street, and money, money, money. New York was still at its nadir. The glitz of Trump Tower, Trump trumpeting his sexual exploits in the tabloids, the insanely extravagant casinos in Atlantic City—none of that had happened yet.

So it is likely that, initially at least, Kislin was less concerned about targeting Trump as a KGB asset and may have been just trying to score a new bulk sale. "I am almost positive that Kislin was not thinking in terms of target, penetration, or recruitment when he first thought of Trump," said Shvets. "The guy is about money. He just saw an opportunity, and he reported to the KGB handler."

And once the contact with Trump had been reported to the KGB, the process had begun.

———

But why should we believe Yuri Shvets? Or, for that matter, any other KGB agent? After all, there's no such thing as a *former* KGB agent, or so the saying goes. But it is also true that when one is investigating the world of intelligence, espionage, organized crime, politics, and other deeply corrupt precincts, the most knowledgeable sources—the ones who often have firsthand information and are familiar with the arcane tradecraft and practices of clandestine operations and criminal conspiracies—are the very same people who are engaged in such practices: spies, criminals, and people who are in one way or another professional liars. Moreover, as anyone who has watched a cop show on American TV knows, it is a verity of our own criminal justice system, and the world of intelligence, that such sources should neither be dismissed nor accepted unquestioningly but should be heard out and their stories corroborated or refuted.

Shvets has considerable experience in such matters, having served in the DC *rezidentura*, a.k.a. Washington station, where he tried—and sometimes succeeded—in recruiting Americans to spy for the Soviet Union. A 1980 graduate of Patrice Lumumba People's Friendship University in Moscow, Shvets went on to do postgraduate work at the Academy of Foreign Intelligence (Andropov Red Banner Institute of the KGB), the prestigious espionage academy that served the Soviet spy agency and its successor, the Foreign Intelligence Service (SVR). There, he and his classmates—Vladimir Putin, among them—were taught the secrets of the espionage trade.

In 1985, Shvets moved with his wife and children to Washington, where he led his double life as reporter for the Soviet news agency TASS who really served in the KGB's First Chief Directorate, the counterintelligence department widely regarded as the most prestigious division in the entire Soviet spy service. And within *that* context, Shvets had one of the most desirable postings in the entire KGB.

Five years later, however, Shvets became deeply disillusioned with the KGB and resigned on political grounds. "It was clear to me and to many of my colleagues that the leadership of the KGB and the Soviet Communist Party were ruining the country," he said in 1999, in testimony before the US Congress.

In the mid-nineties, he was granted political asylum in the United States, eventually settling in suburban Virginia, not far from the Langley headquarters of the Central Intelligence Agency, his once-reviled foe.

A friend and colleague of former FSB officer Alexander Litvinenko, Yuri helped Litvinenko assemble and analyze a dossier linking senior Kremlin officials, including Vladimir Putin, to the Tambov organized crime group, which laundered money and facilitated drug trafficking for the Colombian cartels.[4] In 2006, Litvinenko was poisoned by radioactive polonium-210 in what appeared to be a state-sponsored assassination ordered by Putin.

In 1995, Shvets published *Washington Station: My Life as a KGB Spy in America*, his memoir about recruiting two American spies in the eighties, one of whom had been an aide in Jimmy Carter's administration and the other a journalist in Washington. Two years later, he started a business as a security investigator/consultant with Bob Levinson, a former FBI and DEA agent who disappeared in 2007 after being kidnapped on Iran's Kish Island. (Levinson's death was announced by his family on March 25, 2020.)

In 1999, Shvets testified before Congress, warning the nation about widespread Russian money laundering in the United States as a means through which "high-ranking officials of the Soviet Communist Party, top KGB leadership, and top bosses of the criminal world" had begun to infiltrate the Western banking system. And seven years later, he became a key witness in the investigation into Litvinenko's murder.

Like a number of other former spooks, Shvets now plies his craft in the world of corporate intelligence, providing commercial research and strategic intelligence on the former Soviet Union to American and western European banks, hedge funds, aerospace companies, energy companies, and the like. Long steeped in the particulars of KGB tradecraft, he'd had a front-row seat at the birth of post-Soviet Russia as a Mafia state and on the waves of kleptocrats and oligarchs who have been sweeping into the West, along with authoritarian right-wing populist politicians.

Of course, when the KGB first made contact with Trump, it could not have foreseen his ascent, but it still played the long game, and the simple act of making a bulk sale of television sets to Trump was enough to get the ball rolling. According to Shvets, when Kislin reached out to Trump, he would have had to notify his KGB handler about the transaction. That was standard procedure. Once Kislin's handler had been activated, New York station, in the First Chief Directorate of the KGB, had an opportunity to develop Trump as a new asset.

If they followed that procedure, Shvets said, this is almost certainly the point at which Donald Trump's name first entered KGB files. "I'm ninety-nine percent positive this is how they started their file on Trump," Shvets said. "Kislin would have gone to his handler and said he had an interesting contact. 'The guy is Donald Trump. He is young, ambitious, rich. He might have a future.'"

From the KGB's point of view, the most appealing quality about Trump was probably that he had a personality that was ideal for a potential asset—vain, narcissistic, highly susceptible to flattery, and greedy. It was unclear whether time invested in developing him would pay off, but that's the way the KGB sometimes operated. It was like throwing spaghetti against the wall and seeing what would stick.

In any case, after Kislin met with Trump, a report would have been filed in the KGB's New York *rezidentura*—New York station—and sent to headquarters. A few weeks later, the handler would have followed up with Kislin, and if Kislin had seen Trump or obtained additional information, he would have shared it with the handler. "So you accumulate about ten meaningful reports on the guy," said Shvets, "and you examine them to see if this guy can be cultivated to the point where he can be useful in either of two capacities. Capacity number one: as a trusted contact. Capacity number two, which is more ambitious: as an agent. You want to know if this guy can be cultivated to the point where he can be brought to cooperate."

Assuming they moved forward with Trump, Shvets said, New York station would have had a handler who met with Trump, but who that person was remains an important unanswered question.

Still, Shvets was not the only source saying that Joy-Lud Electronics was secretly an outpost for the KGB. The FBI had it under surveillance because of investigations into the Russian Mafia, which was very much a state actor working in concert with the KGB. "I know guys from Brighton Beach and the Soviet embassy would be spotted going in and out of there," said Kenneth McCallion, a former federal prosecutor who worked closely with the FBI during that era. "There were some surveillance applications at the time, and some of the evidence that was put forward was about the activities at that store."

The bottom line was that the KGB had gotten its foot in the door in what was likely one of its first interactions with Donald Trump—one that was the launching pad for other highly productive and lucrative transactions over the next forty years. "The KGB was happy. Kislin was happy. Everybody was happy," said Shvets. "It was a win-win situation."

Within the new wave of Soviet émigrés, Semyon Kislin came to epito-mize the rags-to-riches immigrant who ended up a billionaire, or close to it. That was the narrative as it generally appeared in the press, but few articles explained the chasm between his humble origins and his vast wealth. The truth is that it was more than being a really good cab driver or business owner.

The first real story on Kislin was published by the Center for Public Integrity, a 1999 article by Pulitzer Prize winner Knute Royce that cited a 1994 FBI file characterizing him as a "member/associate" of the mob organization headed by Vyacheslav Ivankov, the "godfather of Russian organized crime in the United States." By then, Kislin had started Trans Commodities Inc., a firm that, according to the FBI re-port, "is known to have laundered millions of dollars from Russia to New York."* Kislin's firm, Trans Commodities, and Anton Malevsky, a contract killer for the Russian Mafia, were also allegedly tied to oligarch Mikhail Chernoy, who was a major figure in the so-called Aluminum Wars, which were marked by embezzlement, money laun-dering, and murder. Finally, the report said that Kislin was also a "close associate" of the late arms smuggler Babeck Seroush and that he had cosponsored a visa for Malevsky.

By this time, the former Soviet Union had been dissolved, and

---

* Kislin declined to be interviewed by me, but his attorney, Jeffrey Dannenberg, said that there were no such FBI files and that the Center for Public Integrity had disavowed the article long ago. "Not only is the article wrong, but many years ago I spoke with the head of the Center for Public Integrity and told him it was wrong," Dannenberg told me. "They withdrew the article, which was pretty extraordinary for them. They withdrew it."

However, Mei Fong, director of communications and strategy at the center, told me, "We haven't disavowed anything. The article is still on our website." The article, Knute Royce, "FBI Tracked Alleged Russian Mob Ties of Giuliani Campaign Sup-porter," Center for Public Integrity, December 14, 1999, can be found at https://public integrity.org/politics/elections-fbi-tracked-alleged-russian-mob-ties-of-giuliani -campaign-supporter/.

Russia had emerged as the new Wild West, with former mobsters jock-eying for control of steel, aluminum, oil, and other commodities. The Chernoys were among the roughest players in those battles, particu-larly the bloody and brutal Aluminum Wars, during which they claimed to have made a onetime partner of Putin crony Oleg Deri-paska, but ended up in conflict with him.

For his part, Kislin was never charged with any crime, and in 1999 he denied any ties to the Russian mob, insisting, "I have done nothing evil." He has also denied charges that Trans Commodities laundered money for Russian organized crime. In an email for this book, Kislin again disputed Royce's story. "I have never known or had any ties to anyone named Vyacheslav Ivankov, and I have never been involved in money laundering, either directly or through any company," he wrote.

Meanwhile, Kislin donated more than $40,000 to Rudy Giuliani's successful mayoral campaigns in New York in 1993 and 1997, as well as to the campaigns of Giuliani allies, and raised millions more for him at fundraising events for an abortive Senate run.[5] Giuliani appointed Kislin to serve on the New York City Economic Development Corpo-ration from 1996 to 2000, a patronage job the mayor reserved for trusted allies.

And that, according to Shvets, was a very wise decision on his part. "Kislin felt vulnerable," said Shvets, "especially after he became an FBI target because of his connection to Chernoy. He knew he was being investigated and needed some kind of protection. And this is what brought him to Giuliani. He invested money into Giuliani's campaign, and then Giuliani made him an adviser. It was very smart move."

And as we shall see, it enabled Kislin to have a mutually rewarding relationship with Trump as well, one that spanned more than forty years and played a role in the 2019 impeachment and the 2020 election.

———

After the New York *rezidentura* had amassed several reports on Trump and established that Trump was a viable prospect for development as an asset, according to Shvets, an officer of the New York station of the First Chief Directorate would have had to open what's known as a *delo operativnoy razrabotky* (DOR), or file of operational development. DOR files were classified as top secret and given a code name and file number with which to register in the First Chief Directorate's database in its Yasenevo headquarters, just outside Moscow. The database consisted of catalog cards, similar to those found in libraries in the predigital era, and was kept in an especially secure room in the FCD basement. At the time, Shvets said, the KGB's database did not use the real names of their American assets for security reasons.[6]

Nevertheless, this is what happened with people targeted for cultivation like Trump.

According to Shvets, there are three main bases for developing assets: ideology, money, and kompromat. Of them, ideology was long considered the best and most reliable basis for recruitment, but it has not been widely used with Americans since Stalin's crimes were exposed in the fifties, and it was certainly never a consideration with Trump.

In the seventies and eighties, Shvets says, money became very important in recruitment, and it was a key factor in the two most widely publicized cases of that era: CIA agent Aldrich Ames and FBI agent Robert Hanssen, both of whom spied for the Soviets.

Finally, Soviet and Russian intelligence has a long history in acquiring kompromat to hold as leverage over its assets. When the private intelligence report known as the Steele Dossier was published in January 2017, Americans were titillated by the prospect that the Russians had videos of Donald Trump engaged in compromising sexual activities with Russian prostitutes—golden-shower videos and so forth. But more than three years later, none of that has surfaced.

And according to Shvets, that kind of kompromat was rarely used by the KGB because the results were unreliable. Trump was an especially curious case in that he was both spectacularly vulnerable to being cultivated yet so shameless he would have been impervious to pressures most people would feel. Instead, for Trump, the real kompromat was the money trail that connected him to Russian intelligence through massive money laundering.

"Trump was a dream for KGB officers looking to develop an asset,"

Shvets told me. "Everybody has weaknesses. But with Trump it wasn't just weakness. Everything was excessive. His vanity, excessive. Narcissism, excessive. Greed, excessive. Ignorance, excessive."

Shvets's assessment is strikingly similar to those of various CIA officers. "Trump is extremely vulnerable to flattery," Rolf Mowatt-Larssen told me. "He almost defines relationships entirely by who flatters him and who doesn't, as opposed to the intrinsic value of what people say. He doesn't care at all about the fact that Russians are masters at manipulation."

Similarly, retired CIA officer Glenn Carle, who spent twenty years in clandestine field operations, also saw Trump as "incredibly vulnerable" to the Russians. "I thought about how would I approach him if I were a foreign intelligence officer," Carle told me. "The Russians are routine blackmailers, but Trump is hard to blackmail because he is so shameless. Still, there are things that Trump doesn't want to come out—quite clearly his tax returns. So I think they probably have stuff on him, but that the Russian targeting and development of him started decades ago in the classic way."

And indeed, over four decades, whatever else happened between Trump and Soviet/Russian intelligence, the file on Trump would be updated as his life's journey with them went from laundering money for the Russian Mafia through Trump luxury condos, to partnering with wealthy Soviet émigrés in franchising scams, to becoming involved in countless financial irregularities, to creating secret back channels with the Russians, to partying with Jeffrey Epstein, and on and on.

Over time, the Donald Trump operation ripened. "Then," Shvets added, "it paid off much, much more than anyone could possibly have imagined."

CHAPTER FOUR

SPY WARS

By the eighties, Brooklyn's Brighton Beach had become a shadowy subculture filled with mysteries, secrets, and double lives for thousands of Soviet émigrés. There was always something hidden. Drop by a storefront for a late-night pizza and, likely as not, you would uncover a clandestine high-stakes gambling ring in a seedy back room. Passport and marriage license storefronts were everywhere—supplying phony IDs for the asking, as long as you had a few bucks. There were late-night supper clubs like the Odessa and the National and, later, Café Tatiana and Rasputin, with loud, festive nine-course dinners featuring borscht, sturgeon, sable, and more than enough vodka, while garish Vegas-style floor shows were under way. There was techno and disco music, Russian songs, and, on occasion, Iosif Kobzon, a.k.a. the Russian Frank Sinatra, who was notorious for his ties to the Solntsevskaya Bratva, the powerful Russian crime syndicate.

Before long, up-and-coming gangsters from the real Odessa, the so-called Pearl of the Black Sea, arrived in force in "Little Odessa," as Brighton Beach was known—among them people who later became tied to Donald Trump. The El Caribe Country Club, a banquet hall and restaurant in the Mill Basin section of Brooklyn, was owned by Dr. Morton Levine, who shared interests in it with his relatives, including nephew Michael Cohen. Cohen, of course, later became Donald

Trump's attorney, who, at this writing, was sentenced to three years in jail for campaign finance violations, tax fraud, and bank fraud. (As a result of the COVID-19 pandemic, Cohen was allowed to serve part of his sentence in home confinement. He is scheduled to be released in November 2021.)

At night, El Caribe ceded the premises to Russian Mafia kingpin Marat Balagula. The first "modern" don in the Russian Mafia, Balagula, who had strong ties to the KGB, was a pioneer in taking the *organizatsiya* (organization, referring to the Russian Mafia) from relying on extortion rackets, black marketeering, and various other forms of vulgar thuggery into the more upscale, white-collar world of tax scams and pump-and-dump stock swindles on Wall Street. According to Shvets, Balagula was infiltrated to the United States in 1977 by the KGB in the wake of the Jackson–Vanik Amendment.[1]

Just a few years after moving to the United States, Balagula won control over enough gas stations and fuel dealerships to partner with old-school Italian mobsters in operations that became known as the Red Daisy gas tax scam and skimmed millions of dollars in tax revenues from the coffers of hundreds of gas stations. Having arrived in America with no concept of a social contract, they began to go white collar.

Meanwhile, vast sums from the Russian Mafia's various scams had to be laundered. So in 1984, David Bogatin, a Russian mobster who had scored millions in the Red Daisy gas scam with Balagula, went shopping for apartments and ended up at 721 Fifth Avenue, Trump Tower, the glistening new fifty-eight-story building that was the home of Donald Trump.

Bogatin, however, wasn't looking for a home to live in so much as a place to park his excess cash, and at a closing, with Donald Trump himself in attendance, he bought not one but five condominiums, putting down $6 million in cash, the equivalent of more than $15 million in 2020 dollars. According to the New York State attorney general's office, the upshot of the deal was that the Russian Mafia had just laundered money through Donald Trump's real estate.

At about the same time, in early 1984, General Vladimir Kryuchkov launched a newly aggressive campaign to recruit American assets. Thanks to a compendium of his memos during this period, titled "Comrade Kryuchkov's Instructions: Top Secret Files on KGB Foreign Operations," we know that to Kryuchkov, absolutely nothing was more important than recruiting new American assets.[2] By the eighties, however, finding left-wing Americans who were ideological soul mates with the Soviets was increasingly difficult. As a result, he ordered his officers to cultivate as assets not just the usual leftist suspects, who might have ideological sympathies with the Soviets, but also various influential people such as prominent businessmen.

According to Shvets, recruiting American assets was much easier said than done, except in cases where they happened to be walk-ins who approached the KGB on their own, usually for monetary reasons. That was the case with the two new superstar US agents who betrayed the FBI and CIA, one of whom was active in Shvets's turf shortly after he first came to Washington, on April 12, 1985.

At the time, Shvets had just arrived in the United States and presented himself as a journalist working for the Soviet news agency TASS out of the National Press Club Building on Fourteenth Street Northwest— which he was. But more important, he was also working undercover for the First Chief Directorate's Washington station. That meant he went to the *rezidentura* in the Soviet embassy on Sixteenth Street two or three times a week to write reports for KGB headquarters.

After he entered the *rezidentura* for the first time, Shvets immediately went to chief of station Victor Cherkashin and reported for duty. But when Shvets was given his marching orders, they were somewhat puzzling.

"Get lost," Cherkashin told him. "Don't come to the station for three months. Just establish your cover story, and don't show up." Translation: Establishing his cover meant that Shvets should go back to the TASS office and start working as a reporter.

Shvets didn't know it until later, but on April 16, four days after he started, Aldrich Ames, a CIA counterintelligence officer with access to all CIA plans against the KGB and Soviet military intelligence, widely known as the GRU (Glavnoye Razvedyvatelnoye Upravlenie), had walked into the Soviet embassy and established himself for the first time as a double agent selling secrets to the KGB.[3]

At the time, Cherkashin was effectively the day-to-day manager of Soviet espionage operations in the United States. Ames was a huge score for the *rezidentura*—one of the biggest in history. As a result, overseeing Ames was top of mind for Washington station just as Yuri was getting started.[4]

Meanwhile, Shvets had been tasked with two main assignments, the most important of which was uncovering evidence that the United States was preparing for nuclear war with the Soviets. At the Academy of Foreign Intelligence, his instructor had repeatedly asserted that "the United States is capable of wiping our country off the face of the earth."

Such paranoia was not unusual in the KGB. Before his death in 1984, General Secretary Yuri Andropov, former head of the KGB, asserted that "outrageous military psychosis" had taken over the United States, and the Reagan administration, "in its imperial ambitions, goes so far that one begins to doubt whether Washington has any brakes at all preventing it from crossing the point at which any sober-minded person must stop."[5]

Anatoly Dobrynin, the Soviet ambassador to Washington, later explained that Moscow had succumbed to a "paranoid interpretation" of Reagan's policies that saw the Star Wars program—the antiballistic missile system, also known as the Strategic Defense Initiative, which was supposed to shield the United States from missile attacks—as a precursor to an apocalyptic nuclear war.[6]

Similarly, Shvets soon realized that fear of an imminent US attack was largely unfounded and was a dark fantasy emerging from a power struggle between geriatric bureaucrats in the Kremlin more than from facts on the ground. "It took me a couple of months to realize that it was just silly. It was just insane," he told me.

The second of Shvets's main tasks was to recruit new American assets. The pressure to deliver was intense. "It was very rare for a KGB intelligence officer to find, develop, and recruit an American citizen as an agent," said Shvets. "All the agents who had been exposed—like Aldrich Ames, Robert Hanssen, and others—were volunteers who basically offered their services to the KGB for money or complex personal reasons. No one recruited them. To recruit an American citizen as an agent at that time was like for a regular pilot to fly to the moon and back."

One of the first cases Yuri encountered was that of a Soviet agent in Washington who developed a promising American congressman as an asset and used his "phenomenal mastery as a conversationalist," as Shvets describes it in his memoir, *Washington Station*, to penetrate the innermost recesses of his soul.[7]

Before long, the congressman had delivered stacks of documents to the Soviet operative and, Yuri assumed, was well on his way to becoming a new asset of the USSR. But in fact, exactly the opposite was the case: After the very first meeting, the congressman had alerted authorities, so all subsequent get-togethers had taken place under the watchful eye of the FBI.

It wasn't as easy as it looked.

It was an extraordinary period in the spy game—all over the world. In January 1984, five Soviet spies were uncovered in Norway and expelled.[8] In February, Viktor M. Lesiovsky, a Soviet diplomat who was reportedly linked to Soviet intelligence while he was working for the United Nations, died at the age of sixty-three. (In 1979, he told the BBC that Soviet intelligence had achieved a "very substantial" penetration of the UN Secretariat.)[9] In late February, Ethiopia expelled two Soviet diplomats as spies.[10] In May, Denmark expelled two members of a Soviet trade delegation as spies.[11] In October, a Soviet diplomat stationed in San Francisco was outed as a spy,[12] and several Soviet spies were expelled from Washington.

During the next year, 1985, the so-called Year of the Spy, enough espionage took place to keep John le Carré busy for decades. It actually started in December 1984, when Thomas Patrick Cavanaugh, a former engineer at Northrop Corporation, was arrested for trying to sell the core of the technology behind the multimillion-dollar Stealth bomber for $25,000 to undercover FBI agents posing as Soviets. Then the John A. Walker family spy ring, which had operated for seventeen years and sold the Soviet Union information on the US Navy's undersea sensor system, was blown by Walker's mistress. Ronald Pelton, a former analyst for the National Security Agency who had allegedly sold secrets about US electronic listening posts to the Soviets, was identified as a spy by Vitaly Yurchenko, a KGB defector who came over to the American side in August.[13] Later, Yurchenko turned up at a villa secretly owned by the CIA in Virginia and began talking. When that happened, the KGB's network of American agents suddenly began to collapse.[14]

Meanwhile, American intelligence had been suffering huge losses as well, thanks to well-placed moles in both the CIA and the FBI. At the CIA, Aldrich Ames had provided classified information to the KGB identifying hundreds of Western (mostly American) agents, more than twenty of whom were executed or imprisoned.[15] Horrifying as that was, Ames had stiff competition from FBI special agent Robert Hanssen, who, according to a 2002 Justice Department report, was responsible for "possibly the worst intelligence disaster in U.S. history."[16] At this writing, Ames is in prison for life without parole. Hanssen is serving fifteen consecutive life terms.

The Hanssen case may seem light-years away from the urgent national security issues that are related to Trump-Russia. But the way in which Hanssen escaped notice for twenty-two years is remarkably relevant when it comes to the generous treatment afforded to Russian assets by William Barr, first as attorney general in the administration of George H. W. Bush and later in the same position under Donald Trump.

Married with six children, Robert Hanssen was a devout Catholic who was a member of Opus Dei, the deeply conservative Catholic lay organization, and attended Mass almost every day. According to a report by the Justice Department's inspector general (IG), Hanssen had "poor interpersonal skills and a dour demeanor and was an awkward

and uncommunicative loner who conveyed a sense of intellectual su-
periority that alienated many of his co-workers."[17]

The report noted that Hanssen's supervisor characterized him as a
deeply religious social misanthrope who was technically proficient and
analytical but was also repressed, aggrieved, and intent on showing
that he was smarter than his colleagues.[18] He first began to spy for the
GRU between 1979 and 1981, when he transferred to New York to do
Soviet counterintelligence work, which was his specialty for most of
his FBI career. According to the inspector general's report, "Hanssen
quickly began exploiting weaknesses in the FBI's internal information
security" and before long had "gained access to the FBI's most sensitive
human assets and technical operations against the Soviet Union."
Eventually that included information specifying American strategies
in the event of a nuclear war, new weapons technologies, and the identities of active US assets in the Soviet Union.[19]

Hanssen, like Ames, was later captured, tried, convicted, and sentenced to life imprisonment without possibility of parole. But in 1985,
he had just been transferred back to the FBI's New York office, where
he had served four years earlier. According to the New York Times, his
job was to supervise "hundreds of agents in his division who were
consumed by what they saw as all-out war against hostile targets, primarily the Soviet Union."[20]

"The notion that he'd sell out his country as a citizen, as an F.B.I.
agent and as a fighter in the cold war—knowing what he knew, and the
circumstances of what he was doing—is unbelievable," James K. Kallstrom, who knew Hanssen in the mid-eighties when his division supported counterintelligence squads, told the New York Times.[21] "He was
a lieutenant in that war, and the war was being fought in the streets of
New York."

———

Kallstrom, who ended up running the FBI's New York office in the
mid-nineties and oversaw successful investigations into both the Italian Mafia and later the Russian Mafia, had developed friendships with
two key players in the Trump-Russia saga. He worked closely with

then US attorney for the Southern District of New York Rudy Giuliani in the investigation of the Cosa Nostra network that led to the famed Mafia Commission Trial of 1985–1986, which convicted the heads of the so-called Five Families.

Going even further back, Kallstrom had also been friends with Donald Trump since around 1973, when Kallstrom was putting together a parade in New York to honor Vietnam veterans, and Trump came along to fund most of it. "We just got to be friends," said Kallstrom in a 2020 interview as the Trump reelection campaign was just gearing up. (The interview was done for a 2020 documentary about Trump and the FBI called *An American Affair: Donald Trump and the FBI*.)[22] "I went to a few dinners with him, we talked quite often. He was very, very supportive of the bureau. We lose an agent, or somebody gets shot up, he was always there to pay for the food or whatever it took."

According to the *New York Times*, Kallstrom had founded the Marine Corps–Law Enforcement Foundation, a nonprofit that got more than $1.3 million from Trump, an unusually generous offering from the usually parsimonious real estate developer.[23]

Their relationship was such that Kallstrom said things about Trump that were diametrically opposed to the way most Americans saw him. "I would say we were associates who liked each other," Kallstrom added, in the film. "He [Trump] would call me periodically and try to boost my morale, and then I'd call him when he was in the news and try to boost his morale. But he's basically a very, very good person and with a big heart that does a lot of things, ninety percent of which nobody knows about. I mean, we stay in touch even today."

But Trump being Trump, loyalty and generosity came with strings attached. "He [Trump] cultivated FBI people," investigative reporter Jeff Stein, editor of SpyTalk, says in *An American Affair*. "And that's well-known behavior by people who swim in dangerous waters. They want to have a get-out-of-jail card, and that get-out-of-jail is having friendships or being a good source for the FBI."

Kallstrom insisted that Trump was not an FBI informant, but another agent told Stein that Trump was known within the bureau as a "hip pocket" source—that is, someone who was not officially a source and therefore not in the FBI files, but who had curried enough favor to be known as a "friend."

On the one hand, Trump had millions coming in from Russian mobsters like David Bogatin buying luxury condos to launder money. He also had at least a sporadic connection with Kislin, who came to Trump's aid after his massive bankruptcies in Atlantic City in the nineties by issuing mortgages for condos in Trump World Tower, the seventy-two-story luxury high-rise near the United Nations. According to an investigation by *Bloomberg Businessweek*, one-third of the units on the tower's priciest floors had been snatched up by individual buyers or limited-liability companies tied to Russia or the former Soviet Union.[24] (Kislin attorney Jeffrey Dannenberg said the report was untrue.)

Among those who reportedly got Kislin-issued mortgages for Trump condos was Vasily Salygin, who later became an official of Ukraine's pro-Putin Party of Regions, for which Paul Manafort, later Trump's campaign manager, worked. And finally, Kislin partner Tamir Sapir, who lived in Trump Tower until his death in 2014, also helped bail out Trump by funding the ill-fated Trump SoHo development.

Hence, Kallstrom's friendship with Trump set up a curious calculus. Bogatin, Kislin, Sapir, and mobster Vyacheslav Ivankov, one of the most brutal gangsters in the history of the Russian Mafia, who owned a Trump Tower condo in the nineties, all allegedly had ties to the Russian Mafia and/or the KGB. All of them were on the FBI's radar screen, and on Trump's. Who knows what information Trump and Kallstrom exchanged about them?

And Kallstrom wasn't the only person in the FBI who played for both sides. Indeed, as the *New York Post*[25] and *New York Times*[26] reported respectively, FBI special agent Joel Bartow investigated both Kislin and Chernoy and later asserted that neither had ties with the Russian Mafia, that they were both clean.

But as the *New York Post* reported in 1999, Bartow, who left the FBI in 1997,[27] had been hired by Kislin and was also on retainer with Kislin's law firm, Rosenman & Colin. And as the *Times* reported in 2001,

Bartow had begun working for Mikhail Chernoy as well in 2000. And, not surprisingly, now that Bartow had left the FBI behind and was actually on the payroll of the very people he had been investigating, the FBI was not terribly supportive of his conclusions. "He doesn't speak for the FBI," a spokesman for the Bureau told the *Times*.[28]

Similarly, Donald Trump was on both sides of the law. That's the way he liked it. He could afford to be generous with Kallstrom, but he expected something in return. And when it came to his ties to the Soviets, Trump was also being paid back—and quite handsomely. Far from being a unique transaction for Trump, the all-cash sale of condos to David Bogatin became the paradigm. It was an extremely safe and efficient way to launder vast amounts of money. And, as was documented by a 2018 *BuzzFeed News* investigation, more than 1,300 Trump-branded condos in the United States were sold "in secretive, all-cash transactions that enable buyers to avoid legal scrutiny by shielding their finances and identities."[29]

It may be impossible to calculate the exact amount of money Trump reaped from such transactions, but given that the average price of the condos was $1.2 million, the total amount of flight capital being parked in Trump condos was likely more than $1.5 billion, a significant but unknown part of which came from Russians. And that involves the sale of condos only in the United States, and does not include Trump properties in Turkey, Canada, Panama, the Philippines, India, Azerbaijan, or elsewhere.

Later, long after he took up residence in the White House, people asked again and again what the Russians had on Trump. And in a way, it's really quite simple: They owned him.

Meanwhile, throughout the mid-eighties, New York was a hotbed of spies. There was the Russian Mafia in Brighton Beach. The Joy-Lud electronics store. Donald Trump. As yet unidentified moles—Aldrich Ames and Robert Hanssen—were wreaking havoc. And the Soviet Mission to the United Nations was said to be harboring a huge nest of operatives.[30]

When it came to taking on the Soviets, the FBI's New York office was home base. As the FBI's largest office, situated in same city as the UN, its agents were supposed to lead the way in investigating the Soviets. And among them was Hanssen, the worst turncoat in FBI history.

No battlefield was more central than the United Nations. That was because the Soviet Union's Permanent Mission to the United Nations had long been an enormous spy nest in which the vast majority of its 114 staffers reported to the KGB's New York *rezidentura*. The UN was a paradise for spies, a true oasis, because diplomatic cover gave the KGB free run of the place, thanks to UN rules that banned CIA and FBI personnel from the premises. In 1979, former UN undersecretary Arkady N. Shevchenko, a high-ranking Soviet diplomat who defected to the West, confirmed that as many as three hundred KGB officers were stationed in New York. According to *The Spy Next Door*, by Elaine Shannon, the FBI estimated that a third to a half of the Soviet diplomats assigned to the Soviet Mission to the UN were trained KGB or GRU officers.

In addition to the Soviet Mission, the KGB planted hundreds of additional intelligence officers inside the United Nations Secretariat, the executive arm of the UN, which sets the agenda for its various decision-making bodies. According to Shvets, it was relatively high-paying and a highly sought-after job for many a Soviet diplomat. "Working in the UN Secretariat was the wildest dream for any Soviet diplomat or spy," says Shvets. "The salaries they were making there were way higher than any Soviet diplomat in any other embassy in the world."

Typically, specific jobs in the Secretariat were doled out by Soviet representatives who ensured that they went to KGB operatives. Among those jobs, according to a May 1985 report by the US Senate Select Intelligence Committee, *Soviet Presence in the U.N. Secretariat*,[31] working at the UN's Dag Hammarskjöld Library was essentially a cover for KGB operatives, who used it to disseminate Soviet disinformation and implement covert operations.[32] "The Soviets usually begin their efforts to secure slots through the formal UN personnel systems, but they also use a variety of other tactics to gain their ends," the report says.[33] "If the Soviets are particularly interested in a specific position, they will present a well-credentialed, outstanding candidate for the post. This method was used in securing the directorship of the Dag Hammerskjold Library at UN headquarters in New York. When a qualified person is not available, a resume is falsified."

All of which Yuri Shvets saw up close: "I know this firsthand because my colleague worked in this position until back in '82."

In the late seventies and early eighties, he explained, the position in the library allocated to the Soviet Union was held by Lieutenant Colonel Alexander Yelagin of the First Department (North America) of the KGB First Chief Directorate, who worked with Yuri for more than two years. His nickname, Yuri says, was "Old Chap."

When Yelagin returned to Moscow in 1982, Yuri says, he produced a paper titled "Using the UN Library for Collection of Intelligence Information."

But it was one of Yelagin's successors who would prove to play such a key role in cultivating Donald Trump. According to Shvets, from 1985 to 1986 that job was held by Natalia Dubinina, the daughter of Yuri Dubinin, who took over as the USSR's ambassador to the United Nations in early 1986 at the same time his daughter held a vital position in the KGB's First Chief Directorate. Shvets's assertion that Dubinina worked at that post is corroborated by an April 28, 2003, profile of her on the Russian website AIF Express.[34]

Revelations about spies made the headlines day after day in the mideighties, and while Yuri Shvets was not in the news, he was very much on the playing field. After college, he went on to two years of postgraduate studies at what is now called the Academy of Foreign Intelligence (then the Yuri Andropov Red Banner Institute), where, as the Russian-language site Gordon reported, he was a "more talented" scholar than classmate Vladimir Putin and learned the secrets of the espionage trade—how to outwit surveillance, how to load and unload drops, how to execute prearranged clandestine "brush" exchanges.[35] He was taught by the Soviet Union's exalted Cold War heroes, the legendary spies, most of whom were unknown to Americans, who had stolen US atomic secrets and who had handled Julius and Ethel Rosenberg and British spies Kim Philby, Guy Burgess, and Donald Maclean. Shvets had been trained to follow in their footsteps.[36]

As a result, by the time he was twenty-eight, Shvets had become a major in the KGB, within which he worked for the First Chief Directorate, the most prestigious of the five chief directorates in the entire agency. Within the FCD, which was responsible for foreign operations and intelligence, there were sixteen geographical departments, and Yuri had been assigned to the First Department (a.k.a. the North American Department), comprising the United States and Canada.

Finally, within the North American Department, he was stationed at the Washington *rezidentura*, the capital of the "Main Adversary." Within the KGB, there was a certain rivalry between Washington station and its sister *rezidentura* in New York. The former, of course, was in the nation's capital, but the latter had a rich and colorful history as well that involved the Rosenberg case, the theft of atomic secrets, and massive expulsions of Soviet spies from the UN.

Regardless, in the world of Soviet intelligence, Shvets had arrived. And it was an adrenaline-filled realm full of mystery, adventure, and excitement. As he put it, Washington station was "the holy of the holies in the intelligence business."

That said, Shvets was not exactly a dyed-in-the-wool true believer in Soviet communism. Having mastered English, Spanish, and French, he had met people from all over the world, was far more cosmopolitan than the average Soviet citizen, and occupied the vast middle ground between devout adherents of Soviet communism and dissidents.

He had joined the KGB for a very simple reason. "It was the best job a man could have in the Soviet Union," he told me. The pay was good— by Soviet standards, at least. And the perks were fabulous. At a time when ordinary Soviet citizens lived with severe constraints behind the Iron Curtain, he could travel the world. In a country whose national discourse was a tightly controlled creation forged by propaganda and state censorship, Yuri had access to information that ordinary Soviet citizens couldn't get—via the *Washington Post*, the *New York Times*, American TV, and the BBC. Not to mention the secrets men die for.

Finally, he had a mission. When he had trained at the academy, he and his fellow cadets were constantly told that their country was in mortal danger and that they alone could save it. "In the Soviet Union—and now with Russia—to work for intelligence, you're like a national hero," Shvets told me.

And as he explained in his memoir, they were treated as such. "You have an unprecedented opportunity to distinguish yourself," General Dmitri Yakushkin, its celebrated department head, told him. "If there is still some room left for heroism, you can find it in my department."[37]

But after moving to Washington, Shvets gradually became disillusioned. Once he had spent time in the West and had access to media sources that weren't available to ordinary Soviets, Yuri saw Soviet propaganda for what it was. Increasingly, he found himself confronting a rotten, decaying bureaucracy. "What we were trained in the academy had nothing to do with real life," he told me. "And this is where the huge disappointment comes."

It was most notable at work. This was a period during which the most banal rendezvous imaginable could be hyped in reports to win favor with the powers that be in Moscow. All he had to do was take an American out to lunch, discuss the events of the day, and then link it to something he had read in the *Washington Post* that could be passed off as confidential. Again and again, Shvets told me, reports full of phony successes got positive feedback, so much so that another KGB agent explained it to him with a colorful Russian metaphor: "Where there are no birds, even an asshole sounds like a nightingale."[38]

Petrified that if they recruited someone, he would turn out to be a double agent who actually worked for the FBI or CIA, his fellow officers took no risks, and churned out unnecessary paperwork instead. "It turned out that what we were doing, it was for the sake of under-the-carpet bureaucratic fighting of a couple of octogenarians in the

Politburo," he told me. "They were using us, and they finally elected to collapse the entire country. It was disgusting."

When KGB officers were not sipping martinis at second-rate bars in Washington, they were shopping for their dachas back in Russia. Years later, Shvets would find himself asking how on earth such a comically incompetent organization could have actually installed a Russian asset as president of the United States.

CHAPTER FIVE

THE EXPERT

Throughout the mid-eighties, Yuri Shvets, just over two hundred miles away at the Washington *rezidentura*, was regularly in touch with his New York colleagues. Shvets says he is not certain who at the New York station would have been Trump's regular contact, but they almost certainly would have been someone at the Soviet Mission to the United Nations, and would have reached out to Trump at a frequency of roughly once a month. "That was standard procedure," he told me. "It was so standard it was like a cop asking you for your driver's license and registration after stopping your car for a traffic violation."

However, following up on Trump did *not* necessarily mean that the KGB viewed him as a high-value target. The KGB was always hungry for new American assets, and Trump was just one of hundreds of people it had approached. At best, he was a rich and influential businessman. Perhaps he would become more powerful in years to come.

And indeed Trump intended to do precisely that. At the time, the idea of engaging Trump in discussions about foreign policy and nuclear arms sounded downright silly, given his all-too-obvious lack of expertise, but it made sense for one simple reason: Suddenly, in the mid-eighties, for no discernible reason, Trump fancied himself one of the world's leading experts on nuclear armaments. He knew everything about nuclear, or so he said.

Exactly where this fantasy originated is unclear. Trump's uncle John Trump, who died in 1985, was in fact a physicist at MIT who pioneered medical and engineering applications of high-voltage machinery and, together with Robert J. Van de Graaff, developed one of the first million-volt X-ray generators. As reported in *Science for the People*, John Trump had been approached repeatedly to make weapons of all sorts. "What did he do with it?" asked Trump lab director James Melcher. "Cancer research, sterilizing sludge out in Deer Island—a waste disposal facility—all sorts of wondrous things. He didn't touch the weapons stuff."[1]

Donald Trump often cited his illustrious uncle as evidence of the Trump family's genetic predisposition to dazzling intelligence. But there is no evidence to suggest that Uncle John had mentored his nephew on the subject.

As William E. Geist observed in the *New York Times*, with his newly crafted persona as a strategic nuclear arms virtuoso, Trump, briefly at least, left behind the showy attire he had worn earlier (burgundy suits with matching shoes, for example) in favor of dark suits, white shirts, and subdued ties. Suddenly, Trump, the brash, vulgar carney barker, who always projected the aesthetics of Vegas more than Manhattan, had a new side to him. He was thoughtful. He was deep. He thought we might be headed toward a nuclear holocaust. And he wanted to stop it.

Nor was this a passing fancy. In April 1984, Trump told Geist that his concern about a nuclear holocaust had troubled him since he first discussed it with his uncle many years earlier. As a result, he said, he wanted to put his astonishing talents to work negotiating arms agreements.[2]

Similarly, seven months later he surprised *Washington Post* reporter Lois Romano in November 1984 by saying that he should take over the Strategic Arms Limitation Talks with the Soviet Union.[3]

"Some people have an ability to negotiate. It's an art you're basically born with. You either have it or you don't."

Trump made it clear that he thought he had what it takes to handle the negotiations. And as for mastering the nuts and bolts of strategic arms limitations, missiles, nuclear proliferation, and the like—well, that would be child's play. "It would take an hour-and-a-half to learn everything there is to learn about missiles," he told Romano. "I think I know most of it anyway."

Before the interview was over, Trump answered a question that had not been asked. When he did that, it meant he had a special item on his agenda he wanted to get across.

"You know who really wants me to do this?" he asked. "Roy . . . I'd do it in a second."

Roy, of course, was Trump attorney Roy Cohn, who had won notoriety for being the hatchet man for Senator Joe McCarthy (R-WI), the red-baiting demagogue of the fifties.

So now Trump was telling the *Washington Post* that Cohn had been urging him to become involved in nuclear talks. What was that about?

First, it's hard to believe that Cohn, still an unreconstructed McCarthyite Cold Warrior, would get in bed with the Soviets in any way, shape, or form. Or that he would think it was a good idea to have Trump promote himself as an expert on nuclear arms. More likely, Trump, who even then had a creative relationship with the facts, was making it up. With his friend Ronald Reagan in the White House, Roy Cohn's name carried considerable clout in Washington and was certain to get the attention of a *Washington Post* reporter. In Trump's eyes, having Cohn's name attached would have lent the charade gravity.

Then, in 1985, Trump met with a reporter for a stylish, now-defunct monthly business magazine called *Manhattan, Inc.*, which chronicled Wall Street and the "Masters of the Universe" who ran it. In short, the magazine dissected a culture that was all about money, greed, and conspicuous consumption.

By this time, Trump had become a staple in the tabloids' gossip columns. Trump Tower had been the talk of international real estate in the two years since it had opened, and with celebrities such as Michael Jackson, Johnny Carson, Bruce Willis, and Sophia Loren owning condos there, it had begun to define Trump as the ultimate luxury brand in the largely unbranded new sector of high-end condos. Even though one stupendous project after another never reached fruition or failed—a massive domed sports stadium, a 150-story building—Trump's brand skyrocketed.

At the same time, to the media, his intense and unlikely preoccupation with "the Subject," as Trump called the nuclear arms race, and his passion to save humanity from annihilation served up a deliciously ironic stew of new money, glitz, and strategic arms limitation talks—incongruous as a sure winner. With that in mind, the Manhattan, Inc. art director Nancy Butkus told Topic, she decided she wanted "a really nice, formal portrait—with one thing that's weird."[4]

To that end, while Trump was combing his hair in the bathroom, she spoke to him through the closed door and asked him to pose with a bird.

"Because you're so interested in world peace, can you pose with a dove?"

Trump was silent for a few seconds.

"Sure," he replied.

So photographer William Coupon went to work with an eye toward capturing the image of the avian symbol of peace perched atop the impeccably sculpted tonsorial edifice that was otherwise known as Donald Trump's hair.

Which was all well and good until the dove decided to unburden itself on Donald Trump's germophobic hands.[5]

Peculiar as Trump's nuclear fixation may have been, from the KGB point of view, it presented a new opening. "To have any expertise on these issues, Trump would have to be briefed by somebody," Shvets told me. "But as a real estate developer, he wasn't part of any think tank. He didn't work for the State Department or the Pentagon."

Yet Trump was obsessed enough that, in his own peculiar way, he sought out expertise on the matter. In 1986, he met with Nobel laureate Dr. Bernard Lown, who, along with Soviet cardiologist Yevgeny Chazov, had just accepted the Nobel Peace Prize on behalf of the International Physicians for the Prevention of Nuclear War. Knowing that Lown had recently returned from meeting Mikhail Gorbachev in

Moscow, Trump pumped him for everything he knew about the Soviet leader, and then declared that within an hour of meeting Gorbachev, he would end the Cold War. "The arrogance of the man and his ignorance," Lown told me. "The idea that he could solve it in one hour!"

Trump also attended a November 1985 Palm Beach gala put together by Armand Hammer, the wealthy owner of Occidental Petroleum who had long and close ties to the Kremlin.

By the eighties, Hammer was dispensing advice to both President Reagan and Mikhail Gorbachev. And the Soviets loved him for it—enough that, the *New York Times* reported, Brezhnev gave Hammer a luxurious Moscow apartment and suggested that he be appointed US ambassador to Moscow. It was a suggestion that perplexed members of the Reagan administration, one of whom told the *New York Times*, "We simply don't know which side of the fence Hammer is on."[6]

In other words, Armand Hammer might well be a Soviet asset.

There was little doubt that Trump would have loved to be in a similar position to that of the eighty-seven-year-old Armand Hammer—and that presented the KGB with the perfect opening.

When I asked Yuri Shvets and Glenn Carle about how a KGB agent might handle a new asset who was being cultivated, their answers were somewhat similar. "Be good to them," said Shvets. "Give them what they want. Have a good relationship."

As Carle explained, "I think we [as handlers] are dream makers. We fulfill the dreams of our targets. Whatever you lack, we can provide. If you need psychological soothing because you are under stress, come cry on my shoulder. If you need someone to talk to, I'm a listener. If you want a bowling buddy, you know, I really like ten pin. And so forth."

Similarly, it would not have taken a genius to figure out what Trump wanted. "It was like he was created for this," said Shvets. "This is what the KGB is looking for. With Trump, it was so obvious. It was just striking."

One of the great paradoxes of intelligence work is that highly sensitive clandestine work is sometimes done best in plain sight—that openness provides the best cover. As Carle told me, "Good intelligence operations are designed to *not* be punishable in a court of law."

The KGB knew that, of course, and designed intelligence operations accordingly. As a result, KGB tradecraft and protocols slithered in, around, and through the myriad loopholes in America's legal system, government bureaucracies, and regulatory agencies. So Donald Trump bought hundreds of TV sets from Semyon Kislin's electronics store. There's nothing wrong with that. How could he have known that Joy-Lud was under the thumb of the KGB? Or, more important, how could prosecutors *prove* that Trump knew?

Having become a major figure in New York, thanks to Trump Tower, the future president desperately wanted a place on the world stage. For the next step, the strategy was so simple as to be self-evident: Donald Trump was a real estate developer. He developed buildings all over the world.

So it was easy to discuss such matters with Trump without attracting undue attention. There was no reason to suspect that occasional meetings with Russian diplomats were really a way for the KGB to develop Trump as an asset. Trump's new interest in "nuclear" only made the KGB's task easier.

"Trump's contact would have called him and invited him to lunch or dinner on some pretext to discuss having a Trump Tower in Moscow, or to learn Trump's 'valuable opinion' on important war and peace issues," said Shvets. Deeply insecure intellectually, highly suggestible, exceedingly susceptible to flattery, Trump was anxious to acquire some real intellectual validation. In that regard, the KGB would be more than happy to humor him.

Discussions about Trump Tower Moscow could provide a highly credible cover for contacts with Trump that could last for decades. And besides, Trump had long since befriended various people at the FBI such as James Kallstrom, the stalwart Trump supporter who later attacked Bill and Hillary Clinton as being "a crime family." So the FBI was unlikely to do a deep dive into his relationship with the Soviets.

In the end, Trump's dreams of building a Trump Tower in Red

Square were as ludicrous as his putative expertise on nuclear arms. To be sure, Soviet leader Mikhail Gorbachev came to be known as a genial peacemaker who thawed Cold War tensions, but as he reminded a reporter in early 1986, he was still very much a communist, and the communism of Lenin remained "a fine and unsullied ideal."[7]

At the time, the Soviets still zealously guarded the Berlin Wall to safeguard East Germans from the allure of capitalist luxuries in the West. Soviet media were rigorously state-controlled and monitored for the same reason. In that context, how could anyone really think that Soviet communists wanted a garish monument to conspicuous consumption—Trump Tower Moscow—near Red Square? A shrine to American capitalism near the Kremlin?

"The Soviet government was running out of money," Shvets told me. "It was looking to the West for loans because they didn't have enough to feed their own people. To suggest that they were seriously considering building Trump Tower in Moscow was just insane."

Nevertheless, Trump was incapable of resisting sycophantic flattery, so the Soviets humored him and played on his vanity. "No one needed him in Moscow at that time, except the KGB, because they went after everybody who was willing to cooperate," said Shvets.

Trump Tower Moscow would be one of the crown jewels in his empire. Trump Tower in New York had made him a player on the national stage. Building in Moscow would mean he had gone international.

———

For all the unanswered questions, the most "authoritative" official Russian account of how the Trump Tower Moscow project began appeared on the website of the Moscow-based daily newspaper *Moskovsky Komsomolets* (*MK*) at exactly 6:54 p.m. Moscow time on November 9, 2019—nine hours and twenty minutes after Hillary Clinton conceded defeat and Donald Trump was declared the forty-fifth president of the United States.[8]

At that precise moment, *MK*, with a circulation of nearly one million, posted an interview with Natalia Dubinina, the daughter of Soviet ambassador to the United Nations Yuri Dubinin, who, with her father, was among the first Soviet officials to meet Trump in March 1986.

It's worth noting, too, that even though she spoke out so quickly, Natalia was still not the first person to put forth a new version of how Trump's relationship to the Soviet Union began. The day before—November 8, 2016, Election Day in America—Ekaterina Dobrynina was quoted on the Rain, a Russian website, asserting that in 1987 her father, Yuri Dobrynin, then ambassador to the United States (not to be confused with his successor, Yuri Dubinin, who also served as ambassador to the UN), had the idea of building *two* Trump Towers, one in Moscow and one in Leningrad. "My dad tried to promote it here, to Russia, in order to build here—he wanted everything, dreamed of—both here and in Leningrad Trump Towers," she said.[9]

But her account was not nearly as fleshed out as Natalia Dubinina's account in *MK*. "Why did an American businessman come to Russia several times?" the article asks. "*MK* dug up exclusive details of Donald Trump's very first visit to Moscow and learned that it was not politics or the alluring smell of money from new business projects that played a decisive role here, but a combination of circumstances and the wide smile of a Soviet diplomat."[10]

The *MK* version begins in March 1986, when Soviet diplomat Dubinin was appointed the Soviet Union's permanent representative to the United Nations and flew to New York, where his twenty-nine-year-old daughter Natalia was working for the UN. At the time, rigidly enforced Soviet rules did not allow members of the same family to work in the same foreign country at the same time, so Natalia had planned to fly back to the Soviet Union just as her father arrived.

But, according to *MK*, Natalia's flight home was postponed, which meant that she had a rare opportunity to put together a quick tour around New York for him. "I met Dad and offered to show him New York," Natalia recalled. "Still, I had lived there for a long time at that time, and he came for the first time in his life."

According to Natalia, the first stop was Trump Tower on Fifth Avenue, which so impressed her father that he decided he had to meet the creator of this "unprecedented architectural masterpiece."

"This building was the first thing my father saw in New York," Dubinina told *MK*. "He had never seen anything like it, it was a revolution in architecture and approach."

In fact, he was so amazed, Dubinina said, that he decided he had to meet the building's creator immediately, at which point he and Natalia took the elevator up to Donald Trump's office, in what was an extraordinary departure from the Soviet Union's Cold War protocol.

After all, in the context of the ongoing spy wars, the career foreign service officers and "clean" diplomats from the Soviet Union knew all too well that the FBI was scoping them out and making recruitment pitches. According to Shvets, simply being targeted by the FBI pretty much meant the end of a career and an abrupt return to Moscow.

In that context, going upstairs on a whim to meet Donald Trump would have posed a foolish risk to both Dubinina and her father. "The top officials, such as the *rezident* in New York, Washington, or the Soviet ambassador, these are guys who knew a lot of secret information," said Shvets. "The ambassador, for instance, was aware of many other confidential things, and I remember the then KGB *rezident* saying he wasn't authorized to work in the streets of America without a bodyguard. This was an ironclad rule."

In 1984 and 1985, there were two incidents in the Soviet embassy in DC when the FBI tried to recruit officers of the KGB *rezidentura* from the embassy. Shortly thereafter, all Soviet diplomats in the United States, unless they were intelligence officers, were forbidden to make unauthorized unofficial contact with any Americans whatsoever. Merely being approached by the FBI could get them sent home, as the KGB was deeply afraid that the FBI would resort to dire measures to get any information it was looking for.

Nevertheless, Dubinina's account has it that as soon as her silver-tongued father met Trump, he brushed all such protocols aside and took charge. "My father was fluent in English," Natalia told *MK*, "and when he told Trump that the first thing he saw in New York was Trump Tower, Trump immediately melted. He is an emotional person, somewhat impulsive. He needs recognition and, of course, he likes when he gets it. My father's visit had an effect on him like honey on a bee."

About six months later,[11] in autumn, at a luncheon given by cosmetics czar Leonard Lauder, Trump found himself seated next to Dubinin, who had been newly appointed as ambassador to the United States, and Vitaly Churkin, both of whom promoted the Trump Tower Moscow project. As Trump (via ghostwriter Tony Schwartz) claims in *The Art of the Deal*, "One thing led to another, and now I'm talking about building a large luxury hotel, across the street from the Kremlin, in partnership with the Soviet government."[12]

———

To most readers, Dubinina's account may seem relatively anodyne, but in fact it's full of inaccuracies, some of which appear to be intentional—and all of which raise the question of whether there was another agenda behind its publication. The errors are important, Shvets says, because they lead one who understands the KGB modus operandi to believe that "Natalia was a KGB officer and her story in *MK* was an attempt to cover the true nature of the KGB's contact with Trump."

According to Shvets, the real significance of the "gross lies" in the *MK* story is that it is an active measure fabricated by Russian intelligence with two goals. "It was a 'hello' from the Russian human intelligence (HUMINT) to DT, their man at the White House," Shvets texted me. "And it was an urgent attempt to conceal the details of his initial contacts with the KGB foreign intelligence."

Shvets's analysis is based not so much on inside information about the people behind the *MK* article as on his training and knowledge as a former KGB agent who was well versed in the same modi operandi and had seen and run active-measure operations from the inside; who knew how to recruit an American agent and had actually done it himself; and who knew what the tells were in intelligence operations, how to look for them, and how to avoid them. He had acquired this experience working with the KGB in Washington at the same time that Dubinina worked in the sister *rezidentura* in New York. He also worked at the same department with Alexander Yelagin and Yuri Antipov, acting chief of the KGB's NY *rezidentura* in the mid-1980s. As a result, his familiarity with tradecraft and protocols that governed operations for both Yuri Dubinin and his daughter helped uncover inconsistencies in her account that are quite revealing.

Among other things, Shvets noted anomalies in Natalia's life that left the two years after her graduation from Moscow State Institute of International Relations (MGIMO), the prestigious Soviet foreign policy university, shrouded in mystery. That happens a lot, Shvets says, to young intelligence officers who train at the Yuri Andropov Red Banner Institute (the same spy school that trained Shvets) and need to cover up those years with fictitious employment before they engage in operational work. "After graduation, and before you go into operational work, you spend one to three years in training. And you just drop out of sight for a period of time. But then, when you compose your official biography, you need to cover those two or three years."

And when he looked into Dubinina's past, he found plenty of unanswered questions. "In different Russian publications the place of Natalia's employment at the time sounds weird: the Problem Laboratory for Systems Analysis of International Relations (Лаборатория проблемного анализа международных отношений)," he said. "In fact, there was no such lab in the Soviet Union at the time, and the closest name was Scientific Center of Information (НЦИ—Научный Центр Информации), which was the unofficial name of the KGB First Chief Directorate."

Using that as a cover for the time she spent training at the spy school was lousy tradecraft, he pointed out, speculating that Natalia apparently thought no one would bother looking into it. And no one did until *MK* published her interview and Shvets looked into it.

Then there was the question of timing. "Dubinina had kept silent from 1986 until the day after Trump's election," said Shvets. "And suddenly she comes out with a big interview published the very same day. So it had to be prepared in advance. Her interview to *MK* was an important part of a major Russian HUMINT cover-up operation designed to camouflage the roots of DT's contacts with the Russians. Instead, it blew them up."

The publication itself, *Moskovsky Komsomolets*, is of interest as well, because, according to *The Guardian*, it has aided both Soviet and Russian intelligence in the past, including publishing disinformation suggesting that Alexander Litvinenko, the renegade anti-Putin FSB agent who died of polonium poisoning in London, may have been killed by Americans.[13]

Shvets also says that *MK* has been used by the KGB, the FSB, and the SVR for active measures on many occasions. "I know firsthand that *Moskovsky Komsomolets* was used for active measures by the Russian intelligence community," Shvets wrote me in a text message. "I know their modus operandi, because I was trained by the same textbooks as Putin and those who are running Russian intelligence services. The content [in the Dubinina interview] was highly sensitive. It was not something the editor could print without authorization from the Kremlin." He believes the article was edited "to the letter at the top of the Russian HUMINT and scrutinized by the Kremlin" before publication.

Shvets added, "The KGB modus operandi clearly shows that Natalia was a KGB officer, and her story in *MK*, together with some other Russian media publications, indicates that her interview was an attempt to cover up the true nature of the KGB contact with Trump."[14]

In this case, Shvets said, the Dubinina interview reminds him of one that took place in 2009 when Vladimir Putin appointed Patriarch Kirill as the new head of the Russian Orthodox Church, shortly after which a retired KGB agent spoke out to the press about his long friendship with Kirill. "Everyone realized it was an interview with the KGB handler for the patriarch. It was absolutely clear. It was the KGB message to the new patriarch of the Russian Orthodox Church, saying, 'Look, guys. We remember who you were, since you were our agent. Nothing is forgotten, so you must follow the party line.' The same is true with respect to Natalia's interview."

But this time, the FSB was saying hello to Donald Trump, obscuring the origins of his cultivation from journalists and investigators.

Then, as we have already seen, Dubinina's claims that she met her father at the airport on his arrival, took him on an impromptu tour of New York, and went up to Donald Trump's office to meet him violate every protocol in the book. Normal procedure was for the ambassador to be met at the airport by a group of Soviet diplomats and immediately taken to their offices. There were no impromptu outings.

At the time, the same rules applied to the Washington *rezidentura* where Shvets worked and in New York where Dubinina worked. As a result, Soviet diplomats, unless they were intelligence officers, avoided all unauthorized, unofficial contacts with Americans. Intelligence operatives were in a different category because it was their job to make such contacts. After all, how could they possibly recruit spies unless they were out and about?

But according to Shvets, career Soviet diplomats who were *not* spies—the KGB referred to them as "clean"—rarely left their offices unless it was for a hearing on Capitol Hill, a public presentation of some report, or a run to the State Department to pick up official documents. They rigorously avoided face-to-face meetings with Americans, during which the FBI might try to recruit them. So it was fairly easy to tell who among Soviet diplomats and journalists actually worked for the KGB. Only KGB guys were free and active in their contacts in the United States, and by 1985, the FBI had begun to figure that out.

Finally, even if one accepts Natalia's account in which she and her father violated such strictly enforced protocols on his very first day as ambassador, there is another problem—namely, her assertion that her father, with his great command of the English language, dazzled Trump so thoroughly that he "immediately melted."

Quite simply, it's not true.

Far from being fluent in English, Yuri Dubinin's English was so bad that his failure to learn the language was cited in the *Washington Post*,[15] the *New York Times*, United Press International,[16] the *Chicago Tribune*,[17] *Newsweek*,[18] and many other publications as being an unusual and major deficit for an ambassador in such a highly visible position.

According to *Newsweek*, after he arrived in the United States—that is, *after* he and Natalia met with Trump—Dubinin began to study English with a tutor,[19] but even then he had to rely on interpreters to take questions in English at press conferences.[20] In May 1986, just two months after moving to New York as ambassador to the United Nations, Dubinin was given an even more prestigious post as Soviet ambassador to the United States. The *Washington Post* reported that his selection was "a surprise choice" because "Moscow broke with its practice of appointing experts on American affairs and fluent English speakers to its top diplomatic job in Washington."[21]

Similarly, the *New York Times* noted that Dubinin's appointment as the ambassador "startled some diplomats," given that he had the "handicap" of needing "an interpreter in conversing with English-speakers here."[22]

From Shvets's point of view—that of a KGB major working in the First Chief Directorate's Washington station and having regular contact with his colleagues in New York—Dubinin's inability to speak English was no accident, and may even have been one of the reasons he was chosen for such a prominent post.

At the time, Shvets was visiting the Soviet embassy nearly every day. "Because Ambassador Dubinin didn't speak English, he just sat in his cubicle at the embassy without even leaving the premises of the building. He was occupying the third floor, and he lived in complete seclusion. He didn't show up even for meals at the embassy. For meals, his wife would go down to the cafeteria. She would place an order, choosing the meals the ambassador would want, and then she would take them upstairs. He would never go down.

"He was living as a hermit in the Soviet embassy. For at least a year and a half, after becoming the ambassador, he didn't sign any cable coming from the United States to Moscow. Because he said, 'Look, I don't speak English. I don't understand what they're talking about on TV, what they write in the newspapers.'"

Until then, Anatoly Dobrynin, a legend in Soviet diplomacy, had served as ambassador to the United States for twenty-four years, spanning the terms of six presidents and dating back to the Cuban Missile Crisis. But he had been recalled by General Secretary Mikhail Gorbachev to play a key role with the Kremlin in reformulating Soviet relations with the United States. He was so close to Henry Kissinger that he dined with him as often as four times a week and cruised with him aboard the presidential yacht, the USS *Sequoia*. According to Zbigniew Brzezinski, who served as national security advisor under Jimmy Carter, the shift—bringing Dobrynin back to Moscow—was a signal that Gorbachev was ready to pursue an active policy of détente with the United States.[23]

All of which meant that the Kremlin didn't want to replace Dobrynin with a powerful new voice in Washington shooting his mouth off and gumming up the works. So instead they got Dubinin, whom the *New York Times* termed a "gray-faced apparatchik" and whose hard-line positions and attentiveness to tonsorial matters earned him the description "a Molotov with a pompadour."[24]

"Dubinin was supposed to be a Mr. Nobody," said Shvets. "They didn't want a competing voice to be heard in Washington, and that's why they picked a guy who didn't speak any English. His role was to lay low, make no waves."

But if Dubinin didn't speak the language, that meant the initial contact with Trump came from someone else. And *that* leaves Natalia as a likely KGB operative who may have been in contact with Trump during this period.

And if Dubinina was, as she contends, merely another Soviet apparatchik working at the United Nations, she would not have been authorized to meet with Trump, because it was not her job. After all, at the time, the spy wars were still going full blast. With virtually any Soviet citizen considered a ripe target for the FBI, making unauthorized outside contacts with Americans was a fairly certain way to get in trouble with the KGB and win a one-way ticket back to the motherland. Unless, of course, she was already with the KGB at the time.

Mind you, this was a period during which the Soviet Mission to the United Nations was widely seen as a nesting place for the KGB. Indeed, in March 1986, the United States had demanded that the Soviet Mission cut personnel because of concerns they were engaged in nondiplomatic activities including spying.[25] According to the Senate Select Committee on Intelligence, the Soviet Mission had been widely infiltrated by the KGB, which led to the expulsion of twenty-five diplomats attached to the Soviet Mission to the UN later in 1986 and a total of more than one hundred by March 1988.[26]

"They violate our law with impunity," said Senator Daniel Patrick Moynihan (D-NY). "They know that we know they are doing it. Not to stop them invites contempt and in my view deserves contempt."[27]

But back to Dubinina for a moment. It may seem a small thing, perhaps—a self-promoting article in a Russian newspaper with a number of errors and lies. What's the big deal? Why does it really matter so much if Natalia rather than her father reached out to Trump?

The significance of the Dubinina interview, Shvets said, was that it was the "origin story" for Trump's relationship to Russia, the whole point of which was to conceal the ties between Trump and the KGB. But, according to Shvets, Dubinina inadvertently showed her hand "and exposed the fact that, as of 1986, Donald Trump was a contact of the KGB station in New York run out of Moscow by the KGB First Chief Directorate and its key First Department."[28]

And that goes right to the heart of how Donald Trump was cultivated as a Russian asset. Obscuring the real story appears to have been important enough that Russian intelligence would plant a phony story about it thirty years later. "One of the key elements of the article was to camouflage the fact that it was the KGB intelligence that had an original contact with Trump and brought him to Moscow," said Shvets. "This is crucial. If it was Russian HUMINT that established the initial contact, all subsequent contacts with Russian representatives had to be ultimately controlled by the KGB/FSB/SVR and were part of one big intelligence operation, which significantly contributed to his election as the US president in 2016.

"So, Natalia was trying to show it was her father—not her—and the contact was official and had nothing to do with Soviet intelligence. That was purpose number one.

"And number two, the KGB believed that Trump would read this article or translation of this article. It was like a reminder saying, 'Guys, we remember. And you see, we are lying. . . . We are camouflaging our relationship, but we remember everything.'"

Finally, there was the initial premise of the relationship between Trump and Moscow—the Soviet Union's infatuation with the idea of building a Trump Tower in Moscow. "It's all bullshit, because the chances for his Trump Tower in Moscow were zero. But this is how they put people on the hook and say, 'Look, I'd like you to come over and just discuss this thing with you.' And this silly guy, he couldn't understand what's going on in Russia or in the Soviet Union in Moscow. Yes, he is flattered. He is happy. He sees beautiful women. He is like a peacock."

And that, according to Shvets, is the story of how Donald Trump was invited to Russia.

Finally, knowing what we know about Donald Trump, what makes more sense: that Trump was wooed by Yuri Dubinin, then a non-English-speaking man in his midfifties who was renowned as a hardliner, or his daughter, Natalia, an attractive twenty-nine-year-old woman who spoke fluent English and just may have happened to work for the KGB?

Natalia Dubinina declined to respond to multiple phone calls and text messages.

CHAPTER SIX

YASENEVO DAYS

To the general public, the KGB often calls to mind images of Lubyanka, the massive neobaroque Moscow building where Nikolai Bukharin, the Bolshevik revolutionary and foe of Joseph Stalin, was wrongfully charged in 1937 with plotting to kill Vladimir Lenin and Joseph Stalin and sentenced to death in a show trial. More than a thousand prisoners were executed in the basement of the central KGB building between 1944 and the early 1960s.[1] The locus of countless Stalinist purges that has now become a fabled museum of fear, it was also where some of the architects of those purges, such as Lavrentiy Beria, were executed themselves. It has a dark, harrowing history.

By contrast, the home of the KGB's First Chief Directorate in Yasenevo, a suburban district on Moscow's southwest perimeter, is a more obscure, heavily restricted compound in an area surrounded by hills covered with birch trees, green pastures, and, in summer, fields of wheat and rye.[2] As one approaches it by car, the facility is designated by an intentionally vague signs that read "Sanitary Zone" and "Scientific Research Center."[3] A tree-lined driveway takes one to a modern seven-story building that is the headquarters for KGB counterintelligence. The main Y-shaped office building, now adjoining much taller ones, is flanked on one side by a library and an assembly hall and on the other by a clinic, sports complex, and swimming pool.

For all the notoriety and history behind Lubyanka, within the

KGB, Yasenevo had more prestige—and perks. "It was the dream of KGB officers to work in the First Chief Directorate," said Shvets. "It was the elite within the KGB.

"It was Putin's dream, too," he added. "He applied for a job but never got it."

Shvets seemed to say that with a tinge of irony, but it's a matter of some pride that he won admission to this elite assemblage of counter-intelligence professionals, and classmate Vladimir Putin did not.

Referred to as "the Woods," it was the KGB's—and later the SVR's—equivalent of Langley, situated just beyond Moscow's ring road, a beltway like Washington's Interstate 495. Bucolic though it was, the headquarters of the First Chief Directorate was guarded more heavily than the Kremlin, its perimeter ringed with barbed wire and electronic sensors and patrolled by guards with attack dogs.

This was luxury—Soviet-style. The Soviet Union was falling apart economically, but here there were masseuses, lavish private parties, and servants to clean rooms, cook, and tend gardens. There was a swimming pool, tennis courts, a soccer field, saunas, and a gym. As described in Pete Earley's *Comrade J: The Untold Secrets of Russia's Master Spy in America After the End of the Cold War*, the in-house grocery store was stocked with salmon, sausage, cheese, caviar, and fresh produce that were simply not available to the mass of Soviet citizens.[4] "They had cinema showing films, movies in foreign languages just to maintain the professional qualifications," says Shvets. "They had a swimming pool where they had carp, which they would serve for dinner. It was quite a good place for leisure before you took trips abroad. So you would be stationed abroad for three or four years and then come back for two or three years at headquarters."

Within the main building, the North American Department (United States and Canada) of the First Chief Directorate occupied half of the fifth floor in one of the building's wings.[5] This was ground zero when it came to spying on the United States. At the time, there were no computers or high-tech equipment whatsoever—just filing cabinets and standard-issue desks in offices that were about 160 square feet. The chief of the directorate and the deputy chief each had his own private office.[6]

Lavish comforts aside, coming back to Yasenevo was not exactly what Yuri Shvets was expecting career-wise. Throughout the early eighties, Yuri and his colleagues were regularly berated by the top brass for their failure to recruit Americans. "Theoretically, every field officer in the KGB was supposed to look for, identify, develop, and recruit agents," said Shvets, who was tasked to do precisely that in the United States.

Recruit, recruit, recruit—that was the KGB mantra. But in truth, going out cold and trying to win over a new recruit rarely happened. There were plenty of spies in the United States, but most of the double agents working for the Soviets were walk-ins, who sometimes literally walked into the Soviet embassy, as Aldrich Ames did, or devised a system of anonymous cold drops, as Robert Hanssen did; and they did it for the money. In fact, when Shvets looked back over the period between 1970 and 1985 and the hundreds of KGB field officers in Washington, New York, and San Francisco, he could find only one other case of a KGB officer actually recruiting an American spy who was not a walk-in.

The officer who brought in the recruit happened to be none other than General Oleg Kalugin, later the KGB's head of counterintelligence, who had found, identified, developed, and recruited an agent all by himself.

So what kind of reward did Kalugin get for his triumph? He was sent back to the Soviet Union, accused—probably wrongly so—of having recruited a spy who was really an American disinformation agent. In the end, Kalugin was demoted to deputy head of the Leningrad KGB in what was a severe blow to his career.

Which was very similar what had happened to Shvets, who had managed to recruit two sources of political intelligence: the former White House adviser and journalist, who was code-named Socrates, and his wife, also a journalist, code-named Sputnitsa.

Socrates was later identified by Shvets as John Helmer, an Australian native who graduated from Harvard and became a White House aide to Jimmy Carter. His wife, Claudia Wright, a.k.a. Sputnitsa, was an Australian journalist who worked for National Public Radio, the

New Statesman, and other media outlets.[7] (Helmer moved to Moscow in 1989, where he wrote for the *Australian Financial Review, The Australian*, and other newspapers.[8] Claudia Wright died in 2005.) These were the Reagan years, of course, so Helmer was no longer an administration insider, but he delivered intel to Shvets on the Iran-Contra scandal before it became public, on US relations with Libya, and on other foreign policy issues, which KGB analysts assessed as being both highly sensitive and highly valuable.

But, as with Kalugin, instead of being hailed as a hero for recruiting new assets, Shvets was sent back to Moscow in March 1987, where his bosses put him under a microscope. "They were positive Socrates was actually a CIA plant, and it wasn't me who recruited someone; it was the CIA who was trying to develop and recruit me," he told me.

As it happened, Shvets had had the good sense to make sure Socrates was coming in from Washington to Yasenevo a few weeks later. That meant his colleagues would have a chance to cross-examine Socrates themselves. Much of the top brass thought Yuri had been conned by Socrates. Yuri himself said that it was almost impossible to recruit the genuine article. The only way to find out the truth was to spend hours with Socrates, cross-examining him, pumping him full of KGB talking points, and assessing whether he was ready to cooperate.

Shvets and Socrates weren't the only ones being sent to Moscow. Donald Trump was coming, too. In January 1987, Yuri Dubinin, who had already finished his brief two-month term as permanent resident to the UN and had become the chief Soviet envoy to Washington, wrote Trump a letter. According to *The Art of the Deal*, Dubinin told Trump there was "good news from Moscow," namely that Goscomintourist, the leading Soviet tourist agency, "had expressed interest in pursuing a joint venture to construct and manage a hotel in Moscow."

Trump's trip began on July 4, 1987. Independence Day.*[9] *The Guard-*

---

* The Soviets had a propensity for scheduling propitious events on memorable holidays. Notably, in 2018, the Russians hosted eight Republican legislators to celebrate the Fourth of July in Moscow. It also happened to be the same day that British officials said two people had been poisoned by a nerve agent that many speculated

ian's Luke Harding wrote about it in some detail, in *Collusion: Secret Meetings, Dirty Money, and How Russia Helped Donald Trump Win*, as resembling "a classic cultivation exercise, which would have had the KGB's full support."[10] And, as this book will show, new facts have come to light regarding Trump's visit that make it difficult to believe that the trip was anything other than a means of activating Trump's relationship with the KGB.

First, according to Shvets, the letter inviting Trump was written at the behest of General Ivan Gromakov in the First Chief Directorate's *rezidentura* in Washington. Gromakov, who died in 2009, was a high-level operative who headed the Fourth Department of the First Chief Directorate and in the early eighties attended meetings with then–KGB chairman Viktor Chebrikov, First Chief Directorate head Vladimir Kryuchov, and other top brass overseeing the Stasi with East German spymaster Markus Wolf.[11]

"It was an established procedure for the KGB stations in the US to use Ambassador Dubinin to pass on invitations to Americans to visit Moscow," said Shvets. "Usually, those trips were used for 'deep development,' recruitment, or for a meeting with the KGB handlers. In most cases the trips were organized by Goscomintourist, the Soviet government traveler agency that was better known as Intourist and served as a front for the KGB. If the trip included all expenses paid by Intourist, it was a clear indication that the KGB was behind it."

By all accounts, Trump was thrilled with the invitation. But there is no evidence that he was aware of General Gromakov's role or the widely known fact that Intourist was a KGB-run operation that allowed the Soviets to keep an eye on virtually any foreigner who made it to the Soviet Union.

Before Trump was brought to Moscow, Shvets says, the KGB in New York City would have done what they called a "preliminary evaluation" of his personality. For this they got information on him from their human assets in his entourage—Kislin, perhaps; maybe David

---

came from Vladimir Putin, and a day after the Senate Intelligence Committee affirmed that Russia interfered in the election to aid Trump.

Bogatin, who had bought five condos in Trump Tower; or possibly Natalia Dubinina, another alleged operative.

Next came the professional evaluation, for which Trump would have had to meet with an experienced operative at least three or four times. "In terms of his personality," Shvets added, "the guy is not a complicated cookie, his most important characteristics being low intellect coupled with hyperinflated vanity. This combination makes him a dream for an experienced recruiter."

Traveling with his wife Ivana, Trump stayed at the National Hotel, where Vladimir Lenin and his wife had stayed in 1917 and where Trump was almost certainly under constant observation. During the trip, Trump saw half a dozen potential building sites, none of which were as close to the Kremlin as he had hoped.[12]

To the CIA's former Moscow station chief Rolf Mowatt-Larssen, in this relatively early stage of Trump's career, when he was prominent in New York but hardly an international figure, there was no question that the KGB would be all over Trump when he visited Russia. "There's no way they would overlook a guy like Trump," Mowatt-Larssen told me. "He's a prominent American. Any trip—he goes to Moscow—it's going to be a full-court press."

Meanwhile, he was given a grand tour of Moscow and entertained lavishly. Oleg Kalugin, the former KGB counterintelligence head, has speculated that the KGB may have deployed prostitutes as "honey traps" for Trump in hopes of entrapping the future president. Kalugin, who did not claim to have seen such materials, told me, "I would not be surprised if the Russians have, and Trump knows about them, files on him during his trip to Russia and his involvement with meeting young ladies that were controlled [by Soviet intelligence]."[13]

But now that Trump had come to Moscow, the KGB had to figure out what to do with him. "When you have a new source," says Shvets, "you start thinking, How are you going to use the guy? When we were taught how to recruit, they said, 'Recruit us anybody—we'll find how to use him.'"

At the time, the KGB was also concerned about losing aging assets such as Occidental Petroleum's Armand Hammer, who had had an intimate and intriguing relationship with the Soviets that went back decades. Dating back to the early 1920s, Soviet leaders, from Vladimir Lenin and Joseph Stalin to Leonid Brezhnev and Mikhail Gorbachev, had used Hammer as a valuable tool in opening Western capital markets to the Soviets.[14] For decades, he had aided the flow of funds and technology into the USSR, bribed foreign officials, and acted as a facilitator for the Soviet intelligence in such a way that Edward Jay Epstein, the author of the Hammer biography *Dossier*, called the industrialist "a virtual spy" for the Soviet Union. He had continued to get lucrative contracts from the Soviets because he had special skills in laundering money and distributing it to Soviet intelligence.[15]

Among the many categories in Soviet intelligence, it was important to differentiate assets and agents. Agents were recruited and could be tasked to perform specific assignments. They were knowledgeable and self-aware. "Recruitment applies to agents only," Shvets told me. "Recruitment is a procedure where you sit down with a human asset, and you make a deal. Actually, you say, 'Look, I'm KGB officer, and we've been working with you for quite a while, so let's make an arrangement that you work for us and you do something for us, we'll do something for you.'" Agents always understand who they are working for.

But what Shvets called "a trusted contact" was a very different kind of asset. "Trusted contacts are not recruited," Shvets said. "Relations with them are cultivated over time. You just build relations over time with them."

And within that context, Armand Hammer was, according to Shvets, what the KGB called a "special unofficial contact." In Hammer's case, that meant he was an enormously wealthy businessman who had access to the corridors of power in the Kremlin and the White House, and could be called on at various times to perform sensitive favors.

Whether Trump could fill Hammer's shoes was a long shot. But Hammer's best days were clearly behind him. And, according to Shvets, Trump's ongoing fixation with his nuclear negotiations provided an opening to the KGB that made him a highly plausible possibility. "They'd say, 'You have great potential. Someday you'll be a big politician. You have such an unorthodox approach! What great ideas! Such people as you should lead the United States. And then together we can change the world. Maybe we should just be friends and forget about hostilities. There is a growing admiration in the Kremlin about your successes as a businessman, and we are looking for new ideas and opportunities, and I believe that there is an opportunity for your business in Russia.'

"'This bullshit. It looks like he was intoxicated by this. 'We want to explain our position on different issues, and here they are.' He may be taking notes, or he might be given a printout. The KGB called them 'teases,' but you might call them sound bites or active-measure instructions."

According to Yuri, that's what was going on with his own recruit, John Helmer—Socrates—who was being force-fed KGB talking points in meetings with Soviet experts on arms control, foreign policy, and the like. "They would be telling him our views, our sound bites," Shvets told me. "These were our active measures."

Though he had no direct contact with the Trump party when they arrived, Shvets, who was still in Yasenevo, wasn't out of the loop. "The New York desk, where Natalia Dubinina worked, was located just two doors away from the room where I worked. On a regular basis, we had business meetings where we were discussing professional matters. We didn't discuss specific cases in this giant meeting, but you could have an understanding of generally what's going on."[16]

As he saw it, Trump was going through the same process that Helmer had been put through.

And indeed, when Trump returned to New York, he took the opportunity to get the *New York Times* to report, with no attribution, that he had "met with the Soviet leader Mikhail S. Gorbachev. The ostensible subject of their meeting was the possible development of luxury hotels in the Soviet Union by Mr. Trump. But Mr. Trump's calls for nuclear disarmament were also well-known to the Russians."[17]

But in fact no such encounter ever took place. The *New York Times* later posted a correction. In the meantime, however, the paper of record, which plays such a huge role in defining the national conversation, had validated Donald Trump as an expert on nuclear disarmament capable of standing on the world stage with the likes of Gorbachev.[18] That was untrue, of course. He was nothing of the kind.

In addition, Trump's loyalty to Gorbachev—or lack thereof—was another indication that Trump was taking his cues about the Soviet leader from the KGB.

Initially, when Gorbachev became general secretary in 1985, the hawkish Vladimir Kryuchkov, then head of the KGB's First Chief Directorate, got along with him far better than expected. "[Kryuchkov] was like a pussycat to Gorbachev, because he wanted to be promoted to the rank of four-star general," said Shvets.

Widely admired in the West for facilitating the end of the Cold War, Gorbachev was loathed by the hawkish Chekist operatives in the KGB for precisely the same reformist policies that were leading to the collapse of the Soviet Union. In the West, most Americans warmly embraced the Soviet reformer with his new concerns for openness and human rights. But there was one notable exception: Donald Trump.

Of course, when Gorbachev first appeared on the world stage, Trump had nothing but praise for him, and made no secret of it—pestering Nobel laureate Bernard Lown and telling reporters about meetings with the great leader that had never even taken place. In December 1988, when Gorbachev visited New York, Trump sent out word to the *Washington Post* and other outlets "that he had been contacted by Gorbachev's office and informed that the Soviet leader wished to meet him and tour Trump Tower, his Fifth Avenue office-shopping-condo complex, when he comes to New York next week."

"It's a great honor for me," Trump told the *New York Daily News*. "His office called and said it was one of the places he wanted to see. Most likely, I'll show him the atrium, maybe my office and a few apartments."[19]

But, as with Trump's claim of meeting Gorbachev during his 1987 trip to Moscow, the New York meeting never took place. Gorbachev remembered that the Cold War was still on. How would it have looked for the leader of the communist world to promenade about in Trump's Disneyland of conspicuous consumption and luxury goods?

Trump remained so eager for a meeting, however, that on December 7, when a man resembling Gorbachev showed up unexpectedly at

Trump Tower, the future president descended from his twenty-sixth-floor office and greeted him warmly, only to be widely derided later. He had fallen for an imposter, Gorbachev look-alike Ronald Knapp.[20]

In an interview that took place in late 1989, however, Trump dramatically revised his opinion of Gorbachev. As he told *Playboy*, "Russia is out of control and the leadership knows it. That's my problem with Gorbachev. Not a firm enough hand. . . . Yet Gorbachev is getting credit for being a wonderful leader—and we should continue giving him credit, because he's destroying the Soviet Union."[21]

At a time when America was swooning over the Soviet leader, Trump put forth a startling prediction about Gorbachev: "I predict he will be overthrown because he has shown extraordinary weakness."

The timing of Trump's remark was critical. "It would have been a different story if Trump had changed his line on Gorbachev earlier," said Yuri Shvets. "In 1989, only people inside the KGB could suggest someday Gorbachev would be overthrown, because in public he was in a strong position. Everything was fine. Everybody believed that Gorbachev will succeed. You couldn't find anything saying that in the Soviet mass media in 1989.

"So if Trump said this in 1989, it's an indication that he was fed information by somebody with inside knowledge of what was going on—namely, the KGB."

Meanwhile, Vladimir Kryuchkov had gotten his promotion to run the KGB in 1988 and was increasingly appalled at the declining status of the Soviet Union.[22] By 1990, reformers and hard-liners alike had joined Kryuchkov in training their sights on Gorbachev, but for the most part such sentiments were closely held within the intelligence community and were not shared by the general public.

In addition, there was another significant aspect to Trump's trip to Moscow that was not widely noted. It first surfaced on July 24, 1987, just after Trump returned to the United States, in an intriguing report from the unlikely pages of the *Executive Intelligence Review*. The voice of the cultlike Lyndon LaRouche movement, the *Executive Intelligence Review*, as Yale professor and author Timothy Snyder has pointed out, sometimes "echoes Kremlin propaganda," but in this case its journal-

ism is of note because its pages appear to be the first to assert that the
Soviets were looking "more kindly on a possible presidential bid by
Donald Trump."[23] And in fact, Donald Trump did decide to make a
highly improbable, quixotic, and, as it turned out, short-lived explora-
tion of running for president in the 1988 presidential primaries against
George H. W. Bush, then the incumbent vice president.

To get started, Trump turned to Roger Stone, a dirty trickster from
the Nixon era who was then with the firm of Black, Manafort and
Stone, a seamy K Street lobbying outfit that was just becoming known
as the lobby shop of choice for tyrannical dictators all over the world.
In the early eighties, Stone and his colleague Paul Manafort had come
to Trump through hardball fixer Roy Cohn. To help establish himself
as a potential candidate, Trump decided to promote his newly acquired
foreign policy expertise that had been fed to him by the KGB when he
visited earlier that summer.

In early September, after Trump had returned to New York, Yuri
was still in Yasenevo when a new cable came across his desk that today
appears far, far more significant than it did at the time. "I remember
receiving a cable that was an assessment of activities in general terms
of KGB intelligence stations in the United States," he told me.

The cable came from Service A, of the First Chief Directorate in
which Yuri worked. At the time, Service A was led by Major General
Lev Sotskov and consisted of about 120 officers who focused on three
main themes: creating material that would discredit all aspects of
American foreign policy, promoting conflict between the United States
and its NATO allies, and supporting Western peace movements.[24]

"Sometimes we were getting so-called circular cables," says Shvets,
referring to cables that were dispersed to the KGB *rezidenturas*
in New York, Washington, and San Francisco. The term "circular,"
he explained, simply meant that the cables were widely circulated
throughout the First Chief Directorate. "The idea was to show us examples of craftsmanship in recruitment, in analytical work, examples
to follow."

The point of the cable, Shvets said, was not to call attention to the
identity of the new asset, who wasn't considered terribly important at

the time, but to the practices: a successful active-measure operation by which full-page ads voicing KGB talking points were printed in major American newspapers.

Even though the new asset had no security clearance or access to classified documents, Shvets said, the KGB had concluded that he could still be used to channel active measures to influential people in the United States. As a result, they put together a bunch of sound bites to deliver important messages on various political issues that were relevant at the time.

"For each country, there was a specific set of sound bites, and they changed over time, depending on the situation," said Shvets. "There was one set for America, another set with nuances for Britain, a third for Japan, et cetera. For the KGB at the time, the idea of trying to get the US to drop security relations with Japan was one of the long-lasting KGB active measures, which they were disseminating.

"The ad was assessed by the active measures directorate as one of the most successful KGB operations of that time. It was a big thing—to have three major American newspapers publish KGB sound bites."

More specifically, the asset had paid nearly $100,000 for full-page ads in the *Boston Globe*, *Washington Post*, and *New York Times* calling for the United States to stop spending money to defend Japan and the Persian Gulf, "an area of only marginal significance to the U.S. for its oil supplies, but one upon which Japan and others are almost totally dependent."

The ads, which appeared on September 1, 1987, ran under the headline "There's Nothing Wrong with America's Foreign Defense Policy That a Little Backbone Can't Cure," and they put forth a foreign policy that, for all practical purposes, called for the dismantling of the postwar Western alliance. It took the form of an open letter to the American people "on why America should stop paying to defend countries that can afford to defend themselves."

"The world is laughing at America's politicians as we protect ships we don't own, carrying oil we don't need, destined for allies who won't help," the ad said. "It's time for us to end our vast deficits by making Japan, and others who can afford it, pay. Our world protection is worth hundreds of billions of dollars to these countries, and their stake in their protection is far greater than ours."[25]

The positions put forth were and remain quite extraordinary in the context of the history of US foreign policy. In effect, the asset was taking the shared bipartisan foundations of American foreign policy, policies that were the basis for the astonishing ascent of American power after World War II, and throwing them out the window. No wonder the Soviets were so enamored with his ideas.

According to the ad, oil in the Persian Gulf was of "marginal significance"? Right. Of course. This, just a few years after the Carter Doctrine had proclaimed that the United States would use military force if necessary to defend its national interests—a.k.a. oil—in the Persian Gulf. And just a few years *before* George H. W. Bush launched the 1990–1991 Gulf War, which was entirely about control of the viscous amber fluid that powers the world.

Abandon Japan? Sure. After all, why bother to continue a relationship with one of the most pro-American nations in the world, especially when it came to containing the very real Soviet threat to Japan posed by Soviet troops stationed on nearby islands?

America's postwar alliance with Japan was not exactly a burning issue during this period, except perhaps insofar as its auto industry brought Detroit to its knees. But Japanese–American relations were important to the Soviets. As KGB defector Stanislav Levchenko testified before Congress, the Soviets had long hoped to eliminate the possibility of an anti-Soviet triumvirate involving the United States, China, and Japan and to provoke as much distrust as possible between the United States and Japan.[26] So it was indeed a triumph for the KGB to manipulate an American into attacking foundational elements of American foreign policy—and doing it with the KGB's strategic talking points.

Tom Messner, who was part of the team that developed the ad, told the *Washington Post* that the man who took out the ad "wrote the letter himself. The idea of doing it was his. We were merely expediters. We designed the ad, we recommended the newspapers, handled the money and placed it. Our creative input was minimal."[27] So it is unlikely that Messner or others associated with placing the ad were aware that this was part of a much bigger disinformation campaign by the Soviets.

In an unusual twist, the cable Yuri received unavoidably gave away the name of the KGB's latest asset. "In handling assets, security always comes first when it comes to agents. There's always a correlation between objectives and risks," he said. "You can't afford to lose a very important asset in intelligence work. If he had been seen as an important asset, this cable wouldn't have been sent at all. The fact that his name was revealed meant that at the time he was not viewed as a valuable asset. He was not someone who couldn't be exposed."

In this case, that was a good thing, because the attached newspaper ad was signed by the would-be candidate. "He was a nobody at that time for Russia, for the entire Soviet Union. Nobody would have been interested in him other than the intelligence community."

The day after the ad appeared, a piece in the New York Times suggested that the "nobody" in question might enter the 1988 Republican presidential primaries against George H. W. Bush.[28] According to Shvets, earlier that summer the KGB had likely suggested to its new asset that he run for the presidency. It may have been just a whimsical suggestion, but the new asset had actually gone so far as to set up a fall appearance at Yoken's restaurant in Portsmouth, New Hampshire. Appearing at the iconic seafood restaurant—its motto was "Thar She Blows!"—was an obligatory campaign ritual that signaled the asset's quixotic drive to enter the New Hampshire primary for the 1988 Republican nomination, against Vice President Bush, the odds-on favorite to be the GOP nominee.

"There is absolutely no plan to run for mayor, governor or United States senator," a spokesman told the New York Times. "He will not comment about the Presidency."[29]

As it happened, the new asset soon dropped out of the GOP primaries, but to the KGB he had already achieved something extraordinary. This active measure was successful enough that it was cause for a minor celebration. Even though the new asset was, relatively speaking, insignificant, Shvets remembered his name—Donald J. Trump.

PART TWO

PART TWO

CHAPTER SEVEN

OPUS DEI

One summer day in 1990, Bonnie Wauck Hanssen, a school-teacher in her forties, was tidying up the Vienna, Virginia, home she shared with her husband, Bob, and their six children. To her surprise, $5,000 in cash was just sitting there in one of his dresser drawers.

Bonnie was puzzled. Something didn't smell right. Her husband, Robert Hanssen, then forty-six, was supervisor of an FBI technical surveillance squad that specialized in Soviet counterintelligence. He was one of the people the FBI relied on to make sure Soviet spies didn't do too much damage.

With their growing family, the Hanssens could barely scrape by on his modest salary. The amount was far more cash than any FBI agent she knew would have on hand. Bob hadn't mentioned any windfall. Where did it come from? Why did he hide it in his dresser? Everything about it suggested the cash was illicit.

Bonnie's suspicions were amplified by memories of an event that had taken place ten years earlier. In 1980, when the Hanssens lived in Scarsdale, the pricey New York suburb, and Bob had been detailed to the intelligence division of the FBI's New York field office, she came upon him unexpectedly in the basement of their home and saw him frantically trying to hide a letter he was writing.

At first, Bonnie thought that Bob was cheating on her. He had before, so she assumed that he was scurrying about to conceal a love letter to another woman.[1] But when she confronted him, she was stunned by his response—namely, that he had initiated clandestine transfers of information in exchange for cash with Soviet military intelligence—the GRU.

There are conflicting versions of the particulars in that first 1980 conversation between the Hanssens, but it is widely agreed that Bob fed Bonnie a sanitized version of the truth, claiming that, yes, he had put together a deal with the Soviets—and boy, had he taken them for a ride! They had given Hanssen $20,000 or so in cash, he said, and in return he had given them only a bunch of worthless papers. "He told me he was just tricking the Russians and feeding them false information," Bonnie told the *New York Times*.[2] "He never said he was spying. I told him I thought it was insane."

She didn't acknowledge that he was spying, but that's what it was. Robert Hanssen was spying for the Soviet Union.

Even then, Hanssen wasn't telling Bonnie the whole truth. He first began to spy for the GRU in 1979. While he was still assigned to the Criminal Division squad in the FBI's New York office, Hanssen would sneak into the closed file room to read Soviet espionage files, managing, in the process, to figure out who the FBI's most significant assets were. At first, this material was outside his purview, as he had no "need to know." But in New York he soon moved into Soviet counterintelligence work, which became his specialty for most of his FBI career.[3]

During that initial period, and two subsequent periods—in 1985–1991 and 1999–2001—Hanssen gave up the nation's most important military and counterintelligence secrets, including the names of dozens of American assets in the Soviet Union and Russia. He also gave the KGB thousands of pages of classified documents and computer disks that detailed "U.S. strategies in the event of nuclear war, major developments in military weapons technologies, information on active espionage cases, and many other aspects of the U.S. Intelligence Community's Soviet counterintelligence program," according to a thirty-one-page unclassified executive summary report by the inspector general titled *A Review of the FBI's Performance in Deterring, Detect-*

ing, and Investigating the Espionage Activities of Robert Philip Hanssen.
The report was published by the Department of Justice in August
2003.*

Even though Bonnie didn't know the whole story, she was so
stunned that she immediately insisted her husband consult a priest
who ministered for Opus Dei, the Catholic prelature to which she and
her husband belonged.

———

The story of Robert Hanssen, the most damaging spy in the history of
the FBI, is one that has been told repeatedly—in at least ten books, two
movies, thousands of news stories, and countless government documents. Among them, the 2003 IG report is the most complete unclassified official account of Hanssen's treachery, and, as such, is a valuable
document. But as is often the case with government documents, even
more fascinating than what it says is what it conceals, and it omits the
vital subtext of one of the greatest spy dramas in American history.

By that I mean the report largely overlooks the Hanssen family's
close ties to the leadership of Opus Dei (literally "God's work" in
Latin), which learned of Hanssen's espionage as early as 1980 and failed
to report it, thereby enabling him to spy for an additional two decades.

It omits the fact that Hanssen's brother-in-law, who later became an
Opus Dei priest, was working in the Justice Department under Attorney General William Barr and his associate Pat Cipollone during the
George H. W. Bush administration and that, during Barr's tenure from
1991 to 1993, Hanssen was promoted twice *after* having been first discovered. In light of subsequent events, the fact that one of the key sentinels guarding against Soviet—and later, Russian—espionage was a
traitor is disturbing, to say the least. And it is especially disturbing in

---

* The inspector general also produced a far more complete 674-page report that
is classified "Top Secret/Code Word" because it contains highly sensitive classified
information about FBI counterintelligence activities, including information regarding sources in the Hanssen case.

view of the fact that the Soviets were in the midst of developing Donald Trump as an asset.

The report also ignores the fact that Hanssen's brother-in-law reported directly to Paul McNulty, the Justice Department spokesman under Barr who would later be the US attorney who prosecuted Hanssen and somehow agreed not to prosecute Hanssen's wife, allowing her to keep most of her husband's pension, or $39,000 per year.[4]

Finally, the fact that Barr himself, as well as several key associates, allegedly had such close ties to Opus Dei and that, perhaps inadvertently, they helped keep the door open to Soviet and Russian intelligence is particularly disquieting in view of Donald Trump's close ties to Vladimir Putin and the many ways in which Trump has served Putin's agenda.

Indeed, in light of what has transpired in Trump's presidency, one might be forgiven for asking whether Barr had ties to Russia during his first stint as attorney general. But there's no evidence that Barr or Opus Dei had any such ties, and Opus Dei has even declared that Barr is not a member.

Given all these unexplored conflicts, this untold chapter of the Hanssen story can be seen as crucial to opening the floodgates for the Russians. At the same time the KGB was cultivating Trump, it was also undermining the FBI from within. The very institution tasked with protecting America against Soviet espionage was under siege, and one of its key sentinels, Robert Hanssen, was a traitor.[5]

Moreover, during the same period, a handful of powerful attorneys who were closely tied to Opus Dei worked hand in glove with various influential conservative and libertarian members of the Federalist Society, a group that advocates a strict "originalist" interpretation of the US Constitution. Many of these attorneys were based in major white-shoe international law firms whose clients include billionaire Russian oligarchs, Russian money-laundering financial institutions such as Alfa Bank and Deutsche Bank, and the late pedophile/financier Jeffrey Epstein, and whose attorneys have, during the Trump administration, amassed extraordinary power in such formidable bodies as the Southern District of New York, the Eastern District of New York, the FBI, the White House counsel's office, the National Security Council, the Department of Justice, and the US Supreme Court.

This was the birth of the "Praetorian Guard" that would later trample the rule of law in defense of Donald Trump.

The reasons behind Robert Hanssen's treachery range from the banal and money-related to the obscure and twisted motives growing out of a kind of intellectual grandiosity, resentment, and warped egoism. Money was especially likely to be a motive in the pricey New York area, where housing was so costly that agents were forced to live far away and endure marathon commutes to the city. In 1985, FBI agent Earl Edwin Pitts was transferred to Unit 19, a special FBI unit responsible for identifying KGB and GRU spies in the Soviet consulate in New York and the mission to the UN. Once he got to the New York area, the only affordable housing he could find was a two-hour drive to the city. "I earned less than a garbage man!" said Pitts.[6]

Aldrich Ames was paid $4.6 million by the Soviets. As for Hanssen, he was rewarded with more than $1.4 million for more than twenty years of spying. But he was so peculiar that at times the money seemed almost like an afterthought. Nicknamed "Dr. Death" by colleagues because of his grim demeanor, Hanssen was a deeply religious Catholic who attended Mass nearly every day and who was a member of one of the most prominent families in Opus Dei. The IG report characterized him as a misanthrope who was technically proficient and analytical, but was also repressed, aggrieved, and intent on showing that he was smarter than his colleagues.[7]

One way to do that was by spying. So, the report said, "Hanssen quickly began exploiting weaknesses in the FBI's internal information security" and before long had "gained access to the FBI's most sensitive human assets and technical operations against the Soviet Union."[8]

Among the most damaging pieces of information Hanssen said he gave the Soviets was the identity of a prized double agent named

General Dmitri Polyakov. The so-called crown jewel of American intelligence, Polyakov, whose code name was Top Hat, had been spying for the United States since the sixties and supplied key intelligence on the growing rift between the Soviet Union and China, intel that led to President Richard Nixon's epochal decision to open diplomatic relations with China in 1972. He also had delivered data on Soviet-made antitank missiles, information that became vital when Iraq used them in the 1991 Gulf War. As a result, Polyakov had been lauded by intelligence officials as the most valuable American asset of the entire Cold War. But in 1979, he was exposed by Robert Hanssen, who said he told the GRU, Russian military intelligence.[9]

It was not until 1986, however, after Polyakov had also been named by Aldrich Ames, who told the KGB, rivals to the GRU, that Polyakov was arrested.[10] He was executed for treason in 1988 and buried in an unmarked grave by Soviet security officials.[11]

Bonnie, however, claimed that she knew none of this and believed exactly what Bob told her—that he had conned the Soviets into paying thousands of dollars for utterly worthless information. Whether she had been told enough to know he was spying was unclear.

———

Powerful, secretive, authoritarian, and deeply deceptive, Opus Dei is a lay "personal prelature," a bureaucratic entity within the Catholic Church that is not geographic in nature, like a diocese, but that nonetheless is made up of a prelate, clergy, and laity. Founded in Spain in 1928 by Catholic priest Josemaría Escrivá de Balaguer y Albás, Opus Dei was created to promote the idea that people could be holy in their ordinary everyday lives, that work itself could be holy, and that what you do with your friends, family, and colleagues could be sanctified by living the gospel day in and day out.

At least that's what Opus Dei says. But that rather tame description doesn't do justice to a profoundly secretive sect that was closely aligned with Spain's Fascist Party and that, to a real but unquantifiable extent, has become party to a sophisticated assault on liberal democracy and the rule of law, from the US Supreme Court on down to the Department of Justice, the federal judiciary, major corporate white-shoe law firms, and other institutions—including the executive branch.

Indeed, it is not possible to fully understand Trump's success in shattering norms and violating laws without understanding the motivation and mindset of his Praetorian Guard, led by William Barr and a small group of attorneys with ties to Opus Dei.

"They have become, I think, the most effective secret society in American history," said human rights lawyer Scott Horton, a lecturer at Columbia University Law School. "Especially when it comes to changing the nature of the judiciary and filling vacancies with people who are their picks."[12]

Hanssen came to Opus Dei through his wife's family, the Waucks, whose ties to it date back decades to when Bonnie's mother, Frances "Fran" Hagerty (later Frances Hagerty Wauck) married LeRoy Wauck, a professor of psychology at Loyola University who was also a member of Opus Dei, and put together a family of eight children, at least thirty-three grandchildren, and at least twenty-five great-grandchildren whose existence revolved largely around Opus Dei.

"Opus Dei is the best thing that ever happened to the world," Fran told David A. Vise, a Pulitzer Prize–winning reporter formerly with the *Washington Post*, in his book *The Bureau and the Mole: The Unmasking of Robert Philip Hanssen, the Most Dangerous Double Agent in FBI History*.[13] "All of our children have been influenced by Opus Dei. Now they are better than they ever were. God did this, believe me. They send their kids to schools Opus Dei runs. People like the excellence in Opus Dei schools. Teachers get input to do things for the love of God and not just the monetary reward." Both Fran and her daughter Bonnie taught at Opus Dei schools.

Fran wasn't the only one in her family who was devoutly religious. Her brother Reverend Msgr. Robert Hagerty was a well-known Right to Life activist, and her husband LeRoy Wauck was a Catholic psychologist who helped found the psychology department at Marquette University and later became a professor at DePaul and Loyola Universities in Chicago.[14] In his spare time, Bonnie's father translated ancient

Greek scriptures into English-language books sold in Catholic book-stores, as did two of his sons, Mark and John Paul.[15]

As for Bonnie, she taught religion part-time at Oakcrest School, a private all-girls school in McLean, Virginia, operated by Opus Dei, and she convinced her husband[16] to join Opus Dei and raise their children in the faith.[17] The intensely religious family's dinners were often marked by passionate discussions about spiritual issues.[18] Opus Dei was central to their lives, and as longtime personal friends of Father Robert P. Bucciarelli, Opus Dei's vicar and the highest-ranking US official for the prelature, the Wauck family was Opus Dei royalty.

When it came to piety, Hanssen was not to be outdone by his wife or his in-laws. He began tithing a portion of his meager income to the parish and sent all six Hanssen kids to Opus Dei schools—the girls to Oakcrest School and the boys to Heights School in Potomac, Maryland. Hanssen himself went to Mass at the Opus Dei–run Catholic Information Center, just a twenty-minute walk from FBI headquarters in Washington and its center of operations in the district, with a board of directors that boasted, at various times, such legal community power brokers as two-time attorney general William Barr, White House counsel Pat Cipollone, and Federalist Society honcho Leonard Leo, among others.

On Sundays the family attended Mass at Saint Catherine of Siena Church in Great Falls, Virginia—but not because it was conveniently located.[19] Other Roman Catholic churches were closer to the Hanssens' home in Vienna, but more members of Opus Dei attended Saint Catherine's than any other church in the region, and on Sundays one might rub elbows at a Latin Mass with such superstars of the conservative Catholic political firmament as FBI director Louis Freeh, Supreme Court justice Antonin "Nino" Scalia, National Rifle Association president Wayne LaPierre, and Senator Rick Santorum (R-PA.).*

And, of course, there was Robert Hanssen, traitor.

---

* Saint Catherine's is where Santorum famously criticized John F. Kennedy's assertion that he believed "in an America where the separation of church and state is absolute."

Despite all that, Opus Dei is mentioned just once in the entire IG report on Hanssen, in a passage saying that Hanssen "confessed his espionage," as the report puts it, before an unnamed Opus Dei priest.

But was it really a confession?

Confession, of course, is one of the seven sacraments of the Catholic Church, and as such, any conversation that takes place during confession is considered privileged, under both canonical and criminal law. The Church's teaching on this point is unambiguous, and Catholic priests who violate it can be excommunicated.

Similarly, when it comes to criminal law, the US Supreme Court has ruled that privileges protecting private communications between a "priest and penitent, attorney and client, and physician and patient . . . are rooted in the imperative need for confidence and trust."

As it happens, there is considerable controversy over exactly what took place in 1980 after Bonnie Hanssen came upon her husband scurrying about to hide the letter he was writing to the Soviets. According to the 2003 IG report, Hanssen said that just a few days later "he confessed his espionage to an Opus Dei priest who granted him absolution and told him that he did not have to turn himself in but suggested that he donate the money he had received from the GRU to charity."[20]

That's the official account in the unclassified version of the IG report, but it wasn't the whole story, and in fact, it was full of errors. What really happened was this: After Bonnie insisted that her husband consult a priest, they met with Opus Dei priest Father Robert Bucciarelli, who was a cleric at the Overlook Study Center, an Opus Dei–affiliated religious facility in nearby New Rochelle, New York.[*21]

Bucciarelli was not a random choice for such a sensitive matter. A diminutive, dark-haired Harvard graduate, he had known Bonnie's mother since Bonnie was a young child growing up in Park Ridge, Illinois. In addition, Bucciarelli had succeeded Joseph Múzquiz as chief

---

* According to Wise, Hanssen also confessed to another unnamed priest in Indianapolis.

vicar of Opus Dei in the United States, which made him the most powerful person overseeing the American branch of the prelature. The Waucks' friendship with Father Bucciarelli was one measure of their high standing within the secretive sect.

The IG report not only omits Bucciarelli's name; it also presents a confusing picture of exactly what took place at the meeting with Hanssen, Bonnie, and him.[22] A more detailed version of this episode was published in David Vise's *The Bureau and the Mole*, which reveals that Hanssen's "confession" to Bucciarelli was not a "traditional one-on-one confession."

As Vise later explained in the *Washington Post*, "He met with Bob and Bonnie Hanssen together to discuss how to handle the situation that arose when Hanssen began spying in 1980, and Bonnie caught him writing a letter to the Russian military intelligence."[23] At the end of the meeting, Bucciarelli advised Hanssen that the right thing to do was to turn himself in—even though such an act might have resulted in life imprisonment or capital punishment for Hanssen, and humiliation for his family.

Since the sacrament of confession takes place strictly between a penitent and a priest, and since Bonnie was also present at Robert's meeting with Father Bucciarelli, it was more a "consultation" than a confession.

"I'm not clear about what exactly went on," Opus Dei priest Father John Wauck wrote in an email to me. "But this much I can say: If there was a third person present, then it was not a confession."

And if the meeting with Bucciarelli had been a consultation rather than a confession, as such it would *not* have been protected by confessional privilege.[24]

A communications professor at the Pontifical University of the Holy Cross, the university in Rome founded and affiliated with Opus Dei, Wauck is also the youngest brother of Bonnie Wauck Hanssen and the brother-in-law of Robert Hanssen. As a result, he might be said to have a horse in this race.

Although he declined requests for a phone interview, Father John did respond to my emails, and in so doing speculated that there may have been "a proper confession" that took place at another time.

But in the end, no such evidence has materialized.

In addition, the day after the Hanssens' consultation, Bucciarelli did something highly irregular. He called the Hanssens and asked them to return for a second visit. When they arrived, he told them that he had changed his mind about Hanssen turning himself in.[25]

The reasons for Bucciarelli's change of heart are not entirely clear. He had realized, he said, that if Hanssen went to authorities, the entire family, including Bonnie and the Hanssens' innocent children, would be humiliated.[26] That was part of it.

But it is also worth noting that in the insular, cultlike world of Opus Dei, the Hanssen-Wauck families were not just ordinary parishioners. There were only a few hundred members of Opus Dei in the Washington, DC, area, and the huge size alone of the combined members of the Wauck and Hanssen families meant that they were prominent.

In addition to numbers, the Waucks had a real history with Opus Dei that predated even Bucciarelli and could be traced to just after the early years of Opus Dei in America, starting in the late forties, when, having achieved a powerful foothold in Spain, Father Escrivá decided it was time for Opus Dei to go global.

Enter Joseph Múzquiz, a card-carrying member of the Falangist Party who had fought for the Fascists in the Spanish Civil War. Afterward, as a student in Madrid, Múzquiz was introduced to Escrivá's notion of living in celibacy while in the lay world and honoring God through everyday life and work, but was somewhat dubious. The whole idea struck Múzquiz as "something odd and strange that could not succeed."[27]

When they finally met, however, Múzquiz was transfixed by Escrivá and became one of his first apostles, one of the first three members of Opus Dei to be ordained as a priest, and was sent to the United States as a missionary in 1949. There he helped establish Opus Dei centers in Chicago and Washington, and later laid the foundation for Opus Dei to expand into Canada, Japan, and Venezuela.[28]

These were no small tasks, especially in the immediate aftermath of World War II, in which Franco—and by extension, Opus Dei—had supported Hitler, Mussolini, and the Axis powers, and as a result were not held in high esteem in the West.[29]

Múzquiz was not alone when he first came to Chicago in 1949. He brought with him the future Father Salvador Ferigle, then a young physicist working on his doctorate,[30] and together they opened the movement's first center, Woodlawn Residence, in a house near the University of Chicago.

And so with Múzquiz leading the way, and Ferigle as his right-hand man, Opus Dei spread through America. Over the years, Father Ferigle helped build Opus Dei into an organization with more than three thousand members in seventeen cities across the country,[31] as well as in Japan, the Philippines, and Australia.[32] (In 2018, Opus Dei's membership was around ninety thousand worldwide.)[33]

First stop was Chicago,[34] where Ferigle met and later became the confessor to Frances Hagerty Wauck, Bonnie's mother, and to her youngest son, John Paul Wauck, as well as the entire Wauck family.[35] So it was via Múzquiz and his protégé that Frances Wauck first ventured into Opus Dei, brought in her husband, LeRoy Wauck, and later their enormous extended family.

———

As the highest-ranking Opus Dei official in the country, it may have occurred to Bucciarelli that having a loyal member of his flock exposed as a Soviet spy, a traitor, a man who had betrayed his country, might be bad PR for Opus Dei. So one can only wonder whether, between his two meetings with Hanssen, Bucciarelli reached out to other officials in Opus Dei to discuss the matter before reducing Hanssen's penance.

In any case, Bucciarelli, who died in 2016, reversed course and told Hanssen that he should not turn himself in and should instead give the money from the Soviets to a reputable religious charity. As for Hanssen, he took a break from spying for a few years, only to resume later.

He later claimed to have told Bonnie that he gave money to Mother Teresa each month and that he had stopped spying for the Russians. "He said he would stop," declared Hanssen's lawyer, Plato Cacheris. "And Bonnie believed him."[36]

And astoundingly, that was it. Robert Hanssen had sold secrets to the Soviets but managed to walk away scot-free. In addition, as the IG report notes without naming him, Father Bucciarelli, the highest official in Opus Dei, had direct knowledge of Hanssen's treachery. And despite it seemingly not being protected by confessional privilege, Opus Dei kept it secret, thereby allowing Hanssen to continue spying for twenty years. In the process, he revealed the identities of three American assets who were subsequently executed by the Soviets.

It was not until after Hanssen was arrested in 2001 that Opus Dei went into damage control. By this time it was unclear exactly who knew what. In 1999, the Wauck family, including Bonnie and Robert Hanssen, had all traveled to Rome to attend John Wauck's investiture as an Opus Dei priest.

In an email to me, however, Father Wauck said he learned nothing about the Hanssen case until his brother-in-law was arrested in 2001. "Prior to that," he wrote, "it was completely off my radar screen, utterly unimaginable, and I don't see much indication that it was on the radar of anyone else."

Regardless, the Hanssen case is newly relevant because so many key figures tied to Opus Dei have become leading figures in Donald Trump's Praetorian Guard and, deliberately or not, have played key roles in opening the doors to both Soviet and Russian intelligence and enabling Trump.

Unhappy at being linked in the press with Robert Hanssen, Opus Dei officials in Rome wrote to Bonnie Hanssen, counseling her to make no public statements about her husband. With the exception of a few interviews arranged by her attorney, she has remained tight-lipped about her husband's case to this day.

At the time David Wise wrote his book *Spy*, he had no idea that John Wauck was Bonnie Hanssen's brother. When questioned by me,

John Wauck claimed to have no idea who from Opus Dei in Rome contacted his sister. But what remains exceedingly curious is that several key figures on the board of the Catholic Information Center—Attorney General William Barr, White House counsel Pat Cipollone, and the Federalist Society's Leonard Leo, among others—ended up becoming central figures in Trump's Praetorian Guard.

CHAPTER EIGHT

BETRAYAL

I n September 1985, Robert Hanssen was transferred back to the FBI's New York office, where he had served six years earlier. For several years, he had largely stayed away from the Soviets. But the positions he held, first in the FBI Budget Unit and then in the Soviet Analytical Unit at FBI headquarters, gave him access to a broad range of sensitive information from all components of the Intelligence Division as well as the National Security Agency and the CIA.[1]

At the time, the spy wars were heating up. Kislin and Sapir's electronics store was functioning as a KGB front. Donald Trump had laundered Russian Mafia money through real estate, and, though the floodgates had not yet opened for Trump, there was much more to come. Dozens of spies were at the Soviet Mission to the United Nations, and hundreds more were inside the UN Secretariat, the executive arm of the UN, under the cover of being international civil servants. Altogether, the FBI had identified roughly six hundred KGB agents out of about two thousand Soviet officials living in the United States.[2]

Soviet operations were overpowering American counterintelligence. "We don't even have a man-to-man defense," CIA director Bill Casey told the *New York Times* in 1985.[3]

That Hanssen, of all people, had been selected to supervise a division battling Soviet spies was extraordinary. He received favorable performance reviews with the unit, but his supervisor, as noted, made a point of describing Hanssen as the "strangest person" he had ever worked with in the FBI, adding that he was a "kind of cipher who was rigid, dour, and a religious zealot." Colleagues regarded him as distant and arrogant. His subordinates were aware that he mishandled classified information but didn't bother to report it to his superiors.[4]

Over the years since her husband's "confession" with Father Bucciarelli, Bonnie had repeatedly questioned him about whether he was honoring his promises. Each time Hanssen insisted that he was sending checks to Mother Teresa.[5] But in fact the payments had tailed off. He had begun his perfidy in New York in 1979, and now that he had been transferred back, he reverted to his old ways. On a quick trip to Washington in October 1985, just a month after he moved to New York, Hanssen resumed contact with Soviets, though this time it was the KGB rather than the GRU. Using the alias "Ramon" or "Ramon Garcia," he sent a letter to Viktor M. Degtyar, the press secretary for the Soviet embassy in Washington, inside of which was another envelope marked, in uppercase letters, "DO NOT OPEN. TAKE THIS ENVELOPE UNOPENED TO VICTOR I. CHERKASHIN."[6]

As a counterintelligence officer in the KGB's First Chief Directorate, Cherkashin was Yuri Shvets's immediate superior in counterintelligence at the Washington *rezidentura*, and was the case officer for both Hanssen and Aldrich Ames. Inside the second envelope was a letter to Cherkashin in which Hanssen promised to send a box of documents to Degtyar from some of "the most sensitive and highly compartmented projects of the U.S. intelligence community." The documents would be originals, not copies, to facilitate authentication, he said.

"I believe they are sufficient to justify a $100,000 payment to me," Hanssen wrote,[7] and in so doing signed the death warrants of two KGB agents who had been recruited by the FBI—Sergei Motorin and Valery Martynov in Washington. Both men were quickly recalled to Moscow and later executed.

Thanks to Hanssen, Cherkashin may have also learned that the FBI was trying to install tiny bugging devices in the Soviet embassy's

Xerox machines, and also about other state-of-the-art eavesdropping devices beamed at the embassy from the outside.[8]

It was during these next six years—right up until the fall of the Soviet Union in 1991—that Hanssen, according to the Justice Department's IG report, gave so much valuable information to the KGB. In all, officials say, he betrayed a total of nine double agents,[9] and gave the Soviets "some of this nation's most important counterintelligence and military secrets, including the identities of dozens of human assets, at least three of whom were executed." The report added that during the period in which Hanssen served in this position, "both the CIA and the FBI suffered catastrophic and unprecedented losses of Soviet intelligence assets in 1985 and 1986, which suggested that a mole was at work in the Intelligence Community." The mole hunts had begun—but no one seemed to suspect Hanssen.

Except for Bonnie, who knew something was wrong in 1990 when she discovered the money in Bob's dresser drawer. Of course, she had not forgotten his earlier indiscretion, a decade earlier, when he confided to her that he sold secrets to the Soviets. This time, he had just been promoted to supervise an FBI technical surveillance squad that kept an eye on Soviet counterintelligence, and as a result, he had access to intel that could be of great value to the Soviets.

Until this point, with the exception of Father Bucciarelli (and anyone he may have spoken with), Bonnie was the only one who had a clue about what her husband was up to. But Bonnie's sister, Jeanne Beglis, had been close to Bonnie all her life and in 1990 lived just a block or two away with her family. She found out about the $5,000 immediately, and was suspicious enough that she told at least three people about it—her husband, George, an architect; her brother Greg Wauck; and her sister-in-law Mary Ellen Wauck, who had been visiting the DC area with her husband, Mark Wauck.[10] Mary Ellen worked at Northridge Preparatory School, an Opus Dei school outside Chicago, while Mark worked for the FBI.

On the way back to Chicago, Mary Ellen told Mark about this

conversation that she'd had with Jeanne. Then, a few days later, Mark got a call from Greg, who also told him about Hanssen.[11]

According to David Wise's *Spy*, Greg asked, "Do you think this guy [Hanssen] is fooling around with the Russians?"[12]

Mark didn't respond, but he knew the answer was simple. Yes, his brother-in-law might well be a Soviet spy. But Mark was also an FBI special agent. This was a sensitive matter and his brother Greg did not have security clearance, so he brushed him off.

"These were pretty highly classified matters, so I couldn't talk to him about it," Mark told me.

Likewise, Mark says he didn't breathe a word about it to his youngest brother, John. "He's fourteen years younger than I am," Mark Wauck said. "Back when this happened, I would've regarded him as too young. And besides, he had no need to know. I wouldn't discuss [my suspicions about Hanssen] with anybody who didn't have a need to know."

To which his younger brother now says that he wouldn't have known what to make of the information. "Even if I'd have been told about it in 1990, I probably wouldn't have given it a second thought," Father John Paul Wauck explained in an email to me. "It might have seemed somewhat odd, but every day brings lots of other things to deal with, and it wouldn't have seemed like part of an important espionage scenario, because that scenario would never have occurred to me in a million years."

But for Mark Wauck, the discovery of Hanssen's secret cash was the last piece of the puzzle. He had been in the dark about Hanssen and Bonnie's meeting with Father Bucciarelli in 1980, but in the mid-eighties, Mark had been talking to Bonnie on the phone and mentioned that he was studying Polish.

"Oh, isn't that great?" Bonnie replied. "Bob says we may retire in Poland."

Mark was stunned. Poland? Granted, the Wauck family had Polish roots, but that had nothing to do with it. The Cold War was still very much ongoing. For almost any American, much less an FBI agent, to retire in an Eastern bloc country under the dominion of the Soviet

Union, "the Evil Empire" and "the focus of evil in the modern world," as President Reagan famously called it, was utterly insane.

"Retiring to a Warsaw Pact country is what spies would do," Mark told me. "Not normal Americans. And especially not a guy who was working at FBI HQ."

Another factor was that a big mole hunt was under way in the FBI, and Mark knew it. Someone in the Bureau must have been talking to the Soviets. There had been too many losses. "Between those two factors, and then finally hearing about the money, I put two and one together and came up with three," he said.

But this was still a thorny proposition. Mark Wauck had family loyalties. What about his sister Bonnie and her kids? At the same time, he also had loyalty to the FBI and the country—his oath. He talked to his wife about it.

"Do what you think is right," she said.[13]

That meant going to his supervisor, who was head of the FBI's Russian squad in Chicago and whom he saw as a "down-to-earth type of person." The two men had worked together in New York and had even carpooled together at one time. Mark said he brought up three points: namely, that the bureau was searching for a mole, that Hanssen was thinking of retiring in Poland, and the $5,000 in cash.

And a few days later, according to Mark, his supervisor said, "It's handled."

"I thought, 'Okay, fine. It's out of my hands. I've done what I needed to do.'"

But again, nothing happened. According to the IG report, "Wauck provided the supervisor with enough information to warrant some follow-up. Instead, the supervisor readily dismissed Wauck's concerns, in part because there was no policy or procedure mandating that he pass the information on for analysis and possible investigation."

As a result, even after he had been caught with the unexplained cash from the Soviets, Hanssen continued spying for another decade. By this time, more than half a dozen people were aware of Hanssen's activities to one degree or another. And most of them were in Opus Dei.

About twenty-six years old at the time Hanssen's cash was found, John Paul Wauck was the youngest of the eight Wauck children, the baby of the family. He studied history and literature as an undergraduate at Harvard, where he wrote for the *Harvard Crimson*, the university daily. After graduating in 1985, he worked as an editor at an anti-abortion journal called the *Human Life Review* before joining the Justice Department in fall 1991 as a novice speechwriter during the administration of George H. W. Bush. He later won a doctorate from Rome's Pontifical University of the Holy Cross, where he now serves as a professor in literature and communication.

Judging from his messages to me, as well as his various writings, videos, and TV appearances, Father John, who was ordained as an Opus Dei priest in 1999, is cheerful to a fault, gracious, friendly, and disarming—especially for someone who promotes a repressive, book-banning sect that disseminates an authoritarian theology.

Looking like nothing so much as James Norton of PBS's *Grantchester* when interviewed by a reporter for *Rolling Stone*, Father John, ever the hip priest, excitedly brings up *Eminent Hipsters*, a highly regarded rock memoir by Steely Dan's Donald Fagen. Since I trained on the *Harvard Crimson* myself years earlier, he signs his emails to me, "Best wishes from a fellow *Crimson* alum."

Over the years, he has come to play a special role as a bridge between the religious zealotry of Opus Dei and the secular world, speaking out for the sect in the national media—ABC, CBS, CNN, BBC, the *New York Times*, the *Washington Post*, *Time*, and many other outlets—on matters ranging from *The Da Vinci Code* to the canonization of Pope Francis.

As a result, he had preternatural ability to take an extreme right-wing Catholic sect that still observes such esoteric practices as corporal mortification, and which has been caricatured as a secret society of albino assassins, and make it seem, well, almost normal. When it comes to discourse about the authoritarian theology of Opus Dei, he somehow manages to frame its severe, repressive tenets as nothing more than anodyne homilies.

Indeed, part of the morbidly fascinating mystery and intrigue of Opus Dei are the exotic rituals that involve wearing cilices spiked with sharp metal prongs that dig into the flesh of the thigh; self-flagellation, usually on the back, and often drawing blood, as a penance to show remorse for sin; and the subjugation of bodily desires, at times to the point of inflicting serious harm. In fact, acolytes say, the real meaning of mortification is to subdue the desires of the body as part of training the soul to live a holy and virtuous life. As Escrivá puts it in *The Way*, his compendium of 999 axioms for living the Opus Dei way, which serves adherents in much the same manner Mao Tse-tung's Little Red Book served Communist China, "Blessed be pain," which is point number 208 among the aphorisms promoting pain and self-mortification. "Loved be pain. Sanctified be pain . . . Glorified be pain!"

All of which, when framed by Father John Paul Wauck, is normalized. "Corporal mortification used to be universal!" he told *Rolling Stone*.[14] "Until fairly recently, pretty much all religious orders did it. Mother Teresa's nuns still do. It's not something unique to Opus Dei. We just didn't abandon it."

———

For the most part, Opus Dei founder Josemaría Escrivá, who died in 1975, remained relatively unknown in the United States until he was canonized by Pope John Paul II in 2002 as "the saint of ordinary life." At the time, *Newsweek* religion editor Kenneth Woodward noted that Opus Dei prevented critics of Escrivá from testifying at the church tribunals deliberating on his life. "It seemed as if the whole thing was rigged," he said later. "They were given priority, and the whole thing was rushed through."[15]

In more recent years, Escrivá's sect won global notoriety, thanks to the villainous albino assassin from Opus Dei and the mysterious rituals featured in Dan Brown's *Da Vinci Code* potboiler: the wearing of a cilice, a hair shirt or metallic barbed garter that digs into the flesh, and other forms of "corporal mortification"—practices that may sound deeply irrational, mystifying, and superstitious to the secular world but which, adherents say, have been wildly overstated and sensational-ized in the interest of book sales and box-office revenue.

However, the real danger posed by Opus Dei to liberal democracy is not from depraved albino monk assassins, as Frank L. Cocozzelli, the president of the Institute for Progressive Christianity, puts it, but in "its very plutocratic attitude in abhorring dissent. Opus Dei is openly concerned with the economic self-interest of 'friends' who al-ready have superfluous wealth and power often at the expense of the economically less powerful."[16]

Plutocratic? Actually, that's a rather understated characterization of what is really a secretive and forbidding political operation with deep roots in a fascist past.

And the use of the term "fascism" is not hyperbolic. It is history. It dates back to Opus Dei's origin in and collaboration with the fascism of Generalissimo Francisco Franco's Spain in 1936 when Escrivá sent a congratulatory letter to Franco saluting his rise to power—and posi-tioned Opus Dei to play an outsize role in the regime as well.[17]

Three decades later, in 1966, Opus founder Josemaría Escrivá de-lighted in celebrating how Opus Dei had integrated itself into the broader culture in fascist Spain. "It is easy to get to know Opus Dei," he wrote. "It works in broad daylight in all countries, with the full juridical recognition of the civil and ecclesiastical authorities. The names of its directors are well known. Anyone who wants information can obtain it without difficulty, contacting its directors or going to one of its centres."[18]

But finding out the truth about Opus Dei isn't as easy as Escrivá suggested. According to *The Secret World of Opus Dei*, by Catholic historian Michael Walsh, a former Jesuit, that is in part because the principal biographies of Escrivá himself have been so tightly controlled by Opus Dei as to give hagiography a bad name.[19]

Of course, Opus Dei regards its founder-saint as pious, virtuous, and godly, but critics, secular and Catholic alike, including several Opus Dei apostates, have a far more negative take on Escrivá. According to Father Vladimir Felzman, who spent twenty-two years in Opus Dei before resigning, Escrivá feared sexuality, believed everything he wrote "came from God," and even put in a kind word for Adolf Hitler. "He told me that Hitler had been unjustly accused of killing 6 million Jews," Felzman told *Newsweek*. "In fact he had killed only 4 million. That stuck in my mind."[20]

Likewise, in 2006, Terry Eagleton, a radical Catholic professor at Britain's Lancaster University, characterized Escrivá in *Harper's Magazine* as "paranoid, self-aggrandizing, vain, and dictatorial. He was also a mightily ambitious political wheeler-dealer, despite his pious insistence that his organization promoted only 'supernatural' ends, which seem to have included amassing an enormous amount of money."[21]

Devotees insist that both Opus Dei and *The Way* eschew political ideologies of all stripes, but in fact Escrivá's tome is full of aphorisms that can be interpreted as being in service to autocratic, nationalistic, and fascist leaders by glorifying war,[22] secrecy, and blind obedience to authority.

Indeed, perhaps the single most disturbing value promoted in *The Way* is that of authoritarianism. In that regard, as Canadian journalist Robert Hutchison writes in *Their Kingdom Come*, Opus Dei demands that its disciples accept that they were mere children when it came to spiritual matters, an acknowledgment that led to obedience. "Obey intelligently, but blindly," Hutchison wrote.

All of which goes hand in glove with Opus Dei's strict regulation of literature and the arts, the promotion of secrecy and intolerance, and Escrivá's need for secrecy, even deceit, as it became an increasingly powerful force in Franco's regime. Escrivá himself said as much in *The Way*, point number 643: "Be slow to reveal the intimate details of your apostolate. Don't you see that the world in its selfishness will fail to understand?"

Escrivá's history with Franco provides some insight into why he might have wanted to keep "intimate details" secret. Historians quarrel over the extent to which Opus Dei allied with Franco, with its apologists noting that the so-called Red Terror, which came in the wake of Franco's coup d'état, unleashed a massive wave of anticlerical violence that resulted in the deaths of nearly seven thousand people.

Nevertheless, when Franco took over, he ended secular government in Spain. National Catholicism was on the ascent, rejecting everything that was vaguely non-Catholic—Protestantism, Judaism, liberals, and socialists.[23] "Our war is not a civil war," Franco himself declared, ". . . but a Crusade. . . . Yes, our war is a religious war."[24]

To that end, according to Jesús Ynfante, author of *The Founding Saint of Opus Dei*, Escrivá was "an unashamed fascist" and a powerful ally to Franco, who aggressively recruited new members from the wealthiest and most powerful families in Spain and staffed Franco's government with Opus Dei–approved ministers. "He had Madrid under his control, starting with the dictator [Franco]," Ynfante wrote. "Under Franco the clerical fascism of Opus Dei won out over the true fascism of the Falange [Franco's ultra-right-wing political party]."[25]

Nor when it came to commerce were these Opus Dei clerics innocent of the ways of the world. "Opus Dei's hierarchy knows very well that money rules the world and that religious hegemony in a country or a continent is dependent upon obtaining financial hegemony," said Javier Sainz Moreno, a law professor at the Autonomous University of Madrid.[26]

To that end, according to *Their Kingdom Come*, Opus Dei used offshore shell companies and arcane and obscure financial instruments such as *anstalts* and *stiftungs** to keep its business and financial dealings secret from the outside world. A joke around Opus Dei was that one of the secret companies was really a coded word meaning "We take money from unholy souls to finance holy works."

---

* An *anstalt* is a type of corporation that is common in Lichtenstein and is a hybrid between a company limited by shares and a foundation. As an entity, it has no members, participants, or shareholders; no duty to return profit; and no obligation to a beneficiary. A *stiftung* is like an *anstalt* but operates for purely noncommercial purposes.

In other words, Opus Dei and Escrivá didn't care where the money came from so long as it aided Opus Dei. The end justified the means.

Initially, Opus Dei kept a fairly low profile. But in July 1960, according to a report by *New York Times* reporter Herbert L. Matthews, Franco brought three or four ministers into his cabinet who were in Opus Dei. "One is never sure, because the organization works with a high degree of secrecy in names, numbers, and activity," Matthews wrote. "Almost all of its work is done by members acting as individuals, so that the association as such can disclaim direct involvement. . . . The government ministries are believed to be honeycombed with members and 'simpatizantes.'" (English-speaking Spaniards referred to the "simpatizantes" as fellow travelers.)[27]

Matthews's report added that many of the top businessmen and bankers in Spain were Opus Dei. So were the top military officers and the top officials in academia. "They are always seeking men high up in the professions. Many monarchists belong to Opus Dei," the article said. "Opus Dei controls newspapers, magazines, radio stations, movies, and advertising agencies. . . . Politically, it is very conservative and—this is what many Spaniards consider its dangerous side—it is linked to the church and firmly opposes separation of church and state or the weakening of the church's powerful role in education."

Jubilant that Franco was open to such objectives, Escrivá wrote to Franco in the fifties expressing his joy that "the Chief of State's authoritative voice should proclaim that 'The Spanish nation considers it a badge of honor to accept the law of God according to the one and true doctrine of the Holy Catholic Church, inseparable faith of the national conscience which will inspire its legislation.'"[28]

And so, under Franco, God's law ultimately replaced the rule of secular law in Spain. Catholicism, Opus Dei–style, was the state religion. As Escrivá saw it, Opus Dei had won.

Now the challenge was to do the same thing in the United States.

The idea, according to Bucciarelli, was simple. "But the trick," he said, "is how to do it."[29]

CHAPTER NINE

THE NEW PRAETORIAN GUARD

Yes, how to do it.

How to insinuate a tiny, extreme-right-wing Catholic sect within, say, law enforcement and the judiciary, and to do it in plain sight, but quietly without attracting attention, like injecting a toxic virus that slowly poisons the entire body politic.

Opus Dei had done it in Spain, where taking over the courts and the judiciary had been a critical early step in its collaboration with fascism. The United States was different, but here, too, an elite coterie of right-wing Catholic jurists wanted to implement a surgical strike that would in effect take over the US Supreme Court and, at the same time, create an imperial presidency. And they would do it in plain sight without causing a stir from the American public, using a handful of high-powered attorneys tied to Opus Dei, the new Catholic right, and dozens of their fellow travelers. As Bill Barr and his allies often said, the secular left had won one cultural war after another in America—birth control, abortion, gay marriage, and others. So now they were going to rigorously vet prospective judges to roll back the secular tide.

This new Catholic right, in a very different way, was every bit as powerful as the Christian right of the eighties, but instead of relying on the likes of Jerry Falwell, Pat Robertson, the Christian Coalition, and around eighty million Christian evangelicals in the United States, it used a small cadre of savvy right-wing political operatives and sophisticated attorneys who minimized their ties to Opus Dei and buried them in legal theories about "the unitary executive."

This was the new clerisy, an elite group of intellectuals and professionals—highly placed lawyers, politicians, and the like—rooted among the clergy who set out to change the world, whose commitment to theocratic authoritarianism was cloaked in the smoke and mirrors of Opus Dei and other right wing Catholic groups. They allied with the Federalist Society, the immensely powerful conservative and libertarian lobby, and set about stacking the courts with deeply partisan conservative judges who did double duty as economic royalists, ruling in favor of their plutocratic friends.

With about seventy thousand members—mostly law students, lawyers, and law faculty—the Federalist Society is far larger and more visible than Opus Dei, but its leadership in Washington has been dominated by highly partisan lawyers who have transformed the Supreme Court into a rubber stamp for right-wing partisans and taken over both the Justice Department and the judiciary.

In effect, as David Montgomery reported in the *Washington Post*, the Federalist Society now controls the US Supreme Court, boasting seven current or former associate justices: Samuel Alito, Neil Gorsuch, Brett Kavanaugh, John Roberts, Clarence Thomas,[1] and Donald Trump's most recent Supreme Court nominee, Amy Coney Barrett, who had clerked for the late associate justice Antonin Scalia, also a member of the Federalist Society.

Moreover, in addition to overseeing these appointments, Federalist Society executive vice president Leonard Leo, through his work on another right-wing activist group, the Judicial Crisis Network, can take some credit for blocking the appointment of Merrick Garland, President Barack Obama's nominee, to the high court.[2] One of the Judicial Crisis Network's top funders was the Wellspring Committee, led by Opus Dei member Ann Corkery and her husband, Neil Corkery, who has been the JCN's treasurer.[3]

Together, with DC's Opus Dei–affiliated Catholic Information Center, the Federalist Society and various other conservative judicial-activist groups sought out hundreds of deeply conservative candidates at the nation's most prestigious colleges and law schools and cultivated them assiduously from matriculation to clerkship to partnerships, right up until their investitures as federal judges, or even as justices on the US Supreme Court or in the Justice Department—all in service of a right-wing activism that would return the nation's judiciary to a time before contraception, legal abortion, gay rights, and other issues prized by Democrats.

All of which was very much in line with Opus Dei's tenets. According to Michael Walsh's *The Secret World of Opus Dei*, Father Escrivá placed an enormous emphasis on winning converts in Spain, on encouraging people to "whistle," to use an Opus term of art.[4] Each member was expected to have twelve to fifteen friends suitable for recruitment, of whom three or four were considered likely to join.[5] Those targeted for recruitment were largely in the professional class—doctors, lawyers, professionals, merchants, and the like.

When it came to recruiting new disciples in the United States, Opus Dei sought students first at the University of Chicago and later at Harvard, Yale, and Princeton, not to mention Georgetown, MIT, Cornell, and Columbia. Múzquiz met Robert Bucciarelli, then a Harvard student and a fellow Chicagoan—and later, his successor—in Cambridge, Massachusetts.

If the presence of such a deeply repressive, ultra-conservative, secretive sect as Opus Dei at a citadel of secularism as Harvard seems incongruous, well, that was precisely the point. In Franco's Spain, the government ministers who were in Opus Dei came from the elite and had all been schooled at the finest universities in the country.

Bucciarelli explained why targeting Harvard was essential for Opus Dei. "Even if [Harvard] were not Godless, there would be a need for Opus Dei at Harvard," he told the *Harvard Crimson*. "The intellectuals, you know, they have great influence. Like the snow-capped mountains, they're going to irrigate the valleys."[6]

All of which was very much in line with the strategies espoused by Escrivá and implemented—quite successfully, by the way—in Franco's fascist government, where Opus Dei played such a powerful role. You go to those mountains knowing it will trickle down. Or as Escrivá himself put it, using another metaphor in *The Way*'s point number 831: "Among those around you—apostolic soul—you are the stone fallen into the lake. With your word and your example, you produce a first circle . . . and it another . . . and then another, and another . . . Wider each time."

Similarly, the Opus Dei constitution asserts that Opus Dei "is to work with all its strength so that the class which is called intellectual—either by the precept that they are outstanding or by reason of gifts that it exercises . . . is the guide for civil society—adhering to the practice of the commandment of Christ the Lord."[7]

That Opus Dei has such lofty intellectual aspirations is particularly odd in view of its penchant for banning books. Opus Dei denies that it bans books, of course, but that is really a question of semantics and degree. In *The Way*, Escrivá expresses his sentiments on the matter clearly: "Books. Don't buy them without advice from a real Catholic who has knowledge and discernment. It's so easy to buy something useless or harmful."[8]

Moreover, according to John L. Allen Jr.'s *Opus Dei*, Father Guillaume Derville, spiritual director of the prelature of Opus Dei, said that Opus Dei "has a 'database' containing thousands of reactions to books by members over the years, which can be consulted when people want guidance on particular titles." But, he added, it is not an "official list," and the judgments expressed in it are "by definition perfectible."[9]

According to the Opus Dei Awareness Network (ODAN), a nonprofit organization that reviews the sect's practices, Opus members "must ask permission of their spiritual directors before reading any book, even if it is required reading for a university course."[10] All of which allows Opus Dei effectively to say it is not in the business of banning books, but to achieve the same goal of forbidding readership anyway. More specifically, according to ODAN, the database, which, at the time, was called Guía Bibliográfica 2003 (Bibliographic guide 2003), consists of book reviews and recommendations by Opus Dei members as well as a list of some sixty thousand books that are rated in six categories: from category 1, "books that can be read by all, even children"; to category 5, "books that are not possible to be read, except with special permission from the advisory (in New York)"; and category 6, books that are "prohibited reading. In order to read them permission is needed by the Prelate of Opus Dei (in Rome)."*

Similarly, when it comes to politics, Opus Dei spokesmen told me that there's nothing to see. "Opus Dei has no political positions other than simply affirming the teaching of the Catholic Church," said Brian Finnerty, the chief spokesman for Opus Dei in the United States.[11] "If someone were to come to Opus Dei with the idea of harnessing it as sort of some sort of instrument for political ends, then that would be immediately clear. And even if it were for good ends, then that would be an uncomfortable fit. It would be a good indication that the person doesn't really understand that we're all about."

But surely Opus Dei must have *some* political opinions? After all, it's Catholic. Surely, Opus Dei is against abortion? "If you were to ask me on any topic what is the position of Opus Dei," Finnerty told me, "my answer would be whatever the Catholic Church teaches." He then suggested the answers would be in the *Catechism of the Catholic Church*, a publication promulgated by Pope John Paul II in 1992 that sums up the beliefs of the Catholic faithful.

But Finnerty also says that Opus Dei "fully respects the right of our members to formulate their own opinions," and therein lies the rub. Who are Opus Dei's members? What are their political views? And how are they implementing those views?

Ask Finnerty whether various Trump administration officials are

---

* Among the thousands of books that are in the latter two categories are hundreds of the best loved and most hated authors of the last few generations, including Woody Allen, Isabel Allende, Karen Armstrong, Margaret Atwood, Judy Blume, W. S. Burroughs, Joseph Campbell, William Faulkner, Gustave Flaubert, Allen Ginsberg, Nadine Gordimer, Mary Gordon, Günter Grass, Andrew Greeley, Hermann Hesse, Adolf Hitler, John Irving, James Joyce, Carl Jung, Eugene Kennedy, Jack Kerouac, Stephen King, Milan Kundera, Doris Lessing, Sinclair Lewis, Mary McCarthy, Karl Marx, Somerset Maugham, Toni Morrison, Alice Munro, Vladimir Nabokov, V. S. Naipaul, Pablo Neruda, Friedrich Nietzsche, Octavio Paz, Harold Pinter, Marcel Proust, Ayn Rand, Philip Roth, Salman Rushdie, Bertrand Russell, John Updike, Gore Vidal, Voltaire, Alice Walker, Garry Wills, and Tennessee Williams.

in Opus Dei, and likely as not you'll get the same answer I did. "Opus Dei as a matter of policy respects the privacy of its members," Finnerty said.

Then he told me, "I would suggest you talk to them."

But of course they won't say. And that's because Opus Dei is a secret society, and as the secret Opus Dei constitution of 1950 puts it,[12] "It is forbidden for members to reveal they are members without the permission of their Director (N191-50)." Consequently, even members of Opus Dei may not know who their fellow members are unless they have been so informed by higher-ups.

And so long as key details about the sect remain secret, like having as a member a wily lawyer who makes extravagant use of attorney-client privilege, Opus Dei could be insulated from possible disclosures that its members wielded vast amounts of unseen political power they were using to reshape the entire Justice Department and the courts by implementing an authoritarian theology dressed up as the theory of the unitary executive, extending unbridled power to the presidency and allowing Donald Trump to trample the rule of law.

The most important institution in initiating that process has been the Catholic Information Center, which moved to K Street, just two blocks from the White House in 1998, under the direction of Reverend C. John McCloskey, and in doing so became the closest tabernacle to the White House, as the official CIC seal proclaims.[13]

Before long, it became a lively gathering place for conservative academics, politicians, and journalists, thanks in part to a celebrity-studded noon Mass that boasted converts to Opus Dei whom McCloskey had recruited and in some cases baptized, including former Speaker of the House Newt Gingrich, Judge Robert H. Bork, Senator Sam Brownback (R-KS), National Economic Council director Larry Kudlow, and Fox News host Laura Ingraham.[14]

In 2001, Kudlow told the *Washington Times*, "I'd like to unleash him on Capitol Hill. A few doses of Father McCloskey,*[15] and we'll

---

* In 2005, Opus Dei was forced to pay $977,000 to settle a sexual harassment claim against Father McCloskey by a woman who said he groped her while she

turn this country around. He's an old-fashioned evangelical pastor." McCloskey converted Kudlow to Catholicism when Kudlow was recovering from addiction.[16]

In both his writings and his sermons, McCloskey puts forth a vision in which the great cultural battles dating back to the sixties, involving divorce, abortion, gay marriage, and the like, suggest that conservative Catholics and their evangelical allies should prepare for a bloody civil war and perhaps even secede from the United States.[17]

Perhaps because of McCloskey's extreme political views, some Opus Dei members have made a point of distancing themselves from the Catholic Information Center. "I would imagine that there are lots of members of Opus Dei who never go there," Father Wauck wrote to me. "As I say, I rarely went there and don't even recall exactly where it was."

And yet the CIC named its chapel, at which daily Masses are celebrated, after Opus's founder: the Chapel of St. Josemaría Escrivá. The director of the CIC was Opus Dei; he was picked by the American vicar of Opus Dei. It was the go-to place for politically connected right-wing Catholics.

Within that context, no one was more central than Leonard Leo, who had ties to both the CIC and the Federalists. As per its usual policy, Opus Dei won't discuss its relationship with Leo, if any, but it is a matter of public record that Leo is on the board of Opus Dei's Catholic Information Center, which, according to Opus Dei's website, has been "entrusted to the priests of Opus Dei."

Most notably, Leo went on to become executive vice president of the Federalist Society and has led the way for Opus Dei adherents and fellow travelers to ally with the Federalists in reshaping the nation's judiciary. "Leonard Leo was a visionary," Tom Carter, Leo's media relations director when he was chairman of the US Commission on International Religious Freedom (USCIRF), told the *Daily Beast*.[18] "He figured out twenty years ago that conservatives had lost the culture war.

---

sought counseling. McCloskey was relieved of his post at the Catholic Information Center.

Abortion, gay rights, contraception—conservatives didn't have a chance if public opinion prevailed. So they needed to stack the courts."

To that end, Leonard Leo is widely credited with having a hand in the disposition of so many Supreme Court justices that he seemingly has had more influence determining the makeup of the Supreme Court than any single person in the entire country since Franklin D. Roosevelt.[19]

This was the birth of what later became Donald Trump's new Praetorian Guard—the sentinels on the Supreme Court, the men running the Department of Justice—who would trample the rule of law in defense of the president, who would undermine prosecutions of President Trump's cohorts, who would trivialize and undermine the Mueller probe, and who would support one measure after another via pro-Republican decisions on gerrymandering, voter suppression, the theory of the unitary executive, and the limits of presidential power, all of which became vital issues in terms of preserving democracy in the Trump era.

CHAPTER TEN

THE COVER-UP GENERAL

By 1990, as Opus Dei had begun to establish a presence in Washington, William Barr had already begun working his way up the ladder in George H. W. Bush's Department of Justice. Then a thirty-nine-year-old attorney from New York, Barr had grown up on Manhattan's Upper West Side, in a family that supported Republican Barry Goldwater for president at time when his neighborhood firmly supported Lyndon Johnson.[1] According to the *New Yorker*, his mother taught at Columbia and was an editor at *Redbook* magazine, while his father was headmaster at Dalton, the elite co-ed private school on the Upper East Side, and made a name for himself as an autocratic authority figure railing against birth control, feminism, and the social positions of the liberal counterculture of the sixties.

Barr was cut from the same cloth as his father. As Marie Brenner reported in *Vanity Fair*, even in high school at Horace Mann, the venerable private school in the well-heeled Riverdale section of the Bronx, "Barr was the William F. Buckley Jr. of the class of 1967, a droll outlier who lived in a rambling Riverside Drive apartment with a framed 'Goldwater for President' poster in the foyer."[2]

Barr's counterpart, his liberal antagonist in high school, was a classmate named Garrick Beck, the son of Julian Beck and Judith Malina, who founded the Living Theatre, an experimental theater company heavily influenced by European intellectuals and American writers from the Beat generation. In the sixties, there were a number of great face-offs between left-wing and right-wing intellectuals—Gore Vidal versus William F. Buckley comes to mind.

Even as teenagers, Billy Barr, as he was known then, and Beck dove deeply into the issue that has come to define Barr's role in facilitating the rule of Donald Trump—namely, how much authority does the president have as defined by the Constitution. "We argued about the Constitution as it was reflected in President Lyndon Johnson's treatment of the war [in Vietnam]. I argued that Johnson did not have the constitutional authority to enact this war. Billy said, 'All the president needs to declare war is an executive order. That is all!' . . . I really believe that Billy saw the Constitution as concentrating power in the chairs of the committees, and in the cabinet secretaries, the Supreme Court—and the president," Beck told Brenner.

Deeply held as such convictions may have been then, Barr has continued to hold them more dearly than ever—and to implement them even today.

Barr differed from his peers in more than ideology. His overly strict father wasn't just repressive; there was also a religious component to his world view that was highly unusual. Born to a Jewish family, Donald Barr married an Irish Catholic woman, converted to Catholicism, and raised his children in the religion. Young Bill followed in lockstep and took to Catholicism zealously.

Where his father had served in the Office of Strategic Services (the precursor to the CIA) during World War II, after studying at George Washington University Law School, Bill Barr joined the CIA's Office of Legislative Counsel (OLC). At the time, congressional committees led by Representative Otis Pike (D-NY) and Senator Frank Church (D-ID) had been formed to investigate the CIA, FBI, and NSA for decades of abuses in Vietnam, Chile, Iran, and elsewhere.[3]

In the wake of Vietnam, many people were concerned about the so-called imperial presidency and thought the office had become too powerful. Barr thought just the opposite and did everything he could to fight those who were trying to limit the CIA and rein in the executive powers of the presidency.[4] He soon joined forces with a group of ambitious, like-minded people who thought the pendulum had swung too far. In 1976, while working for then CIA director George H. W. Bush, Barr helped write the talking points that Bush used to fend off those congressional investigators who were reining in the intelligence agencies.[5]

Thanks in part to his relationship with the ever-genteel Bush, Barr was often underestimated in terms of his ruthlessness and unrelenting partisanship. Bush was courtly, wrote elaborate thank-you notes, and was so agreeable that he risked being seen as "a wimp," as *Newsweek* famously suggested. Thanks to this genial exterior, he seemed guileless, more concerned with politeness, civility, and accommodation than substantive issues and confrontation.

But beneath that facade, as head of the CIA, George H. W. Bush had mastered the arts of compartmentalization and secrecy. Later, as vice president, under the guise of embarking on a "peace mission" to the Middle East in 1986, Bush secretly undertook an extraordinarily Machiavellian covert operation—which Murray Waas and I wrote about in the *New Yorker*—in which he actually went operational and provided military intelligence to Iraqi dictator Saddam Hussein as a means of facilitating an illegal arms-for-hostages deal with Iran.[6] That duality—polished credentials paired with unyielding partisanship, the iron fist in the velvet glove—was a highly prized prerequisite among Bush's younger acolytes, among them C. Boyden Gray.

A tall, slender figure with notably bushy eyebrows, Gray was the son of Eisenhower's national security advisor and an heir to the R. J. Reynolds tobacco fortune, who had schooled at St. Mark's, Harvard, and the University of North Carolina Law School. He clerked for Earl Warren, then chief justice of the US Supreme Court, and won a partnership at the white-shoe Washington firm Wilmer Cutler Pickering Hale and Dorr.

Then he became counsel to Vice President Bush during the Reagan presidency. Nearly a generation younger than his mentor, Gray was clubbable but more of a shambling, rumpled six-foot, six-inch Ichabod Crane–like figure whose burnished credentials masked a merciless partisanship. In the end, Bush treated Gray like a son.

As for William Barr, he had worked for the CIA between 1971 and 1977 while attending grad school and law school, first as an intelligence analyst and later in the CIA's Office of Legislative Counsel. After Reagan came to power in 1981, Barr became friendly with Gray, who was then counsel to Vice President Bush. The two men worked together on regulatory issues and became close friends.[7]

When Vice President Bush ran for president in 1988, Barr joined his campaign, worked briefly on the transition team after Bush won, and was installed in the Department of Justice as head of the Office of Legal Counsel even before Bush took office as president. As Barr describes it in an interview for an oral history project at the University of Virginia's Miller Center, he got the job "because Boyden Gray thought that that was a very important job and was intent on getting someone in that position who believed in executive authority."

Which Barr did. Later, under Bill Clinton, the OLC became relatively unimportant, with just eight or nine lawyers.[8] But in the George H. W. Bush administration, Barr had no fewer than twenty-six lawyers working full-time to further empower the president.

Gray and Barr got along well. Barr, then in his late thirties, was smart and adroit when it came to navigating complex bureaucracies. He and Gray shared the theory that Article 2 of the Constitution gives the president complete authority over the executive branch, with a wide berth to make war and interpret laws,[9] and that meant Barr finally had a position with which to implement his ideas about the unitary executive. When he took over the OLC, he wrote a formal and oft-cited memo titled "Common Legislative Encroachments on Executive Branch Authority," whose soporific title belied the extraordinary influence it had in delineating "common provisions of legislation that are offensive to principles of separation of powers, and to executive power in particular, from the standpoint of policy or constitutional law."[10]

The memo went on to list ten ways in which he thought Congress had been violating Article 2, arguing, "Only by consistently and forcefully resisting such congressional incursions can executive branch prerogatives be preserved."

He and Gray worked to do precisely that. Asserting that Article 2 of the Constitution gives the president far-reaching powers, Barr lashed out at one "encroachment" on executive power after another by Congress and argued for the broad assertion of executive privilege. Such views, of course, made him particularly hostile to congressional oversight, watchdog positions such as inspectors general, and, of course, independent counsels—or indeed any force that might restrict the president. If fully implemented, the unitary executive theory would allow presidents to take almost any actions they wanted at home or abroad without congressional authorization and would allow them to resist any attempts by Congress to implement oversight or constraints.

"I probably spoke every day to Boyden or someone in his office," Barr said in the University of Virginia's Miller Center interview. "We set up some things because of Boyden's and my own interest in the powers of the Presidency and President Bush's, too, because I think Bush felt that the powers of the Presidency had been severely eroded since Watergate and the tactics of the Hill Democrats over an extended period of time when they were in power. So we set up a group of general counsels under my chairmanship, and we'd bring in all the general counsels of all the executive agencies. I chaired the group. Boyden would come over, and we basically set uniform standards on how you handle document requests, how you serve executive privilege, what Congress can get, what they can't get. We tried to impose a certain uniformity."

Even though what was taking place belied the ostensibly moderate Bush presidency, Barr was among the first to put this all together as coherent ideology and to implement it. In 1990, after Iraqi president Saddam Hussein had invaded Kuwait, Barr, who had been promoted to deputy attorney general, was called to a White House meeting by Bush, who asked if he needed congressional approval to send US troops into the region.[11] Barr insisted that the inherent authority of the president gave him the power to start a war whenever he chose to do so. But, on political grounds, he also advised Bush to get authority from Congress.

And so the theory of the unitary executive giving the White House virtually unlimited power—at least when Republicans occupied the White House—became an elemental part of GOP gospel. At the same time, Boyden Gray, who also happened to be a member of the Federalist Society, kept a close watch on judicial appointments and made sure all the judges fell clearly within Federalist Society guidelines, including Clarence Thomas in his contentious 1992 appointment to the Supreme Court. This new right-wing assault on the judiciary began stealthily, and at the time few people were even aware of who the players were, much less the forces they represented and the ties that were being forged.

After the Gulf War was successfully concluded in 1991, Bush appointed Barr as attorney general. Even at this relatively early stage of his career, this was a man who saw no limits to executive power. He gave voice to the imperial elements of Bush senior's presidency—and amplified them. As the *Village Voice* noted in a 1992 piece by Frank Snepp, Barr was the man who came up with the legal foundation behind the 1991 Gulf War, the invasion of Panama, and the officially sanctioned kidnapping of Panamanian strongman Manuel Noriega.[12]

Barr was also eager to put his views into action, and once he became attorney general in late 1991, he earned the sobriquet "Coverup-General," as conservative columnist William Safire put it in the *New York Times*.[13] To Barr, the tenets of the unitary executive meant shielding the executive branch from congressional oversight in a way that basically allowed them to get away with murder. That included the Iran-Contra scandal, in which the Bush administration defied Congress by illegally selling weapons to Iran and then diverting the funds to support the right-wing Contra rebels in Nicaragua. It included the Iraqgate scandal in which the United States guaranteed grain loans that were used to finance Saddam Hussein's war machine in Iraq. And it included the so-called Inslaw scandal involving a Washington, DC–based tech company named Inslaw that accused the Department of Justice of conspiring to steal its software for use in covert intelligence operations against foreign governments.

And when Bush needed someone to quell the flames from Iran-Contra and Iraqgate that threatened his presidency, time and again,

Barr was Mr. Whitewash, the cleanup man, the guy who kept the secrets and put out the fires. In August 1992, when the FBI uncovered Iraqgate, the House Judiciary Committee called for a special prosecutor who was not beholden to the Bush administration. In response, Attorney General Barr stonewalled the House Banking Committee, asserting that "public disclosure of classified information harms the national security."

As Safire noted in a subsequent column, Barr had personally taken charge of the cover-up. "Despite demands from both Judiciary committees . . . Barr broke precedent and refused to seek independent counsel in the Iraqgate scandal," Safire wrote. "Instead, he hand-picked a whitewasher who dutifully filibustered past the election, ultimately condemning Congress for the arms buildup of Saddam Hussein."[14]

"Why does the Coverup-General resist independent investigation?" Safire wrote earlier. "Because he knows where it may lead: to [former attorney general] Dick Thornburgh, [then secretary of state] James Baker, [former secretary of agriculture] Clayton Yeutter, [National Security Advisor] Brent Scowcroft and himself. He vainly hopes to be able to head it off, or at least be able to use the threat of firing to negotiate a deal."

Safire further asserted that Barr and Robert Mueller, who was then chief of Barr's Criminal Division, could face prosecution "if it turns out that high Bush officials knew about Saddam Hussein's perversion of our Agriculture export guarantees to finance his war machine."[15]

Similarly, to the extent the Barr Justice Department investigated the Inslaw affair—in effect, investigating itself, since it was the Justice Department that allegedly stole the software—the relevant grand jury testimony was heavily redacted.[16] And when twenty-one Democrats on the House Judiciary Committee wrote Barr to ask him to appoint an independent counsel to investigate the Inslaw affair, he declined to follow through.

Finally, that same year, Barr was called upon to advise Bush 41 on whether to recommend presidential pardons for high-level government officials who were actors in the Iran-Contra scandal. So when it came to doling out "punishment" to the principals behind Iran-

Contra, Bill Barr stealthily worked his magic behind the scenes.[17] For Barr, the decision was a no-brainer. As the Nixon presidency had been on the line with Watergate, so the Reagan-Bush legacy was on the line with Iran-Contra.

Barr managed to neutralize the attacks when he urged President George H. W. Bush to grant pardons to six men, including former national security advisor Robert McFarlane, Defense Secretary Caspar Weinberger, and Assistant Secretary of State Elliott Abrams.

When that happened, Iran-Contra special prosecutor Lawrence Walsh was incensed. "The Iran-Contra cover-up has now been completed," he said.[18]

———

At the same time Attorney General Barr launched his crusade to expand the powers of the presidency, the intelligence community was still on the hunt for moles who had been wreaking havoc in American intelligence. The FBI was painfully aware that there had been too many losses, but it didn't know who the culprits were.

Temporarily at least, Hanssen was on hiatus from spying. In the wake of the failed August 1991 coup that attempted to overthrow Mikhail Gorbachev, the Soviet Union was in chaos. Its subsequent downfall meant that Hanssen had nowhere to go until the newly formed Russian Federation and successor agencies to the KGB rose again.

Meanwhile, he was still ready, willing, and able to spy again. And because he was in the FBI, he was ultimately responsible to the Department of Justice and William Barr, and happened to be far, far closer to Barr than anyone seemed to know.

That's because in late 1991, a year after Bonnie discovered the cash in Hanssen's dresser and word got out that he might be a Soviet spy, Hanssen's brother-in-law, John Paul Wauck, got a job writing speeches for then acting attorney general Barr. At the time, Wauck, as he wrote in a series of emails to me, was merely a "27-year-old novice speechwriter [who was] unaware of any speculation about Hanssen being a spy until the day he was arrested."

Older brother Mark, the FBI agent in Chicago, did of course know about Hanssen's cash—and had dutifully informed his superiors about his suspicions. But he didn't tell his younger brother, even when John began working for Barr. "I guess you could say that back then I was rather naive. I didn't assume that the attorney general would be involved in this kind of stuff," Mark Wauck told me. "I think my attitude probably would've been that the attorney general wouldn't have a need to know. Knowing what I know now, I suppose that any kind of investigation of that sort would've been brought to Barr's attention."

As for brother John, he says he didn't have a clue. "For me, as for most people who knew him, his arrest [in 2001] came as a bolt from the blue," Father John wrote. "It never occurred to me that Hanssen might commit treason. Based on what I could see, nothing would have seemed less likely."

And there was William Barr, one of the youngest attorney generals in American history, overseeing the greatest mole hunt in FBI history, yet presumably unaware that the mastermind spy they were hunting was his own speechwriter's brother-in-law, and that all three of them were closely tied to Opus Dei.

Barr's activities with regard to Opus Dei and the judiciary are both murky and intriguing, and when it comes to ducking questions about the subject, Father John doesn't miss a beat. "The very possibility that my name might figure in a book about William Barr seems slightly preposterous to me, and I feel totally out of place in any narrative involving the hypothetical influence of Opus Dei on the US judiciary," he emailed me. "Whether there might be individual members of Opus Dei or people who could be considered connected to Opus Dei who might have an impact on judicial affairs is a question about which I am utterly ignorant."

More specifically, he says that when he started work at the Justice Department in 1991, he had no communication with Barr with regard to Opus Dei. "I was young, new on the job, and on unfamiliar turf," he wrote. And besides, he added, he was not confident that ties to Opus Dei would have left him in good favor. "In 1991, the founder of Opus Dei had not yet been beatified, much less canonized. I don't think I would have taken it for granted that Bill Barr held a high opinion of Opus Dei."

As a matter of principle, Opus Dei *said* it had no role in matters that might have involved the Justice Department. But also as a matter of principle, Opus Dei also said that its members were free to express and act out their own political views and free to conceal their ties to Opus Dei. And if it just so happened that a number of highly placed people tied to Opus Dei played extraordinarily powerful roles in moving the entire judiciary to the right, well, perhaps Opus Dei really had nothing to do with it.

"My impression from afar is that there are a lot of Catholic lawyers in DC (heck, there are a lot of Catholics on the Supreme Court itself), and it would be natural/inevitable for their Catholicism to have an impact in multiple ways (DC is a pretty small town)," Father John wrote. "But it would be inappropriate and, as I say, probably misleading for me . . . to offer uninformed conjectures about whether and how members of Opus Dei might fit into that story."

As befits a secret society, Opus Dei made it increasingly difficult to decipher just who is and who is not a member. Take two-time attorney general William Barr, a devout Catholic who served as chairman of the board of the Catholic Information Center in 2014, and, according to the Senate questionnaire for his confirmation, remained on the board to 2017. But Opus Dei says that did not necessarily mean he was a member of the prelature, even though the CIC was largely staffed by Opus Dei priests and it was the center of the prelature's operations.

But was he anyway—as reported by the *Huffington Post*?[19] When I asked Brian Finnerty, the US communications director for Opus Dei, he suggested that I talk to Barr about it, and repeated his mantra that "Opus Dei as a matter of policy respects the privacy of its members."[20]

But then in December 2019, Finnerty emailed me with a new response, which contained a link to a new posting on the subject that appeared on Opus Dei's website:

"Our normal policy is not to identify members (or non-members) of the Prelature, but rather to leave it to each individual to make known this information. Nevertheless, because there have been recent news accounts referring to the US Attorney General, William Barr, as a member of Opus Dei, we would like to clarify that Mr. Barr is not a member of Opus Dei nor has he ever been one."[21]

However, given Opus Dei's penchant for secrecy, I pressed further. After all, there were different kinds of members—in fact, at least six categories. According to NBC News, of those categories, the biggest, supernumeraries, accounts for about 70 percent of Opus Dei's membership.[22] That designation that includes married men and women who lead traditional family lives and have careers in the secular world while participating in regular meetings, retreats, and fundraising. The next, containing about 20 percent of Opus Dei's membership, are numeraries, a grouping of celibate members who make themselves fully available to serve the prelature. The other four categories are numerary assistants, associates, priests, and cooperators.

This time, Finnerty was more definitive. "William Barr is not now, and has never been, a member of Opus Dei—he has never been a numerary, nor an associate, nor a supernumerary. He has never been a member of Opus Dei, period. Nor has he ever been a cooperator of Opus Dei."[23]

In other words, William Barr had nothing to do with the organization—or so they said. That answers it once and for all, right?

Well, not exactly.

"People have a hard time parsing what Opus Dei is, who's a member, who's not, and all the strange categories they have," said Frederick Clarkson, senior research analyst at Political Research Associates, a nonprofit that tracks right-wing networks, and the author of *Eternal Hostility: The Struggle Between Theocracy and Democracy*.[24] "In a limited sense, it may be true that Barr isn't a member of Opus Dei. But you don't put somebody on the board of directors of your headquarters unless they have some significant relationship here."

There's also the possibility that in explaining that Barr had nothing to do with Opus Dei, the prelature had chosen to enact the Catholic doctrine of "mental reservation," which recognizes "the lie of necessity" and holds that when there is a conflict between justice and truth, justice should win out. As Thomas P. Doyle, a priest in Virginia who is an expert in canon law, told the *Los Angeles Times*, the doctrine has been used in modern times to "claim that it is morally justifiable to lie in order to protect the reputation of the institutional church."[25]

Indeed, according to a former member of Opus Dei, the loyalty of Opus members is constantly tested, and members are expected to implement the Opus agenda at the same time they are denying they are part of it. "You are expected to stand up and tell the world that you are acting in your own name when you carry out the secret indications of your directors," former member Dennis Dubro told ABC News.[26] Dubro had been with Opus for seventeen years before leaving the sect.

That's the nature of a secret society: It's secret. So it's difficult to determine exactly who is a member and who isn't and whether they are operating under strict ideological and/or theological constraints. What we know and see is a small but elite group of powerful attorneys, some of whom were openly part of Opus Dei and some of whom worked with or were associated with the Catholic Information Center and other entities linked to Opus Dei, who are vital parts of the Catholic right.

So it's reasonable to question whether it was merely a coincidence that William Barr later served on the board of directors of the Catholic Information Center, a body that was largely run by Opus Dei, that has a base of operations in the nation's capital, and whose chapel was named after its founder. Was it merely a coincidence that Barr speechwriter John Paul Wauck was an Opus Dei member? That Pat Cipollone, who served as assistant to Barr when he was first attorney general from 1992 to 1993, and later became President Trump's White House counsel, also served on the board of the CIC, as had Barr and Leonard Leo, and that all were in the Federalist Society, close to Trump, and played key roles in helping select judges—including Supreme Court judges—and in defending Trump during his impeachment?[27]

Other members of this so-called Catholic Mafia include Supreme Court Justice Brett Kavanaugh, who, like Barr and Cipollone, was an alum of Kirkland & Ellis; and Fox News host Laura Ingraham, who converted to Catholicism with Cipollone's help and who calls him her godfather.[28]

This was the world Barr had begun assembling—one of powerful cultural warriors, all of whom, including Barr himself, were fierce and vigorous adversaries of the very world he had grown up in: the world of liberal, secular humanism prevalent on Manhattan's Upper West Side. Instead they were fighting for a deeply conservative Catholicism that railed again and again against the boys he had grown up with at Horace Mann.

To that point, an unpublished speech before the Catholic League for Religious and Civil Rights, given just after he became attorney general in 1991, gives a glimpse of Barr's zealotry and rage, with the newly appointed chief law enforcement officer in the country launching a wholesale attack on nonbelievers. "The secularists of today are clearly fanatics," Barr said, as reported by the Associated Press. Their criticism of the "Judeo-Christian moral tradition" has produced "soaring juvenile crime, widespread drug addiction, skyrocketing rates of venereal disease, 1.5 million children aborted each year," he added.[29] Public schools, he said, had undergone a "moral lobotomy."

All of which, he explained in an article in the *Catholic Lawyer*, he blamed on the Enlightenment. "We live in an increasingly militant, secular age," Barr wrote. "We are locked in a historic struggle between two fundamentally different systems of values. In a way, this is the end product of the Enlightenment. On the one hand, we see the growing ascendancy of secularism and the doctrine of moral relativism. . . . First, through legislative action, litigation, or judicial interpretation, secularists continually seek to eliminate laws that reflect traditional moral norms. Decades ago, we saw the barriers to divorce eliminated. Twenty years ago, we saw the laws against abortion swept away. Today, we are seeing the constant chipping away at laws designed to restrain sexual immorality, obscenity, or euthanasia."[30]

And he was determined to fight back.

PART THREE

CHAPTER ELEVEN

THE BOUNCING CZECH

On November 6, 1991, twenty-nine-year-old Ghislaine Maxwell, the youngest daughter of British media baron Robert Maxwell, landed in Tenerife, the largest of Spain's Canary Islands, and quickly made her way to her father's yacht.[1] The day before, her father, the sixty-eight-year-old billionaire publisher, had been seen before dawn, at 4:25 a.m., pacing the deck of the 180-foot vessel off the coast of Tenerife.[2] Later that morning, he was discovered to be missing. It was not until 6:46 p.m. that day that he was found, a search helicopter hovering over his immense three-hundred-pound corpse. "It was naked, stiff, and floating face upward," said a member of the search team. "Not face down which is normal."[3]

Maxwell's body was hoisted from the ocean by helicopter. The next day, reports of his shocking death were in almost every paper in the English-speaking world, including, of course, his own six papers in the Mirror Group, including the *Daily Mirror* in London and the *New York Daily News.*

Ghislaine had been the favorite of her father's nine children—he had even named his yacht, the *Lady Ghislaine*, after her—and soon after she arrived in Tenerife, she joined her oldest brother, Philip, and her mother, Elisabeth, on board. The boat was anchored near Santa Cruz de Tenerife, the island's capital, and they spent much of the day trying to get Maxwell's affairs in order and making plans to fly to

Israel, where he was to be buried. As a Jew, Maxwell had wanted to be buried in the Orthodox tradition, which has it that no burial can take place on the Sabbath. That meant they had to leave right away.[4] So late that night, after a somber dinner, they all disembarked from the *Lady Ghislaine* and took a private plane to Israel with Maxwell's coffin on board.

Ghislaine, like the others, had many unanswered questions about how her father died, but there is reason to believe she had not been left in the dark when it came to his dubious financial machinations and entanglements with certain foreign intelligence services. Before they left the yacht, Ghislaine scoured it for anything that could be detrimental to the family. "Ghislaine rushed through the yacht's lounges and cabins . . . rifled drawers and cabinets, plucking documents from them indiscriminately and throwing them to the ground," wrote *Mirror* reporter John Jackson, who said he saw Ghislaine overseeing the shredding of thousands of pages of documents. "She shouted to the crew, 'I order you to shred immediately everything I have thrown on the floor.'"[5]

Ultimately, three conflicting autopsies left unresolved the big question of whether he had died by suicide or been murdered. Family members discounted the first of those. "He did not commit suicide," Ghislaine said many years later. "That was just not consistent with his character. I think he was murdered."[6]

And if she was right, who did it? And why?

Maxwell's papers—or at least those that had not been shredded—were already packed up in bags that had been flown back to London. One had to wonder if they contained secrets that might answer the mystery of Maxwell's death. According to *Robert Maxwell, Israel's Superspy*, by Gordon Thomas and Martin Dillon, Maxwell's safe on the yacht had been sealed. What was in those papers? What did Ghislaine know about them? Was he stealing from his company's pension funds? Could that have led him to suicide? There were reports that he was involved in illegal arms dealing. Were they true? And had he been laundering money? Did he have illicit intelligence connections?

These questions tantalized the press all over the world as well as his youngest daughter.

———

Born Ján Ludvík Hyman Binyamin Hoch, Ghislaine Maxwell's father was better known as British press lord Robert Maxwell, a larger-than-life figure whose Falstaffian bonhomie dwarfed his enormous crimes and daring exploits. With media holdings including the New York–based Macmillan Publishers, the Israeli daily *Ma'ariv*, the English-language *Moscow News*, the Oxford-based Pergamon Press, MTV Europe, and many other companies, Maxwell was a self-invented Anglicized Citizen Kane of sorts, and a precursor to and rival of Rupert Murdoch. He was also one of the most extraordinary intelligence assets of the twentieth century.

He grew up in a poor, Yiddish-speaking Orthodox Jewish family in what is now the small town of Solotvyno, Ukraine (then known as Slatinské Doly, in what was easternmost Czechoslovakia), became known as "the Bouncing Czech" during his financial travails, and came to occupy an unusually sensitive and pivotal place between the Soviet Union and the West during the last years of the Cold War. On the one hand, Maxwell had ties to Israel dating back to the early 1980s that included close relationships with the most powerful people in Mossad, the legendary Israeli spy agency. On the other, in the Soviet Union, Maxwell's regular visits to the KGB's Lubyanka headquarters went all the way to the top—to the office of the KGB chairman General Vladimir Kryuchkov.

Maxwell's history as a Soviet asset dated back to just after World War II, when, as a fiery young Czechoslovakian Jewish expatriate who had enlisted in the British army, he was sent to Berlin as an interpreter (he spoke eight languages) and first made contact with the Soviets. According to *Robert Maxwell, Israel's Superspy*, he acquired unparalleled access to the most dreaded spymasters of the Eastern bloc over the years, from the KGB's Yuri Andropov to the East German Stasi's Markus Wolf, and knew secrets that could topple governments. Before long, he had begun to indulge in the treacherous game of espionage while simultaneously serving multiple masters—Russia, Israel, and Great Britain. At the same time that Maxwell was working for the KGB, he was also in bed with Israel's Mossad, playing an increasingly dangerous game while he danced on the world stage as a media baron in London, Moscow, and New York.

I first became familiar with Maxwell in 1991 when I traveled around the United States with a rogue Israeli operative named Ari Ben-Menashe, who, among other things, was spreading seemingly absurd tales about how Maxwell was really an Israeli agent who was being used to disseminate Israeli propaganda and disinformation through his media holdings and, even more astonishingly, was actually using his company, the Mirror Group Newspapers, to facilitate the illegal and clandestine sale of Israeli arms to Iran.

I was working at *Newsweek* at the time and had dozens of hours of taped interviews with Ben-Menashe, but one editor after another dismissed his stories as outlandish fabrications. They thought the mere idea that a newspaper publisher was facilitating illegal arms sales from Israel to Iran was ludicrous.

But in fall 1991, Pulitzer Prize–winning reporter Seymour Hersh published *The Samson Option*, reporting for the first time, among other disclosures, on Robert Maxwell's ties to Israeli intelligence and the role of his *Daily Mirror* in secret and illegal arms deals with Iran.

According to the *Sunday Age*, in Melbourne, Australia, on November 2, 1991, a few days after the publication of Hersh's book, an unnamed source close to the Israeli cabinet told Hersh that Maxwell would soon be eliminated. The author did not know how seriously to take the threat.[7] Three days later, Robert Maxwell went missing, until searchers found his naked body floating faceup in the Atlantic.

At the same time that Maxwell's company was being exposed by Hersh, debts from his failing media empire had been spiraling out of control, concealed by creative accounting, unsecured loans, stolen pension funds, and money laundering. Paying no heed to the bottom line, Maxwell had expanded into the United States earlier that year by purchasing the *New York Daily News* and rescuing it from oblivion. To help warm up New York for his imminent arrival, Maxwell had sent Ghislaine to the city to be the advance guard for his foray into New York society.

———

Meanwhile, Maxwell's problematic relationships in the crisis-stricken Soviet Union didn't help matters. At the time, the Soviet Union was in crisis economically and politically, internally and externally. Mikhail Gorbachev had just negotiated a new treaty ceding enormous amounts of power to the Soviet republics, and hard-line Communist Party members who were already opposed to Gorbachev's reforms had had enough.

They included General Vladimir Kryuchkov, the KGB chief who was Maxwell's pal and who orchestrated a coup in August 1991 in an attempt to overthrow Gorbachev.

The coup failed, however, after only three days. Kryuchkov and his fellow conspirators were imprisoned and disgraced. Several killed themselves. If Maxwell, thanks to his ties to Kryuchkov, were in any way linked to a coup that tried to oust the West's favorite Soviet leader, there would be hell to pay from the CIA—not to mention the Kremlin.

In addition, Maxwell's business practices were a disaster. For all his purported wealth, Maxwell had also run up $2.2 billion in debt.[8] *Newsday* reporters went so far as to compare him to another New York con man who was similarly creative when it came to waving pieces of paper prepared by accounting firms that inflated his fortune and made it seem as if he did not have billions in debt. "But all those pieces of paper mean is that the accounting firm got a fee to certify that it had looked at the numbers, not that the numbers are realistic," the paper reported.[9]

Along with his strong ties to the KGB, Maxwell had a long, clandestine history working for Mossad, and as the Soviet Union disintegrated, he provided Mossad with access to the halls of power in the Kremlin and intelligence agencies in various Soviet satellites. A report in his own paper, the *Daily Mirror*, asserted that Maxwell was so desperate for cash he told Mossad that unless they came up with the money, "they could no longer count on his silence."[10]

If that report is true, Maxwell, in effect, was threatening to black-mail Mossad, an act that many people believe was a fatal mistake. Thomas and Dillon's *Robert Maxwell, Israel's Superspy* concludes, "Mossad had decided it could no longer afford to ignore the threat posed by Maxwell."

In life, Maxwell had been feted in Israel as if he were a head of state. In death, he was buried in Jerusalem's Mount of Olives with the splendor and solemnity of a state funeral,[11] attended by Israeli prime minister Yitzhak Shamir and President Chaim Herzog, both of whom gave eulogies, and no fewer than six serving and former heads of Israeli intelligence.[12]

And yet, for all that, Maxwell's killers were likely operating on behalf of Israeli intelligence.

———

Maxwell's entry into the world of intelligence dated back to the immediate aftermath of World War II, when, as a Jewish Czech expatriate, he had interrogated German scientists while serving in the British army. Shortly afterward, with funding from MI6,[13] Britain's foreign intelligence service, he started a scientific publishing firm that soon became the leading authority on Soviet bloc publishing—and a way for MI6 to obtain intelligence about Soviet scientists.[14] In naming the company Pergamon Press, Maxwell, whether he knew its provenance or not, settled on the Book of Revelation's name for Satan's throne—the Pergamon Altar. In return for the funding, Maxwell was to pass on information and help MI6 contact and recruit scientists.[15]

Along the way, Maxwell became so wired into the Kremlin that he knew all the top Soviet leaders personally—Leonid Brezhnev, Yuri Andropov, and Mikhail Gorbachev, among them—and was on speaking terms with the heads of intelligence in one Eastern bloc nation after another, including Bulgaria, Romania, and Czechoslovakia.[16] Which was all well and good, so long as Maxwell wasn't playing both sides and offering similar tidbits to the Soviets, too.

But that was exactly what the FBI feared when they saw Maxwell at the nexus of Soviet and Western science, a highly sensitive place to be just as the Cold War erupted.[17] Indeed, as early as 1953, the year Julius and Ethel Rosenberg were executed after being convicted of providing nuclear secrets to the Soviet Union, FBI director J. Edgar Hoover ordered what became an eight-year investigation comprising thousands of pages of documents that assert Maxwell was "in contact with Russians in East Germany, who were prepared to facilitate trading by their companies with Eastern bloc countries in return for political and economic information regarding policies of the Western Powers."[18]

Throughout the fifties, FBI files show that Maxwell traveled throughout the United States under the aliases of Wallace Chesterton, Ludwig Hock (a variation on his birth name), Enian Robert Maxwell, and others, striking up relationships with top scientists all over the country— including the brilliant mathematician and physicist John von Neumann, commissioner of the Atomic Energy Commission and one of the scientists behind the hydrogen bomb—in the interests of sharing the fruits of international science, translating Russian scientific journals into English, and, as one FBI report had it, "trying to ascertain from various American scientists if they would be interested in publishing an American edition of 'The Journal of Nuclear Energy.'"[19]

At a time when the theft of America's nuclear secrets by Russia was the central narrative in the country that made Robert Maxwell a person of interest. Phone calls were monitored. FBI assets at the Plaza Hotel kept an eye on Maxwell when he stayed in New York.[20] And scores of FBI agents and assets reported on him for the next eight years.

Ultimately, no charges were filed, but Maxwell *had* in fact been cultivating ties in Moscow. The Soviets had given him exclusive rights to publish the work of Soviet scientists. Maxwell translated them, published them through Pergamon, and made millions. In addition, according to *The Independent*, the KGB also paid him to publish a series of groveling hagiographies of Soviet leaders, one volume of which famously had Maxwell tossing a big, fat, slow pitch right across the middle of the plate to the brutal Romanian dictator Nicolae Ceaușescu: "How do you account for your enormous popularity with the Romanian people?"[21] (Maxwell reportedly duped the Soviets about how many copies were printed.)[22]

Soon, Pergamon Press became a major publishing house. In 1964, Maxwell was elected to Parliament as a member of the Labour Party. In 1981, he acquired the British Printing Corporation and later made it a subsidiary of Maxwell Communications Corporation, the umbrella corporation for his other media properties. Three years later, he bought Mirror Group Newspapers, the publisher of six British papers. He had become a major figure in British publishing. Before long, the man who was born Ján Ludvík Hyman Binyamin Hoch, an impoverished Czech Jew who was very much an outsider, had transformed himself into Cap'n Bob, a larger-than-life figure who rattled the cages of Britain's rigidly stratified social world, often to the distress of other socialites.

Maxwell's enormous girth was merely the physical manifestation of an outrageously flamboyant media mogul who knew no boundaries and won extraordinary access to the powers that be in the Kremlin, Downing Street, the White House, Lubyanka, and Mossad headquarters. Not only that, but he wasn't above taking liberties with any or all of them.

Among them, Maxwell's most important relationship may have been with General Vladimir Kryuchkov, the former head of the First Chief Directorate who became head of the KGB in 1988 and won notoriety as a hard-liner whose greatest achievements lay in penetrating US intelligence and launching successful disinformation operations. It was not just that Maxwell and Kryuchkov were on a first-name basis; both men happened to speak Hungarian, which gave them a special bond of sorts. They worked together for years.

Ultimately, the Soviets saw Maxwell as a roguish unofficial ambassador who was comfortable engaging in the highest levels of international diplomacy on the world stage, delivering crucial messages between Margaret Thatcher in London, Mikhail Gorbachev in Moscow, and George H. W. Bush in Washington.[23]

It was a role that Maxwell relished. Prime ministers came and went, but Maxwell was there forever.

These men (and they were mostly men) were part of the Western financial and intellectual elite, members of an exclusive and privileged class who offered access to the West in terms of both knowledge and capital markets, and who would trade favors for operations that were mutually beneficial.[24] In Maxwell's case, as in Trump's, money laundering was a major part of the game. Maxwell also made it clear to the Soviets that he would not tolerate any actions taken against Israel. In return, he offered his trust and loyalty.

In addition, Trump and Maxwell were friends—at least in the transactional sense of the word. They went to the same parties and bought their yachts from the same families. More specifically, in 1986, Maxwell bought the yacht that would become *Lady Ghislaine* from Emad Khashoggi, a wealthy Saudi real estate developer who was Adnan Khashoggi's nephew, and three years later, having just bought Macmillan Publishing, hosted Donald Trump and a plethora of other celebrities on the *Lady Ghislaine* in New York.[25] Other guests included European aristocrats, movie stars, and politicians, including former US senator John Tower (R-TX), whom Maxwell reportedly paid $200,000 a year in return for access to the White House and the defense establishment contacts he had acquired as chairman of the Senate Armed Services Committee.

Less than two years later, Trump bought his 280-foot yacht, renamed the *Trump Princess*, from the sultan of Brunei, who, in turn, had just bought it from Emad's uncle, Saudi arms dealer Adnan Khashoggi.[26] (Emad was the cousin of *Washington Post* journalist Jamal Khashoggi, who was murdered in 2018 by the Saudis. Adnan was Jamal's uncle.)

It is also worth noting that, according to Dylan Howard's book *Dead Men Tell No Tales*, written with Melissa Cronin and James Robertson, Adnan Khashoggi, who was implicated in the Iran-Contra affair that year, was a client of Jeffrey Epstein, the convicted pedophile and finance manager who mysteriously died in jail in 2019.[27]

These were a new kind of superrich. Theirs was a world with opulent villas, costume balls, private jets, and hookers galore. Excess knew no bounds. Yachts were not just important; they were essential. Size mattered. In 1985, Adnan Khashoggi, who was dubbed "one of the greatest whoremongers in the world" by Dominick Dunne in *Vanity Fair*, gave himself a fiftieth-birthday party that reportedly cost $6 million (more than $14 million in 2020 dollars), which he covered by selling an apartment.[28] Trump and Maxwell were both there.

Celebrated in gossip columns the world over, they were also precursors to a new breed of corrupt oligarchs who leveraged ties to intelligence agencies in the United States, the Soviet Union, Israel, Iran, and other countries, all while reaping riches in the world of arms dealing, money laundering, and covert operations related to the Iran-Contra scandal, the Bank of Credit and Commerce International collapse, and various other incidents.

Among those outrages was the so-called Inslaw scandal, which dated back to 1985, when Maxwell set up a tiny publishing company in McLean, Virginia, and hired two senior computer technicians from the Reagan administration's Justice Department. According to a "Memorandum in Response to the March 1993 Report of Special Counsel Nicholas J. Bua to the Attorney General of the United States Responding to the Allegations of INSLAW, Inc.," the technicians were crucial because they were familiar with software known as PROMIS (Prosecutors Management Information System) that had been designed to aid prosecutors in tracking cases as they made their way through the criminal justice system.[29] The program was proprietary software created by a small tech company called Inslaw.

Over the years, the world of investigative reporting has been populated with a number of deep-in-the-weeds rabbit holes, one of the deepest of which is the Inslaw scandal, which won national attention in the nineties, thanks in part to two mysterious deaths. As chair of Pergamon-Brassey's International Defense Publishers, a defense publishing house owned by Maxwell, John Tower put the considerable political capital he had acquired in his nearly twenty-four years in the Senate to work running interference for Maxwell, who had just acquired PROMIS. But on April 5, 1991, Tower died in a plane crash in Georgia, which investigators blamed on the failure of the plane's propeller control unit.[30] Reports of mechanical failure notwithstanding, according to *Robert Maxwell, Israel's Superspy*, Maxwell feared that Mossad was behind the plane crash.

In addition to Tower's mysterious death, there's also the story of a forty-four-year-old freelance reporter named Danny Casolaro, who had been found dead in a bathtub at a Sheraton Hotel in Martinsburg, West Virginia, while he was investigating the Inslaw story.[31]

Casolaro had bled to death from severed arteries in his wrists, which had been slashed ten to twelve times. At first his death was ruled a suicide, but that wasn't the whole story. Casolaro told friends he had finally made a major breakthrough in his reporting and was off to West Virginia to meet a source who would provide solid evidence about what he called "the Octopus," a network of people said to be behind various scandals including Iran-Contra, the collapse of the Bank of Credit and Commerce International, and the theft of PROMIS from Inslaw. He also had been getting death threats. "He told us . . . if there was an accident and he died, not to believe it," his brother Anthony Casolaro told the *Boston Globe*.[32]

Casolaro's death and the mysteries he was trying to unravel were never fully resolved, but several key elements of the scandal were clarified in the "Memorandum in Response to the March 1993 Report of Special Counsel Nicholas J. Bua," which was signed by former attorney general Elliot Richardson, who was then one of Inslaw's attorneys.

According to Richardson's memo, the PROMIS software was first stolen in 1983, when the Justice Department turned over a copy to a visiting Israeli official who came to the Justice Department, introduced himself as Dr. Joseph Ben Orr, and said he was there because Israel hoped to lease PROMIS so that it could computerize its public prosecution offices. About three months later, the Justice Department gave Dr. Orr a copy of the PROMIS software.

As Inslaw finally learned years later, however, "Dr. Ben Orr" was a false identity. The man using that name to get PROMIS was really Rafi Eitan, a legendary Israeli spymaster who at the time was director of a top-secret agency called LAKAM in the Ministry of Defense, which was responsible for the collection of scientific intelligence through espionage.

The memorandum added, "Among the individuals whose companies served as cutouts for the illegal dissemination of PROMIS by Israeli intelligence, according to the author, were Earl W. Brian (a

California businessman who was later sentenced to four years in jail for conspiracy) and the late British publisher, Robert Maxwell."

One of the most distinctive features of the software, in those early days of the computer era, was the fact that PROMIS could integrate numerous databases. But if such features were useful in allowing clients to track cases in the judiciary, they could easily be adapted to help clients track other things. In fact, according to Inslaw founder Bill Hamilton, who worked at the National Security Agency for seven years, PROMIS is especially useful in the world of intelligence, so useful that he heard from multiple informants that hijacked versions of PROMIS had been installed at the NSA, FBI, CIA, and other intelligence agencies.[33]

And when PROMIS was disseminated to other parties, especially to other countries, it was widely alleged to contain a feature that was meant to be secret—namely, a trapdoor engineered by Israeli programmers that enabled Israel and the United States to listen in secretly.[34] In other words, it was an electronic Trojan horse: In solving the software needs of allied or neutral nations, the seller would also be able to steal their secrets.

As Inslaw attorney Elliot Richardson explained to the *Washington Post*, "It's extremely plausible that if the hardware also contained software with which the U.S. was totally committed, it would then be possible to interpret the signal. If the purchaser was a foreign intelligence agency, the U.S. would thus have succeeded in penetrating the intelligence files."[35]

And so, while working with Rafi Eitan—and therefore, Israel—Robert Maxwell used an Israeli computer company he owned, Degem, which was really a front for Mossad, to distribute PROMIS to other countries all over the world. In the end, Maxwell had played a key role in one of the great intelligence scams in contemporary history. In the end, Israel was able to get *paid* by countries from which it was stealing classified information.

Much as he loved Israel, Maxwell at times was equally welcome in the Kremlin. One indication of how high Maxwell had climbed into the upper reaches of the Kremlin comes from *The Diary of Anatoly Chernyaev*, the author of which served as Gorbachev's national security advisor from 1986 to 1991. A key figure in orchestrating the peaceful end of the Cold War, Chernyaev reveals that he finds Robert Maxwell is so close to General Kryuchkov that Kryuchkov constantly pushes Maxwell straight into conversation with Mikhail Gorbachev no matter what else is going on.[36]

As Chernyaev wrote on June 26, 1991: "Maxwell was imposed on M.S. [Mikhail Sergeyevich Gorbachev] by Kryuchkov, they have some business going on! Every time he visits, he is 'presented' to the top. He is impudent: Gusenkov* told me that he was lecturing Gorbachev on how to live in London, how to use the President's time. When I found out from Primakov the day before that Maxwell wants to see M.S., I objected and decided not to tell Gorbachev. But he asked me himself."[37]

Chernyaev added that Gorbachev even confided to Maxwell that he might not run for another presidential term. "Even if he decided not to, he shouldn't spill the news to the West," Chernyaev wrote, because Western leaders might then dismiss him as a helpless and ineffectual lame duck.

According to *Robert Maxwell, Israel's Superspy*, in Maxwell, Kryuchkov had an unusual asset who plied him with gold cuff links, a cashmere coat, hi-fi equipment, and crates of Scotch whisky and champagne.[38] In return, Maxwell was put in charge of laundering money through a special coded account in the Bank of Bulgaria and given wide latitude to do as he saw fit. Kryuchkov created an umbrella of companies to receive and resell technology stolen from the West, leaving Maxwell to launder the profits.

And Maxwell was comfortable working the dark side. General Kryuchkov had put together one of the most ambitious clandestine operations in the history of intelligence, positioning the KGB first to

---

* Vitaly Gusenkov was an assistant to Gorbachev. At the time, Yevgeny Primakov was serving as Gorbachev's special envoy to Iraq during the run-up to the 1991 Gulf War. He subsequently became foreign minister and then prime minister under Russian president Boris Yeltsin.

launder vast amounts of money, and later to rise again after the fall of the Soviet Union—and he brought Maxwell in to help design the financial model that would see the KGB through.

Starting back in the mid-eighties, when the West was welcoming the genial overtures of Mikhail Gorbachev, Kryuchkov, a fearsome hardliner, had secretly launched about six hundred front companies as a safe haven for Soviet leaders and KGB operatives.[39] Buying commodities such as oil, steel, and aluminum from Soviet enterprises at 5 percent of the world market price, these new companies could turn around and sell them in the West at market value. Then, with billions in profits, they could go on to establish authentic trading relationships that went to the heart of Western capitalism—Wall Street, the Paris Bourse, and London's Square Mile and Canary Wharf. In doing so, these KGB-infiltrated companies would gain access to the Western banking system, through which they would learn how to launder billions and navigate the byways of the capitalist world.

Kryuchkov knew that these companies—some of them multibillion-dollar commodity firms—would outlast the disintegrating Soviet Union, and that through them, KGB operatives would rise, phoenixlike, many years later when the dust had settled. Only then, after it had been lulled to sleep with the dream that it had won the Cold War, would the West awaken to find that a Russian asset named Donald Trump was in the White House, and that Trump had been helped by some of Kryuchkov's minions who did business with him many years later.

To assist with the money laundering, Kryuchkov introduced Maxwell to Semion Mogilevich,[40] the legendary figure in the Russian Mafia whom I wrote about in *House of Trump*. "The most dangerous mobster in the world," as the FBI calls him, Mogilevich was renowned as the "Brainy Don," thanks to his mastery of sophisticated financial crimes. Kryuchkov's plan was to divide the spoils of the fallen Soviet Union by taking $50 billion in gold bullion from the Communist Party and putting it in commodity firms and shell companies controlled by Mogilevich, Maxwell, and others.

With Maxwell's help, Mogilevich got an Israeli passport and finally could travel anywhere in the world, at a time when it was difficult for Soviet citizens to leave the country.[41] Off he went to the Channel Islands and the Cayman Islands, to Liechtenstein to set up a new money-laundering operation, to Gibraltar, to Cyprus and other destinations. As I described in *House of Trump*, as part of the operation, years later Mogilevich took over the lucrative Ukrainian energy trade and skimmed a fortune off the top.

The inner workings of Mogilevich's relationship with Dmitri Firtash, the Ukrainian oligarch who served as Mogilevich's front man, were best described in an unusually intriguing memo classified "Secret" by William Taylor, the ambassador to Ukraine who later became a courageous witness against Trump in the 2019 impeachment hearings. In his cable to the State Department, Taylor described meeting Firtash, who at first downplayed his ties to Mogilevich, "stating he needed Mogilevich's approval to get in the business in the first place. He was adamant that he had not committed a single crime when building his business empire, and argued that outsiders still failed to understand the period of lawlessness that reigned in Ukraine after the collapse of the Soviet Union."

Maxwell's eager embrace of Mogilevich was astonishing even for someone with a reputation as an unscrupulous corporate raider. Warfare in the world of international finance and hostile takeovers was one thing, but Mogilevich's world was one of prostitution, human trafficking, arms sales, and drugs—and Maxwell plunged right in. Maxwell courted royalty. But this was a world of transnational organized crime, and Maxwell became a bagman of sorts who moved millions of dollars around at the toss of a hat. He became very close to the Politburo. The information he provided was priceless. He began sharing valuable Western technology with Moscow—stealing it, really—and worked every side of the fence, spending one day in the White House with Reagan, the next in the Kremlin, and then, perhaps, off to Israel.

In effect, Kryuchkov had designated Maxwell as an intermediary between the dark world of organized crime and the KGB and its intelligence services.[42] Later, Putin used these relationships to forge a new

Mafia state. "Some of Maxwell's associates were involved in narcotics, illegal weapons, and contract killings, of which there may be as many as five hundred a year," the late John P. O'Neill, a legendary FBI agent who died in the attacks of 9/11, told a reporter. "They were also into smuggling precious metal and counterfeiting. They had links with the Russian military. Any Russian banker that didn't do their bidding knew what to expect. He got a grenade tossed into his car."[43]

From Kryuchkov's point of view, however, Maxwell was doing just fine. "Maxwell showed how an intricate, complex web of shell companies under a group umbrella could move money around the globe," said O'Neill. "When New York became a target for Eastern Bloc criminal syndicates and we looked at how it operated, the Maxwell model was there for all to see."

By 1987, Maxwell had laundered $1 billion through the Bulgarian Cooperative Bank alone. He laundered more through the *Daily Mirror*. In January 1991, Maxwell bought the ailing *New York Daily News* and allegedly used it to launder Russian mob money as well. Toronto's *Financial Post* reported that the acquisition "made Maxwell a hero in a city that cherishes its heroes, especially flamboyant ones in the mold of Donald Trump. Maxwell, waddling around like a king penguin with a red bow tie, topped every socialite's invitation list."[44]

In 1989, a year after Maxwell bought Macmillan Publishers, both he and Trump were guests at the so-called party of the century, Malcolm Forbes's insanely extravagant seventieth-birthday bash in Tangiers with eight hundred guests, among them Fiat chairman Giovanni Agnelli, opera singer Beverly Sills, broadcasters Walter Cronkite and Barbara Walters, publishers Katharine Graham and Rupert Murdoch, and Henry Kissinger.

The eighties, of course, were the "greed is good" decade, as Gordon Gekko proclaimed in Oliver Stone's *Wall Street*, and nobody captured the zeitgeist better than Trump and Maxwell. In addition to inflating their net worth, both projected outsize personalities as they stood astride the world stage, frequently appearing together in the business pages celebrating their latest extravagant acquisition, all while secretly laundering money for Russian mobsters who, by extension, were playing important roles for Russian intelligence.

Similarly, in 1989, according to the *Chicago Tribune*, Trump attended a party the elder Maxwell gave on the *Lady Ghislaine*, at which Trump saw fit to announce that his yacht, the *Trump Princess*, was bigger than Maxwell's.[45] At roughly the same time, Maxwell had been working with Mogilevich to establish about fifty "legitimate" companies in Israel, Britain, the United States, and Germany, through which they laundered about $40 billion a year for Mogilevich and the Russian Mafia.[46] Working with Mogilevich, Robert Maxwell became the bagman, and one of the most powerful Russian operatives helping the Soviet Union renew its dreams of empire.

Of course, Maxwell wasn't alone in carrying out Kryuchkov's plans. After the fall of the Soviet Union in 1991, Semyon Kislin, who had made the first contact with Trump more than a decade earlier, developed a lucrative relationship with Mikhail and Lev Chernoy, the Uzbekistan-born industrialist brothers, who, according to an Interpol report, used Kislin's firm Trans-Commodities for fraud and embezzlement.[47] The Chernoy brothers became billionaires in the bloody and brutal aluminum wars in the nineties, with Mikhail serving as a mentor to oligarch Oleg Deripaska, who has since become a powerful Putin crony, and who was at various times both allied with and an adversary of the Chernoys. Kislin and his electronics-store partner, Tamir Sapir, were also on their way to becoming immensely wealthy émigrés, and they remained close to Trump.

In 1984, even before Mogilevich consolidated operations in New York, Donald Trump had allowed Trump Tower to launder money for Russian Mafia operatives such as David Bogatin, the alleged gangster who had allegedly participated in the so-called Red Daisy gas tax scam through which billions of tax dollars were siphoned off gas station revenues.

Not long after his abortive campaign for the 1988 Republican presidential nomination, Trump became mired in one bankruptcy after another because of his disastrous overexpansion into Atlantic City casinos that left him $4 billion in debt.

Then, on Christmas Day 1991, Mikhail Gorbachev resigned as the leader of the Soviet Union and handed over the powers of his office to Russian president Boris Yeltsin. At 7:32 p.m. Moscow time, the Soviet flag with its iconic hammer and sickle was lowered from the Kremlin and replaced by the white, blue, and red tricolor banner of the Russian Federation.

The Cold War was over. The West had won. East and West Germany had begun reunification. It was time to declare victory. In his book *The End of History and the Last Man*, political scientist Francis Fukuyama declared victory on behalf of liberal Western democracies. There could be no more argument as to which system was better. Western capitalism, liberal democracy, had won. Pundits discussed how we would spend the peace dividend. Things had never looked rosier. Agents in almost every sector of national security eased up on the Russians. Maybe now they were our friends.

But there were other powerful, unseen forces at work. Like the KGB. In the aftermath of the Soviet Union's demise, attempts to build a market economy in Russia largely lost out to an embryonic Mafia state and an emerging kleptocracy, and wealthy émigrés and oligarchs with ties to the Russian Mafia and the KGB, and later its successor, the FSB, were on the ascent.

As the leader of the abortive coup in 1991 against Gorbachev, Vladimir Kryuchkov was imprisoned for three years and never became active again. But by starting commodity firms that had links to the KGB, he had set in motion mechanisms that were far more successful than he was—and indeed paid off decades later thanks to their ties to Donald Trump. As I reported in *House of Trump, House of Putin*, one of the most notable of those was Seabeco, a successful commodities firm run by Boris Birshtein, a Russo-Canadian businessman who had ties to both the KGB and Russian mobsters Sergei Mikhailov and Semion Mogilevich. As it happened, many years later three principals in Seabeco—Alexander Shnaider, Alexander Mashkevich, and Tevfik Arif—rose from the ashes of the Soviet Union to become enormously wealthy partners of Donald Trump, who bailed him out from his financial woes in the 2000s.

Thanks to the triumphalist tenor of the times, the United States did not exactly have its eye on the ball. Now that the Soviet bear was gone, the national security apparatus no longer saw Russia as a serious national security threat. "We had just had a tremendous success," Rolf Mowatt-Larssen, the former CIA station chief in Moscow, told me. "No one knew our purpose anymore. We were off our game. The Soviets were dead, and that meant the general mood was to question our raison d'être. Our biggest problem was disinterest."

To those counterintelligence agents who had worked the Eastern bloc during Cold War, nothing was what it seemed. "Even after it ended, the Cold War never really ended," said former CIA intelligence officer Glenn Carle.[48] "I thought naively, 'Well, the Berlin Wall has fallen. The Cold War is over. Communism is dead. Now they can just be Russians.' But they were still shaped by seventy years of cultural formation and pressures, and the Russian bureaucracies never really changed. In my experience, as individuals and institutions, they all reflexively took the perspective that relations with the United States in particular were invariably a zero-sum game. That there could be no mutual benefit. That if it helps you, it screws us."

And as it turned out, while the Americans may have thought the Cold War was over, no one told the KGB or its successors. "My understanding," said Carle, "is that there were more Russian intelligence officers active in the United States *after* the fall of the Berlin Wall. They didn't stand down at all—not at all. Whereas the United States had a reduction of twenty-five percent or so."[49]

Likewise, it was the same for the FBI after the collapse of the Soviet Union. There, with William Barr overseeing the bureau as attorney general, the FBI had also decided to focus its attention elsewhere. Even though Mark Wauck had reported his suspicions about Robert Hanssen, according to the inspector general's report on Hanssen, Wauck's supervisor had not followed through. So instead of investigating and exposing Hanssen's perfidy, William Barr's FBI *promoted* Hanssen to program manager in the Soviet operations section at FBI headquarters, where he supervised operational programs designed to counter Soviet efforts to acquire scientific and technical information.

And that wasn't all. Just six months later, in January 1992, Hanssen was *again* promoted to chief of the National Security Threat List (NSTL) Unit, charged with rethinking counterintelligence priorities in the wake of the demise of the Soviet Union. It was the highest-ranking position he held at the FBI. Even though Mark Wauck had reported his suspicions that his brother-in-law was a spy, Hanssen was given these promotions without even a standard background reinvestigation and given access to highly sensitive material.

And thanks in part to his promotions, Hanssen, who wasn't arrested until February 2001, continued to betray some of this nation's most important counterintelligence and military secrets, including the identities of dozens of human assets.

As if that were not enough, Barr went further. Within months of his appointment as attorney general, he transferred three hundred FBI agents, many of them Russian-speaking, from counterintelligence work on the Russian Mafia to investigations of gang violence growing out of the crack cocaine epidemic. The *New York Times* characterized it as "the largest single manpower shift in the bureau's history."[50]

Because the crack epidemic was very real, the manpower shift was a politically popular move. But by transferring so many agents away from work on the Russian Mafia and its growing power, Barr may have helped facilitate one of the greatest national security failures in US history.

Those who remained focused on Russia didn't have a clue what to do. "We didn't know if they were friend or foe," Myron Fuller, a former FBI special agent in counterintelligence, told me.[51]

In the beginning, it wasn't surprising that US intelligence would adopt a holding pattern about what was emerging from the detritus of the Soviet Union. But in the nineties, it gradually became apparent that building a market economy in the former Soviet Union was not as easy as it looked, and that what was taking place instead was the birth of a Mafia state. The fall of the Soviet bloc opened the sluice gates to a torrent of flight capital that could now go into infecting Western democracies with the viruses of a new kleptocracy.

In Washington, K Street lobbyists had created a lucrative cottage industry by fashioning ingenious loopholes in legislation that served powerful corporate interests—Big Oil, Big Pharma, and the like. Now those doors had opened to foreign interests as well. The Russians learned how to work the system. Russian money went to coal mines in Kentucky to keep Senate majority leader Mitch McConnell (R-KY) happy. Billionaire oligarchs like Leonard Blavatnik, who happened to be a naturalized American citizen, could pour millions from their immense fortunes—$31.7 billion for Blavatnik, according to Bloomberg—into America's deeply flawed electoral finance system.

In the decade after the Soviet Union collapsed, KGB operations started by Boris Birshtein and the like began to emerge as forces to launder money, run commodity firms, and help out the likes of Donald Trump. Among them, Birshtein colleague Alexander Mashkevich was later connected to the Bayrock Group, the real estate development company located in Trump Tower that developed Trump SoHo (now the Dominick) in 2002 and pushed unsuccessfully to develop Trump Tower in Moscow. Alexander Shnaider, who was Birshtein's son-in-law, partnered with Trump in building the sixty-five-story Trump International Hotel and Tower Toronto, which opened in 2012. (The hotel has since been renamed the St. Regis Toronto.)

In the nineties, Trump had lost billions by overexpanding in Atlantic City casinos at an insane pace. But now, thanks to the Russians, he was back on his feet. He was ready for his second coming.

CHAPTER TWELVE

GHISLAINE AND JEFFREY

N o one was more stunned by Robert Maxwell's death than officials at the YIVO Institute for Jewish Research, a leading repository of information on Eastern European Jewry that had selected Maxwell and his wife, Elisabeth, to be honored guests at its annual benefit dinner scheduled just over two weeks later.[1]

At first, officials at the institute weren't clear on how to handle the situation and considered canceling the dinner entirely. But when Mrs. Maxwell said she wanted to go ahead with it, the institute decided to turn the evening into "a solemn celebration" of Maxwell's life and his charitable work for Israel.[2] Elisabeth, who was known as Betty, was to be honored as well for her research on the Holocaust.

So on November 24, 1991, Elisabeth arrived at New York's Plaza Hotel, then owned by Donald Trump, with her daughter Ghislaine and her daughter's date. Scheduled entertainment included Mandy Patinkin singing Yiddish songs and an appearance by actor and comedian Tony Randall. New York mayor David Dinkins and Senator Daniel Patrick Moynihan (D-NY) were expected as well.[3]

But none of that meant it was going to be fun. Ghislaine, still finding her legs in New York, had moved to the city after her father bought the *New York Daily News* earlier that year, in March. Her role initially had been to do advance work casting her father as a hero who was rescuing a failing New York institution.

But as must have been clear at the Plaza that night, things couldn't possibly have gone more wrong. The guest of honor was dead. After Maxwell's death, his corrupt empire was finally exposed as the catastrophe it was. The whole Maxwell empire was riddled with scandals being played out in the press—with stories of his tragic death yielding to respectful obituaries, which then gave way to mysteries and scandals that unraveled day by day, and raised the question of whether his demise was the result of murder, suicide, or an accident. Moreover, it was now being reported that before his death, Maxwell had stolen as much as $1.2 billion (more than $2.26 billion in 2020 dollars) from his businesses and his employees' pension funds.[4]

The *Daily Mirror*'s foreign editor, Nicholas Davies, a close confidant of Maxwell's, was shown to have had longtime ties to Mossad. Pressure was mounting on Ian and Kevin Maxwell, two of Ghislaine's brothers who were now running the family business, to satisfy bankers who had been stiffed by their father.[5] All over the world, newspapers headlined stories about the Maxwell meltdown. *The Independent* (UK): "Maxwell's Time Bomb; A Fraud Investigation into Mysterious Events."[6] *The Observer* (UK): "Banks Close In on Maxwell—Pressure Is Mounting for Kevin and Ian." The *New York Times*: "Swiss Bank Is Demanding Maxwell Loan Repayment."[7]

The *Scotsman* put aside the old saw about not speaking ill of the dead: "If he was despised in life, he was hated in death," the newspaper reported. "He was, officially, the biggest thief in British criminal history."[8]

Of course, what made his story even more mesmerizing was the lurid mystery behind his demise. The three pathologists at Maxwell's inquest were unable to agree on the cause of death, and at least one of them, Carlos López de Lamela, left open the possibility of murder. López de Lamela said that a tiny perforation under the publisher's left ear "could have been caused by a syringe filled with some mortal substance. We certainly haven't ruled out foul play." But according to London's *Evening Standard*, López de Lamela kept changing his mind.[9]

Meanwhile, in the immediate aftermath of her father's death, Ghislaine had committed the self-inflicted PR blunder of flying back to New York aboard the luxury supersonic Concorde—in the process, outraging pensioners who had loyally worked for her father and were facing an impoverished retirement, thanks to his extraordinary thievery.[10]

Of all Maxwell's children, Ghislaine was the most sought after by tabloid reporters feasting on the detritus left behind by her father's death. Ghislaine had shown up regularly in the gossip columns before his death, once on the arm of George Hamilton, the debonair and perpetually suntanned Hollywood boy toy. Afterward, Rupert Murdoch's *New York Post*, chief rival to Maxwell's *Daily News*, referred to Ghislaine as the "leggy heiress." Britain's *Mail on Sunday* called her "the youngest and most pulchritudinous of the disgraced tycoon's children."[11]

No wonder she had decamped to New York, where her father's legacy ". . . was less toxic, where she is building a respectability," the *Mail* opined, "which would be impossible in London, where the wounds created by her father cut deepest. In New York, they adore the progeny of felons as much as the felons themselves." And indeed, when Ghislaine was the celebrity invitee at a restaurant opening after her father's death, she was a hit—no apologies necessary.[12]

Oxford-educated, she was smart, sexy, and compelling, a master of the breezy and witty cocktail banter that could win over royalty and posh literary crowds and that delighted even the most jaded New Yorkers. Her pedigree as scion to a corrupt dynasty aside, she had fabulous access to some of the richest and most powerful people in the world on both sides of the Atlantic. She was even able to charm some who hated her father.

"[Robert] Maxwell was an ass-licker," recalled Taki Theodoracopulos, the conservative Greek journalist who has chronicled transatlantic society for more than forty years. "I didn't want to have anything to do with him. But Ghislaine wasn't like that. She was attractive and friendly. She never pulled rank. She was always polite."[13]

A more unlikely fan of Ghislaine's was a former colleague of mine at *Vanity Fair*, Vicky Ward, who famously profiled Epstein in a 2003 article from which reports of his sexual misconduct had been edited out. But in 2011, Ward was back writing about the Ghislaine and Jeffrey for the magazine in a highly flattering piece that extolled Ghislaine's relationship with Epstein, and her vulnerability.

"And Ghislaine?" she wrote.

"Full Disclosure: I like her. Most people in New York do. It's almost impossible not to.

"She is always the most interesting, the most vivacious, the most unusual person in any room. I've spent hours talking to her about the Third World at a bar until two a.m."[14]

But in the end, Ward was most taken by a very different facet of Ghislaine's personality: "When it comes down to things she really cares about . . . Ghislaine shows her vulnerability. And that vulnerability is key to understanding her friendship with Jeffrey.

"'He saved her,' I remember a close friend of mine telling me. 'When her father died, she was a wreck; inconsolable. And then Jeffrey took her in. She's never forgotten that—and never will.'" (When the highly ingratiating profile of Ghislaine was first published, Ward proudly tweeted about its appearance in *Vanity Fair*. But the article is no longer available on her site or the magazine's.)

By the time Ghislaine settled in New York, she had become adept at navigating the transactional nature of New York celebrity society and, in the aftermath of her father's death, played it to the hilt. "She was very funny, very engaging, very sharp. Fiercely bright, intuitive, and fast," said Christopher Mason, a journalist, TV host, and writer of satirical songs whom Ghislaine took on to write songs for Epstein's birthday.[15] "But all of her conversation was about her astonishing access to power. Every conversation involved someone of staggering wealth and power."

All of which were strong cards to play in taking on New York society. And to help her along, Ghislaine had a new man at her side, a new boyfriend, a thirty-eight-year-old financier who provided the kind of support she needed. His name was Jeffrey Epstein.

Having made the journey from the shtetl of Solotvyno, Ukraine, to the top of British society, Robert Maxwell was unrivaled in his ability to leap rigid British class barriers in a single bound, but Jeffrey Epstein may have given him a run for his money. The product of working-class Coney Island—his father had been a municipal parks department employee—Epstein, by the end of his life, hobnobbed with heads of state, Nobel laureates, billionaires, celebrities, and royalty.

He had hundreds of millions of dollars. He owned extraordinary homes all over the world. One, his seven-story, $77 million, fifty-thousand-square-foot Upper East Side town house, was said to be the largest private residence in New York City. Another, situated on a ten-thousand-acre ranch in New Mexico, reportedly made that town house "look like a shack" in comparison. And a third, on El Brillo Way in Palm Beach, Florida, was conveniently located just two miles from Donald Trump's Mar-a-Lago estate, where Epstein and Ghislaine spent much of their time. Finally, Epstein had his own private island, Little Saint James, sometimes known as Little Saint Jeff's, seventy-two acres of paradise off the east coast of Saint Thomas in the US Virgin Islands, replete with a helipad, a lagoon, cabanas, and a luxurious colonnaded villa boasting a large library, cinema, and detached Japanese bathhouse. And, of course, a house staff of seventy.

And then there were the women and young girls—scores of them, dozens of whom were in their teens, and whom Epstein passed around like party favors to some of the world's most powerful men. All the while, he was secretly recording their activities, the tapes of which provided a hammerlock of kompromat, leverage, and influence.

Epstein's ascent began in 1973, when, as a twenty-one-year-old college dropout, he was hired to teach math and physics at Dalton, the posh co-ed private school on Manhattan's Upper East Side at which Donald Barr—the father of Attorney General William Barr—was headmaster. Whether Donald Barr actually hired Epstein before being dismissed himself is a matter of some dispute, but according to *New York* magazine, they were likely no more than ships passing in the night in that Barr was seen as so "authoritarian" and "undemocratic" that he was ousted *before* Epstein started work. "[Barr] was disliked by the faculty, he was highly controversial, he hadn't raised much money, he was very conservative," Dalton's chairman told *New York* magazine.[16]

Barr was also the author of an eccentric 1973 novel called *Space Relations*, a science fiction story that depicts enslaved teenage girls who are forced to have sex with the powers that be, which was published the year before Epstein started teaching at Dalton.[17] (That happenstance was enough to drive the price of a paperback copy of Barr's novel up to $32,207.88 briefly on Amazon in August 2020.)

Dalton was the school of choice for stylish and affluent New York sophisticates. In the movie *Manhattan*, it's where Woody Allen's seventeen-year-old girlfriend, played by Mariel Hemingway, went to school. In real life, it was where John Lennon, director Sidney Lumet, Ralph Lauren, and Rupert Murdoch sent their children. Celebrity alumni include Claire Danes, Chevy Chase, Christian Slater, Jennifer Grey, and Anderson Cooper.

At Dalton, Epstein pushed the envelope in terms of testing how far a teacher could go in fraternizing with students. Wearing gold chains, a fur coat, and open shirts that exposed his chest, Epstein sometimes showed up unexpectedly at student parties and lavished attention on the teenage girls.[18] Students thought he was creepy. As interim headmaster Peter Branch told the *New York Times*, Epstein "didn't come up to snuff, so, ultimately, he was asked to leave."

But before he was fired, Epstein attended a parent–teacher conference at Dalton at which he dazzled a student's father with his brilliance. "This parent was so wowed by the conversation he told my father, 'You've got to hire this guy,'" Lynne Koeppel told the *Miami Herald*.[19] "Give Jeff credit. He was brilliant." (At one point, Koeppel dated Epstein.)

Koeppel's father, the late Wall Street banker Alan "Ace" Greenberg, wasn't just another Dalton parent whose son happened to be tutored by Epstein.[20] He was the feisty tough guy atop Bear Stearns who had built his investment bank into one of the hottest shops on Wall Street. Greenberg didn't care about old money, WASP bloodlines, or the niceties of café society, and instead sought out hungry, young, aggressive, ethnic, bridge-and-tunnel talent that was "PSD," as he put it: poor, smart, and filled with a deep, deep desire to get filthy rich. Epstein fit the bill perfectly.[21]

Greenberg was also friendly with Donald Trump, who, according to *The Art of the Deal*, typically began each morning with a call to him on the trading floor: "Alan is the CEO of Bear Sterns, he's been my investment banker for the past five years, and he's the best there is."

At Bear Stearns, Epstein was Ace Greenberg's protégé and became a limited partner, but he left in 1981 under mysterious circumstances. He later testified before a Securities and Exchange Commission investigation that gossip at his firm claimed that his departure had to with an illicit relationship with a secretary but that the real reason had to do with an improper loan he had made to a friend who was buying stock.

In 1981, Epstein started his own company, Intercontinental Assets Group, and six years later founded a money management firm called J. Epstein & Company. Its name was later changed to the Financial Trust Co., and its headquarters were moved to the US Virgin Islands, chiefly for tax purposes.

By 1986, Epstein reportedly oversaw a $15 billion fund for a list of wealthy clients whose names were a closely held secret, with the exception of billionaire retailer Leslie Wexner, the CEO and founder of the Limited, and, perhaps more famously, the man behind Victoria's Secret. "I was the only person crazy enough, or arrogant enough, or misplaced enough, to make my limit a billion dollars or more," Epstein said.[22] He added that client fees plus his mastery of the currency markets had made him rich.

According to the *New York Times*, Wexner gave Epstein enormous sway "over his finances, philanthropy, and private life" and authorized him "to borrow money on his behalf, to sign his tax returns, to hire people and to make acquisitions."[23]

But that didn't explain everything. To be sure, Epstein was richly rewarded for managing Wexner's money, which, according to Forbes, totaled $1.8 billion in 1988. Over the years, the *Wall Street Journal* reported, Epstein also had relationships with financier Leon Black,

Johnson & Johnson heiress Elizabeth Ross (Libet) Johnson, and hedge fund billionaire Glenn Dubin that proved highly lucrative.[24]

But it didn't add up. At his death in 2019, Epstein's will put his net worth at more than $577 million.[25] It is difficult to make a fortune like that without leaving a bigger footprint. And no one ever saw Epstein work. On Wall Street, the trading desks didn't even know who he was. That in itself was suspect. No one makes that much money without leaving tracks. "He plays 26 hours a day," one of his friends told *New York* magazine.[26]

Friends and associates were mystified as to exactly what Epstein did. Dozens of reporters have tried—and failed—to find Epstein's other clients or other sources of income.

So where did his money really come from? "When I met him in the eighties, for Christ's sake, he was a process server," says Jesse Kornbluth, a longtime colleague of mine at *New York* magazine and *Vanity Fair*, whom Epstein had approached to write a book about him. (The project never went forward.)

At the time, Kornbluth said, Epstein was spending a lot of time with Leon Black, the multibillionaire investor who was then managing director of Drexel Burnham Lambert, at that point one of the biggest investment banks in the country. Black later was cofounder, chairman, and CEO of private equity giant Apollo Global Management, which manages more than $300 billion in assets.

In October 2020, the *New York Times* reported that Black wired Epstein at least $50 million and perhaps as much as $75 million in the years after Epstein's arrest.[27]

"Epstein and I talked a lot about Leon Black," Kornbluth told me. "Leon Black had a huge department of the top tax lawyers in the country. What the fuck did Leon Black need with Jeffrey Epstein? Was Jeffrey a genius beyond anyone he'd ever talked to? Maybe. I have no idea." Similarly, the fact that Epstein had lobbied—successfully!—to get ready access to Microsoft's Bill Gates raised more questions than it answered. "What did Bill Gates see in Jeffrey? Once you've snared Bill Gates, you can't go higher. In order to buy any of this, you have to assume that Jeffrey was an incredible genius."

The Times cited Stephanie Pillersdorf, a spokewoman for Black, who said, "Mr. Black received personal trusts and estates planning advice as well as family office philanthropy and investment services from several financial and legal advisers, including Mr. Epstein, during a six-year period, between 2012 and 2017."[28]

But in the end, it was unclear exactly what services Epstein provided for those fees.

Another associate of Epstein's, the journalist and author Edward Jay Epstein (no relation to Jeffrey), then a columnist for *Manhattan, Inc.*, was also approached by the financier, who was trying to get someone—Ed Epstein, for example—to write about his business.

"What is your business?" Ed Epstein asked.

"I'm sort of a financial bounty hunter," Jeffrey replied.

A financial bounty hunter?

That meant Jeffrey got paid to hunt down money, as Ed Epstein recounted in a column he wrote in *Air Mail*, Graydon Carter's digital weekly.[29] "He described the convoluted network for hiding money in Andorra, Fiji, Gibraltar, and the Cayman Islands in such vivid detail that I thought he might be in the business of hiding as well of finding it. He dropped so many names in the realm of money machinations—such as Adnan Khashoggi, Aristotle Onassis, and Sheikh Zayed bin Sultan Al Nahyan—that his stories, though intriguing, didn't quite add up."

It didn't add up because Khashoggi, Onassis, and Al Nahyan already had plenty of money and needed to hide what they had. *Hiding money*—that was Epstein's game. For all sorts of purposes: tax evasion, laundering illicit riches, marriages that had gone south. If a multibillionaire's marriage was on the rocks, why not stash a few billion away in an offshore shell company just in case he was sued for divorce? Sometimes Epstein said he worked for governments to recover money looted by African dictators. Other times those dictators hired him to help them hide their stolen money.[30]

In addition, sometime in the eighties, Epstein met Steven Hoffenberg, who later ran the *New York Post* but was then head of a collection agency called Towers Financial Corporation.[31] According to *New York* magazine, Hoffenberg had met Epstein through Douglas Leese, an arms dealer about whom little is known except that he made his fortune by putting together defense packages for various governments around the world. (Epstein has claimed he was introduced to Hoffenberg by John Mitchell, the Nixon attorney general and convicted felon.)[32]

According to testimony in Parliament by British MP George Galloway, Leese was a middleman who handled some of the secret commissions for a dubious multibillion-pound deal with the Saudi royal family.

"[Epstein's] a genius," Hoffenberg said Leese told him. "He's great at selling securities. And he has no moral compass."[33]

To Hoffenberg, who went prison for a $450 million Ponzi scheme, that last attribute was an especially desirable trait. Epstein had everything Hoffenberg could want.

Released in 2013 after spending eighteen years in federal prison, Hoffenberg told the *Washington Post* that the entire scam was actually engineered by Epstein, who escaped unscathed and uncharged. "Jeffrey was the best hustler on two feet," he said. "Talent, charisma, genius, criminal mastermind."

"He's got a gift that's extraordinary, where he controls the people he meets and manipulates them totally with his charisma," Hoffenberg says on the four-part Netflix documentary *Jeffrey Epstein: Filthy Rich.* "You can't grasp the magnitude of this man's controlling effect."

Hoffenberg's allegations have not been fully corroborated, but he made similar charges in a 2018 lawsuit, in which he alleged that he and Epstein operated "a classic Ponzi scheme from the late 1980s to mid-1990s. They succeeded in soliciting over five hundred million dollars in investments from participants, all of which they misappropriated for improper and personal uses."[34] In another interview, in *Quartz*, Hoffenberg explained that Epstein's ties to the crime were not explored because he pleaded guilty, and "when you plead guilty, you don't go in for elaborate discovery."[35]

Mind you, this was taking place around 1987, when Donald Trump initiated his long friendship with Jeffrey Epstein and the two of them palled around with real estate investor Tom Barrack, just after Trump made his first trip to Moscow. As Michael Wolff put it in *Fire and Fury*, they were a trio of "nightlife Musketeers" on the New York scene.[36]

Trump later recalled Epstein in those days. "Terrific guy," he famously told *New York* magazine.[37] "He's a lot of fun to be with. It is even said that he likes beautiful women as much as I do, and many of them are on the younger side. No doubt about it—Jeffrey enjoys his social life."

———

Throughout the late eighties, Ghislaine had been involved with a man who had been described as the great love of her life, Count Gianfranco Cicogna, an heir to the Ciga hotels chain who helped mold Ghislaine into a stylish socialite. But that relationship ended in 1990.

By then, Jeffrey Epstein had been sighted in Robert Maxwell's Daily Mirror Building in London's Holborn Circus by Ari Ben-Menashe, the renegade Israeli agent who happened to work with her father on pirating Inslaw's PROMIS software and selling it to third parties.

Ben-Menashe told me that his encounter with Jeffrey Epstein took place during a period when Maxwell was dealing directly with Ehud Barak, then head of Israeli military intelligence (and later prime minister), and sometimes with Yitzhak Shamir, the Israeli prime minister at the time. Maxwell was close to KGB chief Vladimir Kryuchkov during the same period, but such potentially conflicting loyalties fazed Maxwell not a whit.

"Maxwell was with Maxwell," said Ben-Menashe. "He didn't care. He worked for Israel. He worked with the KGB. In Israel, he was a regular in [Prime Minister] Shamir's office. He wasn't working for Mossad, but for Israeli Military Intelligence, when Barak was head of it."

According to Ben-Menashe, Maxwell was trying to figure out a place for Epstein to work that tied him to the Israelis. "Jeffrey Epstein was a young guy at the time, about my age, working with Maxwell," Ari told me. "Nobody at the time put any importance to it. He was just a nice Jewish boy from New York. And nobody really knew what he was up to. And he started a fling with Maxwell's daughter. And to my understanding, they found each other."

The only problem with that story was the source: Ben-Menashe was trouble.

I learned that back in 1991 when I debriefed him as he and I traveled around the United States on *Newsweek*'s dime, with Ben-Menashe spinning tales of how the Reagan-Bush campaign put the fix on the 1980 presidential election, of how Israeli intelligence worked with Robert Maxwell on illicit arms deals to Iran, and of a clandestine Israeli pipeline to arm brutal Iraqi dictator Saddam Hussein.

It didn't take long to figure out that Ben-Menashe was a reporter's nightmare in that he was both knowledgeable and unreliable. Some of the best sleuths in the world debriefed him and cited him in their work, including Seymour Hersh, former National Security Council staffer Gary Sick, and congressional investigators.

Ari had disclosed explosive revelations to *Time* magazine about illegal arms sales to Iran that were later corroborated in the Iran-Contra probe. In Hersh's book *The Samson Option*, Ben-Menashe revealed that Nicholas Davies, one of Robert Maxwell's top editors at *The Mirror*, was involved in illegal arms deals to Iran.[38] Arms dealers and former CIA operatives all over the globe confirmed some of the most sensitive parts of Ari's stories. Much of what he said was true. All of it was startling.

But at the same time, Ben-Menashe was being dismissed by Israel officials as a renegade and fraud who was nothing more than a low-level translator. When Ben-Menashe took a lie-detector test for ABC News, he failed miserably.[39] His stories were said to be riddled with inconsistencies and unproven allegations. Word went out that he was a liar, a fabricator, and a fraud.

In the end, I saw Ari as a freelance arms dealer/operative who implemented operations for Maxwell and others and who often seemed to have an unseen agenda, which, I presumed, was dictated by the highest bidder. In later years, he operated a consultancy out of Montreal called Dickens & Madson that counted Libya,[40] Sudan, and Zimbabwe among its clients. Along the way, he amassed enough money to own a $9.6 million apartment on Park Avenue in New York.[41]

But at the time, no one seemed to know the real story. He had access to so many deeply held secrets that it was impossible to dismiss him. Moshe Hebroni, the deputy director of Israeli Military Intelligence, told me that Ben-Menashe worked directly for him and had "access to very, very sensitive material . . . and that includes material that was not within his authority to know."[42] Similarly, Yehoshua Saguy, the former director of Military Intelligence, corroborated Hebroni's account. And yet, if you listened to Ben-Menashe, trusted him, and printed his story verbatim, chances are your career would go up in flames.

For all that, it was former attorney general Elliot Richardson who convinced me to listen to Ben-Menashe seriously. With his lantern jaw and impeccable Boston Brahmin credentials, Richardson was straight out of central casting as a model of probity. In 1973, during the investigation of the Watergate scandal, he had emerged as a figure of real moral courage when, as attorney general, he stood up to President Nixon by refusing to execute Nixon's order to fire the special prosecutor investigating Watergate—instead resigning from his cabinet post. When I interviewed him in 1991, Richardson, then a partner in the white-shoe law firm of Milbank Tweed, had submitted sworn affidavits by Ben-Menashe on behalf of his client Inslaw, the tech company that had created the PROMIS software. I asked Richardson if he had submitted those affidavits as a legal gambit, a ploy, or if he genuinely believed what Ben-Menashe said. On background, he hemmed and hawed a bit in a way that let me know he couldn't corroborate everything.

Finally, Richardson went on the record. "Ben-Menashe is who he says he is," he said, "and much of what he says is true."

Like any good lawyer, he had parsed his words carefully and, as a result, had left questions unanswered. But then he said something that helped me sharpen the focus of my inquiry. Richardson reminded me that often the people who are most knowledgeable about crime are themselves criminals, which is why it is common practice for prosecutors to get criminals to turn state's evidence. Similarly, in the world of intelligence, the most knowledgeable people are intelligence agents, who, like criminals, are professional liars. So the real question shouldn't be about the rectitude of Ben-Menashe or whether one could "trust" him. His character wasn't the issue. The real question was what really happened.

Back then, in 1991, mobster John Gotti was being prosecuted by the feds, and the key witness against him was underboss Salvatore "Sammy the Bull" Gravano. Reliable? Honest? Truthful? Hardly. Gravano was a sociopathic killer who had confessed to nineteen murders. But his probity—or utter lack thereof—was irrelevant. The larger point was that he was there at the scene of the crime. He knew what happened because he was present. Boy Scouts and choirboys might be ideal witnesses, but they are rarely on-site for mob whack jobs. Thugs like Gravano were. In the end, it was clear that Gravano was knowledge-able, and his testimony, once corroborated, was enough to convict Gotti. That, Richardson suggested, was how I should handle Ben-Menashe: Hear him out. Then corroborate or refute.

Of course that's easier said than done. The specifics of Epstein's ties to Robert Maxwell remain murky, but there are at least three additional pieces of evidence that strongly suggest Maxwell knew Epstein and had transferred a significant amount of his assets to him.

One knowledgeable source told me that Maxwell was involved with Epstein in various business projects, and that in the last year of his life, Maxwell likely put a significant sum—probably between $10 million and $20 million—in Epstein's hands. The reason Maxwell transferred the money to him is unclear, but the walls were caving in on Maxwell, and Epstein may have been trying to keep Maxwell's assets out of the hands of his creditors.

And indeed, the mystery of what happened to Maxwell's millions may also be the answer to questions about Epstein's wealth. "We really don't know anything about Maxwell's ill-gotten gains," says Martin Dillon, coauthor of *Robert Maxwell, Israel's Superspy* with the late Gordon Thomas.[43] "They were never traced. There are people saying that maybe Ghislaine was the kind of conduit for moving money to Epstein. But in the end, my personal view is that Epstein really was a money launderer. He wasn't the great sort of whiz kid of Wall Street."

All of which meshes with a deposition given in 2010 by Maritza

Vasquez, a bookkeeper for the MC2 Model Management agency, in a complaint against Epstein regarding sex trafficking in which she testified she had heard that Epstein "had a relationship with a woman that her father was very wealthy and that's how he started his own money."

Vasquez couldn't remember the woman's name off the top of her head, so she asked the attorney to help her. "And if you tell me the name maybe I can remember."

"Ghislaine Maxwell," came the answer.

"Yes!" replied Vasquez.

That meant Robert Maxwell was the source of Epstein's money—or at least a significant portion of it. But it also raised other questions, one of which was whether Ghislaine and Jeffrey were following in Robert Maxwell's footsteps in terms of having relationships with various intel agencies in Russia and Israel.

Ben-Menashe told me they were later "recruited by Israeli intelligence, but not into the arms business or anything of that nature." That was especially interesting given the fact that former prime minister Ehud Barak, the same Barak who had worked closely with Robert Maxwell, was years later, in 2016, photographed going to Epstein's lavish town house on East Seventy-First Street.

"My guess is that they were probably blackmailing people," Ben-Menashe told me.

I wanted to find out if he was right.

CHAPTER THIRTEEN

SEX, SPIES, AND VIDEOTAPE

When he met Ghislaine, Epstein, then in his midthirties, was not yet a master of the universe, but he was clearly headed in that direction. He had a lot going for him. Looks, for one thing. Frequently compared to Ralph Lauren, Epstein was handsome enough to have been selected as *Cosmopolitan*'s "Bachelor of the Month," and he had made a name for himself accompanying beautiful women in London, New York, and elsewhere.

Smarts, for another. Epstein was a quick study. He soaked up knowledge. To be sure, some thought he was merely a brilliant bullshit artist who embodied the dictum, as Jesse Kornbluth put it, that he was "someone who can talk about any subject for five minutes, but not for six. That was Jeffrey."[1]

But even if that was true, Epstein's bullshit was state-of-the-art bullshit. World-class. That meant it was good enough to attract and ensnare the finest minds of Wall Street and Silicon Valley.

And finally, Epstein had money. According to a report by Vicky Ward in *Vanity Fair*, in 1987, Hoffenberg paid Epstein $25,000 a month, and that was just the start.[2] That was good money, certainly—about $700,000 a year in 2020 dollars—but many people on Wall Street had that kind of money. In the eighties, Epstein didn't yet have great wealth, and he was not yet an integral part of that world. He was still an outsider looking in. Brash, ambitious, obsessed with money, power, and making it big, he had a ferocious hunger to become part of that world; he would do whatever it took.

Enter Ghislaine Noelle Marion Maxwell, daughter of a rich media mogul, Oxford alumna, socialite, friend of British royalty, and Jeffrey Epstein's entrée to society.

Like any great power couple, Ghislaine and Jeffrey were more than the sum of their parts. Even though much of his money appears to have come from her father, Jeffrey had enough to restore the luxurious lifestyle Ghislaine had enjoyed while her father was still alive. And to Epstein, Ghislaine delivered an extraordinarily attractive transatlantic social network that included British royalty, heads of state, and New York and London society. That was Ghislaine at Chelsea Clinton's wedding, in photos with Michael Bloomberg, Donald Trump, and the British royal family, through Prince Andrew, of course, who had hosted them at Windsor, Balmoral, and Sandringham castles and was a frequent visitor in the States.[3]

A key component of the puzzle of Jeffrey and Ghislaine's relationship had to do with her father. Ghislaine had been quite close to him—at least insofar as that was possible for Robert Maxwell, the father of nine who constantly traveled the globe.

Their affinity was mutual. According to *The Final Verdict*, by Tom Bower, a BBC journalist who wrote two books on Maxwell, he once said of his children in an interview for National Public Radio, "I love my youngest daughter, Ghislaine. The rest are a cold lot. Like their mother; and they want to live off what others earn."[4]

Even in her youth, Ghislaine had ambitions to manage the Mirror Group.[5] In the early eighties, Ghislaine, then in her twenties, appeared in Mirror Group newspapers nearly as much as her father—presumably at his behest. And even though he died bankrupt and hundreds of millions of dollars in debt, Maxwell nevertheless was able to grant Ghislaine a $100,000-a-year allowance (about $190,000 in 2020 dollars) when she moved to New York—a sum she continued to receive long after his death.

In the end, however, none of it served her well. Much as he said he loved Ghislaine, according to *The Final Verdict*, she could be intimidated by him, especially when she became the target of his imperious

temper. "I am very sorry that my description of the dinner this morning was inadequate and made you angry," she wrote to him after apparently failing to give an appropriately detailed and respectful report.
"I should have expressed at the start of our conversation that I was
merely presenting you with a preliminary report of the evening and
that a full written report was to follow. . . . Please forgive." All of which
was followed by the requisite litany of sycophantic messages from various makers and shakers.[6]

"I think in his home, she never really learned the difference between right and wrong," said Bower.[7] "She was dominated by him, and
she learned from him to worship wealth and money and power and
influence and really had very little sentiment for what might be called
the little people. . . . By the time he died in 1991, she was a pretty
cracked character. She really was flawed by then."

Toward his last years, Maxwell made sure Ghislaine traveled with
him all around America because he wanted her company. And he
clearly included her in some of his more underhanded undertakings.

No stranger to corporate skulduggery, Ghislaine had acted as a
courier for her father in sensitive matters—especially in the last year
of his life, when he expanded into New York and was facing crushing
debt. According to *The Final Verdict*, it was Ghislaine, then twenty-
eight, who flew over from London on the Concorde with her nine stock
certificates worth about $200 million (about $400 million in 2020 dollars) to take to her father's lawyer, Ellis Freedman, showing that Macmillan Publishing, which Maxwell had bought in 1989, in turn owned
the Berlitz chain of language schools, with hundreds of locations all
over the world.

Freedman instantly got them reissued as twenty-one new certificates with one major change—instead of citing Macmillan's owner-
ship, the certificates were to name the owner as Bishopsgate Investment
Trust, a private company owned by Maxwell. His lawyer may or may
not have realized it, but removing Macmillan from the ownership certificates meant that Maxwell could put the $200 million to work for his
personal use.[8]

But it is still unclear how much Ghislaine really knew about the dark side of her father's world. When she went into her father's *Lady Ghislaine* office after his death and ordered the shredding of his documents, had she read them? Was she privy to his secrets? Did she know about her father's ties to the KGB? To Mossad? Did she understand his ties to Vladimir Kryuchkov and Ehud Barak? How he worked *with* both of them but *for* neither? What did Jeffrey know? And would the two of them play out her father's game?

———

Whatever her plan, Ghislaine had seen Donald Trump as a vital connection for Epstein early on. In the late eighties, she had worked for her father in London, first at Pergamon Press, then in another Maxwell division that specialized in corporate gifts. Thinking Trump would be a great catch as client for her venture, she realized she had a terrific connection through her father, who knew Trump fairly well in the late eighties, as we have seen, as a rival, bidding unsuccessfully to buy the *New York Post*, inviting him to party aboard the *Lady Ghislaine*, and attending hugely extravagant society soirees.[9]

Naively assuming that her father would appreciate her initiative, Ghislaine asked him to call Trump. However, according to Nicholas Davies's *Death of a Tycoon*, even though she was his favorite daughter, Maxwell erupted.

"Have you got your bum in your head?" he said.[10] "Why the fuck would Donald Trump want to waste his time seeing you and your crappy gifts when he has a multimillion-dollar business to run?"

But her father was wrong. In the end, Trump spent plenty of time with Ghislaine and Epstein. In fact, he fit in quite well with them. Arrivistes all—be it Epstein's Coney Island, Maxwell's Ukrainian shtetl, or Trump's Queens—they had all come from the wrong side of the tracks. And at some point in their lives, Robert Maxwell, Trump, and Epstein all had ties to foreign intelligence agencies and to arms dealers like Khashoggi.

For all three men and Ghislaine, as well, the sex trade was part of the equation. Robert Maxwell's sexual appetite was well known to Mossad, and as a result, according to Gordon Thomas's *Gideon's Spies*, the Israeli intelligence service made arrangements during the tycoon's visits to Israel so that "he was serviced from one of a stable of prostitutes the service maintained for blackmail purposes."[11] (Given his immense girth, it was said, Maxwell preferred fellatio.)[12]

And Maxwell, like Epstein and Trump, was not merely a consumer. Through much of the eighties, the Bulgarian cooperative bank that Maxwell owned had laundered millions for Semion Mogilevich, the multibillionaire who was one of the richest and most powerful men in the world of human trafficking.[13]

As for Trump himself, at least twenty-five women have made sexual assault allegations against him, including the rape of underage girls.[14] Many of the charges are still pending and may never come to court. In 2002, when he began partnering with the Bayrock Group, the real estate development company in Trump Tower, he brought into his orbit a host of oligarchs and mobsters involved in money laundering, sex trafficking, and child prostitution. According to documents that were part of an investigation by Turkish law enforcement authorities, in 2010, Bayrock founder Tevfik Arif entertained associates with nine escorts, a couple of whom who were allegedly as young as thirteen and fourteen years old.[15] Arif denied all charges filed and was later acquitted, but the indictment portrays billionaire oligarchs shipping in teenage girls from Russia and Ukraine to have sex with them and their wealthy friends.

Finally, there was Ghislaine, who, at this writing, was jailed in Brooklyn awaiting trial on charges of procuring and sexually trafficking underage girls for Epstein.

It was a world of unimaginable decadence. The epicenter of the operation was Epstein's enormously opulent Upper East Side town house. As a dwelling, it was less a home than a deliberately, extravagantly staged showcase, a calculated spectacle that declared to the world that Epstein, a college dropout from a middle-class Brooklyn family, had been embraced securely in the bosom of the powers that be. And Epstein meant the *real* powers that be.

Indeed, his collection of esteemed friends may have been his most prized possession of all. His notorious "black book" of contacts shows the rarefied circles in which he traveled—Nobel laureates, heads of states, British royals, Wall Street power brokers, and A-listers in every glamour profession.

In the good old days, one might have run into Deepak Chopra or former Israeli prime minister Ehud Barak at Epstein's home while he juggled phone calls from Woody Allen and former treasury secretary and Harvard president Larry Summers. The black book and the passenger manifests for Epstein's private plane—which have shown up in court documents, thanks to evidence obtained from Alfredo Rodriguez, his house manager and a keeper of the black book—a list of about 1,500 people, many of whom are the boldfaced names familiar to tens of millions of Americans.* All of which was compiled largely by Ghislaine and friends with ties to a decaying European aristocracy, New York society, and global celebrities.

For rock and roll fans, there was Mick Jagger, Michael Jackson, Brian Ferry, and Rupert Wainwright. There were actors Ralph Fiennes, Kevin Spacey, and Griffin Dunne; comics John Cleese and Joan Rivers; and arbiters of fashion like designer Tom Ford, supermodel Naomi Campbell, and *British Vogue* editor Hamish Bowles.

From the political set, there was Bill Clinton and his cronies Douglas Band and Ron Burkle; former New Mexico governor Bill Richardson; and boatloads of Kennedys. There were Nobel Prize winners and the top scientists in the world. And royals from Queen Elizabeth on down, including Prince Andrew, a close friend of Epstein's and Ghislaine's, and Andrew's ex-wife, Sarah Ferguson, Duchess of York, and the irrepressible Saudi prince Bandar bin Sultan Al Saud.

There were business, entertainment, and media moguls such as Rupert Murdoch, Conrad Black, and Richard Branson. Associates included Henry Kissinger, British prime minister Tony Blair, and dozens of other household names. The personal framed photos in Epstein's office included shots of Steve Bannon, Bill Clinton, and Mohammed bin Salman, better known today as MBS, the Saudi crown prince who is widely believed to have orchestrated the brutal murder of *Washing-*

---

* According to an affidavit by Rodriguez, the book was compiled not by Epstein himself but by his employees with the assistance of Ghislaine Maxwell.

ton Post journalist Jamal Khashoggi. It was said that MBS was not just an acquaintance, but a real friend of Epstein's.

And of course, there was Donald Trump, who had no fewer than sixteen phone numbers beside his name in Epstein's black book. Within the context of their highly transactional relationships, Trump's friendship with Epstein struck onlookers as a significant mutually beneficial connection. In the nineties, Trump needed friends. He had just gone belly-up in Atlantic City. With personal liabilities exceeding $800 million, he had just been forced to sell off his three Atlantic City casinos and the Plaza Hotel, along with his yacht, the *Trump Princess*.

In addition to helping Trump get back on his feet, Epstein seemed to be the apotheosis of a latter-day version of Hugh Hefner's *Playboy* ideal—surrounded by gorgeous young women, bespoke private planes, and spectacular residences, all while Ghislaine orchestrated a never-ending series of movable feasts—on the Upper East Side, at Epstein's New Mexico ranch, in the Caribbean—at which Epstein would entertain and play courtier to presidents, movie stars, brutal dictators, world-class scientists, Wall Street billionaires, and the like. And he'd have sex with two, three, or more young girls almost every day.

Trump fit right in. Jeffrey and Ghislaine invited him everywhere—and Trump reciprocated. At one highly selective party in 1992 at Trump's Mar-a-Lago resort in Palm Beach, the *New York Times* reported, no fewer than twenty-eight attractive young women were flown in to participate in a calendar-girl competition as entertainment. The organizer, George Houraney, who ran American Dream Enterprise, a small Florida company that staged a calendar-girl contest and other events, was appalled to learn that there were only two male guests—Trump and Epstein.[16]

"Donald, this is supposed to be a party with V.I.P.s," Houraney told Trump, according to the *Times*. "You're telling me it's you and Epstein? . . . I know Jeff really well, I can't have him going after younger girls."

But Trump ignored Houraney's warning and plowed ahead anyway. Houraney's longtime girlfriend Jill Harth later told the *New York Times* that Trump groped her nonstop at a business meeting around the same time. "He was relentless," Harth said, describing how Trump took the couple to dinner, sat beside Harth, and put his hands up her skirt all the way to her crotch. "I didn't know how to handle it. I would go away from him and say I have to go to the restroom. It was the escape route."[17]

———

Trump was often the center of Ghislaine's attention, and women who entered Trump's orbit sometimes ended up being associated with both Trump and Epstein, spending part of their time living in a Trump Tower condo and part in Florida, at Mar-a-Lago or one of Epstein's homes.

Among them was Russian model and beauty pageant contestant Anna Malova,[18] whose journey from the world of beauty pageants and modeling to Trump's Mar-a-Lago and Epstein's island retreat is highly suggestive in terms of how Epstein and his associates began manipulating young women.

In the early nineties, before coming to the United States, Malova had placed well in several beauty pageants—coming in second in Miss Russia 1993 and winning the 1994 Miss Baltic Sea title later that year.[19] Then in 1995 she left Moscow, spent six weeks learning English in St. Petersburg, Florida (not Russia), and was profiled in the *Tampa Tribune* as "reigning Miss Russia."[20] And before long, she met Donald Trump.

Notwithstanding the fact that Trump was still married to his second wife, Marla Maples, Anna moved into a thirtieth-floor condo in Trump Tower on Fifth Avenue.[21] There, according to an item in the *New York Post*, her lavish accommodations were taken care of "courtesy of an unidentified sugar daddy."

Not long afterward, in October 1996, Trump bought three beauty pageants from ITT Corp.: Miss Universe, Miss USA, and Miss Teen USA.[22]

A little more than a year later, in 1998, Malova competed in the Miss Universe pageant representing Russia. According to the *Honolulu Star-Bulletin*, Malova faltered badly when she was asked to compare Russia's television and culture with Ghana's—and couldn't come up with an answer.

Malova was stumped. "She pulled a Chernobyl," said one observer. "She's history."[23]

Malova made the finals anyway, but, as *New York* magazine noticed, there was an anomaly in the very fact she had even entered the pageant. "Oddly, Anna Malova was allowed to compete in this year's contest (1998) even though she was Miss Russia in 1995," the magazine reported. "According to beauty-world sources, it's not a coincidence that the stunning Slav, who wound up a finalist in last month's event, is a friend of Donald Trump, co-owner of the event.

"Did the Donald pull a few strings on his old friend's behalf? . . . While the Miss Universe camp insists that Malova won the Russian event honestly, Malova's agent said, 'I don't think she was Miss Russia this year. She was Miss Russia several years ago.'"[24]

When the magazine asked for documentation that Malova had won the title a second time, the Miss Universe Pageant headquarters declined to furnish it. Trump could not be reached for comment, but a spokesperson said, "I haven't heard about Trump giving any preferential treatment to Malova."

In the meantime, however, she spent time with both Trump and Epstein. According to documents submitted to a Florida court, flight logs showed that in February 1999, Malova, then twenty-seven, flew on board Jeffrey Epstein's black Gulfstream "Lolita Express" with Ghislaine and Prince Andrew from Epstein's Little Saint James (a.k.a. "Pedophile Island") back to Florida.

Over the next two decades, Malova cut an erratic figure. Arrested repeatedly on drug-related charges—including in 2010, criminal possession of narcotics, forgery, and criminal impersonation of a physician—she also appeared in gossip columns as the love interest of men ranging from comedian Garry Shandling to hedge fund billionaire George Soros, some forty-two years her senior.

Anna Malova wasn't the only woman who spent time with both Trump and Epstein. In 1997, Trump, who had just separated from Marla Maples, was photographed with Ghislaine at Ford Models' fiftieth-anniversary party, where he ogled models throughout the evening.[25]

At another event that year, according to the *New Yorker*, Trump, then fifty, seemed to fall for a friend of Ghislaine's, twenty-year-old

London model Anouska De Georgiou, and flew her and Ghislaine to Mar-a-Lago for the weekend, after which he installed Anouska in an apartment in Trump Tower.[26]

But before long, Anouska told NBC News, she was being flown to Epstein's homes all over the world. More than twenty years later, in 2019, Anouska's court testimony was cited in British tabloid *The Sun*, which alleged that she had been abused by Epstein when she was "young and idealistic."[27]

"Jeffrey Epstein manipulated me, corrupted me and sexually assaulted me," she said, adding that the abuse was "devaluing beyond measure" and "lasted several years."

———

Not everyone was terribly fond of Ghislaine. Christina Oxenberg had met her at a wedding years earlier and instantly found her distasteful. "I didn't like her [Ghislaine] when I met her and I liked her less each subsequent time," Oxenberg wrote in an email to me.

The daughter of Princess Elizabeth of Yugoslavia (and sister of *Dynasty* star Catherine Oxenberg), Christina grew up in a royal family—albeit royalty for a country that no longer exists. Nonetheless, that meant she was related to royalty the world over—including the Windsors—in convoluted ways. And when she lived in New York, *Town & Country* reported, her life was "an uptown-downtown cross section of New York society from Andy Warhol's Factory crowd to the Kennedys."[28] (Speaking of which, Christina says her mother had an affair with John F. Kennedy in 1962, nine months before she was born—suggesting, as she intimated at times and as her father told her, that she was President Kennedy's love child.)[29]

Christina had been introduced to Ghislaine through her then husband, a painter named Damian Elwes, who had been friends with Ghislaine years earlier. Christina and she were known to each other and traveled in different social circles that sometimes overlapped. But that didn't mean they were friends.

In Ghislaine, Oxenberg saw the scion of a disgraced family who was desperately trying to hang on to what was left of her dissipated wealth and her position in society, and was doing so by grasping tightly to an extraordinary con man—a man who hoodwinked Nobel laureates, Harvard professors, Clinton, Trump, half a dozen heads of states, and titans of Silicon Valley. She saw Ghislaine as an "ambitious" anomaly in an upper-crust world where she was transforming herself from "her father's snooty sassy daughter" to Epstein's fixer, as she put it in *Secrets*, her online memoir on Patreon, which includes her account of her meeting with Ghislaine. That meant she had begun trafficking in underage girls for him.

At the time, in 1997, Christina had just written *Royal Blue*, a dishy, thinly disguised roman à clef about her own royal heritage, and Ghislaine was desperate to have Oxenberg ghostwrite a similar book for her. Christina told me she wasn't interested in the slightest, but she took the meeting anyway.

After complimenting Christina on her new book, Ghislaine cut to the chase. "I want my ROYAL BLUE! With my name on it," she told Christina.[30] "You will ghost it. I am going to pay you a lot of money. I am going to change your life."

From the start, Christina did not believe a fundamental part of Ghislaine's story. Ghislaine talked and acted as if she and Epstein were lovers, but Christina didn't buy it. Whatever the truth about their relationship, the problem, as Oxenberg saw it, was simple: Ghislaine very much wanted to marry Epstein, but Jeffrey had no interest. "There was no romance and there was no sexual relationship," Christina told me. "Ghislaine was his employee. But she wanted to get married, to be a real power couple."

According to Christina, Jeffrey's disinterest notwithstanding, Ghislaine thought she could win him over by making him part of this upper-crust world. "What you do in London if you're upper class is you give dinner parties," Christina said.[31] "That's what they do. So Ghislaine would have brought her knowledge of that to New York, and she does these dinner parties.

"Generally, the point is just to get drunk and have really good plonk. That's the point of dinner parties. But hers were transactional. She had an agenda. She was creating a life for Jeffrey, trying to present him as, 'Hey, he's got money. He's James Bond. He's someone you should know. He's cool.'

"She's branding him, probably showing him not to wear white sneakers and maybe go with the Oxford low scissor with the tassels. He is a *Pretty Woman*. He doesn't know shit. She believes that she can make herself indispensable to the point where he will marry her."

Or as Ghislaine also told Christina, "The reason Jeffrey keeps me around is because I don't make mistakes."

She could get it all done. On the one hand, she could knit together a social network that brought Bill Clinton and Prince Andrew into Jeffrey's orbit. On the other, she could also administer to his rather unusual needs. Ghislaine told Christina that his sexual appetite was such that she had to make sure that he had a constantly changing supply of young women and girls to make sure he got his three needed orgasms per day.

She could do only so much. "She said, 'I can't keep up with him. I bring in other women and they help pick up the slack.' Those were not exactly her words, but it was definitely the gist of what she was saying."

Then Ghislaine explained how she didn't mind sharing Epstein with other women. She said she personally selected three young girls, but she did not say how young.

Christina was paying rapt attention. "Who are these females?" she asked.

"They're nothing," Ghislaine told her. "They're trash."[32]

"She went into detail, how she drove to the trailer parks of West Palm Beach, how she cruised until she saw what she knew Jeffrey liked. Oxenberg wrote in *Secrets*, "He liked young pretty blondes. Everything Ghislaine was not."[33]

"I found her repellent, and I wanted to get the fuck away," Christina told me. "She cannot talk about human beings like that."

But Ghislaine plowed ahead, making sure Jeffrey was taken care of. In the summer of 2000, she discovered Virginia Roberts Giuffre, then seventeen-year-old Virginia Roberts, working as a nine-dollar-an-hour spa attendant at Trump's Mar-a-Lago while her father worked there as a maintenance manager. According to Giuffre, almost as soon as

Ghislaine introduced her to Epstein, who was a member at Mar-a-Lago until 2007,[34] they began training her to provide sexual services under the guise of being a professional massage therapist.

According to the *Daily Mail*, Giuffre characterized Ghislaine as "the undisputed leader of the girls in Epstein's entourage."[35]

And indeed, to her young recruits, Ghislaine seemed dazzlingly sophisticated. "She's got the whole equestrian attire. She's so elegant," Maria Farmer, who was twenty-six when she met Ghislaine, told *The Guardian*.[36] Farmer added that Ghislaine had the aura of the most popular girl in school who would bestow her favors only upon the anointed.

"Jeffrey Epstein couldn't have done what he did for as long as he did it without the services of somebody like Ghislaine Maxwell," Dan Kaiser, an attorney for alleged Epstein victim Jennifer Araoz, told *The Guardian*. "She is as culpable, in my judgment, as Jeffrey Epstein himself."

"I was scared of ever saying no to her," Giuffre told the *Daily Mail*. "I was always compliant. I knew if I said no to anything, I would be on the street."[37]

Not lacking when it came to derring-do, according to the *Daily Mail*, Ghislaine, as a newly licensed helicopter pilot in 2007, reportedly boasted that she took the controls and flew former president Bill Clinton on Epstein's chopper during a visit to his island.[38] (Later, in a 2016 deposition, Ghislaine denied the report.)

She taunted men with her sexuality. Jesse Kornbluth had met Ghislaine with Epstein and had become friends "in that transactional Manhattan way," as he wrote on *Salon*. Kornbluth recalls then running into Ghislaine at an event one evening, with his wife at his side.

"If you lose 10 pounds, I'll fuck you," Ghislaine told him.[39] That was Ghislaine.

Ghislaine was known for creating a world in which billionaires and royalty could cavort. She was the woman behind the world's greatest Rolodex, an unequaled network of powerful and beautiful people, and she put her talents to work right away. She was all about power and money.

Ghislaine's great contribution to the business of human trafficking was to do it in plain sight, camouflaging it with a guest list that included the great and the near great, thereby making status-seeking journalists, Wall Street financiers, academics, and intellectuals feel like VIP guests who had been admitted to the inner sanctum of Epstein's secretive and elite world of glamour, sex, and power.

No one was more dazzled by the glamour of the Trump-Maxwell-Epstein axis than former Harvard Law School professor Alan Dershowitz, who was so hypnotized by its opulence that he professed not to see anything wrong with it. In fact, it was something you aspired to. "In those days, if you didn't know Trump and you didn't know Epstein, you were a nobody," Dershowitz, who later served on Epstein's defense team, told the *New York Times*.[40]

Another key factor in getting away with it was knowing how to cultivate key journalists. When it came to courting the media, Epstein and Ghislaine didn't miss a beat, whether it was gossip columnists who wrote about them in the New York tabloids, highly paid talent on network TV, or the moguls who owned everything. That was Ghislaine embracing *Vanity Fair* editor Graydon Carter at a society benefit in New York in 2007, with Charlie Rose at the 2009 Earth Awards gala at the Four Seasons in Manhattan, and with Elon Musk in 2014 at *Vanity Fair*'s famous Oscar party.

As reported by Julie K. Brown in a groundbreaking series in the *Miami Herald*, after Giuffre came forward, the FBI found more than three dozen girls who had been underage, some just thirteen years old, whom Epstein had molested in Palm Beach between 2001 and 2005. On a video interview she gave to the *Miami Herald*, Giuffre explained Ghislaine's training. "It was everything down to how to give a blow job, how to be quiet, be subservient, give Jeffrey what he wants," she said. "A lot of this training came from Ghislaine herself, and . . . then there's Jeffrey, who's telling you I want it this way, now go slower, and don't do that and do this.

"You're just thrown into a world that you don't understand, and you don't know how to—you're screaming on the inside and you don't know how to let it come out. And you just become this numb figure who refuses to feel and refuses to speak and refuses—all you do is obey. That's it. And eventually it led to, well, now we're gonna experiment and we're gonna try you with another guy and see how you go. So they sent me to an island with a professor, and I basically had to do what I did for Jeffrey for him. So it's very private. It's the perfect world for a billionaire getting away with what he was doing. He could hold big parties there and have huge orgies there, and nobody would have any idea what was going on."[41]

And who was going to those parties? At one time or another, dozens of names in Epstein's black book had hitched a ride on his private Boeing 727, the Lolita Express, to his Little Saint James in the Caribbean. But in the end, being on Epstein's contact list meant nothing in and of itself. It's far more indicative of the power brokers he and Ghislaine were cultivating than whether they actually had knowledge of or participated in Epstein's nefarious activities.

Nevertheless, the presence of so many rich and powerful people in Epstein's world is of special interest, because when FBI agents raided his homes, they found video recording equipment, hard disks, and the like that Ghislaine and Jeffrey had been stashing away as documentary evidence that could be redeemed at an appropriate time. Compromising material. Kompromat.

Ghislaine said as much to Christina Oxenberg during their meeting in 1997. "I could not believe whatever she was saying was real," Christina told Sebastian Shakespeare in the *Daily Mail*. "Stuff like: 'Jeffrey and I have everyone on videotape!'"

Whatever Epstein's sexual tastes, when it came to recruiting young girls for him, extraordinary youth was highly valued, and not just for whatever pleasure it may have afforded him. After all, if the girls were underage, that spoke to the question of what kind of kompromat was being harvested. Having photos of powerful men, the titans of Wall Street, committing adultery or having sex with escorts was one thing. But having videos of billionaires in the act of pedophilia, raping underage girls, committing crimes that could lead to hard time—that would give even the most powerful among them pause. Perhaps that was why, as Virginia Giuffre related, Ghislaine Maxwell told her, "Jeffrey was very particular in the kind of girls he wanted. First off, the younger the better."[42]

As to who actually engaged in such nefarious behavior, there were clues suggesting who was in the know. According to the *Washington Post*, Rodriguez had circled some of the names in the book in black and identified them as "witnesses."[43] (Rodriguez, who was jailed for eighteen months for attempting to sell the "black book," died in 2015.[44])

Bill Clinton admitted to taking four trips* on the Lolita Express, but his name was not circled. On the other hand, Donald Trump's name was also in the black book, along with no fewer than sixteen phone numbers—and his name *was* circled, as were those of Ehud Barak and Alan Dershowitz. There are still loads of unanswered questions.

Having one's name circled in the black book, of course, was not evidence of participation in or knowledge of any crime. Nevertheless, according to an affidavit filed in the Florida Southern District against him, Rodriguez described the information in the black book as the "Holy Grail" or "Golden Nugget" of the Epstein case.[45]

One male passenger on the Lolita Express who asked not to be identified told me that what was taking place was unmistakable. There were two girls dressed as flight attendants who must have been eighteen to twenty years old—much younger than the average flight attendant. Where were these girls coming from?

By this time, Ghislaine had gotten some of her earliest recruits, Virginia Roberts Giuffre among them, to bring in other young girls. The passenger told me that one of the attendants was former Epstein assistant Sarah Kellen, who has been accused in court papers of recruiting young girls and acting as a pimp for Epstein. Sarah Kellen, Nadia Marcinkova, Lesley Groff, and Adriana Ross were later questioned by lawyers about whether Prince Andrew had any involvement

---

* Each of Clinton's four trips had multiple stops, making a total of twenty-six times that his name appeared as either departing or boarding Epstein's plane. Conservative media outlets have widely (and falsely) reported that Clinton took twenty-six separate trips on the aircraft.

in Epstein's abuse of underage girls. Kellen and Marcinkova have since reinvented themselves as Sarah Kensington and Nadia Marcinko.[46]

Starting in the nineties, Ghislaine and her assistants had been trolling high schools, shopping malls, and trailer parks for strippers, runaways, or girls who were otherwise vulnerable and would serve Epstein's needs. Court records show that it evolved into what was widely called a "pyramid abuse" scheme whereby Epstein and Ghislaine would train victims like Virginia Giuffre to be paid sex slaves and then pay them $200 to $300 for each underage girl they brought into Epstein's lair.

As the Epstein operation continued into the 2000s, things changed. For one thing, Ghislaine had finally given up on marrying Jeffrey and began to date Ted Waitt, the billionaire founder of the computer company Gateway. She was still somewhat in Jeffrey's orbit, but kept a far greater distance.

Meanwhile, Jeffrey began importing girls from the former Soviet Union. After the 1998 Miss Universe pageant, Anna Malova signed up with Karin Models, which had been founded by Epstein friend Jean-Luc Brunel. Known as "*le fantôme*" (the ghost), Brunel, who also owned MC2, was the subject of a 1988 piece that aired on CBS's *60 Minutes* in which several young models accused him of groping them sexually, drugging their drinks, and rape.[47]

The CBS reporter Craig Pyes told the *Daily Beast* that Brunel "ranks among the sleaziest people in the fashion industry. We're talking about a conveyor belt, not a casting couch. Hundreds of girls were not only harassed but molested."[48]

Brunel had worked at a fairly high level in the world of Paris modeling. Claiming to have launched the careers of Sharon Stone, Christy Turlington, and Jerry Hall, he allied with Eileen Ford, the so-called godmother of the modeling industry in New York. "Eileen took Jean-Luc as her son," said fashion photographer and artist Jacques Silberstein. "She let him become very powerful. Jean-Luc's education impressed Eileen. He played the game well. He could be charming."[49]

"I really despise Jean-Luc. . . . This is a guy who should be behind bars," John Casablancas, the late modeling agent, told journalist Michael Gross, whose book *Model: The Ugly Business of Beautiful Women* alleges that Brunel repeatedly drugged and raped models. According to Casablancas, Brunel and his pals "were very well known in Paris for roaming the clubs. They would invite girls and put drugs in their drinks."[50]

And Casablancas, who married a seventeen-year-old when he was fifty, would have known, having used his stature in the modeling business to indulge in similar activities with young girls at a "Look of the Year" modeling competition at the New York Plaza Hotel, with his friend Donald Trump, then the hotel's owner. Trump was closely involved with the contest, in which the average age was fifteen, and, according to *The Guardian*, several of the models said that they were required by their agency to have dinner with Trump and Casablancas.

Trump's behavior at such events is unclear, but, according to *The Guardian*, "The stories we have heard suggest that Casablancas, and some of the men in his orbit, used the contest to engage in sexual relationships with vulnerable young models. Some of these allegations amount to sexual harassment, abuse or exploitation of teenage girls; others are more accurately described as rape."[51]

Which is exactly the kind of thing Jean-Luc Brunel trafficked in. Indeed, according to a court filing by Giuffre, Brunel "would bring young girls (ranging from ages as young as twelve) to the United States for sexual purposes and farm them out to his friends, especially Epstein," the filing states. "Brunel would offer the girls 'modeling' jobs. Many of the girls came from poor countries or impoverished backgrounds, and he lured them in with a promise of making good money."

In response, Brunel issued a statement denying the accusations: "I strongly deny having participated, neither directly nor indirectly, in the actions Mr. Jeffrey Epstein is being accused of. I strongly deny having committed any illicit act or any wrongdoing in the course of my work as a scouter or model agencies manager."

But according to the *Daily Beast*, Brunel's name appeared at least fifteen times on flight logs for Epstein's private plane, and he visited Epstein nearly seventy times when Epstein was jailed in 2008 for procuring an underage girl for prostitution and soliciting a prostitute.[52] As a result of this relationship with Epstein, *Fortune* reported, Brunel's business partner said he was getting a tremendous amount of pushback from major clients, including Macy's, Saks Fifth Avenue, Nordstrom, and Neiman Marcus.[53]

Brunel did not respond to multiple emails requesting an interview. According to news reports, he was spotted in an unspecified country in South America in the summer of 2019.[54]

But according to court documents filed in the US District Court for the Southern District of Florida, Brunel was a key part of Epstein's network, which relied heavily on him and his MC2, a "modeling" agency whose younger models were allegedly part of the Epstein operation.

In addition to whatever legitimate careers Brunel may have fostered, as a "model scout" he also allegedly hired "scouters" to identify, procure, and transport underage girls, many fifteen years of age and under, hire them to give "massages," and train them to give sexual pleasure. Virginia Giuffre claimed she was forced to have sex with Brunel as well, and was forced to watch him engage in "sexual acts with dozens of underage girls."

MC2 wasn't the first company to do something like this, and when it came to determining how to structure such a company—what kind of contractual relationships MC2 would have with employees, and so forth—its management looked to someone who already had experience in the business. Though Brunel was its titular leader, Epstein was really funding the agency and took the initiative when it came to dealing with such issues.

The way such agencies worked, it was normal business procedure to hire scouts to search for and recruit new talent. But how to compensate the scout was another question.

According to a sworn deposition in 2010 by MC2 bookkeeper Maritza Vasquez, directives about those contracts came to her "from the office of Jeffrey Epstein" with instructions that they be forwarded to Brunel as models for MC2's contracts.[55]

Vasquez further testified that Epstein's instruction package contained contracts from another modeling agency that had similar relationships with models, with directions that MC2 should base its contracts after another agency's. Vasquez knew it was run by a famous man, but under oath some five years before he launched his presidential campaign, she momentarily forgot, then remembered, his name.

"Jeffrey Epstein . . . was giving instructions to Jean-Luc [Brunel]," she testified, "saying that he wanted to have the same contracts as, uh—what's his name, of Donald Trump [an apparent reference to Trump Model Management], and that he wanted to have the same kind of benefits for the scouters. So he was giving instructions to Jean-Luc on what to do."[56]

In other words, according to Vasquez, Epstein saw Trump Model Management as a prototype to emulate while working with Brunel to lure minor children in to participate in sexual activity for money. After all, if you were looking for success in the world of sex trafficking, what better role model than Donald Trump? Epstein wanted MC2 to use the same system of incentives that drove "model scouts" and models at the Trump agency. (Trump Model Management discontinued operations in 2017.)

———

As the Epstein operation chugged along, Donald Trump, who had married three models—Ivana, Marla, and Melania—and in 1999 started his own agency, Trump Model Management, was very much part of Epstein's picture. According to court records, message pads confiscated from Epstein's home showed that Trump often called Epstein's West Palm Beach mansion. Asked under oath in a September 2016 deposition whether he ever socialized with Trump in the presence of females under the age of eighteen, Epstein punted. Rather than answer the questions, he took the Fifth.

Trump Model Management allegedly indulged in many of the dubious practices that MC2 did, such as violating immigration laws and illegally employing young foreign girls. Three former Trump models, all foreigners, told *Mother Jones* that Trump Model Management profited by using foreign models who came to the United States on tourist visas that did not allow them to work here. And two former models said that Trump's agency suggested they lie on customs forms about where they planned to live. All of which meant they were perpetually scared of getting caught and pretty much at the mercy of the agency. All of which was ironic indeed, given Trump's hard-line immigration policies as president and his assertions that undocumented immigrants are taking American jobs.[57]

Meanwhile, Trump himself became known for hosting parties in suites at the Plaza Hotel, which he owned at the time, where older rich men were introduced to young women and girls who assumed "they'd get somewhere" by joining the party, as one partygoer, a fashion photographer, told Michael Gross, writing in the *Daily Beast*. "Of course, it never happens."[58]

According to the photographer, the girls were as young as fifteen.

"[They were] over their heads, they had no idea, and they ended up in situations," the photographer added. "There were always dramas because the men threw money and drugs at them to keep them enticed. It's based on power and dominating girls who can't push back and can be discarded."

Trump has publicly talked about how attracted he is to his own daughter and has often made troubling remarks about being drawn to young girls. Once he pointed out a ten-year-old girl and joked about dating her in the future. He would "go from room to room," said the photographer. "It was guys with younger girls, sex, a lot of sex, a lot of cocaine, top-shelf liquor."

Meanwhile, in April 1999, Ghislaine and Jeffrey invited Trump to a party for Prince Andrew. "Recruiting Prince Andrew as a great friend was *very* strategic," Christopher Mason, the journalist and TV host, told me. "He was an ideal target for manipulation."[59] And the presence of royalty, needless to say, gave a glamorous sheen to the man from Coney Island.

In Palm Beach the following February, Trump staged a pro-am tennis tournament at Mar-a-Lago and appeared with Jeffrey, Ghislaine, and his latest girlfriend, Melania Knauss, whom Epstein claimed to have introduced to Trump.[60] Epstein's claim was reported in the *New*

York Times, which noted that "while Mr. Trump has dismissed the relationship, Mr. Epstein, since the election, has played it up, claiming to people that he was the one who introduced Mr. Trump to his third wife, Melania Trump, though neither of the Trumps has ever mentioned Mr. Epstein playing a role in their meeting."[61]

Jeffrey and Ghislaine knew Trump's secrets, and he knew theirs. And secrets were the ultimate currency in the decadent and highly transactional world they lived in. As Michael Wolff reports in *Siege*, "Trump often saw the financier at Epstein's current Palm Beach house, and Trump knew that Epstein was visited almost every day, and had been for many years, by girls he'd hired to give him massages that often had happy endings—girls recruited from local restaurants, strip clubs, and, also, Trump's own Mar-a-Lago."[62]

Similarly, Epstein was privy to some of Trump's unorthodox business customs, such as his practice of accepting fees to act as a front man in order to mask real beneficial ownership in a real estate transaction.

But in 2004, after a friendship of roughly seventeen years, the two men had a serious falling-out when Epstein sought to buy a spectacular oceanfront mansion in Palm Beach called Maison de l'Amitié (House of Friendship) that was being sold out of a bankruptcy auction. The property, a nearly sixty-two-thousand-square-foot neoclassical palace, had once been owned by Leslie Wexner, the billionaire retailer who was so close to Epstein.[63] Epstein had his heart set on the house, but he planned to make at least one major renovation project once he bought it: He wanted to relocate the swimming pool, and he brought Trump to the property to give him advice on how to do it.

But before the sale was finalized, Epstein was horrified to see that Trump, who was still underwater financially from his Atlantic City bankruptcies, outbid him with an offer of more than $41 million for the property. The purchase was financed by Deutsche Bank, which was already holding dubious loans for Trump.[64]

Epstein was apoplectic and became even more enraged when Trump soon thereafter put the house up for sale for $125 million. Finally, Trump sold the house to Russian oligarch Dmitry Rybolovlev for

$96 million in 2008—never having lived there—and Epstein threat-
ened to sue him. The two men never spoke again. And from then on,
whenever Epstein's name was mentioned to Trump, the whole tenor of
the conversation instantly changed.

And that wasn't the end of it. In 2005, the Palm Beach Police Department began investigating Epstein's relationship to the young
women around him. According to someone who knew him, Epstein
believed Trump got the police to investigate him in retaliation for
threatening to sue.

Their friendship frayed beyond repair, Epstein became less discreet
as the keeper of Trump secrets and was not averse to showing off potentially compromising photos of him and Trump. An associate of
Epstein's who asked not to be identified told me that Epstein showed
him one photo of Trump with a topless young girl. In another, the
source said, Trump is with two young girls who are said to be laughing
as they point out what appears to be a wet spot in an unfortunate location on his pants. The description of the photo suggested that it was a
semen stain—but the photos have never been released.

————

Brunel, who had earlier signed Anna Malova to Karin Models, now
began to bring in more models from the former Soviet Union, some of
whom were as young as twelve. These were said to be girls who had no
real chance of becoming big-time models in New York, and because
they were so vulnerable financially, the risk of debt slavery made them
easy prey for Epstein. According to the *Daily Beast*, Brunel received a
$1 million wire transfer from Epstein in September 2004, which he
used to set up a new venture with Elite Models.[65] The listed address was
457 Madison Avenue—the same as Epstein's investment firm, J. Epstein & Co. It is unclear whether the transfer represented a gift, a loan,
or an investment in Brunel's operation.[66]

Nevertheless, Brunel's girls became frequent guests on Epstein's
private jets. Flight manifests show that Brunel made dozens of trips to
Epstein's homes in New York, Palm Beach, and Little Saint James. According to a complaint filed in the US District Court for the Southern

District of Florida, Brunel began working with Epstein and Maxwell "in a pattern of racketeering that involved luring minor children through MC2, mostly girls under the age of 17, to engage in sexual play for money."

Epstein and Brunel obtained visas for the girls and charged them rent once they arrived. According to a 2010 deposition of MC2 book-keeper Maritza Vasquez, Epstein "was the one who said who stays in what apartment."

With Ghislaine less of a presence, Epstein increasingly went to the Russians for young girls. Brunel was not alone in his endeavors and reportedly worked with Peter Listerman, the "roly-poly pimp" from Moscow, as author Peter Pomerantsev has called him, who is celebrated as a procurer, or "matchmaker," as he prefers, for Russian oligarchs such as the late Boris Berezovsky.[67]

Yuri Shvets worked with Berezovsky from 2002 to 2007 as a secu-rity consultant and said he had personal knowledge that Listerman provided girls to Berezovsky when the oligarch lived in London. "Ev-ery other day [Berezovsky] was receiving a new one from Russia, and that was just for one day. She spends the day and overnight and then she goes. He has another one, etc. It was Listerman. He helped FSB to film videos, sex parties of his clients with hookers, and then this infor-mation was used by the FSB to blackmail people."

Wearing an Astrakhan fur hat, Listerman, or someone who looks a lot like him, was photographed entering Epstein's mansion in Janu-ary 2016, according to the *New York Post*.[68] In a 2019 interview with the *Daily Beast*, Kristina Goncharova, Miss Teen Ukraine in 2010, de-scribed Listerman, with considerable distaste, as "the world's famous seller of young models to oligarchs."[69] At the Miss Teen Ukraine pag-eant, Goncharova had been first approached by Listerman, who wanted an introduction—and she was just fourteen years old.

As a visitor to Epstein's New York town house told *New York Post* columnist Richard Johnson in 2016, increasingly the young women and girls at Epstein's seemed to be coming from the remains of the Eastern bloc. "Half of them are from the former Soviet Union and the other half are a mix of Americans and Europeans," the source said.

"When the Russian girls arrive in the city, they already have Jeffrey's phone number."

A well-known figure in Russia who has thrived under Putin, Listerman, sometimes known as Uncle Petya, got his start in the nineties recruiting young girls for modeling agencies—which he supplemented by getting them work as part-time "girlfriends" escorting affluent businessmen. According to a source who knew both men, Brunel had known Listerman for some time and had helped him set up a legitimate modeling agency many years earlier. *Kommersant*, Russia's biggest business daily, reported in 2003 that one could see them together in marijuana smoking clubs in Paris, where Listerman arrived, two models in tow: one of whom was the top model Natalia Vodianova, from Emmanuel Ungaro's show in the Louvre, and the other of whom was Listerman's wife and, not incidentally, the face of Christian Dior, Kristina Semenovskaia.[70]

The men found they could make good money from superstar models, but second-tier models often had trouble bringing in revenue. Once the Soviet Union collapsed, however, and the ascent of the oligarchs began in Russia, a new market emerged. "Listerman figured out he could make a shitload more money by turning his modeling agency into a pimp agency," said the source. "So basically there were about a hundred Russian oligarchs who had a constant stream of girls Listerman supplied."

In other words, whatever the season, if an oligarch wanted young party girls for the chic Alpine ski resorts in Davos or Courchevel or for yacht parties in Ibiza, Mykonos, or Saint-Tropez, Listerman was the man. "Everybody used Listerman. He was the go-to guy for the Russian oligarchs. That's how they got all the girls on their boats."

By the nineties, Listerman had become a well-known figure in Russia, and according to the *Daily Beast*, in 2000, after Vladimir Putin had been elected president, he went on vacation in Courchevel with multibillionaire oligarch Vladimir Potanin.[71] Deputy Prime Minister Boris Nemtsov, an opposition leader in the Duma, was staying in the same hotel.[72] (An outspoken critic of Putin's, Nemtsov was assassinated in 2015 near the Kremlin.)

After they got settled in a small chalet in the mountains, Putin led everyone to dinner, whereupon about "ten long-legged girls" showed up in tow with "famous promoter" Petya Listerman.

"Petya, what is this?" Nemtsov asked.

"Well, you guys too, after all," Listerman said.

Thoughtful and considerate as ever, he had brought extra girls for everyone.[73]

As Listerman put it in an interview on a Russian website, "In the 20 years that I have been doing my job, I have become the best in the world [for Russian girls] I am a brand! I created a brand! The coolest, richest people who love all the most beautiful, the most expensive and want new ones . . . to be fucked—they all come to me."[74]

Listerman had started out as a ski instructor in the posh Dombai winter resort in the Caucasus and then moved to Paris, where he started recruiting young girls for modeling and earned extra money by making them work as escorts for affluent Western businessmen.[75]

In the mid-nineties Listerman was arrested on stolen car charges, and when he was released from a French prison after several months, he began to develop a new business model in which, in addition to their providing sexual services, he allegedly used his girls to steal highly sensitive information from the political and business elite they were serving.[76] According to Russian newspaper *Sovershenno Sekretno*, before long, Listerman's girls became regulars at Davos, Switzerland, and the Côte d'Azur, in France, and would return with a boatload of confidential information. Before long, Listerman met with oligarch Boris Berezovsky to implement a new kind of "model espionage" where, in addition to their sexual activities, young models would engage in intelligence operations by allowing themselves to be photographed with their patrons in compromising positions or by stealing secrets.*

---

* In 2013, Berezovsky died by hanging at his home in England under mysterious circumstances, amid much speculation that Russian intelligence may have been involved. After the inquest, coroner Peter Bedford issued an open verdict, saying, "I am not saying Mr. Berezovsky took his own life, I am not saying Mr. Berezovsky was unlawfully killed. What I am saying is that the burden of proof sets such a high standard it is impossible for me to say."

With Listerman delivering the goods for him, Berezovsky soon became a key supplier of kompromat to President Boris Yeltsin through Yeltsin's bodyguard, Alexander Korzhakov. In the end, Shvets told me, "Listerman became an agent of the FSB. I know this firsthand because I used to know Boris Berezovsky pretty well when Listerman was supplying him with girls."

According to Shvets, Berezovsky said Listerman helped the FSB shoot videos of his clients' sex parties with hookers and allowed the kompromat to be used by the FSB to blackmail people.

As the Russian website FBI Media reported, "Listerman has not been a 'free bird' since the 90s. His girls are actively involved in the FSB's program to collect incriminating evidence against top businessmen and politicians."[77]

That meant ultimately his boss was Vladimir Putin.

CHAPTER FOURTEEN

WHO'S GOT THE KOMPROMAT?

At a time when Jeffery Epstein and Ghislaine Maxwell were courting the titans of Wall Street and Silicon Valley, internationally known academics, and European royalty, they were also injecting the virus of human trafficking into the American body politic and weaponizing it in the form of dirty little secrets of the richest and most powerful people in the world.

But exactly who used these secrets as leverage and against whom was unclear. Were they using the girls as perks to woo new clients, lending them out like trinkets to entertain billionaires? Were they using them as leverage—extortion, perhaps—by keeping sex videos as potential blackmail? Were they trading them to foreign intelligence services in Israel or Russia? No one really knew.

Some men close to Epstein actually said they thought that what was going on was far more innocent than the press has made it out to be. According to *Mother Jones*, Stuart Pivar, a scientist and cofounder of the New York Academy of Art, who also served as Epstein's longtime friend and art adviser, said Jeffrey was suffering from satyriasis, an affliction characterized by an insatiable sexual appetite.[1] There was no grand strategy behind Epstein's operation, another associate of his told me, insisting that what was going on was merely that a bunch of rich guys were constantly looking for girls for their own pleasure and amusement. Epstein's massive homes—in New Mexico, on his Caribbean island, in his Upper East Side mansion—were all part of an operation that was really just a latter-day version of Hugh Hefner's Playboy Mansion, but on steroids. In other places, in other times, rich and powerful men would gather in wood-paneled, smoke-filled rooms and trade tall tales over fine whiskey and Cohibas. Jeffrey was offering up young girls instead.

But that rationale doesn't quite work. For one thing, there was no reason to doubt that Ghislaine and Jeffrey regularly documented the sexual escapades of their guests. Christina Oxenberg told me that Ghislaine had told her about the videos in 1997. In 2015, Virginia Roberts Giuffre filed an affidavit in court asserting that she believed federal prosecutors had videos and photos of her "as an underage girl having sex with Epstein and some of his powerful friends."[2]

There was the Epstein acquaintance who told me Epstein had shown him photos of Donald Trump with young girls. And in 2019, according to Bloomberg News, after the FBI raided Epstein's Upper East Side mansion, prosecutors said that FBI agents had assembled a "vast trove of lewd photographs of young-looking women or girls" as well as compact discs labeled "Misc nudes 1" and "Girl pics nude."[3]

So there was no doubt that this was kompromat on a grand scale. But so many questions about it were unanswered. And there was always the possibility that Epstein's operation itself was not secure. A former deputy sheriff in the Palm Beach County Sheriff's Office told me he had possession of more than four hundred videos that were presumably taken by Epstein and Ghislaine.[4] Epstein's lawyers—and there were many of them—presumably had access to the materials or at least knew some of their contents. So did prosecutors and their investigators.

Moreover, exactly who was in these videos, who had been compromised, has never been fully revealed. As noted, Epstein's black book and his planes' flight logs listed hundreds of celebrities and power brokers of one sort or another. Between them, the two documents, also as noted, showed that Bill Clinton and Donald Trump, former Israeli prime minister Ehud Barak and former British prime minister Tony Blair, billionaire industrialist David Koch, and countless other luminaries had hitched rides with Epstein on the Lolita Express. There were also scores of celebrities from the worlds of art, entertainment, and media, including Mick Jagger, Alec Baldwin, Courtney Love, and Charlie Rose. Not to mention less glamorous but nonetheless powerful titans of the media industry, Wall Street, and politics.

In addition to his huge operation on Little Saint James, Epstein oversaw an equally elaborate operation in his East Seventy-First Street mansion in New York, and maintained a special set of apartments to house the girls just a few blocks away. Then, of course, there were his massive homes in New Mexico, Paris, and elsewhere. Scores of people worked for him and could not fail to notice the nude photos, erotica, dildos, and sex toys, not to mention all the tall, lithe, attractive young girls.

The girls themselves knew what was happening—or at least parts of the story. And there were hundreds of them. The black book alone listed dozens of masseuses in New York, Paris, New Mexico, the Virgin Islands, and other locales. With Ghislaine at the top of Epstein's "sexual pyramid scheme," dozens of girls like Virginia Giuffre serviced Epstein and then recruited others to do the same. Courtney Wild, in the Netflix documentary *Jeffrey Epstein: Filthy Rich*, claims she was first molested by Epstein when she was fourteen and subsequently brought Epstein forty to sixty girls, for which she was paid $200 each. Girls including Lesley Groff, Sarah Kellen, Nadia Marcinkova, and Adriana Ross recruited others as well.

Giuffre has given sworn testimony about her alleged sexual encounters with Epstein, Prince Andrew, and Alan Dershowitz. The other girls she worked with told similar stories. And so did the girls who recruited them—all the way to the top of the pyramid. In addition, there was Jean-Luc Brunel, his "models," and his staff at MC2; and Peter Listerman, who had direct ties to the FSB and firsthand experience dealing with sexual espionage—Russian-style.

But when all was said and done, it was still unclear who had been captured on the videos, who had actual possession of them, and how they might be used. Had Epstein hidden them before he was taken into custody in 2008? Were they locked down in the custody of law enforcement officers and attorneys? Had Ghislaine hidden them? Were they seized by the sheriff's office? The FBI?

And who would be interested in such kompromat?

Wall Street insiders, for sure. Israel was another possibility. Former Israeli prime minister Ehud Barak had allegedly been seen with both Robert Maxwell and Epstein shortly before Maxwell's death in 1991. And he later got financing from Epstein for Carbyne, a company he started that handles emergency-response services.[5] Barak had been a visitor to Jeffrey Epstein's Upper East Side residence in 2016.

The Saudis were another possibility. That photo of Crown Prince Mohammed bin Salman, a.k.a. MBS, was not there just for show, as one Epstein associate told me. They were genuinely close friends.

There was also Iran, the United Kingdom, and, of course, Russia, which realized that the rewards were potentially huge. In addition to Listerman, Russia had ties to Epstein through dozens of girls from the former Soviet Union who were participating in the Epstein operation. Reached by text in October 2020, shortly before publication, Listerman wrote back that he was suffering from COVID-19 and would not be able to respond to my questions until after the book's deadline. In the past, according to the *New York Post*, he has told reporters, "I'm not a pimp, just [a] matchmaker."[6]

Epstein's ascent as a philanthropist in science and technology started even before he had been convicted for soliciting minors and served time. But after he got out of jail in 2009, the zeal with which the most prestigious academic institutions in the world accepted his largesse became vital to his quest to rehabilitate his reputation.

In 2003, the Jeffrey Epstein VI Foundation—VI, as in Virgin Islands—established the Program for Evolutionary Dynamics (PED) at Harvard, and Epstein donated $6.5 million to the program that year, the largest single donation he made to Harvard. After serving only thirteen months of an eighteen-month sentence in prison for procuring a girl under the age of eighteen for prostitution, he began using his association with Harvard and PED to rehabilitate his image, and, according to a review by Harvard's Faculty of Arts and Sciences, likely made more than forty visits to the PED office in Cambridge to that end.[7]

According to the *Harvard Crimson*, the report also found that mathematics and biology professor Martin A. Nowak approved posting "flattering and false descriptions of Epstein's philanthropy and support of Harvard." Nowak was put on paid administrative leave as a result.

Starting in 2011, three years after his conviction, Epstein began meeting occasionally with Bill Gates, who, according to the *New York Times*, visited Epstein's Seventy-First Street town house at least three times, staying into the night on one occasion. Employees of the Bill and Melinda Gates Foundation went there as well. Epstein had begun discussions with the Gates Foundation and JPMorgan Chase about overseeing a proposed multibillion-dollar philanthropic fund, an arrangement that could potentially be enormously lucrative for Epstein.[8]

Before long, Epstein had carved out a serious reputation for himself as a science and technology philanthropist. His credentials helped. A former member of the New York Academy of Science and a board member of Rockefeller University, he had also served on the advisory board of the Harvard Society for Mind, Brain, and Behavior.[9]

With tall young girls everywhere, most often blond, and his bathrooms stocked with penis- and vagina-shaped soaps, Epstein had created a world that served two wildly differing purposes. In addition to being the site of his sexual massages—often three times a day—and sex parties, Little Saint James was home to the Jeffrey Epstein VI Foundation (which Epstein endowed with a $30 million grant affiliated with Harvard) and hosted conferences on medical research, theoretical physics, string theory, and the like with world-renowned scientists such as Stephen Hawking.

In January 2012, the Jeffrey Epstein VI Foundation announced its sponsorship of a conference organized by MIT's Marvin Minsky, a pioneer in artificial intelligence, with the headline "Top Scientists Meet to Discuss Greatest Threats to the Earth." A key figure at MIT's Artificial Intelligence Lab, Minsky, according to the *Verge*, co-wrote, with Seymour Papert, a groundbreaking 1969 book on self-training algorithms, *Perceptrons*, and later developed a computer display that was a forerunner to modern virtual-reality and augmented-reality systems.[10]

Two and a half months later, in late March, the Jeffrey Epstein VI

Foundation put out a press release declaring "Science Philanthropist, Jeffrey Epstein, Convenes a Conference of Nobel Laureates to Define Gravity." In April, his foundation put out yet another bulletin: "Jeffrey Epstein, Science Philanthropist, Organizes a Global Doomsday Conference." In 2013, he told journalist Edward Jay Epstein that he was funding a group in Hong Kong that was building the world's smartest robot.

In 2014, he funded NeuroTV, an online network devoted to neuroscience. In 2015, as Gabriel Sherman reported in *Vanity Fair*, LinkedIn cofounder Reid Hoffman, who later apologized for his role in rehabilitating Epstein's image, brought Epstein out to Palo Alto, California, for dinner with Mark Zuckerberg, Elon Musk, and Peter Thiel, among others.[11]

Epstein had wormed his way into Musk's world after he initiated regular contact with Kimbal Musk, who serves on the boards of two of his brother Elon's companies, Tesla and SpaceX, and whom Epstein introduced to a woman he had previously dated. "It almost seemed a little more transactional," one source told *Business Insider*.[12] "The rumor has always been that Epstein facilitated introductions to beautiful women, looking for deal flow or access to capital."

Of course, close ties to the heavyweights of the tech sector carried considerable clout in terms of legitimizing Epstein in the eyes of Silicon Valley, and Epstein pulled out all the stops to win them over. He told the *New York Times* that even though Silicon Valley techies "had a reputation for being geeky workaholics," he found that they were hedonistic and regular users of recreational drugs, and he personally witnessed "prominent tech figures" taking drugs and setting up sexual assignations.[13]

It's unclear what, if anything, Epstein intended to do with that knowledge. According to *Mother Jones*, Epstein put together lavish dinner parties with the likes of paleontologist and evolutionary biologist Stephen Jay Gould and cognitive psychologist and linguist Steven Pinker as a way of creating his own "mini-university."[14] He had an extraordinary ability to assemble a group of great scientists and intellectuals.

But in the end, of course, he had really bought his way into their world. Scientists liked sex and money as much as anyone. Joichi Ito, the former head of MIT's prestigious Media Lab, and Harvard biologist George Church, of the Human Genome Project, were among those who had support from or regular contact with Epstein. In September 2019, Ito resigned after acknowledging he had received $1.7 million from Epstein, including $1.2 million for his own outside investment funds.

And ultimately, Epstein was Epstein, and when the conversation drifted outside his interest and he got bored, he was known to interrupt by referring to a topic that occupied his thoughts a great deal of the time.

"What does that got to do with pussy?" he'd ask.[15]

———

Epstein wasn't the only one who was obsessed with artificial intelligence. Vladimir Putin was, too. "Artificial intelligence is the future, not only for Russia, but for all humankind," he said in a speech that was broadcast on RT, the propagandistic Russian TV network, in 2017.[16] "It comes with colossal opportunities, but also threats that are difficult to predict. Whoever becomes the leader in this sphere will become the ruler of the world."

To that end, according to Intelligence Online, in October 2019, Putin signed Russia's new National Strategy for the Development of Artificial Intelligence by 2030, calling for the "establishment of a security system during the design, development, the installation and use of artificial intelligence."[17]

Already, Russia has implemented enormously disruptive campaigns against the United States using unconventional weapons, including disinformation attacks and cyberwarfare—campaigns that were vital to installing Donald Trump as president in 2016.

But a report from the Brookings Institute concluded that in the future, Russia's use of AI as a weapon can make that look like small potatoes. "AI has the potential to hyperpower Russia's use of disinformation—the intentional spread of false and misleading information for the purpose of influencing politics and societies," the report says.[18] "And unlike in the conventional military space, the United

States and Europe are ill-equipped to respond to AI-driven asymmetric warfare (ADAW) in the information space."

In fact, according to Yuri Shvets, you can't fully understand the scope of Russian intelligence until you understand that Putin sees artificial intelligence, supercomputers, and control of advanced computer technology as Russia's most vital national security issue. "This is, for Putin, as essential to the survival of his regime as it was for Stalin to get the A-bomb," Shvets told me. "There are seventeen thousand Russian IT guys working in the United States, and a great number of them are connected with Russian intelligence—bright people who've been working inside Apple, Microsoft, and other companies for years.

"For Russian intelligence, it would have been like a Klondike to penetrate Epstein's network of tech people who work on artificial intelligence and supercomputers. It would have been the equivalent of penetrating the Manhattan Project in World War II."

Enter, into Jeffrey Epstein's world, Svetlana Pozhidaeva, better known as Lana, a striking young Russian multi-hyphenate—scholar, model, women's empowerment activist, and tech entrepreneur—who had ties to both Epstein and procurer Jean-Luc Brunel, and has her own suitably curious background in Moscow.

Raised in a Moscow apartment complex built for staffers of the NKVD, the Stalinist precursor of the KGB, Pozhidaeva was educated at the Moscow State Institute of International Relations (MGIMO), the prestigious academy run by the Ministry of Foreign Affairs that is a training ground for Russian diplomats and intelligence officials.[19] Reputed to be the most elite university in the country, MGIMO has been dubbed the "Harvard of Russia" by Henry Kissinger because it has trained so many figures in Russia's political, intellectual, and financial elite.

According to the Italian edition of *Maxim*, Lana gave up a promising tennis career at the age of sixteen to become the youngest freshman at MGIMO, where she graduated with the equivalent of summa cum laude, having mastered, along the way, French, English, Italian, and Spanish, as if she were on course to join the Foreign Ministry.[20]

Her stellar academic credentials notwithstanding, Pozhidaeva somehow ended up in the orbit of alleged Epstein pimp Brunel by being represented by his modeling agency MC2. As a model, she was featured prominently in *Maxim Italia* and *Ukraine Vogue*, moved to the United States, and began her association with Jeffrey Epstein.

Unlike the very young local Florida girls Ghislaine and her team had recruited from broken homes and trailer parks, Lana was older—at this writing, thirty-five—and very well educated, self-possessed, and refined enough to play hostess to distinguished academics and Silicon Valley titans.

Once Pozhidaeva got to New York, she became president of a New York–based charity called Education Advance, which received most of its $56,000 in funding from Epstein in 2017 to support education science and technology. Pozhidaeva later told the *Daily Beast* that Epstein's donation "helped develop an impactful program at MIT."[21]

With Epstein's help, Pozhidaeva also founded a New York–based monthly event series for female entrepreneurs and professionals called WE Talks. ("WE" stands for Women's Empowerment, Encouragement, and Entrepreneurship.)

She took on a partner in Moscow named Victoria Drokova, who had also been educated at MGIMO, and whose CV raised exactly the same questions Lana's did. But Drokova had another feature in her biography that Pozhidaeva did not: Her sister Masha Drokova was a celebrated pro-Putin activist in Russia.[22]

Best known as "the Girl Who Kissed Putin," Masha, whose story is related in the 2012 documentary *Putin's Kiss*, had been an activist in Moscow and a leader of the Nashi, the pro-Putin youth movement that critics have compared to Hitler Youth and have dubbed "Putinjugend." She became famous when she spontaneously planted a kiss on Putin's cheek during a Nashi rally after joining the group in 2005.

As a teen, she had her own online pro-Putin TV show in which she asserted that serving Russian intelligence is an honorable pursuit.[23] "I really liked Putin, especially after I learned he liked me," she later told *Mashable*.[24] "When you're a teenager . . . and the president of the country pays you attention and remembers you, it proves to you that you're important."

Russian foreign minister Sergei Lavrov (left), Donald Trump, and Russian ambassador to the United States Sergey Kislyak met in the Oval Office at the White House on May 10, 2017. Trump told the Russians that he had just fired "real nut job" FBI director James Comey, who had begun investigating Russian interference in the 2016 election. No American journalists were allowed to record the meeting—just one photographer from TASS, the Russian news agency that has frequently provided cover for Russian intelligence agents. *(Alexander Shcherbak/TASS/Getty Images)*

President Donald Trump met with Russian president Vladimir Putin in Helsinki on July 16, 2018, and stunned observers when he sided with Putin over the FBI, which had concluded Russia had attacked America's 2016 elections. *(Brendan Smialowski/AFP/Getty Images)*

Donald Trump's obsession with nuclear arms and his insistence he could negotiate between Ronald Reagan and the Russians provided an opening for the KGB to cultivate Trump. *(Courtesy of the Ronald Reagan Library)*

(Above left) In July 1987, Trump is seen here with first wife, Ivana, at the Hermitage Museum in St. Petersburg during his first trip to the Soviet Union. According to Yuri Shvets (right), a former major in the KGB, Trump's trip was initiated and set up by the KGB, which oversaw the entire trip. *(Maxim Blokhin/TASS/Getty Images), (Courtesy of Yuri Shvets)*

Semyon Kislin was co-owner of Joy-Lud Electronics, which was allegedly controlled by the KGB and sold hundreds of TVs to Trump more than forty years ago. According to Yuri Shvets, Kislin appeared to be a "spotter agent" who opened the door for the KGB to develop Trump. *(Screenshot/Semyon Kislin's YouTube Channel)*

In the '90s, New York mayor Rudy Giuliani, who later became President Trump's lawyer, marched with the future president on Fifth Avenue in the Steuben Day Parade. Semyon Kislin, who allegedly first identified Trump as a potential target for the KGB, had become a major Giuliani supporter. *(Evy Mages/NY Daily News Archive/Getty Images)*

At left, a mug shot of Robert Hanssen, the FBI agent and Opus Dei member who spied for the Russians, and at right, his brother-in-law Father John Wauck, an Opus Dei priest who also served as a speechwriter for Attorney General William Barr in the administration of George H. W. Bush. *(FBI), (Antonello NUSCA/Gamma-Rapho/Getty Images)*

William Barr just after being sworn in as attorney general in 1991. His religious zealotry merged with his absolutist interpretation of the "unitary executive" to help forge policies that gave President Trump almost dictatorial powers. *(Scott Applewhite/AP Images)*

Opus Dei founder St. Josemaría Escrivá de Balaguer (center) prays with other Opus Dei officials in June 1974. A small number of officials with ties to Opus Dei played key roles in establishing a new Catholic right that gave unbridled power to the presidency. *(Opus Dei Archive for Franco Origlia/Getty Images)*

Leonard Leo, executive vice president of the Federalist Society, on the steps of the Supreme Court in Washington, DC, March 2017. Leo and the Federalist Society have overseen the selection of hundreds of conservative judges, including those on the Supreme Court. *(Mark Peterson/Redux)*

The so-called Bouncing Czech, Robert Maxwell (left), shown here with USSR general secretary Leonid Brezhnev, had access to the corridors of power all over the world and often acted as a friend of the KGB, among other intelligence agencies. *(Bettmann/Getty Images)*

Maxwell, with daughter Ghislaine, in 1984, long before she became an alleged sex trafficker and partner of Jeffrey Epstein. Her father often said she was the favorite of his nine children. *(Mirrorpix/Getty Images)*

British media mogul Robert Maxwell at the Houses of Parliament in London to take up his seat after being elected MP in 1964. *(Keystone/Hulton Archive/Getty Images)*

Trump at an event with John Tower, former senator from Texas; veteran broadcaster Mike Wallace (second from right); and media baron Robert Maxwell. Tower became a fixer for Maxwell and opened doors for him in America's intelligence apparatus.

Immediately after Robert Maxwell's death in 1991, his daughter Ghislaine Maxwell went to her father's yacht, *Lady Ghislaine*, and ordered documents to be shredded. *(Matthew Polak/Sygma/Getty Images)*

Jean-Luc Brunel, a French model agency boss who allegedly trafficked young girls with Jeffrey Epstein, snuggles up with Ghislaine Maxwell in 1992.

Ghislaine Maxwell dated Jeffrey Epstein and was allegedly a co-conspirator in his sex-trafficking ring that lasted for more than two decades. Here, they attend a benefit in New York in 2005. *(Joe Schildhorn/Patrick McMullan/Getty Images)*

Donald Trump and his model girlfriend, Melania Knauss, future first lady; financier and convicted sex offender Jeffrey Epstein; and British socialite Ghislaine Maxwell, at the Mar-a-Lago, Palm Beach, Florida, February 12, 2000. *(Davidoff Studios/Getty Images)*

Jeffrey Epstein (left) and Donald Trump were close friends for fifteen years. Here, they pose together at the Mar-a-Lago, Palm Beach, Florida, 1997. *(Davidoff Studios/ Getty Images)*

Jeffrey Epstein with one of his attorneys, former Harvard professor Alan Dershowitz, September 8, 2004. Dershowitz was also accused of sexual assault in the Epstein scandal. He denies the accusations and he has countersued. *(Rick Friedman/Corbis/Getty Images)*

In June 2018, Russian model Svetlana Pozhidaeva attends a swimsuit launch for Sofia Resing in New York. Earlier, she had worked with Jeffrey Epstein, becoming president of a STEM education nonprofit he funded. *(Lev Radin/Pacific Press/Alamy)*

At right, Anna Malova, the former Miss Russia who was tied to both Donald Trump and Jeffrey Epstein. For a time, she lived in Trump Tower, and also spent time on Epstein's Little St. James Island. *(Richard Corkery/New York Daily News Archive/Getty Images)*

Masha Drokova, who briefly worked as Jeffrey Epstein's publicist and became a rising star in the tech world, started out as a leader of Nashi, a pro-Putin youth group. *(AF Archive/Alamy)*

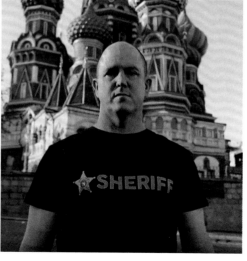

Former deputy sheriff John Mark Dougan claims to have 478 videos from Jeffrey Epstein's stash. Above, he meets with Pavel Borodin, a member of Putin's inner circle who had oversight of a vast amount of Russian assets. At right, Dougan poses in Red Square. He is the fourth American to receive asylum in Russia. *(Facebook)*

Attorney General William P. Barr speaks with reporters at a news conference in Washington, DC, December 19, 1991, flanked by acting principal associate attorney general Robert Mueller. Barr squashed the Mueller Report when it was released, but his friendship with the former special counsel dated back to Barr's first term as attorney general in 1991. *(Barry Thumma/AP Images)*

Barr speaks at an April 18, 2019, news conference to discuss Special Counsel Robert Mueller's report on Russian interference in the 2016 US presidential election. Barr claimed—falsely—that the Mueller Report exonerated Trump. *(Jonathan Ernst/Reuters)*

Special Counsel Mueller testifies before the House Permanent Select Committee on Intelligence on his findings of Russia's 2016 US election attack. His report contained evidence of criminal misconduct by the Trump campaign, but it failed to deliver the promised counterintelligence investigation into Donald Trump's four-decades-long dealings with Russian mobsters and intelligence operatives. *(Salwan Georges/*The Washington Post*/Getty Images)*

Longtime associates Attorney General William Barr (left) and White House counsel Pat Cipollone, both alumni of Kirkland & Ellis, played key roles in awarding expansive authoritarian powers to Donald Trump. *(Alex Brandon/AP Images)*

Donald Trump with Attorney General William Barr in the Oval Office on May 28, 2020. *(Doug Mills-Pool/Getty Images)*

In a defiantly authoritarian act, Donald Trump marches from the White House for a photo-op in front of St. John's Episcopal Church on June 1, 2020. He had called out federal troops to subdue peaceful protests against racial inequality following the killing of George Floyd by police. *(Tom Brenner/Reuters)*

Federal officials use tear gas and brutal tactics on peaceful protesters to clear the way for Donald Trump to walk to the church. In the wake of the killing of George Floyd, police officers wearing riot gear push back demonstrators outside of the White House. *(JOSE LUIS MAGANA/AFP/Getty Images)*

Trump stands in front of St. John's with US attorney general William Barr, National Security Advisor Robert O'Brien, and White House press secretary Kayleigh McEnany after clearing away protesters. *(Tom Brenner/Reuters)*

Trump walks back to the White House, having made his point that he is willing to use American troops against American citizens on American soil. *(BRENDAN SMIALOWSKI/AFP/Getty Images)*

Federal agents used crowd control munitions to disperse Black Lives Matter protesters at the Mark O. Hatfield United States Courthouse on Monday, July 20, 2020, in Portland, Oregon. Tactics included kidnapping of protesters by unidentified federal officers in unmarked cars. *(Noah Berger/AP Images)*

Trump used Portland as a testing ground to deploy these unidentifiable federal agents in major cities as the presidential election approached. *(Paula Bronstein/ Getty Images)*

Hundreds of Black Lives Matter protesters hold their phones aloft in Portland, Oregon, on July 20, 2020. *(Noah Berger/AP Images)*

She has said that her personal mentors have included Putin himself and Vladislav Surkov, the brilliant puppet master who merged theatrical techniques with PR to alter the way reality is perceived in Putin's Russia.[25]

But she says that she later fell out of love with Putin and took a more critical view of rising Russian nationalism.[26] Whether that "disillusionment" was real is open to question, however. By 2015, she had moved to New York and gone into public relations, serving various tech firms and clients—doing well enough to set up shop in 2017 as Day One Ventures, a venture capital and public relations firm where she was an angel investor in early-stage tech start-ups in Silicon Valley. Day One Ventures has invested more than $30 million in tech start-ups since 2016.[27] In addition, she served as vice president of communications for Acronis, a data-protection firm founded by Russian venture capitalist Serguei Beloussov that claims to protect the data of more than five million consumers and half a million businesses. Masha also did public relations for a number of clients—including Jeffrey Epstein.

———

Drokova's ties to Epstein are of special interest because Vladimir Putin was obsessed with artificial intelligence, supercomputers, and other forms of cutting-edge technology, and Jeffrey Epstein's operation just happened to provide a perfect entry point. After all, technology was high on Epstein's agenda, and his salon of Nobel laureates, Silicon Valley heavyweights, and celebrated academics constituted a fabulous assemblage of great minds—especially for a college dropout who had studied for two years at Cooper Union.

One of Pozhidaeva's first WE Talks salons, in May 2018, featured Masha Drokova as a panelist addressing the challenge that only 2 percent of the venture capital raised goes to female founders.[28]

As an intelligence officer, Shvets had to constantly analyze case files as part of his job, and, according to him, Pozhidaeva's story, much like Natalia Dubinina's, does not quite compute. "She was in one of the best, most prestigious academic institutions in Russia," said Shvets. "She could make a breathtaking career in the Foreign Office or in any foreign company working in the Moscow office. She would make a great career. But instead she goes into the so-called modeling business?"

"Each intelligence officer operates under a so-called legend or a cover story," he said. "This is like their official work history, which they show to the world. The purpose of this legend is to cover up years you spent training at the KGB or FSB."

What was most striking about Pozhidaeva was that she had a terrific academic career in Russia and then threw it away on something completely unrelated. She attended, as she says, a top college in Russia, like Stanford in the United States, said Shvets. "And she was a straight-A student. This is important to understand. She sacrificed four years and then two more years for a master's degree. It's an achievement."

But suddenly after this, Shvets noted, "She says, 'Fuck it all. Fuck my previous six years. Fuck everything I was doing.' I mean, it's amazing—it just does not happen in real life."

According to Shvets, it all started with Peter Listerman. "It was Listerman who introduced her to Brunel, and Brunel introduced her to Epstein," Shvets told me. "Of course, we know what Epstein was doing with the ladies. But in this particular case, Epstein takes her and introduces her to renowned American and international scientists."

How could someone as intelligent and well educated as Pozhidaeva become an activist for women while possibly seeking patronage from Jean-Luc Brunel and Jeffrey Epstein, who directed and participated in human trafficking and the rape of underage girls for more than two decades?

According to Shvets, the only answer is that it all must have been part of a deliberate effort to introduce Lana to a network of scientists and to help her set up a charity that made lots of donations to companies associated with artificial intelligence. And that leads Shvets to believe that she worked as a penetration agent with the assistance of Jeffrey Epstein. "She penetrated the network in the United States related to supercomputer and artificial intelligence," he told me. Pozhidaeva did not return phone calls or emails from me.

CHAPTER FIFTEEN

TWO NEEDLES IN A HAYSTACK

Even before Epstein was convicted in 2008, it was widely known within Epstein's entourage, law enforcement circles, and various intelligence services that Jeffrey, Ghislaine, and company had been making videos of grave sexual crimes taking place under Epstein's aegis and were keeping them safely guarded—just in case. According to the *New York Times*, Virginia Giuffre had written an unpublished memoir in which she noted she had found a room in Epstein's New York mansion where monitors displayed surveillance footage. Similarly, Maria Farmer, who accused Epstein of assaulting her sexually in the nineties, said that Epstein had pointed out tiny cameras in room after room and told her, "We keep [recordings]. We keep everything."[1]

Why were they doing this? The people who knew weren't talking, of course. There was speculation that it was used to facilitate deals with Wall Street power brokers and to cement the loyalty of various actors in the drama, be they high-powered lawyers, heads of state, royalty, billionaires, media moguls, or operatives in any intelligence service. But no one outside Epstein's circle seemed to know the specifics: who was involved, what sexual acts may have been recorded, how Epstein or Ghislaine may have used the recordings, whether the subjects who were in them were aware of them.

But it was leverage—and powerful leverage at that. "I'm sure many people wanted him dead," Epstein accuser Chauntae Davies says in Netflix's *Jeffrey Epstein: Filthy Rich*. "He had a lot of information on a lot of people. A lot of blackmail—videos and pictures."

With countless bold-faced names in his black book—Donald Trump, Bill Clinton, Tony Blair, Ehud Barak, Prince Andrew, and so many more—this was kompromat paradise, and the FSB couldn't possibly pass it up.

Potentially, the FSB had access to Epstein and his kompromat through the likes of Peter Listerman and the Russian girls who had come through Listerman and Brunel—Lana Pozhidaeva, Masha Drokova, and others. But when the Epstein case entered the court system in 2005 and his computers and videos became evidence, more people suddenly had access. A new avenue that the FSB began to explore was through a former deputy sheriff named John Mark Dougan, who had served in the Palm Beach County Sheriff's Office (PBSO) from 2002 to late 2008.

With his shaved head and the sturdy build of a former US Marine, Dougan has taken a turbulent journey over the last decade, from Donald Trump's and Jeffrey Epstein's Palm Beach playground to Moscow. There, he now claims to be in command of no fewer than 478 videos taken from Epstein's Palm Beach residence—perhaps the most valuable assemblage of kompromat on the planet.

As a military man and an ex-cop, Dougan is the sort of macho antihero of questionable reliability one often encounters in the comic Florida crime fiction of Carl Hiaasen and Elmore Leonard. Like them, Dougan has a rather patchy job history that has taken him laterally from police work to horse transportation to database design to piloting.[2] The word "disgruntled" follows Dougan wherever he goes. A hapless and quixotic underdog, he has reinvented himself as an avenging angel/whistleblower who has been taking on the powers that be, in Palm Beach County at least, since he resigned in 2009.

Dougan is of interest in the Epstein saga because from 2005 to 2009 he served as deputy sheriff in the Palm Beach Sheriff's Office District 3, an area that includes Jeffrey Epstein's house at 358 El Brillo Way, as well as Mar-a-Lago and the Trump International Golf Club.

But Dougan had never been a happy camper in the PBSO. He did not endear himself to the top brass. At his best, Dougan has taken on racist and corrupt cops on his home turf in Palm Beach, where he occasionally won praise from his superiors for his "surveillance skills" and "thinking outside the BOX."

"Deputy Dougan's interpersonal skills need improvement," one lieutenant wrote in an evaluation, "as he does not know how to pull back from a brewing issue."

According to Neil Barnett, who runs Istok Associates, a London-based intelligence and investigation consultancy, Dougan was also clearly "an aggrieved individual with a fragile ego and a sense of his own grandeur. In other words, Dougan was openly present on the Internet as a former PBSO officer who exhibited a number of the classic traits of a suitable target for recruitment by a hostile intelligence service."

That meant the Russians.

In Palm Beach, Dougan was already getting in trouble—for good reasons and bad. Among the various controversies he got involved in, one was, as noted, taking on a gang of racist cops that he said were assaulting people they arrested, especially those who were nonwhite. "They were just beating the minorities bloody," Dougan told the *Daily Beast*.[3] "It was just awful."

Fed up with his colleagues' racist behavior, he resigned and sent off pseudonymous emails to his department superiors about what was going on.[4] But little was done in the way of punishing the malefactors. In the end, Dougan was so dismayed they got away with it that he was on his way to becoming a whistleblower.

Before long, he launched PBSOtalk.org, a secure whistleblower forum that allowed cops and other law enforcement officers to talk anonymously and circulate exposés of alleged abuses and corruption within the byzantine, internecine politics of the Palm Beach Sheriff's Office. At this writing, his site has more than fifty thousand posts.

On a phone call from his one-bedroom apartment in west Moscow, Dougan told me the site was necessary because the cops would make life "a living hell" for anyone who crossed "that blue line" to report corruption in the Palm Beach Sheriff's Office.[5] Over time, Dougan did more than merely expose malfeasance among law enforcement officials; he began to use his technical expertise to attack his foes with doxing and an array of social media attacks.

Whether one saw him as a whistleblower or as an aggrieved former employee, Dougan clearly had access to secrets, and he wanted to talk. More than that, using the Internet persona BadVolf, Dougan, the renegade American ex-cop, had taken on the guise of a Russian hacker. Using a voice changer, he pretended he was a woman and carried on an intimate ten-day telephone relationship with a law enforcement official. According to the *Daily Beast*, he doxed no fewer than fourteen thousand federal agents, judges, cops, and intelligence agents, posting their home addresses on the web.

And you could learn all about BadVolf's exploits on his site, BadVolf.com, which features a short promotional video by RT, the propagandistic Russian TV network, heroically portraying him as a David taking on Goliath in the form of the awesome power of the Palm Beach Sheriff's Office. (The video shown was a short promo film for *Breaking Bad Wolf*, a full-length documentary that can be seen on YouTube.)[6] Between BadVolf and PBSOtalk.org, Dougan says he was so effective that his work led to the arrest and firings of countless police officers. But his work also led to serious ruptures with the powers that be, with the PBSO and FBI trying to put him in jail, he says, to "have me tortured and killed."[7]

Some time around 2010, about a year after Dougan left the force, having established a reputation as someone who provided a secure outlet for like-minded cops to speak out, Dougan got a call from Joseph Recarey.

Recarey was a former detective with the Palm Beach Police Department and had been a detective on the force in 2005 when Dougan still worked there. During that period, a woman came into the station and charged that Jeffrey Epstein had paid her fourteen-year-old stepdaughter $300 to strip to her underwear and perform an "erotic massage." This was the beginning of legal proceedings in the Epstein case, and Joe Recarey was chief detective. Dougan had had absolutely nothing to do with the case when he was with the PBSO, and he had zero interest in it—or so he said.

But Recarey was deeply committed to the investigation. According to Julie K. Brown's reporting in the *Miami Herald*, in the first seven months of his investigation, he discovered twenty-one possible victims. Eventually, the probe had identified at least thirty-five underage victims, and there were more cases still being investigated. Epstein was a pedophile. There was no question about it.

As the evidence snowballed, internal pressures to drop or downgrade the investigation mounted. But according to the *Miami Herald*, Recarey and Palm Beach police chief Michael Reiter stood fast as courageous cops who were willing to risk their careers to go after Epstein.

Then, in 2010, about five years into the Epstein case, Recarey called Dougan. The two men did not know each other well, but they had worked for the same employers and Dougan thought highly of Recarey. "He was a serious guy," Dougan told me. "But not so serious where he couldn't take a joke. He was really nice and down-to-earth."

"'I've got some stuff I want you to keep for me,'" Dougan says Recarey told him.

As the founder of PBSOtalk.org, Dougan often got requests like that. "I just became the guy who everybody used to give stuff to. Everybody knew that I designed the system to keep everybody absolutely confidential, and the sheriff hated it. So people would give me things like a deposition where the sheriff got caught stealing a gun from the evidence room. I was like the dumping ground for stuff."

So, Dougan says, Recarey came over to his office on Olive Avenue in Palm Beach with a cartful of boxes. "One of the boxes was a bunch of DVDs—the blank kind that you record your own media on," Dougan recalled. "They were labeled by date and spanned from 1994 to 2005 or so. I asked Recarey what they were, and he told me they were concerning Jeffrey Epstein, but he didn't elaborate about the contents."

According to Dougan, Recarey said his investigation was being sabotaged by both Epstein and his powerful allies, and he wanted to make sure he had copies in case they tried to make the originals disappear. After all, they had to know the kind of evidence Recarey had assembled.

Recarey's fears were also reported in the *Miami Herald* by Julie K. Brown and David Smiley in an article noting that Epstein had hired investigators to tail both Recarey and Chief Reiter. Recarey said that he often switched vehicles in an attempt to throw Epstein's team off. "At some point it became like a cat-and-mouse game," he told the *Herald*.[8] "I knew they were there, and they knew I knew they were there. I was concerned about my kids because I didn't know if it was someone that they hired just out of prison that would hurt me or my family."

In May 2018, shortly after his interview by the *Herald*, Recarey, then fifty, died after a brief illness. In the meantime, according to a report by Kevin Poulsen of the *Daily Beast*, Dougan's website continued to publish dirt about Palm Beach's finest. Some of it was true; some of it was not. There was the story of the former SWAT commander who was accused of "stealing painkillers from a dying deputy; purchase orders showing the office spent nearly $80,000 on barbecue grills; a photo of officers posing with a topless woman on a Palm Beach golf course."

But he also published loads of disinformation and accusations about Sheriff Rick Bradshaw and other PBSO brass, including a fake pedophilia confession that appeared under the fraudulent byline of a top department official.

Meanwhile, Dougan had struck up an online relationship with a Russian woman on Facebook. It was the beginning of a virtual romance that he hoped to transform into a real one, so in February 2013 he went to Moscow for the first time. Dougan loved Moscow immediately, citing its sense of ungoverned freedom. "It was like the Wild West meets New York City," he said.[9]

As for the romance, he told me he has not seen nor communicated with the woman in several years, and he declined to reveal her name.

About a week after he arrived in Moscow, Dougan posted a photo on his Facebook page of himself having lunch at the Bison Steakhouse in Moscow with an unusually intriguing companion—former Kremlin official Pavel Borodin. (The photo has since been removed.)

Up until this time, Dougan had vacillated between the worlds of a small-time huckster who created revenge-fantasy websites laced with disinformation and a legitimate whistleblower decrying racism and corruption. Whether one thought Dougan was legit or a con man, everyone could all agree on one thing: In either case, in the context of world affairs, John Mark Dougan was small-time. Insignificant. A nobody.

But the photo he posted on Facebook suggests something else entirely. Pavel Borodin is not a familiar name to Americans, but in Russia he's a major figure. In fact, he's so close to Vladimir Putin that one has to ask why one of the most important figures in Putin's inner circle would waste time lunching with Dougan.

"Borodin is no small fry," says Yuri Shvets. "This is the guy who brought Putin to Moscow, to the Kremlin."

Dubbed "Putin's mentor" by *Time*,[10] Borodin had overseen the Presidential Affairs Department during the Boris Yeltsin administration in the nineties, and so was in charge of the upkeep of the Russian Federation's assets.

And which of Russia's assets was he overseeing? You may ask.

Actually, just about *all* of them.

As the *New York Times* reported, Borodin had oversight of Russia's land, Russia's farms, Russia's dachas. Its automobiles, its aircraft, and its yachts. Russia's hospitals, Russia's buildings, its antiques, its art, and more. More than two hundred profit-making companies. And he had oversight of things you might overlook because they didn't fit neatly into categories—such as a stake in a $12 billion Arctic diamond mine.

All told, Borodin was in charge of supervising some $600 billion in assets—nearly $1 trillion in 2020 dollars. "Mr. Borodin is unequivocally, far and away the Russian that people would most love to bribe," the *New York Times* reported. "Forget Russia. Few people on earth have this much largesse at their fingertips."[11]

And even fewer people were in such a pivotal position at the birth of the untamed gangster capitalism in Russia and were able to do something that truly marked a turning point in world history. In 1996, at a time when efforts to develop a real market economy were failing, and Russia was devolving into a Mafia state, Borodin hired Putin as his deputy and put him in a vital strategic position that allowed him to broker the new rules of a nascent kleptocracy, the relationships between the oligarchs and the Kremlin, and the rise of the Mafia state. It has been widely speculated in the Russian media that if anyone has kompromat on Putin, it would be Pavel Borodin from this period.[12]

And when the state prosecutor started investigating Borodin for his alleged role in a multimillion-dollar bribery and money-laundering scam, Putin, who had become FSB chief by this time, showed his great loyalty to Borodin by ousting the prosecutor, Yuri Skuratov, using secret footage that allegedly showed Skuratov cavorting with prostitutes.[13]

When Putin became president in 2000, he then gave Borodin the post of state secretary of the union of Russia and Belarus, a largely ceremonial position that had the highly valued perquisite of guaranteeing him legal immunity in Russia. Then, in 2002, Borodin was convicted of money laundering by a Swiss court, and the Putin administration paid $3 million bail for his release.

Immunity is a good thing to have when you have access to hundreds of billions of dollars.

After Dougan's lunch with Borodin, a company called MD International Holdings put out a press release announcing that the company CEO, Mark Dougan, had traveled to Moscow "to meet with Russian Secretary of State, Pavel Borodin." (In fact, Borodin was state secretary for the Russia Belarus Union.)

The release added that "Secretary Borodin presented Mr. Dougan with a very beautiful and very limited leather and gold book about the history of the Kremlin, as well as signing the book under his chapter in the book." The purpose of the meeting was said "to establish cooperation in various aspects of business, including facilitating American investments into the robust Russian business environment and to engage into markets that would be considered 'frontier' to Russia."

An Internet search on the Wayback Machine suggests that MD International Holdings was not really a going concern and that its site may have been constructed for the sole purpose of publicizing Dougan's meeting with Borodin.

So what was a big fish like Borodin doing with a small fry like Dougan? According to Dougan, the meeting was perfectly innocent, and Borodin was just another Facebook friend. "I wanted to start a business in Russia, I started looking at Facebook profiles and saw that this person was sitting in front of the Russian parliament," he told a Russian reporter.[14] "I added him as a friend and started chatting with him on Facebook. I asked him to meet. When you are American, it's easy to organize meetings with people."

Sure. The man Vladimir Putin trusted to oversee more than $600 billion in assets was sitting around waiting for a former Palm Beach deputy to become his Facebook friend. That makes lots of sense.

When I asked Yuri Shvets what he thought of Dougan's narrative, he laughed. "It's like two needles meet each other in a haystack," he said. "Pavel Borodin is searching Facebook, waiting until the guy comes from Florida to Moscow? This is what I would trust: The guy with a massive collection of video comes to Moscow, and he gets in touch with Borodin and the FSB. That is what is happening . . . [Dougan] is in the selling business."

And as for Borodin, he is in the buying business. "Putin was a nobody until Borodin brought him to Moscow. So that means Borodin has direct contact with the Kremlin, with the FSB."

According to Neil Barnett, Dougan presented himself as a ripe target for recruitment by the FSB, and his first trip to Moscow "would have allowed Russian intelligence to fully recruit Dougan. . . . It is likely that they presented the 'co-operation' as a way for them to support his campaign against PBSO, and that they slipped in requests relating to Epstein as an apparent afterthought or contextual matter."[15]

When he returned to Palm Beach, Dougan moved on to other matters. He continued to have a relationship with his Russian girlfriend for a period of time during which each of them made two or three trips between Moscow and Palm Beach. At the same time, he says, Joe Recarey continued to give him more documents from the Epstein investigation through 2015.

Meanwhile, Dougan also escalated his war with the local powers that be. It became increasingly sophisticated. Over the next three years, he played email pranks on politicians, disseminated fake news, and created a website to show how to keep the FBI from accessing a computer.[16] "He became adept at creating fake news sites to propagate false stories," said Barnett. "He also apparently worked out how to reverse engineer access to confidential data, which he then released in order to cause maximum damage. It appears that he benefited from the assistance of more sophisticated people."[17]

But in his book about his adventures, *BadVolf*, Dougan insists that he is not an asset of the Russian government, nor has it tried to recruit him. In an interview with the *Daily Mail*, Dougan also asserted that he has not shared any materials with the Russian government and that he does not intend to blackmail anyone with his information.[18]

———

By March 2016, however, Dougan's massive doxing rampage had apparently gone too far. Early in the morning of March 14, 2016, Dougan woke up and fed breakfast to his two kids as they prepared for school. As Dougan himself describes it in *BadVolf*, at the front door, he noticed a black Ford FX2 pickup truck idling in front of his house. The pickup had black-tinted windows, which are illegal in Florida and suggested to him that the truck was an undercover vehicle.[19]

Dougan went back indoors, put on a shirt, and went outside to see what they were doing. The truck's doors opened. FBI agents wearing tactical vests burst out. Agents started coming out of the bushes, behind buildings—everywhere.

Within moments, Dougan was cuffed and on the ground. One agent immediately grabbed Dougan's cell phone and passed it to another, "presumably because they knew my phone was encrypted and had to act fast to ensure they could suck all the data out of it before it locked."[20]

Before long, the FBI began wheeling in machinery, which Dougan surmised had "portable batteries and an inverter that would enable the FBI to keep the computer running while they unplugged it. That way, they could extrapolate the encryption key at a later date."[21]

One of the agents asked, "Who are your Russian friends? You

should tell us because it's going to be a lot easier if you tell us what we want to know."[22]

They seized his passport and put him on the no-fly list, so no commercial air travel or private travel outside the country was possible. The raid, he said, was "the most significant 'holy shit' moment of my life."[23]

As for the so-called Epstein videos, what about them? According to Dougan, when the FBI seized his computers in 2016, they got everything Recarey had given him.

If Dougan's videos were the real deal, that meant that the FBI had possession of Jeffrey Epstein's prized kompromat, and with it, the secrets of the most powerful men in the world.

When the FBI finally left and had not arrested him, Dougan knew his troubles weren't over. So nine days later, on March 23, 2016, he went down to Islamorada Key in South Florida, about 150 miles south of Palm Beach, and rented an eighteen-foot boat from Bud N' Mary's Marina. He intended not to return the boat but instead to embark on a spectacularly dangerous three-hundred-mile trip to Cuba on the "barely-buoyant shitbox," as he referred to it.[24]

Before he took off, however, Dougan noticed a handful of FBI agents at the marina on his tail. Dougan immediately realized that meant even if he were able to survive the stormy seas, the FBI would have Homeland Security or the Coast Guard on him in no time.

That meant it was on to plan B. Now that he realized he was still under such intense surveillance, Dougan deactivated all his mobile devices, including a burner phone he had bought.[25]

In *BadVolf*, Dougan's account of what happened next as he escaped from the United States is brief, but it is full of holes. "A few days after I left the marina," he writes, "I donned a blond wig on my bald head and a pair of light prescription glasses, evading capture by the FBI and fleeing the United States. After renting a small plane and faking a medical emergency to slip into Canada, I made my way to Toronto. I flew Turkish Airlines to Moscow, where I became the 4th American in history to obtain political asylum in Russia."[26] (Before Dougan, Edward Snowden had been the most recent.)

He arrived in Russia on April 6 or 7, he told me, and applied for asylum a few days later. "It took a few days for me to get my head on straight and apply for asylum."

According to Barnett, Dougan's departure from the United States bore all the hallmarks of "a professional exfiltration plan put together by an intelligence service. First, Dougan got a car with no documented connection to him and drove it to the Canadian border. He then chartered a light aircraft to overfly Canada. During the flight he claimed he was having a heart attack, and then ran off when the pilot made an emergency landing. From Toronto, he bought a ticket to Istanbul, and from Istanbul bought a new ticket to Moscow."

And why Moscow? "There are very few governments around the world that the US won't mess with, and that the US can't somehow strong-arm into returning a political dissident," he told a Russian reporter.[27] "Russia happens to be one of them. And I can't think of another government that's more powerful that would protect me."

And indeed, on arrival, Dougan was granted temporary asylum in Russia, which was later changed to permanent status.[28]

When I talked to him, he added a rhetorical question: "Where else am I going to go that my country can't extradite me back? You've got North Korea. You've got Africa. China. Forget it. I like this country very much."

And what about the kompromat?

In confiscating Dougan's computers, the FBI and the PBSO now presumably had copies of the Epstein videos that Dougan says Recarey had brought to him for safekeeping.

Dougan told me he had paid scant attention to the files Recarey had left with him, and on the rare occasion when he opened a video file, all he saw was footage of an empty room with coverage from an old-fashioned low-resolution closed-circuit TV camera. "You have to remember, in those days, CCTV was poor quality and some of the earlier files had the telltale signs that they were burned to the disks from VHS tapes."[29]

When I asked if I could see any of the files, he demurred and said he was not going to broadcast child pornography over the Internet.

Because the taped sessions regularly began with the camera survey-ing an empty room, Dougan says, he never saw any activity and as-sumed they were ordinary surveillance videos. Nevertheless, he told me that he knew the files were about Epstein, so he made an extra set—which would have made him an extraordinarily valuable asset to the Russians.

"If Dougan really has these videotapes, they would be priceless," said Yuri Shvets. "Hundreds of videotapes with famous people in the United States with underage girls. It's hard-core kompromat."

Because of their value, Dougan claims he took extraordinary pre-cautions. "The FBI and other intelligence agencies may be surprised to have discovered that I kept an off-site backup that was sent to me in 2017, after I was safely established in Russia."[30]

Initially, he says, he put all the Epstein videos into a TrueCrypt container, which moved from server to server over the years as insur-ance that the data would stay fresh and safe from data loss. When TrueCrypt discontinued its software in 2014, Dougan switched to VeraCrypt and rotated encrypted backups on a regular basis.[31]

Later, he says, he distributed the data to unidentified contacts who did not know each other and who lived on five different continents and are unable to read the files because they do not have the decryption keys. "I do not have a physical copy in my immediate possession, be-cause of security reasons," he told me. "This is to make sure my family and friends remain safe. I have made arrangements that it can only be decrypted in the event of my arrest, if I go missing for an extended time, or in case of my unusual or untimely demise. I have a system in place to connect people with the encrypted containers to those who have the decryption keys."[32]

According to the *Daily Mail*, "Dougan, who said he has received death threats since fleeing the United States, added that he had no in-tention of ever revealing the contents stored on encrypted drives. 'I am not going to reveal them and I am not going to blackmail anyone. If I give them up then I lose all my leverage and I do not want that to happen.'"[33]

In other words, the kompromat was perfectly safe. Unless, of course, the FBI, the Palm Beach Sheriff's Office, Ghislaine Maxwell, or some other unidentified parties could break the codes.

And, of course, there was the question of whether Dougan had made a deal with the FSB. For all the indications that he may be a con man or an eccentric, in Britain, MI6 was taking Dougan very seriously indeed as someone who may be working directly with Russian intelligence. The chief reason, the *Daily Mail* reported in September 2019, had to do with his meeting with Pavel Borodin.

The paper cited a Western intelligence source saying that Dougan had all the classic traits that made him vulnerable to recruitment by "a hostile intelligence service." It also noted that "his knowledge of the Epstein case would have been of great interest to Russian intelligence."[34]

But the fate of the kompromat remained uncertain.

CHAPTER SIXTEEN

THE LAWYERS

John Mark Dougan wasn't the only one who had access to Epstein's kompromat. There were lawyers on both sides of the case—the prosecution team and those defending Epstein would have had access as well. And as the Epstein investigation in Palm Beach metastasized into a probe of a major pedophilia and human trafficking operation, Epstein and his attorneys launched a no-holds-barred campaign in the interests of damage control and tamping down the investigation.

Even before the Palm Beach investigation began, Epstein had tried to ingratiate himself with the local police by donating $50,000 to the Palm Beach Police Scholarship Fund, offering tuition help to the children of law enforcement officers, and $90,000 to the Palm Beach Police Department in 2004—all while ramping up his sex trafficking operation right under their noses.[1]

Epstein's generosity to the police recalls Trump's magnanimity with the FBI's James Kallstrom—although it was not as successful. By fall 2005, with the Epstein probe fully under way, Palm Beach police chief Michael Reiter and detective Joe Recarey felt that something fishy was going on to impede their investigation. One sign came on October 20, 2005, after police had clearly established probable cause and executed a search warrant at Epstein's Palm Beach home, only to find that computers and other electronic equipment that had vital evidence had been removed. That suggested Epstein had been tipped off.[2]

According to *Perversion of Justice*, the award-winning series in the *Miami Herald* by Julie K. Brown and Emily Michot, just as the investigation began to snowball, word got back to Epstein that the police had been questioning some of the girls. In response, Epstein hired Alan Dershowitz,[3] the Harvard Law School professor and, by Dershowitz's account, a close friend.

Virginia Giuffre, who alleged that she was recruited by Epstein when she was sixteen, also charged that she was forced to have sex with Dershowitz on six occasions, and she sued him, alleging that "Defendant Dershowitz was Epstein's attorney, close friend, and co-conspirator. Dershowitz was also a participant in sex trafficking, including as one of the men to whom Epstein lent out Plaintiff for sex." She also accused him of making "false and malicious defamatory statements" against her.[4]

Dershowitz has denied the charges and countersued Giuffre, claiming that Giuffre "conspired with her lawyers to publish her false and defamatory claims of and concerning Dershowitz with a knowing or reckless disregard of their falsity," according to his lawsuit. "She has done so with the specific intent and design that her statements be a source for the media so that the media will publish her false allegations of and concerning Dershowitz that he had sex with her while she was underage as part of Epstein's criminal sex trafficking of minors."

Like Epstein, Dershowitz was a middle-class Brooklyn Jew who had ascended to the national stage, albeit in a very different way. Raised in an Orthodox Jewish family in Borough Park, Brooklyn, he initially built a reputation as a prominent civil libertarian and had become, at twenty-eight, the youngest full professor in the history of Harvard Law School.

But what was most notable about Dershowitz was his overweening desire to deliver polemics on behalf of the most offensive, controversial, and, often, richest clients on the planet. When it came to defending free speech, Dershowitz's clients were neo-Nazis and pornographers. Similarly, when it came to violence against women, he assembled a client list that reads like the Hollywood Walk of Fame for misogynistic criminals. There was Claus von Bulow, the Danish-German-British socialite who was convicted and later acquitted of attempting to murder his wife and leaving her comatose. There was O. J. Simpson, the football great who was acquitted of murdering his wife and her friend, but was found responsible for their deaths in a civil trial. There was heavyweight boxing champion and convicted rapist Mike Tyson, film producer/sex criminal Harvey Weinstein, and, finally, Donald J. Trump, president of the United States, who, according to *Business Insider*, has been accused of rape, sexual assault, and sexual harassment by at least twenty-six women.[5]

And now there was Dershowitz's newest client, Jeffrey Epstein, whom he regarded so highly that, as Connie Bruck reported in the *New Yorker*, Epstein was the only non-family member Dershowitz trusted to read rough drafts of his books.[6]

Dershowitz wasn't a member of the Florida bar, but he agreed to take on the case and helped assemble a high-powered legal team for Epstein consisting of big-name attorneys who covered all the bases politically. He started off by giving Epstein a list of lawyers he "worked with in the past that had been exceptionally able and Jeffrey picked from the list," Dershowitz told the *Daily Beast*.*

---

* In the interests of full disclosure, I've had my own run-in with Dershowitz. It took place in the nineties, when I was the editor of *Boston* magazine and Dershowitz wrote a regular column for us. At the time, the magazine had just published a summer guide to Martha's Vineyard that mentioned nude beaches on the island that were popular with local celebrities—including Dershowitz.

Just after the issue came out, Dershowitz called me—livid. "What is this crap about me being on a nude beach?" he shouted. It wasn't true, he said. He demanded an apology and a retraction.

For the moment, I was mortified. To have made a factual error regarding one of the magazine's contributors would have been especially embarrassing. After hanging up, I immediately went to the author of the piece to get to the bottom of it. But before I could chew her out, she reached into her desk and took out a photo that, more than twenty years later, I have still been unable to erase from my memory bank. It was a full-frontal shot of Alan Dershowitz, accompanied by an unidentified woman, walking nude on a beach. It appeared that some kind of green goop, sunscreen perhaps, had been slathered over his genitals.

One of the first people Epstein chose was Ken Starr, then a partner at Kirkland & Ellis, and the former solicitor general in the administration of George H. W. Bush. "Starr had experience in investigating sex investigations," Dershowitz said.[7] "He had experience as the solicitor general and as a judge. He had all the bases covered."

Epstein also brought on Roy Black, Miami's most famous criminal defense lawyer, who won renown in 1991 when he got an acquittal for William Kennedy Smith, a nephew of Senator Ted Kennedy who had been charged with rape. He has also defended actor Kelsey Grammer, sportscaster Marv Albert, and bombastic right-wing talk radio host Rush Limbaugh.

Finally, Epstein also brought on Jay Lefkowitz, another partner at Kirkland & Ellis; former US attorney Guy Lewis; and criminal defense lawyer Gerald Lefcourt.

Meanwhile, Dershowitz flew to Florida and met privately with the state attorney of Palm Beach County, Barry Krischer, who at the time was said to be intent on prosecuting Epstein aggressively. According to the *Miami Herald*, Epstein immediately struck back and that's when, Palm Beach detective Joe Recarey said, "the shenanigans" began. Police reports show that Epstein's investigators began to impersonate cops to conduct interviews, picked through Michael Reiter's trash in search of incriminating material, and followed the girls and their families.[8]

Initially, according to Reiter, Barry Krischer had been saying, "We'll put this guy away for life." But before long, Epstein's high-powered legal team went to work, and Krischer eased off.[9] Epstein's teenage victims were really high school girls who were being assaulted by a man who

---

I immediately called Dershowitz back and told him about the photo.

"That's not me!" he yelled. He had not yet seen the photo, so I'm not sure how he came to that conclusion, but he was still livid.

Dershowitz, the distinguished Harvard Law School professor, an author of thirty-five books, and a cable-news media star, was so convincing that I immediately returned to get a second look. Yes, it was still Dershowitz. Definitely. And as for the unidentified woman accompanying him, her name turned out to be Carolyn Cohen, Dershowitz's wife. Dershowitz subsequently became a vocal proponent of nude sunbathing.

was forty years older, but Krischer suddenly started to act as if they were seasoned prostitutes looking for clients.[10]

After Reiter realized that Krischer was going to indict Epstein only on the relatively minor charge of soliciting prostitutes, rather than on far more serious charges of sex trafficking and pedophilia, he was so fed up that he released a letter calling on Krischer to remove himself, and he called in the FBI. Bringing in the feds meant that Alexander Acosta, then US attorney for the Southern District of Florida and a Republican, would now prosecute the case.

Acosta had also been a partner at Kirkland & Ellis, and the fact that Epstein defense attorneys Ken Starr and Jay Lefkowitz were from the same firm was not incidental. It was smart politics to have defense attorneys who were close to the prosecutors, and that kind of thing happened a lot with Kirkland.

In addition, Ken Starr's presence on Epstein's team carried with it enormous political clout. Having served as solicitor general, a prestigious post that made him the government's top lawyer arguing before the Supreme Court, Starr had also won nationwide notoriety as the independent counsel who spent four years, from 1994 to 1998, building a case against Bill Clinton that ultimately led to his impeachment.

Given Starr's past involvement in cases involving sex, there was a certain unspoken irony in having such a prim, devoutly religious man defending a pedophile who was one of the great sex criminals in American history. In prosecuting Clinton with his deputy Brett Kavanaugh, Starr refashioned a probe about an Arkansas real estate deal that went south into one about consensual oral sex between Bill Clinton and White House intern Monica Lewinsky.* The so-called Starr Report he oversaw marked a momentous point in the history of salacious government documents, with its explicit accounts of oral sex, a cigar in a vagina, and Monica's famous semen-stained blue dress.

---

* In prosecuting Clinton, Starr had argued that even sitting presidents were not immune from civil suits. But he apparently felt that rule was only applicable to Democrats, and when Trump became president and faced impeachment, Starr conveniently changed his position.

Insistently professing his religious adherence to family values, Starr emerged as something of a prissy, schoolmarmish scold, albeit one with real political clout in Washington. Later, in 2016, Starr was fired from his post as president of Baylor University for ignoring at least seventeen women on campus who reported sexual or domestic assault involving nineteen football players.[11] And now he was in the corner of one of the most notorious and decadent sex-trafficking pedophiles in US history, who just happened to have a mother lode of secrets.

From the moment of his arrival at Kirkland & Ellis, Starr was one of its big guns. For many years Kirkland had been a relatively nonpolitical Chicago-based firm whose Washington, DC, office was regarded as little more than an unexceptional outpost. But that changed dramatically when Starr came to Kirkland in 1993. His stint as solicitor general meant that Starr was a serious catch for any number of top firms. His presence changed Kirkland's brand identity from that of a middle-of-the-road establishment firm into one that had a powerhouse Washington office newly filled with ambitious young conservatives who had clerked for Supreme Court justices Antonin Scalia, Clarence Thomas, and Anthony Kennedy. It has since become the biggest law firm in the world by revenue, with more than $4 billion in billings in 2019.[12]

In the Epstein case, Kirkland's lawyers were everywhere, on both the prosecution and the defense, and for the defense, Kirkland's Jay Lefkowitz made mincemeat of a fifty-three-page indictment the feds had put together that accused Epstein of being a serial child molester and sex trafficker—and should have made Epstein spend the rest of his life in jail.

Instead, in October 2007, Lefkowitz had breakfast with former Kirkland partner Alexander Acosta, who would be his adversary in prosecuting the case.[13] At Kirkland & Ellis, Acosta had specialized in employment and labor issues, and Lefkowitz, a domestic policy adviser and special envoy to North Korea during the administration of George W. Bush, had specialized in litigation. More to the point, according to the website Above the Law, the two men had been good friends at Kirkland, which made Lefkowitz the perfect choice to lean on Acosta.[14]

On the face of it, Acosta had an extraordinarily powerful case against Epstein. It was based on depositions of dozens of girls telling essentially the same story about how they were groomed and recruited to be "sex slaves" to Epstein when some of them were as young as thirteen or fourteen years old.

"This is not a 'he said, she said' situation," Palm Beach police chief Michael Reiter told the *Miami Herald*.[15] After all, more than fifty girls all told essentially the same story.

But even with such a strong hand, Acosta essentially caved and gave Lefkowitz an astounding amount of latitude to write up a "non-prosecution agreement" for Epstein. Under its terms, Epstein would plead guilty to two prostitution counts and serve his sentence in the county jail.

Moreover, as part of the agreement, Epstein was allowed to leave jail for twelve hours a day, six days a week. In 2009, the deal was actually modified and made even more lenient, allowing Epstein to leave jail up to sixteen hours a day, seven days a week, including two hours a day at his Palm Beach mansion, where much of the abuse had taken place.[16] Epstein's regular visitors included Sarah Kellen and Nadia Marcinkova, who was widely said to have participated in sexual encounters as his "sex slave" with him and the underage girls she had recruited.

Whatever was going on, this was *not* hard time. Acosta had given new meaning to the term "sweetheart deal."

Even more astounding, the non-prosecution agreement granted immunity to Kellen and Marcinkova, who had been named as potential co-conspirators, and other co-conspirators both named and unnamed. That essentially killed the ongoing FBI investigation into other young women and girls who had been Epstein's victims. Clearly, Epstein's operation involved international sex trafficking on a huge scale, but Acosta had agreed to give it a pass. No investigation into pedophilia, sex slavery, or human trafficking. No investigation into Ghislaine Maxwell. And the same for Jean-Luc Brunel, and all the young women who had facilitated Epstein's operation. Dozens of other people were involved, but now they were all off the hook.

Bradley Edwards, an attorney representing two of Epstein's victims, described the deal as a "conspiracy between the government and Epstein" that was intended "to make the whole thing go away as quietly as possible. In never consulting with the victims, and keeping it secret, it showed that someone with money can buy his way out of anything."[17]

Finally, in apparent violation of a federal law, Acosta agreed that the terms of the non-prosecution deal itself should be sealed when it was approved by the judge, thereby preventing any chance for the victims to show up in court and object. No one would know—not even the victims who'd had the courage to come forward.

And in fact, it remained secret until it was first exposed by the *Miami Herald* reporter Julie K. Brown in November 2018.

————

So why did Alexander Acosta cave so easily? At a press conference on July 10, 2019, he said simply, "We did what we did because Epstein needed to go to jail."[18]

But journalist Vicky Ward, who wrote about Epstein for *Vanity Fair* (which declined to print her allegations about Epstein's relations with young girls), had a more intriguing explanation. According to Ward's story in the *Daily Beast*, in 2016, when Acosta was being interviewed by the Trump transition team, he was asked about Epstein and "explained breezily, apparently, that back in the day he'd had just one meeting on the Epstein case. He'd cut the non-prosecution deal with one of Epstein's attorneys because he had 'been told' to back off, that Epstein was above his pay grade."[19]

According to Ward, Acosta told the Trump team that he "was told Epstein 'belonged to intelligence' and to leave it alone." The Trump team apparently thought that was good enough, so they took him on as secretary of labor.

Of course, the assertion that Epstein "belonged to intelligence" raised far more questions than it answered. Which intelligence service? It seemed unlikely that Epstein would have been working for the CIA or FBI, unless he had been an FBI cooperator back in the eighties when he was running scams with Steven Hoffenberg. Or did this have something to do with relationships that dated back to the days when Epstein supposedly was working with Ghislaine's father, Robert Maxwell? Did Epstein have ties to Russian intelligence, as Maxwell had? What about the Israelis and his ties to Ehud Barak? Or were Epstein and, presumably, Ghislaine just keeping the kompromat around for the right moment when it would come in handy, or selling it to the highest bidder?

Similarly, Epstein's ties to intelligence became an issue in 2013 when he had a meeting with journalist Edward Jay Epstein, who asked him about his business and wrote about the episode in the *Mail on Sunday*, the British tabloid.

"I manage money for a few select clients," Epstein said.[20]

Ed pointed to photos on the wall of Epstein with Saudi prince Mohammed bin Salman and Emirati prince Mohammed bin Zayed, and Jeffrey allowed that some of them were.

"What about Russia?" Ed asked. "Any clients there?"

With that, Epstein just shrugged and said he often went to Moscow to see Vladimir Putin.

But no one ever knew if Epstein was telling the truth.

Those issues aside, the Epstein plea deal was the product of high-powered lawyers from Kirkland & Ellis working for both the prosecution and the defense. For one thing, in order to get such a deal approved, Acosta would have had to run it up the flagpole with the Department of Justice in Washington. However, at the time, in October 2007, Alberto Gonzales had just resigned as attorney general and had not yet been replaced. According to the *New York Daily News*, another Justice Department official who signed off on Epstein's non-prosecution deal was Mark Filip, who was then a senior official at the Justice Department and had shuttled back and forth between the DOJ and Kirkland & Ellis, where, at this writing, he is a partner.[21]

Kirkland & Ellis lawyers were everywhere.

Whether it was the Epstein case or various aspects of Trump's

Russia scandals and impeachment, many of the attorneys representing Trump were based in major white-shoe international law firms such as Kirkland & Ellis and Jones Day, whose clients, together, include billionaire Russian oligarchs and Russian money-laundering financial institutions such as Alfa Bank and Deutsche Bank, and whose attorneys have, during the Trump administration, amassed extraordinary power in such formidable bodies as the Southern District of New York, the Eastern District of New York, the FBI, the Department of Justice, and the US Supreme Court.

And dozens of them went on to hold powerful positions in the Trump administration. These would be Trump's enablers, the men—and they were almost all men—who facilitated Trump in dismantling the elaborate system of checks and balances that reined in authoritarianism, who gave Trump counsel during impeachment proceedings in 2019, who helped him implement the doctrine of the unitary executive, who tried to rewrite the history of the Trump-Russia saga as if it were a hoax, who blithely ignored subpoenas, and who abolished oversight by Congress and inspectors general at the drop of a hat.

Under Trump, norms were violated so frequently that conflicts of interest became the rule rather than the exception. The thieves and kleptocrats, or their lawyers, really, were in control.

Historically, there had been an invisible and inviolable firewall between the White House and the Department of Justice to ensure that the ruling party didn't use the criminal justice system for its own political agenda—or at least that was the norm. As a measure of the extent to which things had changed, during the Clinton administration only four people in the Clinton White House—the president, the vice president, the White House counsel, and the deputy White House counsel—were empowered to take part in discussions with the Justice Department regarding pending criminal investigations and criminal cases, and only three Justice Department officials were allowed to talk to the White House. But that changed dramatically under the aegis of White House adviser Karl Rove in the George W. Bush administration, when, according to Senator Sheldon Whitehouse (D-RI), 417 White House officials and at least 30 Justice Department officials were so empowered—a staggering increase that politicized the Justice Department as never before.[22]

Now, with Trump in command, the Justice Department was further transformed into an institution that embraced the most extreme interpretation of the unitary-executive doctrine imaginable by making the president truly above the law.

In the private sector, no firm played a bigger role in enabling Trump than Kirkland & Ellis. Trump's affinity with the firm began just two months after his inauguration when former Kirkland partner John Eisenberg, the top lawyer for the National Security Council, and his deputy, Michael Ellis, inappropriately shared classified intelligence files with House Intelligence Committee chairman Devin Nunes (R-CA).

At the time, the House Intelligence Committee was investigating Trump's ties to Russia, and the episode, while perfectly legal, was an early indication that when it came to overseeing Trump's transgressions, Nunes and other House Republicans were delighted to do Trump's bidding.

Two years later, in 2019, Eisenberg was still at it, in a key episode of the Trump-Ukraine scandal. In the famous July 25, 2019, phone call that led to his impeachment later that year—the "perfect phone call," as the president characterized it—Trump urged newly elected Ukrainian president Volodymyr Zelensky to announce investigations into his chief political rival Joe Biden and his son Hunter if he wanted to receive almost $400 million in previously approved military aid.

Specifically, Trump wanted Zelensky to investigate Burisma Holdings, a large Ukrainian natural gas company whose board members included Hunter Biden.

In effect, Trump was saying, If you won't help my campaign by drumming up a phony investigation against my opponent, I'll let the Russians do as they please. Given that Ukraine desperately needed the aid because it was at war with Russian troops occupying the eastern part of the country, Trump's demand was nothing less than an extortionate quid pro quo.

A number of White House aides were deeply disturbed by the phone call, and in an effort to make sure the Trump-Zelensky phone call stayed secret, Eisenberg ordered that a transcript of it be moved to a highly classified server. Eisenberg later was subpoenaed to testify before the House of Representatives but declined to appear on advice of counsel.[23]

The charges against Michael Ellis are even more damning. Citing the testimony of Lieutenant Colonel Alexander Vindman, Ryan Goodman in *Just Security* reported, "It was Ellis who came up with the idea of moving the memorandum of the phone call to the highly classified server. After the Ukraine call, Vindman and his brother (an ethics lawyer on the NSC) had an urgent meeting with Ellis and Eisenberg. Vindman testified that he told the lawyers that he thought what happened on the call was 'wrong,' that Ellis first raised the idea of placing the call summary into the highly classified system, and that Eisenberg as the senior official in the room signed off on the idea giving it 'the go-ahead.'"[24]

Of course, Kirkland & Ellis wasn't the only major firm sending multiple attorneys to the White House. Don McGahn, who served as White House counsel from Trump's 2017 inauguration until October 2018, was a partner at Jones Day, another enormous firm that, on Inauguration Day, issued a press release that thirteen of its lawyers were joining the Trump administration.[25]

Jones Day had represented at least ten major corporations and organizations close to Vladimir Putin, and as a result had a highly significant "oligarch practice" whose clients included Oleg Deripaska's Basic Element; the Alfa Group and Leonard Blavatnik's Access-Renova Group, which jointly own billions of dollars in oil and gas assets; Alfa Bank, the largest commercial bank in Russia; Letterone, a $30 billion holding company; Rosneft, one of the largest oil companies in the world; the Sapir Organization, which partnered with Trump to build Bayrock's Trump SoHo; and, of course, Donald Trump himself—not to mention the Trump 2016 and 2020 Presidential Campaign Committees, Trump for America, and certain Trump-related political action committees, as well as the Republican National Committee.[26]

As the *Washington Post* famously reported, Jared Kushner, the president's son-in-law, tried to set up a secret and secure back channel between the Trump team and the Kremlin.[27] But Jones Day had plenty to offer along those lines, all of which could take place under attorney–client privilege.

Consider that when Steven Brogan, the firm's powerful managing partner, sat down with Jones Day partner Don McGahn and Vladimir Lechtman, the head of Jones Day's Russia practice, he was talking to both Donald Trump's attorney and a man who, when it comes to Kremlin–White House affairs, is almost certainly the single most trusted corporate counsel to Putin's oligarchs, all of whom are completely beholden to Putin. Lechtman has been said to be one of the first bicultural corporate lawyers, a man who understands the way murder, bribery, and honey traps work in the former Soviet Union and also is familiar with its more civilized analogues in the West, like lobbying, campaign contributions, and the like. In any case, when Russia wanted to retaliate against US sanctions, those companies now had advocates deep inside the White House, advocates whose careers were tied to Jones Day or Kirkland & Ellis and had friends from the firm in the White House, the Justice Department, or other agencies.

Kirkland & Ellis attorneys helped grease the wheels for the Trump-Russia relationship, but in a different sector—the judiciary. One could see Kirkland partners start to flood into key positions in the administration starting in the last half of 2018.

On July 9, 2018, after consulting with the Federalist Society's Leonard Leo, Trump nominated former Kirkland partner Brett Kavanaugh, who had worked with Kirkland partner Ken Starr investigating and impeaching President Clinton, to the US Supreme Court. Two other Kirkland partners, Brian Benczkowski as head of the Department of Justice's criminal division and John Bolton as national security advisor, joined the administration. And that December, Kirkland partner Pat Cipollone replaced Don McGahn as White House counsel.

Benczkowski's appointment was unusual for two reasons. One was that he had never tried a single criminal case in his entire life, which made him an unlikely choice to oversee nearly seven hundred lifelong prosecutors. "This goes beyond an unqualified nominee," Senator Whitehouse said during Benczkowski's confirmation hearings. "This is a nominee exhibiting a flashing array of warnings that there may be mischief afoot here. No Senator should take this vote unaware of these obvious warnings. In the name of the integrity and independence of the Department of Justice, Senators should vote no because of the contamination risk Mr. Benczkowski poses, even if he were highly qualified for the post. . . . He may be the weakest candidate ever put forward to oversee the Criminal Division."[28]

Another issue that made Benczkowski suspect was that one of his clients at Kirkland was Alfa Bank. Alfa was especially sensitive in that two of its key figures, Mikhail Fridman and Petr Aven, were rich and powerful oligarchs, whose wealth and standing was entirely contingent upon acting in Vladimir Putin's interests.

In addition, Alfa was presumably being investigated by Special Counsel Robert Mueller for its mysterious communications with a special computer-network server in Trump Tower during the 2016 presidential campaign.[29] The relationship between the Trump server and the Russians was unclear, but journalist Franklin Foer reported in *Slate* that the link suggested that there may have been ongoing secret communications between the Trump campaign and the Russians.[30]

Regardless, the fact that the FBI was investigating the issue meant that any high-ranking Justice Department official who had been a beneficiary of Alfa's largesse would have a serious potential conflict of interest.[31] "We know from our correspondence with the [Justice] Department that the Russia/Trump collusion investigation is being run under DOJ procedures that require approval by the Criminal Division for a wide array of investigative and prosecutorial steps," Whitehouse explained. "That gives Benczkowski, if he is confirmed, not just a window into the Russia/Trump collusion investigation, but the ability to interfere."

Of course, those caveats did not sway Republicans, and on July 11, 2018, more than a year after he had been nominated, the GOP-controlled Senate voted to confirm Benczkowski 51–48 along a nearly straight party-line vote.

Which is exactly what happened again and again. By mid-2020, as the next presidential election approached, so many compromised attorneys had taken powerful positions among Trump's lawyers that it was as if Trump had created his very own Praetorian Guard.

Trump rued his appointment of Jeff Sessions as his first attorney general—largely because Sessions had recused himself from overseeing Robert Mueller's Trump-Russia probe because he had been on Trump's transition team. But that meant Trump could not count on Sessions to rein in the investigation. Now he made sure he was not going to make the same mistake twice. He wanted an attorney general who would do his bidding.

Enter Kirkland & Ellis partner William Barr, in his second stint as head of the Justice Department, and a host of other Kirkland attorneys. Kirkland senior partner Jeffrey Rosen came in as deputy attorney general. Steven Engel came in as assistant attorney general for the Office of Legal Counsel.[32] Kirkland's Robert Khuzami became deputy US attorney in the Southern District of New York, even though he had been general counsel at Deutsche Bank, which loaned Donald Trump more than $2 billion at a time when several of his businesses had filed for bankruptcy and no other Western bank would lend to him. (Deutsche Bank was also involved in a $10 billion Russian money-laundering scheme.)

Pat Cipollone had been a board member of the Opus Dei–affiliated Catholic Information Center, where Barr and Leo (a non-Kirkland attorney) had also been board members, as was Kirkland partner Thomas Yannucci, who had been the longtime chair of Kirkland's Firmwide Management Committee.

Similarly, Kirkland's Viet Dinh, who wasn't in the Trump administration, nonetheless played an extraordinarily powerful role as a close friend of Rupert Murdoch and his son Lachlan Murdoch, cochairman of News Corp. Dinh was godfather to one of Lachlan's children[33] and the chief legal and policy officer of Fox Corporation, a position that gave him real clout. "Lachlan has delegated much of the running of the company to Viet Dinh, a high-powered Republican lawyer without much experience in the media business, people who work with them said," the *New York Times* reported. "Mr. Dinh earned more than $24 million in salary and stock last year as the company's chief legal officer."[34]

These were Trump's lawyers—Kirkland, Kirkland, and Kirkland. And there were many more. Of course, Kirkland was so big, with more than 2,300 lawyers, that it would have been unusual if *none* of them ended up in the Trump administration. It would also be unlikely if none of them were involved in episodes that had the appearance of conflict of interest. In fact, according to the Trump Town database, coproduced by ProPublica and the Columbia School of Journalism, no fewer than two hundred former Kirkland & Ellis attorneys ended up in the Trump Justice Department.[35]

This was the start of a horrendously corrupt new calculus in the Justice Department. "There's extraordinary power within some of these law firms and the social connections they have," says Richard Painter, the chief White House ethics lawyer in the George W. Bush administration and a professor of law at the University of Minnesota. "And the restrictions against that revolving door through the private sector and the government are really very weak."[36]

Consider, too, that these were highly paid lawyers. According to *Bloomberg Law*, the average equity partner at Kirkland made more than $5 million in 2019, and it was not unheard of for the uppermost tier to top $10 million.[37] It paid Robert Khuzami $11.1 million for his work at the firm between late 2016 and early 2018, according to his financial filing.[38] And he was by no means the only partner in the eight-figure bracket.

So why then would Khuzami leave behind such handsome paychecks later that year to serve as deputy US attorney for a salary certain to be under $200,000? That's a 98 percent pay cut.

"That's the way it works in Washington," Painter told me.[39] "If your party gets in power and the executive branch, you are expected to go into the government, take the pay cut." Even though the firm can't explicitly promise that you can return, he said, it is understood implicitly that you can, and when you do, someone else from the firm will then go into government.

As for potential conflicts of interest, Trump ignored them. Since he first got into business, one of his strategies was simply to say, "So sue me." He had brought that tactic from his real estate empire into the White House, ignoring one subpoena after another and issuing countless waivers regarding ethical conflicts, knowing how easy it was to tie one's adversaries up in courts for years. There were loads of potential conflicts of interests with the Russians, thanks to Kirkland's representation of Alfa Bank, not to mention sanctioned oligarchs such as Petr Aven, Mikhail Fridman, and German Khan. For his part, Aven, in his interview with Mueller, said he had to report to Putin regularly. Kirkland's London office also represented Oleg Deripaska's En+ Group, a Russian energy and metals company that controls the world's largest independent hydropower generator, and Deripaska, of course, was very close to Putin.

If you were making millions of dollars from Putin's oligarchs, in effect you were representing Putin himself.

So when these Putin allies were pressing for sanction relief, they knew they would have friends in the Justice Department. This was the kind of Justice Department an autocrat would love—if he wanted to kill investigations into any dealings he'd had with Russia, any money laundering, secret communications, or the Epstein case, with Kirkland partners working on both sides of it. That was Ken Starr and Jay Lefkowitz, among others, for the defense, representing Epstein by making a super secret, super sweetheart deal with ex-Kirkland partner, US attorney, and prosecutor Alexander Acosta, which all but got Epstein off the hook, thereby enabling Kirkland to control huge amounts of potentially toxic material that Epstein and Ghislaine assembled as kompromat and that could be used in any number of ways—with various intelligence services—be they American, British, Russian, or Israeli, suppressing or merely hoarding damaging information and holding it over any number of powerful figures.

————

Which brings us back to Jeffrey Epstein, who had returned to New York after his sweetheart deal in 2008 and resumed the profligate lifestyle to which he was accustomed. But in the wake of the *Miami Herald*'s reporting, Epstein was arrested on July 6, 2019, when his private plane touched down at Teterboro Airport outside New York and charged with sex trafficking by the US attorney's office of the Southern

District of New York. Viewed as a flight risk, he was detained without bail at Metropolitan Correctional Center (MCC), the notorious and terrifying rat-infested New York jail, which had been at one time home to such notorious criminals as Mexican drug lord El Chapo, mob boss John Gotti, and fraudster Bernie Madoff. It was a striking counterpoint to the decadent and extravagant life Epstein had led.

Then, just over a month later, early in the morning of August 10, a prison guard at MCC went to check on Epstein and found him hanging in his cell, dead, surrounded by orange bed linens. The New York City medical examiner ruled that the cause of Epstein's death was suicide by hanging.

The anomalies in the events leading up to Epstein's death have been widely reported, but it is worth recalling that two weeks earlier, on July 23, Epstein had been found half-conscious in his cell. He claimed he had been assaulted by his cellmate, a muscle-bound ex-cop named Nicholas Tartaglione, who had been charged with four murders. Nonetheless, prison officials concluded it was a suicide attempt and put him on suicide watch.

Six days later, however, after a session with a prison psychiatrist, Epstein was taken off suicide watch and returned to his cell. On the day before his death, his cellmate was released from jail, leaving Epstein there as the sole prisoner in his cell, with two officers on watch who had been instructed to check on him every thirty minutes. However, the two guards allegedly falsified records and didn't check on him for eight hours—thereby violating the most basic operational aspect of their jobs. They were charged with conspiracy and record falsification.

When Epstein was found dead at about 6:30 a.m., they immediately rushed him to New York–Presbyterian Lower Manhattan Hospital, in the process once again violating protocol that dictates suicides should be treated with the "same level of protection as any crime scene in which a death has occurred."[40] To make matters worse, prison personnel failed to photograph Epstein's body as it was found.

All of which leaves many unanswered questions. Why on earth would they put the high-profile, high-value prisoner they had in the same cell with a man accused of a quadruple murder? Why had Epstein been taken off suicide watch? Why had he been left alone without a cellmate, especially given such overcrowded conditions at the prison? Given those circumstances, and the fact that Epstein was one of the most notorious inmates in the nation, how is that the two guards just happened to leave him unattended? Why were so many bedsheets in his cell—another violation of protocol? And what about surveillance? Was it just another coincidence that the two surveillance cameras looking into Epstein's cell happened to malfunction during this period?

One surveillance camera outside his cell was working, but, according to federal prosecutors, the video was permanently deleted, apparently because MCC officials mistakenly saved video from a different floor.

Attorney General William Barr described the events leading up to Epstein's death as "a perfect storm of screw-ups."

But others raised the question of murder. Epstein's lawyer David Schoen, who met with Epstein just a few days before his death, said he believed his client did not die by suicide. "The reason I say I don't believe it was suicide is for my interaction with him that day," Schoen told Fox News.[41] Epstein was described as "upbeat and excited."

The mystery of Epstein's death became presidential fodder nearly a year later, in July 2020, just after Ghislaine Maxwell was finally arrested and President Trump wished her well, making good use of the tough guy syntax of a mob boss making a not-so-veiled threat. During an interview with news program *Axios on HBO*, Trump was reminded that Maxwell had been arrested on charges of child sex trafficking and was asked why he wished her well.

The unspoken context, of course, was that many people wondered if Epstein would "flip" and tell who he had kompromat on—heads of state, Wall Street billionaires, or even Donald Trump, but he had ended up dead under mysterious circumstances.

"Her friend or boyfriend [Epstein] was either killed or committed suicide," he replied. "She's now in jail. Yeah, I wish her well. I'd wish you well. I'd wish a lot of people well. Good luck. Let them prove somebody was guilty."

Trump repeated that Epstein was killed three times in the interview. As for the facts behind Epstein's death, former New York chief medical examiner Michael Baden, who was retained by Mark Epstein, Jeffrey's brother, to attend the autopsy and give a report, found other anomalies—most notably three fractured bones in his neck that were more consistent with "homicidal strangulation" than with suicide.

"Going over a thousand jail hangings, suicides in the New York City state prisons over the past forty to fifty years, no one had three fractures," Baden told *60 Minutes*.[42]

Other experts disagreed with that analysis. And although he felt homicide was the more likely cause of death, even Baden stopped short of being conclusive. For that, he awaited more evidence, but that was being withheld pending an ongoing Justice Department investigation against the two guards who had left their posts.

All of which left the Epstein matter—or what remained of it—in the hands of William Barr, who promptly dismissed it as a suicide and "some irregularities at the [Metropolitan Correctional Center]."

But that wasn't the end. On the morning of Epstein's death, thousands of previously sealed documents from a lawsuit filed by Virginia Giuffre against Ghislaine Maxwell were released online, including depositions, police reports, flight logs, photos, and other materials.

However, that was only the tip of the iceberg. Far more damaging material was hidden away. Who knew what secrets were still concealed? Epstein had been silenced. Others may have had kompromat—the pimps, the girls who scheduled Epstein's "massages," Ghislaine, John Mark Dougan, and others—but most of them were lying low.

And there was always the age-old question, Cui bono? Who benefits? Certainly, Epstein's high-profile friends—those who had indulged in sexual activities that he handed out like party favors—could breathe easier. And one had to wonder whether that included Donald Trump. After all, in an indiscreet moment, Epstein had shown photos of Trump with young girls to a friend.

That left law enforcement authorities at the FBI, the Justice Department, and US attorneys offices in Florida and New York, who had been investigating Epstein for years. All of which led to one inescapable conclusion: William Barr was in charge.

CHAPTER SEVENTEEN

BARR JUSTICE

Among all the key figures in Trump's Praetorian Guard, no one loomed larger than William Barr. No one was more effective in counteracting the complex web of checks and balances that reined in the powers of the presidency. No one was better at negating and eliminating oversight of the executive branch, not just by Congress but also by inspectors general in one bureaucracy after another. In short, no one played a bigger role in opening the floodgates to allow a narcissistic, sociopathic autocrat who was a Russian asset to bring US democracy to the brink.

Aside from a deep ideological commitment to the principle of the unitary executive, Barr's motives puzzled many, but religion may have been a factor. As Peter Steinfels, a former *New York Times* religion columnist and codirector of the Fordham Center on Religion and Culture, explained in an email to me, the authoritarian theology of Opus Dei and other institutions on the Catholic right has a considerable amount in common with the ideology of Barr and his associates. One calls for blind obedience to the catechism, the other to the president.

"Opus Dei's structure is definitely top-down, controlled by a clerical leadership, not conducive to internal debate, and hostile to secular modernity," Steinfels wrote. He added that this suggests an affinity between Opus Dei, Barr's interpretation of the doctrine of the unitary executive, and "his broader jeremiads on the dangers of secularism."[1]

Colonel Lawrence Wilkerson, former chief of staff to Secretary of State Colin Powell, addressed the question of Opus Dei's role in the Trump administration on the *Background Briefing with Ian Masters* radio show, asserting that the "Opus Dei Catholics were there, first and foremost, to reverse *Roe v. Wade*. . . . They believe everyone should be Catholic by the way, that a kind of authoritarianism, a kind of tyranny, is what's necessary to get this country back in order again. And what do they mean by 'back in order again'? They mean white, male, with the wife following along behind as the Bible says she should, and basically rich elite. That's what they mean."[2]

In the end, Barr's religious zealotry led him to go so far as to call for the end of secular democracy, to call for it to be replaced by God's law, and to develop his theory of the unitary executive as a blueprint for an autocratic presidency in which Donald Trump would have virtually dictatorial powers. In October 2019, Barr told students at Notre Dame Law School how he really felt about "militant secularists" and "so-called progressives" who were doing everything they possibly could to destroy American society and create crises as part of their war against religion. "This is not decay," Barr said, in his assault on America's popular culture. "This is organized destruction. Secularists and their allies among the 'progressives' have marshaled all the forces of mass communications, popular culture, the entertainment industry, and academia in an unremitting assault on religion and traditional values.[3]

"Virtually every measure of social pathology continues to gain ground," he claimed. "Along with the wreckage of the family, we are seeing record levels of depression and mental illness, dispirited young people, soaring suicide rates, increasing numbers of alienated young males, an increase in senseless violence and the deadly drug epidemic." He charged that the government was trying to keep parents from "passing on of the faith" to their children and added that "for the government to interfere in that process is a monstrous invasion of religious liberty."

As Joan Walsh observed in the *Nation*, this was "scary shit."[4]

The speech closely resembled one Barr gave twenty-seven years earlier, on October 6, 1992, to the Catholic League for Religious and Civil Rights, in which Barr went so far as to call for the imposition of "God's law," because "to the extent that a society's moral culture is based on God's law, it will guide men toward the best possible life.

"There is a battle going on that will decide who we are as a people," he added, and he made clear the enemy in that battle were "modern secularists."[5]

At the time, you may recall, one of Barr's speechwriters was John Paul Wauck, more recently known as Father John, the Opus Dei priest who became a professor at the Pontifical University of the Holy Cross in the Vatican. In a series of emails, he first distanced himself from the speech, and then wrote to me again. "I didn't mean to give the impression that I had nothing 1992 [sic] to do with them; I just don't remember them."

Then he suggested that Barr's attack on secularists was not very Opus Dei–like. "Within Opus Dei—in the writings of St. Josemaría [the founder of Opus Dei], for instance—'secularity' is generally a positive thing."

Wauck, however, neglected to mention that when St. Josemaría Escrivá spoke so warmly of "secularity," he was speaking of Generalissimo Francisco Franco's fascist Spain, in which Opus Dei had an enormously powerful role in overseeing the judiciary.

When it came to Russia, however, Barr, too, had Russian ties. In his financial disclosure report, Barr noted that he received between $5,001 and $15,000 in dividends from the Vector Group, a company that had strong links to Russia and whose president, Howard Lorber, accompanied Trump on a 1996 trip to Moscow that attempted to get a Trump Tower Moscow project under way.[6]

Similarly, Barr held between $100,000 and $250,000 in assets in Deutsche Bank.[7] In 2018, he resigned from the board of Och-Ziff Capital Management, whose management had run afoul of the Kremlin. And, of course, he was counsel at Kirkland & Ellis, which handled Russia's Alfa Bank.

When it came to overseeing issues relating to Trump's ties to Russia, these ties represented potential conflicts of interest. "The legal standard is really clear about these issues. It's not about actual conflict, it's about the appearance of a conflict, about the appearance of bias," Jed Shugerman, a professor at Fordham University's School of Law and an expert on judicial and government ethics, told *Newsweek*.[8] "The problem is that we have so many flagrant conflicts that are so obvious, we get distracted from what the legal standard is."

That said, Barr came to Trump's defense early on in his administration, starting on May 12, 2017, just five months into Trump's presidency, when he wrote an op-ed for the *Washington Post* defending Trump's firing of FBI director James Comey. At the time Comey was dismissed, he was overseeing the ongoing FBI investigation into Trump's ties to Russia, and Barr baldly asserted that "Comey's removal simply has no relevance to the integrity of the Russian investigation as it moves ahead."[9]

If the op-ed did not suffice in currying favor with President Trump, Barr took a bigger step thirteen months later. As his firing of Comey showed, Trump desperately wanted to have one of his allies in control. After Comey was fired, Deputy Attorney General Rod J. Rosenstein appointed Robert Mueller to be special counsel investigating Trump's links to Russia. And Trump was now displeased with Attorney General Jeff Sessions, who had recused himself from overseeing the Trump-Russia probe.

On June 8, 2018, Barr offered up a nineteen-page memo addressed to Rosenstein that was widely seen as a way of auditioning to be Sessions's replacement. Even though Mueller was a close friend, and the Muellers had been guests at the weddings of Barr's daughters, Barr held back nothing and assailed Mueller's theory of obstruction of justice as being "premised on a novel and legally insupportable reading of the law." Barr added, "Moreover, in my view, if credited by the Department, it would have grave consequences far beyond the immediate confines of this case and would do lasting damage to the presidency and to the administration of law within the executive branch."[10]

Specifically, Barr argued that Trump, as president, had the power to hire and fire FBI director Comey, and even if doing so was an attempt to obstruct the investigation, Mueller should not be allowed to investigate the Comey firing, because to do so would limit the president's authority over government agencies. "Apart from whether Mueller [has] a strong enough factual basis for doing so, Mueller's obstruction theory is fatally misconceived," Barr wrote.

This was the theory of the unitary executive again—this time on steroids. "The unitary executive idea is an important idea within our constitutional framework, but it does not justify the sort of absolute control over every conceivable action taken by anyone in the executive branch that Barr's interpretation would give it," said Donald Ayer, who served in the George H. W. Bush Justice Department as deputy attorney general in 1989 and 1990.[11]

According to Ayer, back when Barr was in the Office of Legal Counsel under President Bush, he pushed many of the same ideas he is pushing today. "The big difference," Ayer told me, "is that as head of the OLC and then as attorney general under Bush, Barr didn't have the ability to implement his idea of an autocratic president who has essentially unrestricted powers because George H. W. Bush didn't aspire to be an autocratic president. So Barr couldn't do that. Whereas today we have a president who, we all know, wants to be able to do anything he wants, and Barr is busily engaged in advancing the cause."

Donald Trump, of course, was not one for reading nineteen-page memos. But the bottom line was that Barr believed that the president should have a vast array of powers and that if the president wanted to do something, by and large it would be legal. It went without saying that Donald Trump would appreciate that position.

———

On December 5, 2018, while waiting in line for a shuttle bus to go to George H. W. Bush's funeral at the National Cathedral, William Barr ran into his old mentor, C. Boyden Gray.[12] Gray, you may recall, oversaw Barr's hiring in the Office of Legislative Counsel in the Bush Justice Department. According to the New York Times, Gray knew that Barr's name was in the mix to succeed Jeff Sessions as attorney general, but he didn't know the details. The two men spent much of the day together, but Barr never let on that the decision had been made. His appointment became public the next day.

By the time the Mueller Report was released, Barr had replaced Jeff Sessions as attorney general and was finally in a position to give Trump the far-ranging powers he sought. With his ferociously Manichaean approach to scandals and lawsuits—deny, deny, deny, and attack, attack, attack—Roy Cohn had epitomized the archetype Trump sought in a wartime consigliere. He had done it so well that even more than thirty years after Cohn's death, Trump, a president who was deeply angered by Sessions's refusal to tamp down the Mueller investigation, was known to shout, "Where's my Roy Cohn?," a plaintive cry that so perfectly crystallized Trump's dilemma that it became the title for a 2019 documentary movie.

Now, in William Barr, Trump had found his new Roy Cohn. As Trump's presidency devolved into authoritarianism, liberals were arguing that US institutions were strong and that the rule of law would prevail. What Barr did belied all that.

America was just starting to enter a period in which a cascading series of historic events, each one of which in ordinary times would have been monumental enough to define an era, began to take place—before being lost in the growing mountain of crises engulfing the country.

Was former national security advisor Michael Flynn a traitor in his dealings with the Russians? Did Trump pay hush money to a porn star? Was Trump crony Roger Stone in touch with Julian Assange, and was Assange's WikiLeaks a proxy for Russia in releasing Hillary Clinton's emails? Had Jared Kushner set up back channels to Russia? Was Trump campaign manager Paul Manafort a Russian spy? How big a role did Russia play in installing Trump as president? Why was Trump sharing intelligence with Russia? Was Trump's firing of Comey an attempt to obstruct justice? How could the Republicans have an impeachment trial and not call a single witness? Indeed, the Senate Intelligence Committee Report, which was not released until August 2020, made it clear that even in the Republican-controlled Senate, Trump's loyal supporters were well aware of his treachery.

Beginning in 2017, when Republicans held the White House and both houses of Congress, Special Counsel Robert Mueller, with his lantern jaw and by-the-books G-man demeanor, became the last best hope of the enfeebled Democrats. As such, they had designated him to be their knight in shining armor, riding in on his white steed to save the day.

But that's not what happened. Since his first term as attorney general under George H. W. Bush, Barr had been out of the limelight for more than twenty-five years, and the intensity of his radical, hard-line positions, the way he had covered up and swept under the rug the Bank of Credit and Commerce International, Iran-Contra, Iraqgate, and Inslaw scandals, had largely been forgotten. Few Americans knew or cared about the doctrine of the unitary executive. Mueller had run an airtight investigation without a single leak—this while the Trump administration was leaking like a sieve. As a result, the entire country was on tenterhooks, awaiting the results of Mueller's two-year investigation.

It began with Barr's presentation of it on March 24, 2019, which may go down as one of the most artfully deceptive and effective undertakings in the history of spin control. In this masterpiece of disinformation, Barr completely stole Mueller's thunder, misrepresented it, and presented Trump forces with a victory they used to label the entire Trump-Russia scandal a hoax.

The Mueller Report failed in many respects—but not completely. Its 448 pages contain a number of explosive revelations, especially in terms of obstruction of justice. It disclosed at least ten episodes in which the president appeared to be obstructing justice, including trying to stop the investigation into former national security advisor Michael Flynn; Trump's reaction to the appointment of Mueller as special prosecutor ("Oh my god. This is terrible. This is the end of my Presidency. I'm fucked"); and the events surrounding the firing of FBI director Comey. There were also Trump's multiple efforts to fire Mueller as a way of shutting down the probe, principally through White House counsel Don McGahn, who refused—knowing that to do so would provide fodder for impeachment. As the report put it, "The President's efforts to influence the investigation were mostly unsuccessful, but that is largely because the persons who surrounded the President declined to carry out orders or accede to his requests."[13]

Even though Mueller had uncovered ample evidence of obstruction of justice, he declined to indict the president and cited a memo from the Justice Department's Office of Legal Counsel, which ruled that a sitting president could not be indicted. And if no charges were brought against Trump, the Mueller Report said, asserting that Trump had committed crimes would be unfair because he would have "no such adversarial opportunity for public name-clearing before an impartial adjudicator."

At the same time, Mueller did not exonerate Trump and wrote that if his team "had confidence after a thorough investigation of the facts that the President clearly did not commit obstruction of justice, we would so state." They did not.

When it came to a conspiracy to sway the election, Mueller dissected the role WikiLeaks played with Russian military intelligence in releasing the Democrats' emails that had been hacked.

The report noted "that the Russian government perceived it would benefit from a Trump presidency and worked to secure that outcome, and that the Campaign expected it would benefit electorally from information stolen and released through Russian efforts." But it added that "the investigation did not establish that members of the Trump Campaign conspired or coordinated with the Russian government in its election interference activities."

According to a piece by Jeffrey Toobin in the *New Yorker*, throughout the investigation, Mueller was directed by the Justice Department to confine his probe "to individuals who were reasonably suspected of committing crimes."[14]

"I love Ken Starr," Rosenstein told Mueller, according to people present who spoke with Toobin. "But his investigation was a fishing expedition. Don't do that. This is a criminal investigation. Do your job, and then shut it down."

"A fishing expedition." That was a key Republican talking point. Going after Trump's ties to Russia was a "fishing expedition."

And yet, in the beginning, Rosenstein had very different marching orders for Mueller that were spelled out simply on one page of the deputy attorney general's stationery under the heading "ORDER NO. 3915-2017 APPOINTMENT OF SPECIAL COUNSEL TO INVESTI-

GATE RUSSIAN INTERFERENCE WITH THE 2016 PRESIDEN-
TIAL ELECTION AND RELATED MATTERS."

The document was signed by Rosenstein and dated May 17, 2017. It
authorized Mueller to serve as special counsel "to conduct the investigation confirmed by then-FBI Director James B. Comey in testimony
before the House Permanent Select Committee on Intelligence on
March 20, 2017."

The rest of the wording was somewhat vague and unclear, perhaps,
but it said Mueller's mandate was to investigate national security
issues—specifically "any links and/or coordination between the Russian government and individuals associated with the campaign of
Donald Trump."[15]

The mandate goes on to authorize Mueller "to prosecute federal
crimes arising from the investigation of these matters." So to some
extent, it is a criminal investigation. But that was a by-product of its
primary goal: a counterintelligence operation, which, as we know, was
buried or never even took place.

As Representative Adam Schiff (D-CA), chairman of the House
Intelligence Committee, later told the *Washington Post*, "This all began
as an FBI counterintelligence investigation into whether people around
then-candidate Trump were acting as witting or unwitting agents of a
foreign power. So it began as a counterintelligence investigation, not as
a criminal investigation."[16]

In other words, the Justice Department was pulling a bait and switch
on the American people, and that meant Trump had been successful in
shutting down the intelligence probe. In a March 27, 2019, letter to Attorney General Barr, Deputy Attorney General Rosenstein, and FBI
director Christopher Wray, requesting access to Robert Mueller's "findings, and, underlying evidence, and documents," both Schiff and Congressman Devin Nunes, the ranking Republican on the Intelligence
Committee, clearly specify that the "Special Counsel's investigation
originated with the Federal Bureau of Investigation ('Bureau') as a
counterintelligence probe."

But their requests were never answered. This was no minor detail. That's because a successful intelligence operation could inflict

enormous damage on US national security without necessarily breaking the law.

So if you made millions of dollars from dealing with Russian oligarchs, good for you. Chances are it was perfectly legal. On the other hand, if you were president, it meant you were completely compromised.

"It may not be a crime for a candidate for a president to seek to make money from a hostile foreign power during an election and mislead the country about it," Schiff said. "But the counterintelligence concerns go beyond mere violation of criminal law. They're at one time not necessarily a criminal activity and at the same time potentially far more serious than criminal activity, because you have the capacity to warp U.S. policy owing to some form of compromise."[17]

It was perfectly legal, for example, for Trump to buy hundreds of television sets from an electronics store in lower Manhattan, as he did some forty years ago. And if the store is owned by a KGB "spotter" agent who is looking for new assets, that may still be legal—but it is grounds for a very serious counterintelligence investigation.

Similarly, it's perfectly legal to take out full-page ads in the *Washington Post*, *New York Times*, and *Boston Globe* putting forth unconventional foreign policy talking points, even if they happen to have been crafted by the KGB. And it's legal to sell multimillion-dollar condominiums to Russians through anonymous shell companies, to get $3 billion loans through Deutsche Bank when you've filed for bankruptcy multiple times, and to reap billions from partnerships with oligarchs who are in Putin's pocket. But if Trump is effectively bailed out of bankruptcy by the Russians and made a billionaire again, isn't he somehow compromised by that?

Throughout the probe, however, Mueller was repeatedly steered toward confining his investigation narrowly to the criminal sphere. In addition, he declined to probe Trump's finances, which might have revealed the extent to which Trump relied on Russia in extricating himself from multiple bankruptcies.

Finally, even when Trump stepped over the line of legality, it was very hard to prove, because one had to prove Trump's state of mind, one had to prove that he *knew* he was laundering Russian money, that he *knew* that the money came from illicit sources, that he *knew* the talking points in his newspaper ads had come from the KGB, and so forth.

But at Barr's presentation in March, all that was off the table. No counterintelligence. The Mueller Report had concluded that "the investigation established that the Russian government perceived it would benefit from a Trump presidency and worked to secure that outcome, and that the Campaign expected it would benefit electorally from information stolen and released through Russian efforts."

Barr, however, omitted that passage and instead quoted the one in which Mueller said that "the investigation did not establish that members of the Trump Campaign conspired or coordinated with the Russian government in its election interference activities."

Similarly, Barr opined that "the evidence now suggests that the accusations against [Trump] were false." But that was not what Mueller wrote. Instead, the report said, "The first volume of the report details numerous efforts emanating from Russia to influence the election. This volume includes a discussion of the Trump campaign's response to this activity as well as our conclusion that there was insufficient evidence to charge a broader conspiracy."

And so it went, one misrepresentation after another. Later, on *Just Security*, Ryan Goodman published a side-by-side comparison of Barr's statements with Mueller's. Barr: "The accusations against [Trump] were false. . . . There was in fact no collusion." Mueller: "There was insufficient evidence to charge a broader conspiracy."[18]

Barr: "Special counsel Mueller did not indicate that his purpose was to leave the decision [to indict] to Congress." Mueller: "The [Justice Department's Office of Legal Counsel] opinion says that the Constitution requires a process other than the criminal justice system to formally accuse a sitting President of wrongdoing."

And on it went. Clearly, Barr had lied, and in doing so he had been terribly effective. His words sounded exculpatory, they were widely disseminated, and because Barr did not allow the release of the Mueller Report—and a redacted version of it at that—until nearly a month later, for many Americans it was now official: Trump had done nothing wrong. He was exonerated.

All of which gave Donald Trump and Fox News and the right-wing echo chamber license to tweet and shout that the whole thing had been a hoax. Trump-Russia had been nothing more than "fake news!"

Stunningly, the Senate Intelligence Committee Report put the lie to such misrepresentations by explicating at length the story of Trump campaign manager Paul Manafort and his longtime ties with Konstantin Kilimnik, a Russian intelligence officer; Roger Stone's communications with WikiLeaks; and the fact that Natalia Veselnitskaya, a Russian lawyer who met with Trump campaign officials in June 2016, had much closer ties to Russian intelligence than had been reported. But by then, for millions of Americans, the die had already been cast.

———

What had taken place was extraordinary, not just because Robert Mueller fans were so sorely disappointed, but also because William Barr had just begun. In May 2019, President Trump said that he thought Joe Biden and his son Hunter should be investigated and it would be appropriate for him to discuss it with William Barr to get such an investigation under way. Biden, of course, was Trump's likely rival in the 2020 election. What better way to get the campaign started than to have the attorney general discredit your adversary?

Meanwhile, on May 13, Barr had already begun rewriting history for Trump. When he appeared on Fox News, being interviewed by devoted Trump supporter Laura Ingraham, Barr was especially in his element. "What happened to him [Trump] was one of the greatest travesties in American history," he said. "Without any basis they started this investigation of his campaign. And even more concerning, actually, is what happened after the campaign, a whole pattern of events . . . to sabotage the presidency."

Having already asserted that Trump had been wrongfully accused, Barr now raised the question of whether federal agents had abused their authority in their investigation. "I think spying did occur," he told a Senate panel. "The question is whether it was adequately predicated. And I'm not suggesting that it wasn't adequately predicated. But I need to explore that."

To that end, Barr assigned the top federal prosecutor in Connecticut, John Durham, the task of discovering if there was a conspiracy among those investigating Trump to harm his political prospects.[19] In addition, Trump granted Barr an enormous range of new powers including "full and complete authority" to declassify government secrets about the Russia investigation. Trump had labeled the probe a "political witch hunt," and now Barr was doing his bidding to write that into the history books.

Equally disturbing, by granting Barr new powers, Trump was entering dangerous territory. "Stripping the intelligence leaders of their ability to control information about sources and methods, and handing that power to political actors, could cause human agents to question whether their identity will be protected," Jeremy Bash, a former CIA chief of staff during the Obama administration, told the *Washington Post*.[20]

In June, Barr widened the scope of his investigation. He began interviewing high-level CIA officers. He took on a bigger and bigger role in erasing the damage from the Trump-Russia probe and in fabricating a new history in which Trump was the victim of rogue liberals in the FBI who had conjured up a phony scandal to smear Trump in the fake news media. Trump's tweets were endless, calling it a "witch hunt," a "hoax," and "fake news."

When necessary, Barr came to the rescue of Trump aides such as Paul Manafort, making sure the former Trump campaign manager did not suffer the indignity of being sent to the notoriously harsh and violent New York prison complex on Rikers Island. Manafort, who deposited $75 million in offshore accounts he got from carrying water for Vladimir Putin in Ukraine, had been sentenced to a seven-and-a-half-year sentence for tax and bank fraud. (In May 2020, Manafort was released to home confinement in view of concerns about the COVID-19 pandemic.)

Meanwhile, Barr continued his campaign to negate any evidence there had been compromising ties between Trump and Russia, to characterize the investigators in the FBI as highly partisan rogue liberals who were using their positions as political weapons, to discredit the media that had printed the stories as fake news—to find, create, and, if necessary, invent a new narrative, a new reality in which Trump was a martyr, a victim of a "deep state" that was filled with liberals out to get him.

To that end, on October 1, 2019, as impeachment hearings heated up, bringing forth more and more damning information against Trump, Barr took off for London to meet with British intelligence in hopes of finding anything that would discredit reports showing that Russia had interfered on Trump's behalf in the 2016 presidential election. As one British official told the UK's *Independent*, Barr's wish list "is like nothing we have come across before, they are basically asking, in quite robust terms, for help in doing a hatchet job on their own intelligence services."[21]

In rapid succession, there was the impeachment of Trump; followed by a phony Senate acquittal in which there were no witnesses; a raging pandemic that the administration had neither the competence nor the will nor the desire nor the common sense to control; and a powerful mass movement for racial justice, which the administration insistently opposed. News cycles could be measured in nanoseconds. Historic events—impeachment!—quickly faded from memory, buried in mountains of earth-shattering news.

On the afternoon of Monday, June 1, 2020, at 6:04 p.m., the White House communications office sent out an alert to reporters that President Trump would hold a news briefing eleven minutes hence in the Rose Garden.

Spontaneous, out-of-the-blue press conferences were unusual under Trump, but now he needed to speak to the nation. Six days earlier, on May 25, in Minneapolis, Minnesota, George Floyd, a forty-six-year-old black man, had been killed by a white police officer who coolly kept one hand in his pocket as he forced his knee down on Floyd's neck for eight minutes and forty-six seconds. At the time, Floyd was handcuffed, on the ground, and pleading for his life, and his casual but brutal murder was captured on video for all the world to see, instantly igniting hundreds of massive, largely peaceful demonstrations in all fifty states and in other cities all over the world. All because Floyd was suspected of passing a counterfeit twenty-dollar bill.

The murder of George Floyd and the demonstrations that followed happened at a time when the Trump administration was already coming apart at the seams.

With more than four hundred Trump officials having resigned or been dismissed by this time, the administration was a revolving door, and such episodes were too numerous to keep track of. Top cabinet posts—including the secretaries of the Departments of Defense, State, Health and Human Services, Energy, and Homeland Security—were at various times filled by "acting" secretaries whose status did not require that they be approved by the Senate, thereby obviating congressional oversight.

After William Barr had become Donald Trump's attorney general, he immediately became a one-man wrecking ball in service to allowing Trump to fully enjoy the vast scope of powers afforded by Barr's expansive views of the unitary executive.

And, of course, there was Trump's catastrophic management of the COVID-19 pandemic that appeared to be deliberately structured so as to make sure as many Americans died as possible. Even before the virus hit, the Trump administration had dismantled the global health team on the National Security Council and repeatedly dismissed dire warnings from the secretary of Health and Human Services, the Council of Economic Advisers, and the nation's intelligence services. "The Coronavirus is very much under control in the USA," he tweeted on February 24, after the virus had hit US shores. "Stock Market starting to look very good to me!"

This, seventeen days after he had already told journalist Bob Woodward that the coronavirus was far more deadly than the flu.

Trump, of course, explained the discrepancy between his public dismissal of the COVID threat and his taped interview with Woodward by asserting that he didn't want the entire country to panic. But the truth was more political. Increasingly desperate about his reelection chances, Trump cast his political fortunes as the victim of the disease, proclaiming at a campaign rally in South Carolina,

"The Democrats are politicizing the coronavirus. . . . This is their new hoax."

As if hundreds of thousands of people dying were a hoax.

Meanwhile, as the deadly virus rapidly spread throughout the country, instead of forging a coherent national response to the crisis, Trump put the responsibility on the plate of the nation's fifty governors. He flaunted his refusal to follow his own administration's guidelines by rarely wearing a mask, and transformed a relatively effective and benign safety precaution into a potent weapon in the culture wars, in which mask-wearing citizens were disparaged as politically correct. Trump falsely claimed a vaccine would soon be available. He touted dangerous and bizarre alternative health measures: Taking hydroxychloroquine! Putting powerful ultraviolet lights inside your body! Ingesting disinfectants to kill the virus.

Trump even blamed the high incidence of cases in the United States on testing itself. "If we stop testing right now," he said, "we'd have very few cases, if any."

As if being deliberately oblivious to the virus would somehow make it disappear.

Now Trump had a plan that he hoped would reverse his political woes, and his trusted attorney general William Barr would play a key part in it.

———

By the time of Trump's June 1 news briefing, one hundred thousand Americans had died, the economy was in free fall, forty million had lost their jobs, and even more had been housebound for weeks, if not months. With the presidential election just five months away, Trump had already begun dropping in the polls.

And now, on top of all that, came massive demonstrations across the country—regarding another issue that Trump was equally ill-suited to handle. Asked why he thought so many people were demonstrating, Trump's response to a Fox newscaster consisted largely of an incoherent word salad. "Protesters for different reasons," he said. "You're protesting also because, you know, they just didn't know. I've watch—I watched very closely. Why are you here? They really weren't able to say, but they were there for a reason, perhaps."

For the most part, the demonstrations were peaceful, but they had erupted in at least 140 cities, and according to the *New York Times*, at least five people had died in the protests.[22] So rather than deal with racism and police brutality, Trump focused on the very few acts of disorder, tweeting, "The United States will be designating ANTIFA as a terrorist organization."

That, even though ANTIFA was not really an organization. "Antifa," short for "antifascists," refers to a left-wing ideology that resists neo-Nazis and white supremacists. It has been falsely portrayed as a single organization, rather than a movement, by right-wing activists and Trump officials, and there have been frequent attempts to discredit it via false-flag attacks from right-wing adversaries.

Earlier that day, White House press secretary Kayleigh McEnany had added fuel to the fire by telling reporters, "The President has made clear that what we are seeing on America's streets is unacceptable. Violence, looting, anarchy, lawlessness are not to be tolerated, plain and simple. These criminal acts are not protest. They are not statements. These are crimes that harm innocent American citizens."

Then McEnany raised the ominous specter that Trump would deploy the vast resources of the military to take up arms against American citizens. "There will be additional federal assets deployed across the nation," she said.[23] "There will be a central command center, in conjunction with the state and local governments. That will include [Chairman of the Joint Chiefs of Staff] General [Mark] Milley, Secretary [of Defense Mark] Esper, and AG Barr."

McEnany declined to further specify exactly what was taking place. Nor did she mention another major event in Trump's schedule that day—namely the phone conversation he'd had with Vladimir Putin. According to Putin's office, the call was initiated by Donald Trump.[24] The two men discussed the successful launch of the SpaceX rocket that week, and Trump repeated his invitation to Putin to attend the G7 conference in September, a move that was widely disapproved of by other members of the group.[25]

There is no evidence that Trump discussed with Putin his latest woes regarding ongoing nationwide protests, but Trump nonetheless prepared a ferocious Putinesque response. He was furious about the demonstrations and angry that the National Guard had not yet been deployed in Washington. During his brief announcement, Trump said that he was "your president of law-and-order" and "an ally of all peaceful protesters," but he asserted that the demonstrations "are not acts of peaceful protests. These are acts of domestic terror. The destruction of innocent life, and the spilling of innocent blood, is an offense to humanity and a crime against God."

In general, the law forbids using the military as a domestic police force, thanks to the Posse Comitatus Act, which gives state governments the authority to keep order within their borders. But Trump, without citing its name, was essentially invoking a rarely used law called the Insurrection Act of 1807. It was originally signed by Thomas Jefferson to halt a plot by Aaron Burr; it allows the president to deploy US military troops within the United States and had not been cited since 1992, when riots broke out in Los Angeles after the acquittal of four white police officers charged with using excess force in the beating of Rodney King, an unarmed African American. At the time, William Barr was serving as attorney general under George H. W. Bush.[26]

"If a city or state refuses to take the actions necessary to defend the life and property of their residents, then I will deploy the United States military," Trump said.

"Thank you very much," he concluded. "And now I'm going to pay my respects to a very, very special place." His remarks lasted less than seven minutes—roughly two minutes less than the time it took the officer to kill George Floyd.

———

The "very, very special place" to which Trump was referring was Saint John's Episcopal Church, across Lafayette Square, a seven-acre park north of the White House. Because it had been damaged by vandalism and fire during the demonstrations, Trump wanted a photo op there, holding a Bible (upside down, as it turned out), in an apparent attempt to create an iconic image of himself as the president of law and order who was going to be the savior for people of faith. The only problem was that getting there in the midst of the ongoing demonstrations meant clearing out hundreds of peaceful protesters in Lafayette Square.

Lafayette Square was sometimes known as "the public square" because it had hosted countless First Amendment protests for more than a hundred years. It was the place where freedom of speech, freedom of assembly, and the right to petition the government landed on the president's front door—whether the cause was women's suffrage, LGBTQ rights, reproductive rights, or civil rights.

But on this occasion, Attorney General William Barr said the protests "were so bad that the Secret Service recommended that the President go down to the bunker."[27] Consequently, Barr began to transform the area immediately surrounding the White House into "a veritable fortress," as the *Washington Post* put it, with barricades erected by police and federal authorities blocking off various entrances so that they would be in complete control. This "public square" was for anything but the public.[28]

As Trump prepared to speak in the Rose Garden, Barr made his way to Lafayette Square, where he met briefly with assembled security forces and told them that a decision had been made to extend the security perimeter a block to the north. At about the same time, the *Washington Post* reported, a White House operations official told the Secret Service that the president would make a brief, impromptu visit to the church in just a few moments.

The damage to the church had taken place the previous evening when it had been briefly set afire, thereby outraging a number of White House aides. In response, presidential adviser Hope Hicks, a thirty-one-year-old former child model who had served as White House director of communications, had concocted a plan to have Trump walk over to the building for a photo op.

According to protocol, that meant the Secret Service had to bring in other law enforcement agencies to help clear the park—and that included the National Guard, mounted federal police, US Park Police, military police, Bureau of Prisons Special Operations Response Teams, and

Secret Service officers. All this when church officials had not even been notified of the plan and were generally horrified by the aggressive riot-control tactics that were being used on a crowd that was peaceful.

In an interview with the Associated Press, Barr said he did not give the order to Park Police and the National Guard to begin sweeping protesters out, because he "was not involved in giving tactical commands like that."[29]

But that contradicted an earlier statement by White House press secretary Kayleigh McEnany, who said, "AG Barr had determined that we needed to expand the perimeter by one block on each side."

At 6:18 p.m., the Secret Service began moving onto H Street. Three minutes later, according to the *Washington Post*, law enforcement officers checked on the status of personnel who had training in deploying pepper balls and other irritants. Barr then left the park as a barely audible announcement ordered the crowd to disperse. At 6:32 p.m., military police on the southern edge of the protest area moved forward in a face-to-face confrontation with the protesters.[30]

By 6:35 p.m., police in riot gear with shields and clubs began forcing the protesters back, away from Lafayette Square, just as Trump had begun speaking from the Rose Garden.

According to a statement by Park Police, at that point, "Violent protesters on H Street NW began throwing projectiles including bricks, frozen water bottles and caustic liquids. The protesters also climbed onto a historic building at the north end of Lafayette Square that was destroyed by arson days prior. Intelligence had revealed calls for violence against the police, and officers found caches of glass bottles, baseball bats and metal poles hidden along the street." But a review of video footage by the *Washington Post* showed only water bottles being thrown, and no bricks or caustic liquids.

Meanwhile, in the Rose Garden, Trump's rhetoric rose to new heights as he threatened to deploy US armed forces to cities or states that do not take actions to halt the protests, saying the military will "quickly solve the problem for them."[31]

Vice President Mike Pence said that he would have been "happy to walk shoulder to shoulder" with Trump and Barr in their sojourn to Saint

John's but that he was "encouraged to stay at the White House out of an abundance of caution," because protocols dictate that US presidents and vice presidents should not be in the same place during volatile times.

At 7:01 p.m., Trump began walking across the north lawn of the White House to the southwest corner of Lafayette Square toward Saint John's, accompanied by Barr, Secretary of Defense Mark Esper, and General Mark Milley, chairman of the Joint Chiefs of Staff. Tear gas residue lingered in the air.

When he arrived at the church, Trump spent a few minutes posing for photos both alone and with Attorney General Barr, the radical right-wing Catholic who was appropriating the Episcopal church for Trump's photo op without even consulting its clergy. Trump held a Bible, awkwardly, for the photo shoot, and when someone asked if it was his, President Trump responded with the only two words spoken during this episode.

"A Bible," he said, putting deliberate emphasis on the first word. Other than that, Trump did not say a thing.

Trump's presence in front of Saint John's and the fact that he was holding a Bible, seemingly as a prop, outraged Mariann E. Budde, the Episcopal bishop of Washington. "He did not pray," she said. "He did not mention George Floyd, he did not mention the agony of people who have been subjected to this kind of horrific expression of racism and white supremacy for hundreds of years. We need a president who can unify and heal. He has done the opposite of that, and we are left to pick up the pieces."

As if it were not enough that Trump used the church as a political prop, Reverend Virginia Gerbasi, the rector at Saint John's, found that Trump's forces had transformed the park adjacent to the church from a place of peaceful contemplation to a tear-gas-filled field of violence and mayhem. "I literally COULD NOT believe it," Gerbasi wrote, on her Facebook page, according to the *Washington Post*. "WE WERE DRIVEN OFF OF THE PATIO AT ST. JOHN'S—a place of peace and respite and medical care throughout the day—SO THAT MAN COULD HAVE A PHOTO OPPORTUNITY IN FRONT OF THE CHURCH!!! PEOPLE WERE HURT SO THAT HE COULD POSE IN

FRONT OF THE CHURCH WITH A BIBLE! HE WOULD HAVE HAD TO STEP OVER THE MEDICAL SUPPLIES WE LEFT BEHIND BECAUSE WE WERE BEING TEAR GASSED!!!!"[32]

Meanwhile, a dramatic confrontation had begun. Protesters were hit by riot-control grenades and rubber bullets. Clouds of tear-gas covered scores of "Black Lives Matter" signs. There were smoke canisters, pepper spray, and flash-bang canisters. Police assaulted reporters. Five civilians were injured, as were a handful of cops. And fifty-four arrests were made.

The amount of damage aside, a line had been crossed: The American military was attacking American citizens, and it was being done at Trump's and Barr's behest.

Of course, Barr claimed that nothing could be further from the truth. In an interview with CBS News, the attorney general went so far as to assert that the police operation moving the perimeter of the protesters back from the White House had absolutely nothing to with the fact that President Trump wanted them out of the way so he could have a photo op.

"This was not an operation to respond to that particular crowd," Barr said. "It was an operation to move the perimeter one block."

Translation: It was pure coincidence that federal troops were using rubber bullets and tear gas to forcibly move protesters at the same time and place Trump was staging his photo op. And it was an especially odd coincidence given that the military police had allegedly asked the National Guard for flesh-melting heat guns called Active Denial Systems, which are said to make "targets feel their skin is on fire."[33]

But a lot of people didn't buy Barr's explanation. "I think we need a thorough investigation about what occurred there," Washington police chief Peter Newsham told the *Washington Post*. "Why was the crowd cleared? Who did it? Was it legal?"[34]

What was particularly disturbing was not just the aggressive tactics used; according to former DOJ attorneys, it was also that Barr had used "federal law enforcement officers throughout the country, and especially within the District of Columbia, to participate in quelling lawful First Amendment activity."[35]

In a letter to Donald Trump, Speaker of the House Nancy Pelosi asserted that the use of such forces posed a grave threat to American democracy. "The practice of officers operating with full anonymity undermines accountability, ignites government distrust and suspicion, and is counter to the principle of procedural justice and legitimacy during this precarious moment in our nation's history," Pelosi wrote.

Initially, it had not been clear exactly which "federal law enforcement officers" had been brought in for the occasion. In fact, Barr had inundated Washington with agents from the FBI, the Department of Homeland Security, the Bureau of Prisons, and the Bureau of Alcohol, Tobacco, Firearms and Explosives. And according to Pelosi's letter, this was just the beginning. Barr "was mobilizing agents from the Federal Bureau of Investigation (FBI); the Federal Bureau of Prisons (BOP); the US Marshals; the Bureau of Alcohol, Tobacco, Firearms and Explosives; Drug Enforcement Administration (DEA); and possibly other agencies, against peaceful protests."

At Lafayette Square, many of them, especially teams from the Federal Bureau of Prisons, wore only generic, unmarked riot gear and were unidentified. Some observers compared them to Russia's "little green men" who invaded eastern Ukraine wearing unmarked uniforms to obscure their identities.[36]

In this case, Barr had brought in only about three thousand such law enforcement officers, but when one understood the thicket of federal agencies under Barr's command, those forces seemed ominous indeed. In 2016, the federal government had 132,000 law enforcement officers at its command, and the number had grown significantly since then. According to an article by Garrett M. Graff in *Politico*, in all, there were more than eighty different federal agencies with trained officers—not just well-known agencies like the FBI, Secret Service, and DEA, but also the federal US Capitol Police, the Park Police, the USPS police, Amtrak police, and the Bureau of Engraving and Printing Police, all of which could potentially be enlisted by Barr in "what amounts to a federal army of occupation."

Increasingly, it was clear that there was no bottom. That there was no line that Trump and Barr wouldn't cross. That they would not hesitate to use militarized forces against American citizens if it helped their cause. And that, with the entire country still in an uproar following George Floyd's murder and hundreds dying daily in the ongoing COVID-19 pandemic, as the presidential election approached, the question of how Trump and Barr might utilize such militarized forces suggested a dark and bloody future.

In the immediate aftermath of the episode, more than 1,250 former attorneys for the US Justice Department, Republicans and Democrats, called for Justice Department inspector general Michael Horowitz to investigate what role Barr had played in overseeing the aggressive tactics used at Lafayette Square.

Similarly, General Milley, the chairman of the Joint Chiefs of Staff who had accompanied Trump and Barr in walking across Lafayette Square, expressed regret for his presence at the event. "I should not have been there," he said in a prerecorded video commencement address to the National Defense University. "My presence in that moment and in that environment created a perception of the military involved in domestic politics."

Other high-ranking members of the military joined in. Secretary of Defense Esper asserted that the Insurrection Act should be invoked only in the "most urgent and dire of situations," adding that "we are not in one of those situations now."[37]

Retired four-star general and former chairman of the Joint Chiefs of Staff Martin Dempsey tweeted, "America is not a battleground. Our fellow citizens are not the enemy." Michael Mullen, who held the same post under President George W. Bush and Barack Obama, wrote in *The Atlantic* that he was "sickened" by the use of troops to accommodate the president because "our fellow citizens are not the enemy, and must never become so."[38] And General James Mattis, Trump's former secretary of defense, said he was angry and appalled at seeing troops ordered "to violate the constitutional rights of their fellow citizen."[39]

For his part, Trump was said to be furious with Milley and Esper. But this was merely the beginning of what was clearly going to be a long summer of discontent. The game wasn't over yet.

CHAPTER EIGHTEEN

AMERICAN CARNAGE

The explosion of the Black Lives Matter movement didn't take place in a vacuum. It materialized in the midst of the greatest health crisis of the century—the COVID-19 pandemic. And in the United States, the pandemic was being handled with all the proficiency that one might expect to find in a corrupt and dysfunctional regime led by a superstitious, science-defying authoritarian leader of a banana republic who had decided to let the people fend for themselves—and die accordingly.

Notices about COVID-19 had appeared in the president's daily briefings (PDB) as early as January 2020, but, as was usually the case with PDBs, Trump didn't bother to read them. He had long since disregarded the entire intelligence apparatus as "deep state," and was preparing to do to it exactly what he had done with the Justice Department by installing a loyal lieutenant who would put forth exactly the kind of self-serving intelligence he wanted.

And when it came to the pandemic, despite repeated warnings from various officials, Trump exempted the federal government from overseeing the fight against it and instead delegated it to the fifty states and hundreds of municipalities. The resulting patchwork quilt of wildly varying strategies allowed the virus to bounce back and forth from one state to another as it spread throughout the country for month after month after month.

Trump was consistent in this approach to the pandemic. He did everything within his powers to pump up the economy—or at least the stock market (which is not the same thing)—but he did next to nothing when it came to stopping the spread of the virus. When a reporter asked about the administration's failure to test Americans for the virus as it first spread throughout the country, Trump said, "I don't take responsibility at all."

And so, the nation that put the first man on the moon, that created mass consumer culture with automobiles, telephones, televisions, and iPhones, and that led the world in so many sectors of science and technology, cast science aside for Trump's cultlike magical thinking. Maybe we could save ourselves by somehow putting ultraviolet lights "inside the body, either through the skin or some other way."

It was a death cult. Trump suggested injecting bleach as a cure. He asserted that the virus would disappear "magically." He taunted those who wore protective masks as being "politically correct." Trump campaign workers removed social-distancing stickers at his rally in Tulsa. Rarely wearing a mask himself, Trump demonized protective measures as an unnecessary capitulation to cultural elites. He urged governors to open up their states even if they were not operating within the guidelines set forth by the Centers for Disease Control.

In other words, America was in crisis and there was no coordinated national health policy. And worse, like a slow-motion Reichstag fire, the disease itself was being weaponized and politicized by Trump and his followers. Much like the 1933 arson attack that allowed Germany's newly elected chancellor Adolf Hitler to consolidate power, the pandemic provided cover for Trump and Barr to do likewise. In rapid succession, they fired no fewer than five inspectors general, cut back on sharing intelligence between Congress and the director of National Intelligence, appointed a Trump megadonor as head of the U.S. Postal Service, who issued orders to destroy equipment, removed mail drop boxes, and slowed down mail delivery (especially of mail-in ballots), and more—all to help Trump's reelection chances.

Throughout the spring and early summer of 2020, depending on one's location, Americans were either in lockdown or partying at bars and restaurants, dying en masse in nursing homes or taking spring break in Fort Lauderdale—all with little to no federal guidance and haphazard regulations varying from state to state, municipality to municipality.

As a result, by August, the United States had more casualties than any country in the world. More than 6.3 million Americans had been confirmed infected, 189,000 people had died, and infections were still accelerating at a rate that was worse than the European Union's by a factor of ten. At one point, Florida, with 21 million people, had nearly twice as many new cases per day—about 10,000—as the entire European Union, with its 446 million people.

Tens of millions of people were newly unemployed. Economic repercussions were certain to be dire and long-lasting, the "rocket ship" economic recovery promised by Trump having been scrubbed at liftoff.

The United States was a nation in free fall. The George Floyd murder, in conjunction with the killings of Ahmaud Aubrey, Rayshard Brooks, Breonna Taylor, Jacob Blake, and many other African Americans, ignited more than 450 major demonstrations led by Black Lives Matter all across the United States and three continents in what appeared to be a historic rebirth of the civil rights movement, with as many as 26 million Americans participating. According to the *New York Times*, that may have made it the biggest movement in American history, bigger even than the antiwar movement and turbulent counterculture wars of the sixties.[1]

Injuries had been minor at Lafayette Square, to be sure, but Trump's intentionally tone-deaf nonresponse suggested a reckoning was at hand. Attorney General Barr had set a precedent for more to come: Federal troops were being used against American citizens. Biden moved ahead in the polls. But Trump was considering other ways of holding on to power.

———

Meanwhile, with the entire nation consumed by the fight against a massive deadly pandemic and systemic racism, there was still the question of Trump's relationship to Russia. We may never be privy to all the conversations Trump and his surrogates had with Putin and influential Russian contacts, but it would be an understatement to say that those interactions appear to have had their desired effect.

A case in point dated back to October 2016, just before Trump's election, when, as you may recall, Donald Trump Jr. gave his speech in Paris before the Kremlin-linked Center of Political and Foreign Affairs. Immediately afterward, Randa Kassis, a Syrian whose husband had sponsored the event and who is herself the leader of a Syrian group endorsed by the Kremlin, had flown off to Moscow to brief Foreign Minister Sergei Lavrov and the Russian Ministry of Foreign Affairs (MFA), which then issued press statements about Trump Jr.'s speech.

Almost immediately after he was installed in the Oval Office, Donald Trump showed he clearly had gotten Russia's message. In March 2017, just two months after his inauguration, Trump reversed Barack Obama's policy that had made the departure of Syrian president Bashar al-Assad a key American goal.[2] Then, in July 2017, Trump terminated a CIA program arming anti-Assad rebels.[3] And in December 2018, Trump announced the departure of *all* remaining American troops from Syria—even though it meant abandoning America's Kurdish allies and strengthening the Assad regime.

The move effectively ceded control of the area to the Syrian government and Russia.[4] "Putin likely can't believe his luck," a Western military official who served in Syria told *Business Insider*.[5] "A third of Syria was more or less free of ISIS, and its security was good without any involvement of the regime or Russia, and now because of the Turkish invasion and American pullout, this area is wide open to return to government control."

Once again, Trump had given Putin everything he wanted.

And why was Trump doing that?

The answer, I believe, is that John Brennan, Michael Morell, Michael Hayden, and James Clapper were right when they said that Donald Trump was a Russian asset; that, as Yuri Shvets explained, when

Trump bought hundreds of TV sets from Semyon Kislin for the Grand Hyatt more than forty years ago, he had been identified as a potential asset by the KGB, and that evolved into a series of intelligence operations that paid off far, far more handsomely than anyone in the KGB could have imagined.

As the relationship continued over the years, Trump had been rescued from multiple bankruptcies when boatloads of Russian cash were laundered through Trump real estate in the eighties and nineties. In the 2000s, he became wealthy again, thanks to his partnership with Bayrock, which brought in hundreds of millions of dollars in Russian money to finance and develop buildings franchised under Trump's name. And now that he was president, it was Trump's time to pay the piper—knowing, of course, that the Soviet Union could document any or all of his ties to them if they so choose.

But when it came to giving Putin what he wanted, Syria was just the beginning of his wish list. "The Russian objective is to separate the United States from NATO," says Glenn Carle, "to undermine NATO, to expand Russia's sphere of influence, at least regionally, and to remove the United States as an immediate rival. Those are the strategic objectives."

Putin, after all, had famously characterized the collapse of the Soviet Union as the biggest catastrophe in world history and would do anything to re-create his new Russian empire in its image. To that end, whether it was czarist Russia or the Soviet Union, Moscow's imperial ambitions had always begun and ended with Ukraine. Ukraine was essential if Russia was to be an empire.

In that regard, Trump answered more of Putin's prayers than the Russian leader could possibly have imagined, inflicting more damage on NATO during the first three years of his administration than all its foes during its entire seventy-year history.

It began even before Trump took office, at the 2016 GOP convention, the *Washington Post* reported, when Team Trump famously weakened the Ukraine plank of the Republican platform, removing language that called for "providing lethal defensive weapons" and replacing it with the phrase "appropriate assistance."[6]

"Since then, it's been very obvious that on many occasions he's been acting in the Kremlin's interests, even when it's not in America's interests, and that is extremely troubling regardless of the relationship between Donald Trump and the Kremlin prior to 2016," Biden adviser Mike Carpenter told me.

"There's just a litany of things you can tick off the list, from calling Putin a terrific guy, to maligning our closest democratic allies—Europe, like Angela Merkel or Emmanuel Macron—withdrawing troops from Germany, saying that Putin offered a strong denial of his interference in the US election when clearly there was absolutely not a shadow of doubt amongst all the disparate US intelligence agencies that he had done so."

NATO, of course, had been the foundation of the Atlantic Alliance, the most powerful deterrent to Russia and, before that, the Soviet Union for seventy years. As result, weakening NATO—or even better, destroying it—was answering Vladimir Putin's prayers.

"It's not hard to figure out how the Russians would have approached him," says Carle. "Let's assume that Trump is actually a controlled asset. They couldn't say, you know, here are your tasks today and here are your tasks tomorrow. Instead they would say, 'We're interested in establishing security in Europe, and we don't really want to have a clash. We just want to have good relations. And we can help you with your real estate development, and so forth, but it would be good if you were to focus on, uh, you know, the fact that Europe is really screwing the United States over and they aren't paying their fair share of NATO.'"

Not long after Trump became president, some twenty-four years after he had taken out those full-page ads saying NATO was taking advantage of the United States, he picked up the theme again—the same one, according to Shvets, that he had been taught by the KGB—and repeatedly criticized NATO members for not paying enough in dues.

Before long, Trump made it clear that the United States, which had long been the most powerful component of NATO, was no longer a reliable partner.[7] In July 2018, after a private two-hour meeting with Putin in Helsinki, where he strongly suggested he believed Putin's denials about the 2016 election, Trump was interviewed by Fox News' Tucker Carlson, who questioned one of the most basic tenets of NATO, Article 5, which requires member states to treat an attack on one member as an attack on all members and to response appropriately. "So, let's say Montenegro, which joined [NATO] last year, is attacked. Why should my son go to Montenegro to defend it from attack? Why is that?" Carlson asked Trump.

"I understand what you're saying. I've asked the same question. Montenegro is a tiny country with very strong people," Trump replied. "They have very aggressive people. They may get aggressive, and congratulations, you are in World War III."

By rejecting Article 5, Trump was thereby practically inviting Putin to invade the tiny Balkan country. Without American support, Europe would likely refrain from coming to Montenegro's aid, a scenario that would render NATO toothless.[8]

Meanwhile, according to the *New York Times*, Trump repeatedly told administration officials that he wanted to withdraw from NATO.[9] And he continued to distance himself from the alliance. In October 2019, after Trump announced the planned withdrawal of US forces from northern Syria, French president Emmanuel Macron told *The Economist*, "What we are currently experiencing is the brain death of NATO," because the United States is "turning its back on us."[10]

———

Worst of all, in terms of Trump's stunning deference to Putin, on June 26, 2020, the *New York Times* published reports that Russia was offering lucrative bounties to the Taliban to target remaining American troops in Afghanistan. According to the *Times*, intelligence officials say the program was run by an arm of Russian military intelligence (GRU) known as Unit 29155, with money going directly to middlemen who apparently had large sums of money sitting around the house.[11]

Russian aid to the Taliban had been a concern of the Pentagon since 2017, when then secretary of defense James Mattis raised concerns. But Trump never said a word, so the Russians continued and upped the ante by ordering the assassinations of Americans.

It was not immediately clear whether American soldiers had been killed by the program. What was clear, however, according to the *New York Times*, was that intelligence assessments of the program had been included in the President's Daily Brief by no later than February 2020—and he had done exactly nothing.

When Republicans and Democrats alike expressed alarm at both the news and the president's lack of response, the White House, at various times, said that the president had not read the briefing—as if that explained it.

Regardless, according to *The Economist*, in March, the report was taken seriously enough that it had been discussed at a National Security Council meeting, and potential plans for reprisals were discussed. But the matter was never discussed in the Oval Office.[12] And why would they? After all, Trump, according to CNN, had made it clear that he did not want to hear any more bad things about Russia.

Moreover, his antipathy toward the military was crystal clear. As the *Atlantic* reported, he had bridled at being forced to go to an American military cemetery near Paris. Trump said, "Why should I go to that cemetery? It's filled with losers." Separately, he had referred to 1,800 marines who died in battle as "suckers."[13]

Meanwhile, according to a report by Ryan Goodman of *Just Security*, Trump went even further to win Putin's favor by directing the CIA to share intelligence on counterterrorism with Russia. "There was a consistent push for CT [counterterrorism] cooperation with Moscow, coming from the White House, despite near universal belief with the IC [intelligence community] that this effort would be one sided and end up being a waste of time," Marc Polymeropoulos, who had worked for the CIA's Senior Intelligence Service, told Goodman. "I cannot think of anything of value that the Russians provided us."[14]

He added that the "myth that Russians could be a good CT partner—which former National Security Advisor [Michael] Flynn first perpetuated and then became the cornerstone of for this farcical engagement strategy—was by 2019 met with near total derision and eye-rolling in the IC."

As part of his assault on NATO, Trump had essentially seized control of US intelligence and had, in effect, muted counterintelligence reporting on his ties to Russia. He fired FBI director James Comey, attacked and humiliated FBI agents Lisa Page and Peter Strzok as "dirty cops" and "lovers," and fired FBI deputy director Andrew McCabe—the latter just two days before he was eligible to collect a full early pension from the FBI, thereby sending a loud and clear message to all FBI agents who might be investigating the president.[15]

"Among FBI people I know, the worst job to have right now is to be Russia counterintelligence in DC," says national security analyst Clint Watts, the author of *Messing with the Enemy: Surviving in a Social Media World of Hackers, Terrorists, Russians, and Fake News*.[16] "That's because if you find something, you're going to get told to ignore it; and if you advance it, then you're going to be smeared publicly by someone. Especially if it touches the election, it's just a terrible assignment to get."

And by installing John Ratcliffe as director of national intelligence in May 2020, Trump took over the Department of Intelligence as completely as he had taken over Justice with William Barr. And it is hard to imagine agents in the CIA or FBI bothering the president with additional reports that were critical of Putin's Russia. How could the FBI, the CIA, or our military possibly protect us from our gravest national security threat when it came from the man they had pledged to serve?

Meanwhile, Trump did whatever he could to exculpate Russia from its role in the 2016 election attack, reverting to an oft-debunked conspiracy theory falsely suggesting that Ukraine was behind the attack on the Democratic National Committee server. Just as Trump had taken out newspaper ads in 1987 to promote KGB talking points, he was now using the bully pulpit of the Oval Office to do the same thing.

At the same time, with Barr's assistance, Trump took the opportunity to strip the federal government of its internal watchdogs. On April 3, 2020, Trump fired Michael Atkinson, the intelligence community inspector general who had received the whistleblower complaint that had led to his impeachment. Throughout the entire administration, inspectors general, the officials who are in charge of oversight of specific institutions and provide some of the checks and balances to guard against corruption, became an endangered species. In addition to the intelligence community inspector general, Trump fired IGs in the Department of Transportation, the State Department, the Department of Defense, and the Department of Health and Human Services.[17] Five were gone within a period of six weeks.

Loyalty replaced expertise throughout the entire administration. That was nowhere truer than in the intelligence sector, where Ratcliffe was appointed director of national intelligence, overseeing the CIA and sixteen other intelligence agencies, and became widely known as the least qualified director of national intelligence in history.

In a job whose previous applicants had been Rhodes Scholars, served on the National Security Council, run the National Security Agency, headed Pacific Command, served as ambassador to the United Nations, held decades of intelligence experience, and generally attained a career full of celebrated accomplishments, Ratcliffe had distinguished himself in Congress as a Republican who was known for his unswerving loyalty to Trump and for having served as mayor of Heath, Texas—population 7,590.

"We saw him dance around direct questions," Senator Ron Wyden (D-OR) said on the Senate floor shortly before the confirmation vote. "If you're John Ratcliffe, the intelligence really doesn't matter. All that matters is that he makes Donald Trump happy. And if Donald Trump doesn't want to acknowledge that the Russians helped him, then those are John Ratcliffe's marching orders."

With the watchdogs out of the way, Trump and Barr continued inventing richly detailed but fictitious narratives that absolved Putin and Russia of interference with the 2016 election. For Barr, it wasn't enough that he had buried the entire counterintelligence investigation and released material only on criminal prosecutions. Now Barr set about helping out even those who had been convicted by investigations stemming from Mueller's probe. In February 2020, when Trump friend and consultant Roger Stone, the bad boy of political consulting, was given a sentencing recommendation of seven to nine years, Barr's Justice Department intervened to lessen the sentence. (In July, Trump commuted Stone's sentence.) Barr dropped charges against former national security advisor Michael Flynn, who had pleaded guilty to lying to the FBI—only to be rebuffed later by a federal appeals court, which reinstated them. After the coronavirus pandemic struck, Barr let Trump campaign manager Paul Manafort, who had been sentenced to seven and a half years, out on home confinement. Similarly, Trump attorney Michael Cohen, who had been allowed to serve time at home because of the pandemic, was briefly sent back for refusing to agree not to write a book about Trump. However, a federal judge soon overruled the order.

Meanwhile, Trump continued developing a narrative that blamed President Obama for "spying" on Trump's 2016 candidacy, that cast Trump not as a villain but as a victim of pro-Hillary Democrats in the FBI, the fake news, the liberal elites. Led by Rudy Giuliani, Trump proxies shuttled back and forth to Ukraine to generate sham investigations and disinformation they hoped would torpedo Joe Biden.

These false narratives had begun almost immediately after Trump's inauguration with an assertion—a tweet, naturally, on March 4, 2017, just over six weeks after his inauguration—in which Trump wrote, "Terrible! Just found out that Obama had my 'wires tapped' in Trump Tower just before the victory. Nothing found. This is McCarthyism!"

Donald Trump was the victim!

A key problem with making that case, of course, was that the facts didn't quite mesh with the theory, and they would have to be changed to make it work. That included much of the Mueller Report, thousands of newspaper articles, and the conclusion—shared by all US intelligence agencies—that Russia interfered in the 2016 election on Trump's behalf.[18] So as each component of the Trump-Russia scandal came to light, it would be turned on its head by Trump, Putin, and company through extensive operations that spanned the globe from Moscow to Kiev to Washington and that cast pro-Putin operatives as heroes in the fight against corruption and depicted FBI investigators as diabolical Democratic operatives in a massive multifaceted disinformation operation.

To that end, in May 2019, just two months after taking office, Attorney General Barr had designated John Durham, the US attorney in

Connecticut, to investigate whether the FBI or other officials in any way engaged in misconduct during their probe, code named "Crossfire Hurricane," into Trump's ties to Russia. Its goal was to assert that the Obama administration had illegally spied on Trump.

The next month, Trump attorney Rudy Giuliani got together two pro-Putin Ukrainian operatives, Lev Parnas and Igor Fruman, to share back-channel "information" that, according to Giuliani, included "enormous allegations of criminality by the Biden family."[19]

Thus Ukrainegate, the scam for which Trump had already been impeached, was reborn. Before Biden even nailed down the Democratic nomination, Trump had set out to destroy him. At the heart of Trump's impeachment was the infamous phone call—"the perfect phone call," as he called it—in which President Trump threatened to withhold previously authorized and desperately needed military aid to Ukraine unless President Volodymyr Zelensky put together a sham investigation of Joe Biden and his son Hunter. In his phone call, Trump explicitly asked Zelensky to interfere in the 2020 election in a way that would benefit Trump. According to the *New York Times*, no fewer than ten former White House chiefs of staff, both Republican and Democratic, said it was unprecedented for an incumbent president to "personally apply pressure to foreign powers to damage political opponents."[20]

Of course, Trump was summarily acquitted by the GOP-controlled Senate—in a trial in which the Republicans refused to allow a single witness. But from Russia's point of view, Trump had already aided Putin by undermining and endangering Ukraine, and by making clear to President Zelensky that he couldn't count on American support as long as Donald Trump was in power.

During impeachment, former White House adviser Fiona Hill noted, "Some of you on this committee appear to believe that Russia and its security services did not conduct a campaign against our country—and that perhaps, somehow, for some reason, Ukraine did. This is a fictional narrative that has been perpetrated and propagated by Russian security services themselves."

But Trump and his allies were not about to abandon their narrative.

Giuliani had opened the door to making more charges against Biden, who, as vice president, had fought corruption in Ukraine by taking a stand against Prosecutor General Viktor Shokin, an ally of pro-Putin oligarchs who was widely seen as an obstacle against fighting corruption—and whose two fellow prosecutors had been caught with heaps of diamonds, cash, and other treasures in their homes.[21] As a result, Biden had pushed for Shokin's firing in coordination with anti-corruption reforms supported by the US State Department, the International Monetary Fund, and the European Union.[22]

In February 2020, just after Trump was acquitted, Giuliani went to Kiev, where former prosecutor general Shokin opened a criminal case against Joe Biden for his role in getting Shokin fired.[23] By March, websites such as TheSaker,[24] said to be a GRU front, were retailing wild conspiracies about how the FBI conspired with Ukrainian hackers to hack the Democratic National Committee and blame the break-in on Trump-Russian collusion.

And so it went, one disinformation scam after another, stitched together with the help of a dizzying array of Putin operatives and promoted heavily by Fox News and the right-wing press, but with diminishing efficacy as the toll from COVID-19 mounted.

Then, as the coronavirus spread throughout the country in spring 2020, the new amorphous, fluid, ever-changing narrative known as Obamagate began to emerge. "You know what the crime is," Trump said. "The crime is very obvious to everybody."[25]

"It was the greatest political crime in the history of our country," Trump told Fox Business's Maria Bartiromo in May. "It is a disgrace what's happened. This is the greatest political scam, hoax, in the history of our country."

Meanwhile, Giuliani continued making the case against Biden, with the help of Andrii Telizhenko, a former Ukrainian official and Giuliani ally who asserted that he might testify before the US Senate prior to the November elections and drop major bombshells against Biden in the form of secret recordings involving him and former Ukrainian president Petro Poroshenko.

By May, several websites of dubious provenance had sprung up, citing unauthenticated recordings of then vice president Biden in conversation with Zelensky's predecessor, Petro Poroshenko, with Poroshenko essentially taking orders from Biden—to fire Prosecutor General Shokin and squash the investigation against his son, Hunter; to sign over a billion-dollar loan guarantee to Ukraine; and more. "The smoking gun has just been found," said a pro-Trump site called Creative Destruction Media.[26]

But that was clearly not the case. As the *Washington Post* reported, the recordings show, as Biden has previously said publicly, that as vice president, he linked loan guarantees to Ukraine to firing Shokin. But the tapes that have been released thus far don't corroborate Giuliani's charge that Biden's motive was to stop an investigation of Burisma Holdings, which had hired Hunter Biden.[27]

Secret recordings, videos, a criminal complaint against Biden, phony websites, disinformation—all raised the possibility of dramatic last-minute preelection show trials against Biden in the Senate, with testimony from pro-Kremlin witnesses and documentation, recordings, and videos of questionable provenance.

Biden foreign policy adviser Michael Carpenter in the *Washington Post* called the tape clips that were being released "a KGB-style disinformation operation tied to pro-Russian forces in Ukraine, whose chief aim is to make deceptive noise in the U.S. election campaign to advance the interests of their oligarchic backers, the Kremlin, and the faltering Trump campaign."[28]

These were dark times. Trump, remember, had campaigned in 2016 on insults and fear—taking aim at women, Mexicans, Muslims, immigrants, Gold Star mothers and fathers, and others. He had started his administration with an inaugural address that put forth a dark dystopian vision of "American carnage," as he put it—that is, an America he saw with "mothers and children trapped in poverty in our inner cities; rusted-out factories scattered like tombstones across the landscape of our nation; an education system, flush with cash, but which leaves our young and beautiful students deprived of knowledge; and the crime and gangs and drugs that have stolen too many lives and robbed our country of so much unrealized potential."

Unlike any other inaugural addresses, which generally have tried to project visions of unity after divisive campaigns, Trump spoke solely to his base of aggrieved white supporters. Where past Republican presidents had evoked "a city on a hill" or "a thousand points of light" as images, Trump's vision of American carnage was so dark that Hillary Clinton, in an appearance on Howard Stern's radio show, recounted the remarks of former president George W. Bush.

"Well," he said, "that's some weird shit."[29]

But that was just been the beginning. After more than three years in office, thanks to impeachment, to the pandemic, and to the racial justice movement, for all his obstinacy, the curtain had gradually been pulled back to reveal more and more of Trump. Of course politicians lied, but Trump was a sociopath, who, by the count of *Washington Post*'s "Fact Checker" had given false or misleading statements more than twenty thousand times in office through July 2020—and he hadn't even started campaigning yet (that's an average of twelve false or misleading claims a day).

By this time, Trump's assault on reality and his somewhat demented self-aggrandizing tweets were widely discounted by most Americans—fewer than three in ten believed his false claims, according to the *Post*'s "Fact Checker" poll.[30] Nevertheless, he had cultivated tens of millions of unwaveringly fervent supporters who were cultlike in their suspension of disbelief.

And as the 2020 presidential campaign got under way, Trump, having brushed off impeachment, now confronted presumptive Democratic nominee Joe Biden. In fact, Trump's acquittal by the Senate gave him even more latitude to exercise his basest impulses. But he also now faced the COVID-19 pandemic and the resulting economic disaster.

Perhaps the most salutary effect of the pandemic was that the curtain had been pulled back on the Wizard of Oz, revealing a doughy reality-TV host well past his prime, playing at being president in an infantile way, making up lies, saying whatever came into his head, changing his version of reality on a whim, as if he alone determined reality for all of us. But by now, millions of Americans had begun to see past the buffoonery and clownlike behavior that masked a real tyrant, a real demagogue, a force of evil on a mythic level, a Shakespearean evil, a dictator in waiting who would intentionally allow hundreds of thousands of his fellow citizens to die so long as it helped him stay in power.

Even though the pandemic was clearly hurting Trump's chances at reelection, the White House response to it essentially boiled down to this: Let people die and hope no one minds. Let's hope they become numb.

As one former administration official told the *Washington Post*, the White House's thinking was that Americans will "live with the virus being a threat." Another added, "They're of the belief that people will get over it or if we stop highlighting it, the base will move on and the public will learn to accept 50,000 to 100,000 new cases a day."[31]

Refusing to wear a mask, taunting those who did as being "politically correct," Trump and his supporters occasionally paid the price, as did former Republican presidential candidate Herman Cain, who attended Trump's indoor rally in Tulsa and died from COVID-19 a bit more than a month later.

Trump had banned immigrants, separated families, put children in cages, and acted as if he were above the rule of law, as if he had monarchical powers. And for Trump, staying in power was an existential crisis because, more likely than not, he would end up in jail if he lost. As a result, it was clear he would stop at nothing. But the election was approaching. He was sinking in the polls, and his campaign embodied a murderous stupidity that defied common sense and magnified the risk of grave illness and death for his supporters by politicizing the most benign commonsense safety measures, such as wearing protective masks.

A train wreck was coming. But no one knew how it would play out.

Geopolitics is sometimes—too often, perhaps—compared to three-dimensional chess. In this case, it would be more accurate to say that to the extent the cascading forces at play—Trump's tyranny, the forthcoming election, the Trump-Russia scandal, the pandemic, the economic crisis, the assault on American democracy—resembled three-dimensional chess, it was the end game of a blitz chess match, with ferocious assaults coming in from every direction at blinding speed.

By early fall, conventional wisdom had it that Trump would lose a free and fair election—in the highly unlikely event that such an event took place. The pandemic took center stage, and as it raged throughout the summer, Trump insisted that parents send their kids back to school in the fall—a potential super-spreader event at a time when a second wave was expected to strike. Eschewing protective masks, staging super-spreader events, encouraging the entire country to get back to work, no matter how unsafe the conditions, Trump appeared to be deliberately fueling the pandemic so much that voting would be unsafe, and the curtailed postal service would undermine the integrity of the election.

It is hard to top America's greatest health crisis and racial justice as enormously powerful and important issues, but for both Donald Trump and America, something even bigger was at stake. As long as he was in office, and William Barr's generous interpretation of the unitary executive prevailed, he was, for all effective purposes, beyond the reach of the law.

Which meant that for American democracy, the election was existential as well. We had already seen how Trump and Barr had stripped bare elemental institutions like the Department of Justice, the State Department, and FBI counterintelligence, and fired inspectors general in one sector after another—in the process all but destroying the checks and balances and congressional oversight that had kept the executive branch in line for more than two centuries. One more term, it seemed, and Trump's authoritarianism would be irrevocable.

And so Trump's whitewash continued. To that end, he granted clemency to Roger Stone, who had been convicted of no fewer than seven felony counts—of obstructing a congressional inquiry, of perjury, of witness tampering—all to cover up his effort to get information about Democrats' emails hacked by Russians to help Trump win in 2016. Trump clearly benefited from Stone's crimes, and for all we know, he may have ordered them.

But commuting Stone's sentence was not merely an act of cronyism, of Trump doing a favor for a friend. Stone had the goods on Trump but didn't talk. He had been convicted of lying to protect Trump. If Trump let him languish in jail, especially with the ongoing pandemic, he might talk. So in letting Stone walk, Trump was protecting himself.

And in the end, that's what it was all about—keeping secrets. Keeping Roger Stone happy so that he wouldn't talk. And that would help keep Trump in power, which was essential to Trump, because as a private citizen he could be prosecuted. That meant keeping any compromising materials—kompromat—out of the public eye. It meant keeping transcripts of Trump's private conversations with Putin in the vault, on the top-secret White House server. It meant keeping Trump's financial records secret. Keeping the Jeffrey Epstein files in safe hands.

As for the judiciary, when Ruth Bader Ginsburg died on September 18, the Supreme Court was very much in play, with Trump, Barr, Leonard Leo, and company not even waiting until she had lain in state before Trump announced the appointment of Amy Coney Barrett to take Ginsburg's seat. This, of course, was the same Republican-controlled Senate that had blocked President Obama's nomination of Merrick Garland in the last year of Obama's final term.

Her appointment could guarantee the right control of the high court for the next generation, in which it would likely roll back *Roe v. Wade* and perhaps even decide the outcome of the 2020 election if it were contested. Although she was not a member of Opus Dei, Barrett, who had clerked for Justice Antonin Scalia, was both a member of the Federalist Society and a deeply conservative Catholic, a lifelong devotee of the charismatic, largely Catholic group People of Praise, another right-wing secret society with a highly authoritarian structure.

On September 27, in a major investigation into Trump's finances, the *New York Times* revealed that Trump had paid no federal income taxes whatsoever in ten out of the last fifteen years, that he was disastrous as a businessman, and that he owed $421 million, most to

Deutsche Bank, which, of course, had a long history of money laundering with Russia. How could Trump *not* be deeply compromised?[32]

Then, in his catastrophic September 30 debate with Biden, Trump,
who interrupted the former vice president with a continuous stream of
mockery and lies, made one thing abundantly clear: The bottom line
was that he would not play by the rules. Refusing to rebuke white
supremacists—specifically, the Proud Boys, a far-right, neofascist group
that resorts to violence—he instead told them, "Stand back and stand
by." In doing so, he held on ever more tightly to his racist base—while
not attracting the independents or converts he desperately needed.

Instead, it had become clear that he was running against the election itself. Trump's message was that voting by mail was fraudulent,
that the entire electoral system was rigged, and as a result, he refused
to say he would accept the results if Biden won. His new plan was
chaos and violence, disrupting and delegitimizing the election so that
multiple states run by Republicans could conceivably refuse to certify
their ballots with the Electoral College, thus moving the election to the
House of Representatives and possibly the Supreme Court. So it was
essential for Trump and Mitch McConnell to ram Amy Coney Barrett's nomination through the Senate before the election so that the
Republicans would have an extra vote on the court.

———

On October 1, two days after Trump's presidential debate with Joe
Biden, came yet another October surprise: Donald tested positive for
COVID-19. The man who mocked people wearing masks, who said the
virus would disappear, who suggested injecting bleach to kill it, who
flouted his own health agencies' recommendations, and persuaded his
own political base to indulge in such magical thinking had himself
contracted the virus.

At the time, Democratic nominee Joe Biden had begun to open up
a lead, which would gradually grow to more than ten points over
Trump in the polls by the middle of the month. As for Trump, he went
to Walter Reed hospital on Friday, October 2, was pumped full of the
latest pharmaceutical cocktails designed to bring down the COVID-19

virus, and returned to the White House, where he made an appearance on the South Portico balcony, staged like a great cinematic spectacle, with the kind of lighting that wins Oscars, punctuated by President Trump dramatically removing his mask and giving onlookers a double thumbs-up, before returning into the White House, his mask stuffed into his pocket.

This is what has become known as Trump's Mussolini moment. This was Donald Trump on steroids. Literally. Dexamethasone, to be precise.[33] Whether Trump's manic behavior over the next few weeks was steroid induced or just Trump being Trump is unclear. What was certain was that he could strut about as though he had fought the disease like a man and had triumphed. "Don't be afraid of Covid," he tweeted. "Don't let it dominate your life. . . . I feel better than I did 20 years ago!"

He tweeted a video proclaiming, "Don't let it dominate you. Don't be afraid of it. You're going to beat it. We have the best medical equipment, we have the best medicines—all developed recently."

All of which were readily available—if you were president of the United States.

Fueled with steroids, Trump went back on the campaign trail. "I feel so powerful. I'll walk in there, I'll kiss everyone in that audience. I'll kiss the guys and the beautiful women, just give you a big fat kiss," he said, as his personal physician, Sean Conley, released dubious reports regarding whether Trump was still infectious.

Meanwhile, the White House, the most heavily protected building in America, had become a hot spot for the coronavirus. A week earlier, on September 26, Trump had hosted an event in the White House Rose Garden honoring Supreme Court nominee Amy Coney Barrett, who, it turned out, had tested positive for COVID-19 earlier in the summer. Though the event was outdoors, most of the more than two hundred people attending did not wear masks, and failed to observe pandemic protocols. According to *Newsweek,* at least thirty-seven cases of the new coronavirus were confirmed within twelve days after Barrett's Rose Garden event. In addition to President Trump and First Lady Melania Trump, former New Jersey governor Chris Christie, California pastor Greg Laurie, University of Notre Dame president John Jenkins, White House press secretary Kayleigh McEnany, former Trump counselor Kellyanne Conway, Utah senator Mike Lee, and North Carolina senator Thom Tillis tested positive.[34] It was, perhaps, Ruth Bader Ginsburg's revenge.

And so, with Biden seemingly pulling away in the polls, Trump had barnstormed Florida, Arizona, and Michigan, staging one superspreader rally after another, as if there were no risks. It was a death cult, of sorts, but Dr. Anthony Fauci, director of National Institute of Allergy and Infectious Diseases, was more politic. "We're all glad that the president of the United States did not suffer any significant consequences of it," said Fauci. "But . . . because he is such a visible figure, it amplifies some of that misunderstanding that people have that it's a benign disease and nobody has anything to worry about."[35]

The coronavirus numbers surged. And with cold weather coming, epidemiologists fear the worst. The rate of infection was rising in thirty-seven out of fifty states.

Meanwhile, in the Senate, Republican majority leader Mitch McConnell tried to ram through Barrett's Supreme Court nomination before it was too late. The stakes were enormous. Her presence would create a 6–3 conservative court, and with vital votes looming, *Roe v. Wade* could be overturned. The Affordable Care Act was at risk—at a time when Americans needed health care more than ever. Gay marriage could be overturned. The Republicans had succeeded at court packing, and Federalist Society–approved justices might be ruling the Supreme Court for a generation unless the Democrats returned the favor.

And then there was the election itself, which, at this writing, was still not one hundred percent clear. What if Trump and company managed to tear the election out of the hands of the electorate and throw it into the courts. There was still the possibility that Amy Coney Barrett, Trump's newly appointed associate justice of the United States Supreme Court, might cast a decisive vote in his favor.

Trump had made clear that there would be no transfer of power. That's what Trump said. It meant the end of democracy. Dictatorship.

Tyranny. The end of America as I knew it. Whether Trump would achieve that was another question.

―――――――

Given the magnitude of the pandemic, it was not surprising that Trump's failed COVID response became such a huge part of Biden's campaign. After all, the virus was a matter of life and death. As a result, Russia and Trump's relationship was scarcely mentioned during the campaign, which meant that one of the greatest national security failures in American history—allowing a Russian asset to become president of the United States—was almost completely ignored.

For decades, Americans had almost always gotten final results at night, just hours after voting ended. This time, however, there would be a wait, and the suspense was heightened by the fact that for years Trump had said American elections were corrupted by massive voting fraud. During this campaign, he had insistently denounced mail-in voting as fraudulent. He had even admitted that he was undermining the United States Postal Service to make it harder to deliver mail-in votes[36] and discouraged his supporters from using the mail. As a result, Democrats voted by mail far more than their Republican counterparts.

As the polls closed across the country on November 3, the initial results were far too close to comfort Democrats. In the crucial battleground state of Pennsylvania, for example, at midnight, four hours after the polls closed, Trump held a lead of around 550,000 votes over Biden, and it was hard to see how the Democratic nominee could catch up.[37]

As it happened, when Pennsylvania tallied its votes, it had begun counting mail-in votes only *after* other votes had been counted. As a result, the votes that came in late overwhelmingly favored the Democrats, and Biden gradually ate away at Trump's lead.

Finally, late Saturday morning, November 7, after four days of vote counting and nail-biting suspense, Pennsylvania was called for Biden. In rapid succession, one news division after another finally called Joe Biden president-elect.

Astoundingly, in the end, Trump garnered over seventy-three million votes—almost eleven million more than he got in 2016. Nevertheless, the outcome was not nearly as close as it initially appeared. There had been a strong turnout for both sides. At this writing, with votes still being counted, Biden was leading Trump by nearly six million popular votes, and had won the electoral college 306 votes to Trump's 232. He had flipped the crucial battleground states of Pennsylvania, Wisconsin, and Michigan that Hillary Clinton had lost in 2016. By winning Georgia, Biden had established a beachhead in the Republicans' "Solid South." It was not the overwhelming landslide many Democrats had sought. But Biden had won a clear and decisive victory. It was indisputable.

And so, for one brief moment at least, on Saturday, November 7, after days of intense uncertainty and confusion, there was wisdom, light, hope, and all the rest. Millions of people took to the street spontaneously. With honking car horns, cowbells, and loud music, exuberant celebrations erupted all across the country and continued through the weekend.

———

And yet.

Even before the election, Trump had said he would not concede. "People will not accept this Rigged Election!" he tweeted. "Nevada is turning out to be a cesspool of Fake Votes," read another. Many such tweets were accompanied by warnings from Twitter: "This claim about election fraud is disputed."

More than anything, Trump detested "losers," and now that the election results were in and the American people had forced him to join that wretched tribe, an elaborate spectacle unfolded, a tragicomic clown show, really, starring an infantile narcissist whose shameless ability to deny reality had been weaponized.

For his part, Trump spent much of his time doing what he did best—tweeting and golfing. As Philip Bump reported in the *Washington Post*, in the two weeks after the election, Trump's public calendar was virtually empty.[38] At the time, the US led the world in COVID-19 deaths, having exceeded 250,000 fatalities. At least 130,000 of those deaths, according to a Columbia University study, could have been avoided if President Trump had taken more serious measures to prevent the spread of the disease.[39] That was nearly four times as many fatalities as the US suffered in Vietnam. More than eleven million Americans had been infected. And as the rate of infections soared to more than a million[40] a week, Trump said nothing. Instead, he went golfing four times, tweeted constantly, and filed numerous lawsuits and procedural motions in a desperate attempt to reverse the outcome of the election. For the most part, he stayed out of the limelight, the most famous person in the world, holed up at the White House, as if he were ashamed to show his face, branded as a loser.

As for Twitter, in the two weeks between the election and November 17, Trump sent forth no fewer than four hundred tweets,[41] the vast majority of which asserted that he had won the election, that Biden's victory and the entire election were racked by fraud. "In Detroit, there are FAR MORE VOTES THAN PEOPLE. Nothing can be done to cure that giant scam. I win Michigan!," he tweeted. Many such tweets were again accompanied by warnings from Twitter: "This claim about election fraud is disputed."

Similarly, when it came to his lawsuits, team Trump charged that poll watchers were not allowed to "meaningfully" monitor the vote count in Philadelphia. In Arizona, they alleged that the use of Sharpies on ballots somehow screwed up the vote count. In Nevada, they cited "lax procedures for authenticating mail-in ballots."[42]

And so it went, in one lawsuit after another, mainly in battleground states where Biden had won and the vote was close, where Trump's attorneys went to court with almost no evidence. By November 19, Trump had not won a single meaningful victory out of more than two dozen lawsuits and motions.[43] Even with the Federalist Society, Opus Dei and the new Catholic Right, Leonard Leo, and William Barr on Team Trump, it seemed, the Republicans had not taken over the entire judiciary.

Nevertheless, Trump still had the support of almost the entire Republican Party. Two full weeks after Election Day, only five out of fifty-three Republican senators accepted Biden's status as president-elect.[44] Nor were such sentiments limited to the Senate. On November 10, when asked how the State Department would interact with the Biden transition team, Secretary of State Mike Pompeo puckishly declared, "There will be a smooth transition to a second *Trump* administration."[45]

Having lost, the Republican Party had, in effect, declared war on the election itself. The entire party was committed to fighting *against* democracy. Republican senator Mike Lee, of Utah, had said as much, even before the election. "Democracy isn't the objective; liberty, peace, and prosperity [sic] are," he tweeted. "We want the human condition to flourish. Rank democracy can thwart that."

Headlines in the *Washington Post*, *The Guardian*, *New York Magazine*, and *The Nation*, among other media, referred to Trump's battle to retain power as an attempted "coup," a fight to overturn Biden's victory. Others compared it to a second civil war. This was a season in which far-right militiamen took guns to state capitols and planned to kidnap and murder a governor—in this case, Michigan governor Gretchen Whitmer, a Democrat who had taken strict measures in an effort to stem the spread of the COVID pandemic. It was a time when QAnon conspiracy theorists peddled theories that Democrats were Satan-worshipping pedophiles, and managed to get elected to Congress, as did Marjorie Taylor Greene, a Republican QAnon believer from Georgia.[46] Subscribing to fantasies of paranoid conspiracies was no longer a hindrance to winning a Congressional seat.

And the Republicans were never more clown-like than on November 7, four days after the election, when Rudy Giuliani booked a press conference at the Four Seasons in Philadelphia in which he was to present a purported witness to voter fraud. But instead of booking the posh Four Seasons Hotel, Giuliani's team staged the event at Four Seasons Total Landscaping, situated conveniently between a sex shop and a crematorium, with Giuliani presenting as his star witness a man who happened to be a convicted sex offender.[47] All of which led the landscaping company to tout "Lawn and Order" merchandise and vow to "Make America Rake Again."

Such farcicalities notwithstanding, the Trump administration still had more than two months in power, and continued to do what it could to thwart Biden. Georgia secretary of state Brad Raffensperger, a Republican, said Senator Lindsey Graham (R-SC) asked him if he could throw out *legally* cast mail-in ballots in various counties.[48] Trump invited Republican state legislators from Michigan to the White House in an effort to block the certification of Biden's victory there.[49] And when it came to the transition of power, Emily Murphy, the head of the General Services Administration, declined to accept Biden as president-elect even two weeks after his victory, thereby putting a hold on government resources and briefings for the transition of power to the incoming administration.

Having already installed the outrageously unqualified John Ratcliffe as director of National Intelligence, Trump now began to decapitate the surveillance state. On November 9, Trump fired Secretary of Defense Mark Esper. The next day, Trump appointed Ezra Cohen-Watnick, a steadfast Trump loyalist, as acting undersecretary of defense for intelligence.

Similarly, in the Justice Department, Attorney General Barr had removed Brad Wiegmann, a well-regarded career public servant, as deputy assistant attorney general and replaced him with Trump loyalist Kellen Dwyer in a position that, some observers believed, gave him power to determine when it is and isn't appropriate for the Justice Department to make public statements about election interference.[50]

There were many others. So now, in the intelligence world, as it was in the Justice Department, the most groveling loyal Trump sycophants had the keys to the kingdom. They were now in charge of the kompromat. Who knew what secrets they would uncover about their foes? Who knew how many compromising documents they had begun to shred? Or would they be able to use their power to stay in office?

In June 2015, Trump took his famous escalator ride down to the Trump Tower atrium, where he launched his seemingly improbable presidential campaign. In the ensuing five years, he had, to a considerable extent, turned the country into an American version of Putin's Mafia state. It wasn't just that his drive for personal enrichment and power put a stranglehold over democracy as Americans had built and lived it. As an asset who benefited from Russia while a sitting US president, he was also a principal in one of the greatest national security failures in American history. The real damage he had wreaked was just beginning to be understood, as an incoming administration began to prepare to move into the White House.

As to Trump's fate, that was still unclear. Having lost the election, he would be in serious legal jeopardy, potentially facing numerous civil and criminal charges, once he left the White House. Still, at various times, he vowed he would run again in 2024. More than seventy-three million people had voted for him. More than any candidate in history save Joe Biden. And, at this writing, there was still Trump's slow-motion coup, what appeared to be the last gasps of his attempts to block the certification of the vote in key states that Biden had won.

In the end, it would be some time before Americans got to the bottom of exactly how damaged their country was. Trump had been so compromised, for so long, that the treasured things Americans had were not yet clear.

But president or not, Donald Trump was still the Republican Party. He was still a beneficiary of kompromat's power, and at risk from its danger. He had made it clear that he intended to remain a powerful political force. He was not going away.

AFTERWORD

July 5, 2021

I t was not until Saturday, November 7, four interminable white-knuckle, nail-biting days after the 2020 election, that Joe Biden's triumph was finally in the books. With a margin of more than seven million popular votes over Trump, Biden's victory turned out to be significantly bigger than many people initially thought. Several states had been squeakers, but Biden still ended up with a reasonably comfortable margin in the Electoral College, 306 to 232. It was now confirmed by the *New York Times*, the *Washington Post*, Associated Press, ABC, NBC, and CBS, among others. Even Donald Trump's reliably right-wing friends at Fox News conceded that Biden had accumulated more than the 270 electoral votes "to become the forty-sixth president of the United States."[1]

But one formality remained before Biden could be inaugurated. On January 6, a joint session of Congress was scheduled to certify the electoral votes from each state. Vice President Mike Pence was slated to preside. What was supposed to have taken place was essentially procedural, an administrative technicality. Each of the fifty states already had certified its electoral votes. Theoretically at least, Congress's role was to be nothing more than the simple addition of electoral votes from each state as they were announced. That meant this was an event in which partisan political biases were to play no role whatsoever.

At least, that was the idea. Four years earlier, on January 6, 2017, the shoe had been on the other foot when it came to certifying Donald Trump's 2016 victory. On that occasion, the certification of electoral votes was interrupted no fewer than eleven times—all by Democrats making quixotic attempts to derail Trump's shocking victory over Hillary Clinton[2] by asserting that the electors were "not lawfully certified" given Russia's illegal interference in the election and "massive voter suppression" by the Republicans, among other reasons.

But the Democrats got nowhere. That was because objections to certification needed to be signed in writing by both a member of the House and a member of the Senate, and, according to CNN, every House member who objected did so without a senator's signature.[3] As a result, the presiding officer in the Senate, then Vice President Joe Biden, repeatedly gaveled down his own party for failure to observe the rules.

"It is over," Biden told congresswoman Pramila Jayapal (D-WA) when she tried to object.

"The debate is not in order," he told another congresswoman.

"There is no debate," Biden told yet another congresswoman. "There is no debate. There is no debate."

In the end, Biden wouldn't budge. He had strictly observed congressional protocols, the electoral votes were certified by Congress, and Donald Trump was to be sworn in as president.

Now, four years later, the calculus had changed radically. This time, it was Biden who was supposed to be sworn in. And instead of Democrats trying to obstruct the process, you had Donald Trump and the seventy-four million people who voted for him, refusing to accept his defeat, insisting that Trump had won—and by a landslide, at that.

As a result, they had arrived en masse in Washington to "Stop the Steal" and prevent Biden from becoming president. That meant they were committed to ending America's uninterrupted history of peaceful transitions of power from one administration to the next. Like two trains racing toward each other on the same track, Trump supporters and his foes were poised for a massive head-on collision.

And that's exactly what happened on January 6, 2021, two weeks before Inauguration Day, when Trump rallied thousands of his followers on the National Mall in Washington, DC, in an event that for some may have been simply a march in support of their president and for others was far, far more serious—a veritable call to arms to engage in combat with the powers that be and stage an insurrection, a coup d'etat rejecting the outcome of the November election and installing Trump as president for a second term.

According to the *Times*, in the days leading up to January 6, there were more than a million posts on social media about storming the Capitol.[4] People discussed what weapons to bring. Baseball bats, ammunition. Maps of the building's layout were widely distributed—presumably to help facilitate lines of attack. They discussed which lawmakers should be targeted: Speaker of the House Nancy Pelosi, Senate Minority Leader Chuck Schumer, and Vice President Mike Pence, among others. QAnon, the far-right conspiratorialist cult that was fueled in part by support from Russian trolls,[5] joined in, asserting that satanic, cannibalistic pedophile Democrats—"drinking their blood, eating our babies"—had conspired against Trump to steal the election.[6] The equally far-right paramilitary Oath Keepers arrived in force, clad in body armor. The nationalist Proud Boys attended as well. Misogynists, white supremacists, anti-Semites, homophobes—all were welcome. Many saw themselves as patriots who were fighting for their country, in much the same way that Confederate soldiers did during the Civil War. Living deep within the right-wing bubbles in their siloed social media, they all bought into the evidence-free lie that Donald Trump had really won the election, and they were determined to change the course of history.

And so began the historic and violent storming of the United States Capitol, in which Trump supporters rammed through the barricades manned by ill-equipped and understaffed law enforcement officers to breach the Capitol in no fewer than eight locations. Having learned that Vice President Pence, like Biden before him, had refused to disrupt the proceedings, rioters chanted, "Hang Mike Pence! Hang Mike Pence!" In the ensuing insurrection, more than 140 people were injured. Rioters trampled one fellow protester to death. In all, five people lost their lives, including one police officer.

———

In the end, of course, the insurrection failed. Biden was inaugurated as scheduled on January 20, and a new era began. No longer center stage, Trump had lost both his bully pulpit in the White House, and—horror of horrors—had even been banned from his Twitter account, Facebook, Instagram, and other social media.

With Trump absent from the national stage—relatively speaking, of course—Russia was no longer a key part of the national conversation. But that didn't mean the conflict was over. For one thing, the Republican Party was still very much Trump's party, populated by millions of deeply nativist white supremacists who believed in their own alternative reality, which just happened to be perfectly synchronized with Putin's narrative that American democracy is corrupt, a fraud, and a hoax. "This is the Russian active measure narrative—Stop the Steal," Yuri Shvets told me.[7] "This party is still under Trump's influence, so the whole party has become a Russian intelligence asset. They are doing one Russian active measure after another."

Again and again, Putin had asserted that American democracy had been corrupted. Now the Republican Party was repeating his words in unison, as if echoing its puppet master. "It's unbelievable," said Shvets. "The Republican Party became a channel for the implementation of Russia's active measures. They are saying exactly the same things. The KGB would not have thought this possible in its wildest dreams."

And Trump's deference to Putin was constant. Though little noted, the GOP's Stalinist purge of Liz Cheney (R-WY), a hawk on Russia's aggressions, from her leadership post as chair of the House Republican Conference, was yet another Trump-ordered win for Putin. Accepting Trump's false claims of electoral victory, the Big Lie had become a prerequisite for Republicans.

So it was not surprising in June when Rep. Andrew S. Clyde (R-GA) described the assault on the Capitol as resembling "a normal tourist visit."[8] In fact, as London's *Independent* reported,[9] photos of the siege appeared to show Clyde screaming in terror, hands in the air, "his face contorted in fear." Nevertheless, his remarks parroted those of Vladimir Putin's, who had previously characterized the insurrectionists as people who merely "took a stroll to the US Congress," for which they face as much as twenty-five years in jail.[10] Like Rep. Clyde, Putin omitted the fact that the rioters were in the middle of executing a failed coup d'etat.

Andrei Illarionov, a former economic adviser to Putin who was also senior fellow at the Cato Institute's Center for Global Liberty and Prosperity, went even further in trying to exculpate the mob that assaulted the Capitol by asserting, falsely, of course, that the insurrection had actually been a Reichstag Fire–like false-flag operation—a trap deliberately set by the Democratic mayor of Washington, DC, and the police, aided by provocations by Black Lives Matter activists.[11]

By this time, tens of millions of emotionally exhausted Americans desperately wanted to leave behind the twin traumas of the Trump presidency and the COVID-19 pandemic and return to the rich and varied lives they once had. In the first quarter of 2021, with Trump leaving the White House, ratings for CNN, MSNBC, and Fox News, which had soared in 2020, plummeted by as much as 68 percent.[12] Trump and Russia indeed were no longer front and center in the national conversation. And long accustomed to thinking of intelligence operations in cloak-and-dagger terms of spies being caught red-handed making a dead drop, Americans were largely oblivious to the stratagems of hybrid warfare that Russia was employing.

Under relative cover of darkness, Russia's hackers went to work and compromised not just our nation's secrets but its essential services as well. In February 2021, the water treatment plant just outside Tampa, Florida, was hacked by unidentified cyber terrorists, resulting in the amount of sodium hydroxide (lye) in the drinking water being dramatically ramped up. Had the breach not been discovered in time, thousands of Florida residents would have been sickened.

That attack was not clearly linked to Russia, but three months later, on May 7, 2021, Colonial Pipeline, a private company that supplies nearly half the liquid fuels for the East Coast and controls a major part of the US energy infrastructure, was hit by a ransomware cyber attack that temporarily shut down the pipelines completely, thereby underscoring the vulnerability of critical sectors within the US infrastructure.

According to NBC News, hackers attempt to penetrate American companies 260 times per week[13] in the utility sector alone—and that's just what we *know*. In 2018, the *New York Times* reported accusations by the Trump administration that Russia had orchestrated a series of cyber attacks on nuclear power plants, water, and electric systems, that gave them the power to sabotage "or shut power plants off at will."[14]

"We now have evidence they're sitting on the machines, connected to industrial control infrastructure, that allow them to effectively turn the power off or effect sabotage," Eric Chien, a security technology director at Symantec, a digital security firm, told the *Times*.

"From what we can see, they were there. They have the ability to shut the power off. All that's missing is some political motivation," Chien said.[15]

The biggest breach of all had begun during Trump's last year in office, when Russian hackers secretly broke into Texas-based SolarWinds' systems and added code that further penetrated the systems of up to 18,000 SolarWinds customers who had installed software updates.

Given that SolarWinds' software helps large companies and other organizations manage their networks, the implications were far worse than they may have sounded. Its customers included virtually all of the gigantic multibillion-dollar companies on the Fortune 500: the Pentagon, the Federal Bureau of Investigation, the Department of Homeland Security, the US Cyber Command, and many other[16] huge agencies and government bureaucracies with millions of employees. Access to highly sensitive material had been breached, and US intelligence had determined the hack was officially authorized by the Russian government.

To this day, the depth and breadth of the damage is not fully known. But according to Microsoft president Brad Smith, the SolarWinds hack was "the largest and most sophisticated attack the world has ever seen."[17]

Not surprisingly, high-stake questions about cyber warfare were very much on the table on June 16, 2021, when President Joe Biden met Vladimir Putin in Geneva for their first summit meeting. In light of Donald Trump's excruciating servility to Putin, the mere fact that Biden agreed to meet face-to-face with the Russian leader raised the issue of whether he would appear to be ceding parity to Putin as a world leader.

But Biden insisted. "It was important to meet in person so there could be no mistake about or misrepresentations about what I wanted to communicate," he explained in a press conference immediately after the summit.[18]

"The tone of the entire meeting was good, positive," he added. "The bottom line is, I told President Putin that we need to have some basic rules of the road that we can all abide by."

According to Biden, the two men spent most of their time discussing cybersecurity, with Biden outlining no fewer than sixteen sectors of critical infrastructure, including energy and water, that should be out of bounds for cyber war. "I talked about the proposition that certain critical infrastructure should be off limits to attack, period. By cyber or any other means," Biden said.[19]

But such strictures meant nothing, of course, unless they were enforced, and Biden said he told Putin that the US has significant cyber warfare capability and would respond appropriately to future cyber attacks. "He knows there are consequences," Biden said of Putin.[20] "He knows I will take action."

He added that he told Putin, "Well, how would you feel if ransomware took down the pipelines from your oil fields?"[21]

Of course, the threat that American hackers might retaliate and go after Russia's precious oil could not possibly have taken place under Trump. "I believe Biden did the right thing," said Yuri Shvets. "He clearly set red lines and said what would happen to Putin if he crossed those lines. He didn't make the same mistakes of George W. Bush, who said he looked into Putin's eyes and saw his soul. He didn't make the same mistakes as Obama, who sought a reset."

And all that left the ball in Vladimir Putin's hands in terms of how to deal with America now that its leader was much, much tougher than Donald Trump and far more savvy. All of which, of course, presupposed that Joe Biden and the Democrats would be successful in fighting off the insurgent Republicans and continue to hang on to power.

But that premise was by no means certain. First, the upcoming November 2022 congressional elections were to take place under circumstances that would make it extraordinarily difficult for the Democrats to hold on to their slim majority in the House of Representatives. After all, Democrats held only 220 seats in Congress, just two more than the 218 seats necessary to keep a bare majority. And historically, it was a virtual certainty that the party in power lost seats in mid-term elections. In 2006, 2010, 2014, and 2018, for example, the ruling party lost 30, 63, 13, and 40 seats, respectively.[22] It was a trend that would be difficult to reverse.

Meanwhile, the GOP had focused on consolidating power in statehouses throughout the country for decades, and had been so successful that they now controlled no fewer than 32 state senates and 29 state legislatures in the fifty states.[23] As a result, they could take charge of redistricting in those states and carve out new Republican majority districts via continued creative use of the gerrymander. "We have redistricting coming up and the Republicans control most of that process in most of the states around the country," Rep. Ronny Jackson (R-TX) told a conference of religious conservatives. "That alone should get us the majority back."[24]

Writing in *The Guardian*, David Daley, author of *Ratf**ked: Why Your Vote Doesn't Count*, noted that Democratic congressional candidates won 4.7 million more votes than Republicans in 2020, and only narrowly held power. But under the newly Republican-drawn maps that will be operative in 2022, the GOP will win control even if voters behave exactly the same way.[25]

And if the Democrats were somehow able to overcome the inequities of gerrymandering, the Republicans had yet another powerful weapon: voter suppression. Indeed, by July 2021, Republicans had crafted more than 400 voter suppression bills in various localities throughout the country, bills that restricted voting hours, access to mail-in ballots, or the number of vote drop boxes—and all of which just happened to have the likely effect of reducing turnout in heavily urban (and usually Democratic) districts. Typical was Texas's bill limiting early-voting hours, curtailing local voting options, and adding restrictions to voting by mail. "We should just be blunt about this," Democratic senator Bob Casey told *Newsweek*. "These voter suppression bills are about white supremacy."

In other words, the Republicans could only win if they were successful in suppressing the Black vote.[26] And the 6 to 3 conservative majority on the United States Supreme Court was in a position to facilitate their strategy. In early July 2021, the nation's highest court upheld two bills restricting voting in Arizona, so it seemed like the Republicans were off to a good start when it came to drawing up wildly unrepresentative districts, constructing elaborate obstacles and inconveniences to hinder voting by Blacks and Hispanics.

Less clear to Americans, and far more ominous, was the fact that the leader of their party, Donald Trump, once and always a KGB asset, was following a path that appeared to be straight out of the Kremlin playbook. He effectively had transformed the GOP, once the Party of Lincoln, into an American version of the Party of Regions, the notoriously corrupt and treasonous Ukrainian political party that looted Ukraine's coffers and blindly followed the dictates of Vladimir Putin. And with their hands on the levers of powers in the statehouses, the entire judiciary, the nation's highest courts, and more, they were still very much a powerful force to be reckoned with. The battle was not over yet.

ACKNOWLEDGMENTS

This book would not have been possible without the help of many people. At Dutton, once again I was privileged to have excellent editing by John Parsley, who oversaw the book from start to finish. I am also grateful to Dutton publisher Christine Ball and president Ivan Held, and a terrific team that treated the project with great professionalism. They include Andrea St. Aubin, Emily Canders, Stephanie Cooper, Tiffany Estreicher, Brent Howard, M. P. Klier, LeeAnn Pemberton, Amanda Walker, Cassidy Sachs, Ryan Richardson, Linda Rosenberg, Susan Schwartz, Dora Mak, Sabila Khan, Leigh Butler, and Chris Lin. I'd also like to thank Penguin Publishing Group president Allison Dobson. My thanks as well to Yuki Hirose for her legal review.

Once again, my literary agent, David Kuhn, did a superb job of shepherding the project from its inception to publication. He, Nate Moscato, and Arlie Johansen at Aevitas were enormously supportive throughout. I'm also deeply indebted to researcher Olga Lautman, with whom I was fortunate to work again and whose language skills and deep knowledge of Russian and Ukrainian politics are invaluable. Similarly, I'd like to thank other members of my team, including fact-checker Ben Kalin, photo researcher Cynthia Carris Alonso, and my friend the photographer James Hamilton for the author's photo. Peter Alson was a terrific help as a reader editor and as a friend as well.

Among the many people who were either interview subjects or gave me assistance, I'd like to thank first and foremost Yuri Shvets for sharing with me so much of his time, his experiences in the KGB, and related expertise. Through many hours of interviews, he always proved an extraordinary, engaging, candid, and courageous subject who has spoken out against Putin, even after the murder of his colleague, Alexander Litvinenko, and the mysterious death of his employer, Boris Berezovsky.

In addition, I'd like to thank Donald Ayer, Neil Barnett, Ari-Ben Menashe, Glenn Carle, Michael Carpenter, David Carr-Brown, Frederick Clarkson, Jeff Dannenberg, Martin Dillon, John Mark Dougan, Edward Jay Epstein, Brian Finnerty, Myron Fuller, Bill Hamilton, Oleg Kalugin, Semyon Kislin, Christopher Mason, Kenneth McCallion, Rolf Mowatt-Larssen, Christina Oxenberg, Richard Painter, Peter Steinfels, Taki Theodoracopulos, Father John Paul Wauck, and Mark Wauck, for their time.

I'm especially indebted to a number of people who asked not to be mentioned, but who nonetheless contributed greatly to the book.

I also want to thank friends and colleagues for generously sharing related materials or contributing much-needed moral support. Anders Aslund, Gabe Benincasa, Sidney Blumenthal, the late Patti Bosworth, Marie Brenner, Jack Bryan, Nina Burleigh, Andy Cohen, Edmundo Desnoes and Felicia Rosshandler, Alan Heilbron and Kerry Malawista, Robert Kaufelt and Nina Planck, Jesse Kornbluth, Todd Gitlin, Ryan Goodman, Steve Halliwell, Scott Horton, Martin Kilian, Michael Mailer, Don and Marji Mendelsohn, Clara Mulberry, Cody Shearer, James Sheldon and Karen Brooks Hopkins, Jeff Stein, Neal Stevens, Paco Underhill, Jonathan Winer and Libby Lewis.

Finally, thanks to my extended family including Chris, Shanti, Thomas, Marley and Miles; Jimmy, Marie-Claude, Adam, Mel, Noah, Rose, and Otis; Matthew and Jacelyn; Harlow and Richard, Romy-Michelle and Gregg.

NOTES

CHAPTER ONE: THE MONSTER PLOT

1. Allan Smith, "Trump on Peaceful Transition If He Loses," NBC News, September 23, 2020.
2. Fintan O'Toole, "Donald Trump Has Destroyed the Country He Promised to Make Great Again," *Irish Times*, April 25, 2020.
3. "Fact Checker," *Washington Post*, updated August 27, 2020.
4. Michael J. Morell, "I Ran the C.I.A. Now I'm Endorsing Hillary Clinton," *New York Times*, August 5, 2016.
5. "The Lead with Jake Tapper," CNN, August 9, 2016.
6. Christopher Woolf, "Former CIA Chief Calls Trump 'Moscow's Useful Idiot,'" *PRI's The World*, December 16, 2016.
7. "The Lead with Jake Tapper," CNN, December 18, 2017.
8. US Central Intelligence Agency, "A Fixation on Moles: James J. Angleton, Anatoliy Golitsyn, and the 'Monster Plot'; Their Impact on CIA Personnel and Operations," *Studies in Intelligence* 55, no. 4 (December 2011).
9. Author's interview with Yuri Shvets.
10. Author's interview with Glenn Carle.
11. Author's interview with Michael Carpenter.
12. Yuri Felshtinsky, "Who Is Dimitri Simes and Why Is He Trying to Sink Mayflower?," *Gordon*, August 22, 2018.
13. Ben Smith, "Nixon's Name," *Politico*, April 19, 2011.
14. Jay Solomon and Benoit Faucon, "Donald Trump Jr. Was Likely Paid at Least $50,000 for Event Held by Hosts Allied with Russia on Syria," *Wall Street Journal*, March 2, 2017.
15. Brian Ross, Matthew Mosk, and Rym Momtaz, "For Donald Trump Jr., Lingering Questions About Meeting with Pro-Russia Group," ABC News, March 2, 2017.
16. Jay Solomon, "Donald Trump Jr. Held Talks on Syria with Russia Supporters," *Wall Street Journal*, November 23, 2016.
17. Julian Borger and Raya Jalabi, "US Syria Policy: Signs of Shift as Trump Son Meets Pro-Damascus Figure," *The Guardian*, November 23, 2016.

18. Michael S. Schmidt, "Comey Memo Says Trump Asked Him to End Flynn Investigation," *New York Times*, May 16, 2017.
19. Julie Vitkovskaya and Amanda Erickson, "The Strange Oval Office Meeting Between Trump, Lavrov and Kislyak," *Washington Post*, May 10, 2017.
20. Matt Apuzzo, Maggie Haberman, and Matthew Rosenberg, "Trump Told Russians That Firing 'Nut Job' Comey Eased Pressure from Investigation," *New York Times*, May 19, 2017.
21. Greg Miller and Greg Jaffe, "Trump Revealed Highly Classified Information to Russian Foreign Minister and Ambassador," *Washington Post*, May 15, 2017.
22. Michael S. Schmidt, "Justice Dept. Never Fully Examined Trump's Ties to Russia, Ex-Officials Say," *New York Times*, August 30, 2020.
23. Rebecca Jennings, "The Mueller Report Renders Thousands of T-Shirts Irrelevant," *Vox*, March 25, 2019.
24. Philip Bump, "What Happened to the Trump Counterintelligence Investigation? House Investigators Don't Know," *Washington Post*, May 15, 2019.

CHAPTER TWO: THE SPOTTER

1. Charles V. Bagli, "Trump Sells Hyatt Share to Pritzkers," *New York Times*, October 8, 1996.
2. Celestine Bohlen, "From Russia, with Love for U.S. Goods," *New York Times*, January 10, 1989.
3. Stuart W. Elliott, "A Cabbie's Climb to Buy 11 Madison," *Real Deal*, March 1, 2004.
4. Shtemler Ilya Petrovich, "Breakfast in Winter at Five in the Morning," *WikiReading*.
5. Caleb Melby and Keri Geiger, "Behind Trump's Russia Romance, There's a Tower Full of Oligarchs," *Bloomberg Businessweek*, March 20, 2017.
6. Georgy Luchnikov, "Uncle Sam in Kiev. What Says the SBU's Enemy of Ex-President Poroshenko and Trump's Personal Friend," *Ukraine.ru*, August 15, 2019.
7. "Semyon Kislin, or Just Sam: What Is Known About the American Citizen of Odessa Who Accused Poroshenko of Large-Scale Corruption—'Timer,'" *Ukraine.ru*, March 29, 2019.
8. *Russian Money Laundering: Hearings Before the Committee on Banking and Financial Services*, 106th Cong., first session, September 21–22, 1999.
9. Author's interview with Yuri Shvets.
10. Interview of Oleg Kalugin by researcher Olga Lautman.
11. Interview of Kalugin by researcher Lautman.
12. Kalitin Andrey, "Shark Capitalism," *WikiReading*.
13. Author's interview with Shvets.
14. "Georgian Businessman's Hollywood Story—from Taxi Driver to Billionaire," *Georgian Journal*, May 13, 2014.
15. Text message to the author from Yuri Shvets.
16. Petrovich, "Breakfast in Winter at Five in the Morning."
17. Matthew Swibel, "The Boomerang Effect," *Forbes*, March 31, 2006.
18. Author's interview with Kenneth McCallion.
19. Author's interview with Rolf Mowatt-Larssen.

CHAPTER THREE: THE ASSET

1. Ondrej Kundra and Jaroslav Spurny, "New Respect: Why Trump Found Himself in the STB's Sights," *Respekt*, October 29, 2018.

2. Luke Harding, "'A Very Different World'—Inside the Czech Spying Operation on Trump," *The Guardian*, October 29, 2018.

3. Harding, "'A Very Different World.'"

4. Natalia Dvaly, "Putin's Groupmate, a Former KGB Spy: You Seriously Think That Putin, Who Is Making a Facelift, Will Unleash a Nuclear War? His Botox Will Melt from the Fear," *Gordon*, May 1, 2015.

5. Tom Topousis, "Rudy Donor Linked to Russian Mob," *New York Post*, December 22, 1999.

6. Text message to the author from Yuri Shvets.

CHAPTER FOUR: SPY WARS

1. Text message to the author from Yuri Shvets.

2. Christopher Andrew and Oleg Gordievsky, *Comrade Kryuchkov's Instructions: Top Secret Files on KGB Foreign Operations, 1975–1985* (Stanford University Press, February 1, 1994).

3. Senate Select Committee on Intelligence, *An Assessment of the Aldrich H. Ames Espionage Case and Its Implications for U.S. Intelligence*, 103rd Cong., second session, November 1, 1994.

4. Christopher Andrew and Vasili Mitrokhin, *The Mitrokhin Archive: The KGB in Europe and the West* (Allen Lane/Penguin Press, 1999), 220.

5. Christopher Andrews and Vasili Mitrokhin, *The Sword and the Shield: The Mitrokhin Archive and the Secret History of the KGB* (Basic Books, 1999), 214.

6. Andrews and Mitrokhin, *Sword and the Shield*, 243.

7. Yuri Shvets, *Washington Station: My Life as a KGB Spy in America* (Simon & Schuster, 1995), 32.

8. Reuters, "Norway Expels Five Russians," *New York Times*, February 2, 1984.

9. "Soviet Defector, on BBC, Says Moscow Agents Have Penetrated the U.N.," *New York Times*, September 24, 1979.

10. United Press International, "Around the World; Ethiopia Expels 2 as Spies for Moscow," *New York Times*, March 8, 1984.

11. Associated Press, "Around the World; Denmark Expels Two in Soviet Group as Spies," *New York Times*, May 25, 1984.

12. UPI, "Soviet Diplomat Named in Spy Case," *New York Times*, October 13, 1984.

13. Anne Saker, "1985 a Bumber [*sic*] Year for U.S. Spy Catchers," United Press International, December 17, 1985.

14. Shvets, *Washington Station*, 38.

15. Andrew and Mitrokhin, *Mitrokhin Archive*, 220.

16. Commission for Review of FBI Security Programs, *A Review of FBI Security Programs*, US Department of Justice, March 2002.

17. Office of the Inspector General, *A Review of the FBI's Performance in Deterring, Detecting, and Investigating the Espionage Activities of Robert Philip Hanssen* (Washington, DC: US Department of Justice, August 14, 2003).

18. Office of the Inspector General, *Espionage Activities of Robert Philip Hanssen*.

19. Office of the Inspector General, *Espionage Activities of Robert Philip Hanssen*.

20. Benjamin Weiser, "A Search for Answers: The New York Years; Spy Chasers Feel Betrayed by One-Time Top Gun," *New York Times*, February 22, 2001.

21. Weiser, "Search for Answers."

22. *An American Affair: Donald Trump and the FBI*, documentary film, courtesy of David Carr-Brown and Fabrizio Calvi, Pumpernickel Films and Allumage for France Télévisions & SWR, 2020.

23. Garrett M. Graff, "The Real F.B.I. Election Culprit," *New York Times*, July 13, 2018.

24. Caleb Melby and Keri Geiger, "Behind Trump's Russia Romance, There's a Tower Full of Oligarchs," *Bloomberg Businessweek*, March 16, 2017.

25. Tom Topousis, "Biz Man: Mob Leak Meant to Smear Rudy," *New York Post*, December 30, 1999.

26. William A. Orme, Jr. "Intrigue Derails a Public Offering; Israel Halts Sale of Phone Company," *New York Times,* April 3, 2001.

27. Topousis, "Biz Man."

28. Orme, Jr. "Intrigue Derails a Public Offering."

29. Thomas Frank, "Secret Money: How Trump Made Millions Selling Condos to Unknown Buyers," *BuzzFeed News*, January 12, 2018.

30. David Wise, "When the FBI Spent Decades Hunting for a Soviet Spy on Its Staff," *Smithsonian*, October 2013.

31. Senate Select Committee on Intelligence, *Soviet Presence in the U.N. Secretariat*, United States Senate, May 1985.

32. "United Nations Library: Putting Soviet Disinformation into Circulation," Heritage Foundation, February 18, 1986.

33. Senate Select Committee on Intelligence, *Soviet Presence in the U.N. Secretariat*.

34. "Woman with Character," *AIF Express*, April 28, 2003.

35. Natalia Dvaly, "Putin's Groupmate, a Former KGB Spy: You Seriously Think That Putin, Who Is Making a Facelift, Will Unleash a Nuclear War? His Botox Will Melt from the Fear," *Gordon*, May 1, 2015.

36. Shvets, *Washington Station,* 22.

37. Shvets, *Washington Station,* 33.

38. Shvets, *Washington Station,* 20.

CHAPTER FIVE: THE EXPERT

1. "Scientists Who Have Said No," Science for the People, January/February 1988.

2. William E. Geist, "The Expanding Empire of Donald Trump," *New York Times*, April 8, 1984.

3. Lois Romano, "Donald Trump, Holding All the Cards: The Tower! The Team! The Money! The Future!," *Washington Post*, November 15, 1984.

4. David Goldenberg, "Trump and the Dove," *Topic* (n.d.).

5. Goldenberg, "Trump and the Dove."

6. Edward Jay Epstein, "The Riddle of Armand Hammer," *New York Times*, November 29, 1981.

7. Tony Judt, *Postwar: A History of Europe Since 1945* (Penguin, October 2005).

8. Tatiana Antonva, "'Trump Immediately Melted': The Intrigue of the First Visit of the US President to the USSR," *Moskovsky Komsomolets*, November 11, 2016 (Google Translate).

9. Lilya Yapparova, "Trump's Russian Trace: From the Real Estate Market in Moscow to Gaidai's Films and Ukupnik's Songs," *The Rain*, November 8, 2016 (Google Translate).

10. Antonva, "'Trump Immediately Melted.'"

11. Luke Harding, *Collusion: Secret Meetings, Dirty Money, and How Russia Helped Donald Trump Win* (Vintage, 2017), 221–222.

12. Donald Trump, *Art of the Deal* (Random House, 2009), 27.

13. Martin Sixsmith, "Different Name, Same Tactics," *The Guardian*, November 20, 2006.

14. Text message from Shvets to the author.
15. Gary Lee, "Soviets Name Veteran Diplomat to UN," *Washington Post*, March 14, 1986.
16. G. Luther Whitington, "Soviet U.N. Ambassador Named to U.S. Post," United Press International, May 20, 1986.
17. Thom Shanker, "Soviets' Man in UN Now Envoy to U.S.," *Chicago Tribune*, May 21, 1986.
18. "Moscow's New Man on the Potomac," *Newsweek,* June 2, 1986.
19. "Moscow's New Man on the Potomac," *Newsweek.*
20. Thom Shanker, "New Ambassador," *Washington Post,* May 20, 1986.
21. Gary Lee, "Moscow Names U.N. Envoy Ambassador to Washington," *Washington Post,* May 21, 1986.
22. Elaine Sciolino, "Man in the News; New Russian in Capital: Yuri Vladimirivich Dubinin," *New York Times,* May 21, 1986.
23. Bernard Gwertzman, "Embassy Row; For Dobrynin and Washington, 'End of an Era,'" *New York Times,* March 7, 1986.
24. Elaine Sciolino, "Washington at Work; Tale of Two Yuris: For Soviet Ambassador, These Are the Best of Times," *New York Times,* November 27, 1989.
25. O. C. Doelling, "U.S. Orders Cuts in Soviet U.N. Missions," Associated Press, March 8, 1986.
26. Stephen Engelberg, "Aide to U.N. Chief Called Soviet Spy in Senate Report," *New York Times,* October 8, 1986.
27. "Moynihan: Soviet Spying Must Be Stopped," United Press International, January 11, 1986.
28. Memo from Shvets to the author.

CHAPTER SIX: YASENEVO DAYS

1. "The Former Execution Chamber," Genocide and Resistance Research Centre of Lithuania.
2. Christopher Andrews and Vasili Mitrokhin, *The Sword and the Shield* (Basic Books, 1999), 7, 8.
3. David Wise, "Closing Down the K.G.B.," *New York Times,* November 24, 1991.
4. Pete Earley, *Comrade J: The Untold Secrets of Russia's Master Spy in America After the End of the Cold War* (Thorndike Press, 2008), 62.
5. Yuri Shvets, *Washington Station: My Life as a KGB Spy in America* (Simon & Schuster, 1995), 173.
6. Author's interview with Yuri Shvets.
7. Daniel L. Wick, "Another Ex-KGB Spy Spills the Beans: Yuri B. Shvets Claims He Recruited a Former Carter Adviser," *San Francisco Chronicle,* March 12, 1995.
8. Dave D'Alessandro, "Weekend Reading Assignment: A Russian Tale," *New Jersey Star Ledger,* January 10, 2010.
9. Dana Milbank, "Eight Republicans Pick the Worst Possible Place to Celebrate July 4," *Washington Post,* July 6, 2018.
10. Harding, *Collusion,* 223.
11. "Ministry of State Security (Stasi), 'Note About the Talks of Comrade Minister [Mielke] with the Chairman of the KGB, Comrade Chebrikov, in Moscow,'" Wilson Center Digital Archive, February 9, 1983.
12. Seth Hettena, *Trump/Russia: A Definitive History* (Melville House, 2018), 14.
13. Craig Unger, *House of Trump, House of Putin* (Dutton, 2018), 50.

14. Edward Jay Epstein, *Dossier: The Secret History of Armand Hammer* (Random House, 1996), 8.

15. Epstein, *Dossier,* 123.

16. Author's interview with Shvets.

17. Michael Oreskes, "Trump Gives a Vague Hint of Candidacy," *New York Times*, September 2, 1987.

18. Paula Span, "When Trump Hoped to Meet Gorbachev in Manhattan," *Washington Post*, December 3, 1988.

19. William C. Trott, "Trump's Communist," United Press International, December 2, 1988.

20. Natalie Schreyer, "The Trump Files: When Donald Couldn't Tell the Difference Between Gorbachev and an Impersonator," *Mother Jones*, July 5, 2016.

21. Glenn Plaskin, "The *Playboy* Interview with Donald Trump," *Playboy*, March 1, 1990.

22. "Vladimir Kryuchkov: Plotter Against Gorbachev," *The Independent*, November 26, 2007.

23. Kathleen Klenetsky, "Soviets 'Intensely Interested' in 1988 U.S. Campaign," *Executive Intelligence Review*, June 24, 1987.

24. Christopher Burgess, "Russia: Skilled Political Warfare Adversary," *Security Boulevard*, November 7, 2017.

25. Unger, *House of Trump*, 51.

26. John F. Barton, "Defector Details KGB Activity in Japan," United Press International, December 11, 1982.

27. Howard Kurtz, "Between the Lines of a Millionaire's Ad," *Washington Post*, September 2, 1987.

28. Michael Oreskes, "Trump Gives Vague Hint of Candidacy," *New York Times*, September 2, 1987.

29. Oreskes, "Trump Gives Vague Hint."

CHAPTER SEVEN: OPUS DEI

1. David A. Vise, "From Russia with Love," *Washington Post*, January 6, 2002.

2. James Risen, "Spy's Wife Speaks, After Taking a Lie Test," *New York Times*, May 16, 2002.

3. Office of the Inspector General, *A Review of the FBI's Performance in Deterring, Detecting, and Investigating the Espionage Activities of Robert Philip Hanssen* (Washington, DC: US Department of Justice, August 14, 2003).

4. Eric Lichtblau, "Spy's Wife Apologizes, Finds His Life Sentence 'Appropriate,'" *Los Angeles Times*, July 13, 2001.

5. Office of the Inspector General, *Espionage Activities of Robert Philip Hanssen.*

6. Elaine Shannon, *The Spy Next Door* (Little, Brown, 2002), 60.

7. Office of the Inspector General, *Espionage Activities of Robert Philip Hanssen.*

8. Office of the Inspector General, *Espionage Activities of Robert Philip Hanssen.*

9. Vise, "From Russia with Love."

10. Anthony Zanontian, "Your Complete Guide to the Russian KGB—Key Players," http://www.math.ucsd.edu/~crypto/Projects/AnthonyZanontian/azkgb.htm.

11. Elaine Shannon, "Death of the Perfect Spy," *Time*, June 24, 2001.

12. Author's interview with Scott Horton.

13. David A. Vise, *The Bureau and the Mole: The Unmasking of Robert Philip Hanssen, the Most Dangerous Double Agent in FBI History* (Grove Atlantic, 2001), 41–42.

14. Graydon Megan, "Dr. LeRoy Wauck: 1920–2009," *Chicago Tribune*, January 9, 2009.

15. Adrian Havill, *The Spy Who Stayed Out in the Cold* (St. Martin's, 2001), 45, 154.

16. Eric O'Neill, *Gray Day: My Undercover Mission to Expose America's First Cyber Spy* (Crown/Archetype, 2019), 174.

17. Michael F. Flach, "Opus Dei Members 'Shocked, Saddened' by Hanssen's Arrest," *Arlington Catholic Herald*, March 1, 2001.

18. Shannon, *Spy Next Door*, 38–39.

19. Vise, *Bureau and the Mole*, 1.

20. Office of the Inspector General, *Espionage Activities of Robert Philip Hanssen*.

21. David Wise, *Spy: The Inside Story of How the FBI's Robert Hanssen Betrayed America* (Random House, 2002).

22. Office of the Inspector General, *Espionage Activities of Robert Philip Hanssen*.

23. Vise, "From Russia with Love."

24. Wise, *Spy*, Kindle location 494.

25. Wise, *Spy*, 26.

26. Vise, *Bureau and the Mole*, 48–49.

27. John F. Coverdale, *Putting Down Roots: Father Joseph Múzquiz and the Growth of Opus Dei, 1912–1983* (Scepter, 2009), 6.

28. "Who Was Father Joseph Muzquiz?," Opus Dei, July 13, 2017.

29. Robert Hutchison, *Their Kingdom Come: Inside the Secret World of Opus Dei* (St. Martin's, 1997), 101.

30. Coverdale, *Putting Down Roots*, ix.

31. Wolfgang Saxon, "Salvador Ferigle, 73, Priest Who Brought Opus Dei to the U.S.," *New York Times*, January 17, 1997.

32. Fr. Roger J. Landry, "The Captivating Sanctity of Fr. Sal," *The Anchor*, January 13, 2017.

33. Personal Prelature of Opus Dei.

34. Coverdale, *Putting Down Roots*, 47.

35. Email from Fr. John Paul Wauck to the author.

36. Wise, *Spy*, 26.

CHAPTER EIGHT: BETRAYAL

1. Office of the Inspector General, *A Review of the FBI's Performance in Deterring, Detecting, and Investigating the Espionage Activities of Robert Philip Hanssen*, US Department of Justice, August 14, 2003.

2. David Wise, "When the FBI Spent Decades Hunting for a Soviet Spy on Its Staff," *Smithsonian*, October 2013.

3. Joel Brinkley and Leslie H. Gelb, "U.S. Frustrated in Efforts to Counter Soviet Spying," *New York Times*, June 16, 1985.

4. Office of the Inspector General, *Espionage Activities of Robert Philip Hanssen*.

5. Rob Boston, "Of Spies and Saints," *Church and State*, May 2006.

6. David Wise, *Spy: The Inside Story of How the FBI's Robert Hanssen Betrayed America* (Random House, 2002), Kindle location 50.

7. Wise, *Spy*, 50.

8. Elaine Shannon, *The Spy Next Door* (Little, Brown, 2002), 90.

9. Brooke A. Masters, "Hanssen Admits Spying, Avoids Death Penalty," *Washington Post*, July 7, 2001.

10. Author's interview with Mark Wauck.

11. Author's interview with Mark Wauck.

12. Wise, *Spy*, 125.

13. Author's interview with Mark Wauck.

14. Mark Binelli, "Pope Francis: The Times They Are A-Changin'," *Rolling Stone*, January 28, 2014.

15. James Martin, S.J., "Opus Dei in the United States," *America: The National Catholic Weekly*, February 25, 1995.

16. Frank L. Cocozzelli, "The Politics of Schism in the Catholic Church," Political Research Associates, September 6, 2009.

17. Kirsten Biondich, "Operation Lemonade: Opus Dei's Public Relations Campaign Against the Da Vinci Code" (thesis, University of Florida, 2007).

18. Robert Hutchison, *Their Kingdom Come: Inside the Secret World of Opus Dei* (St. Martin's, 1997), Kindle location 61.

19. Michael J. Walsh, *The Secret World of Opus Dei: An Investigation into the Controversial Sect at the Heart of the Roman Catholic Church* (Grafton, 1989).

20. Kenneth Woodward, "A Questionable Saint," *Newsweek*, January 12, 1992.

21. Terry Eagleton, "The Fraternal Corrections: Opus Dei and the Catholic Church," *Harper's*, April 1, 2006.

22. Josemaría Escrivá, *The Way*, number 311.

23. Walsh, *Secret World of Opus Dei*, 20.

24. Hutchison, *Their Kingdom Come*, 73.

25. Giles Tremlett, "Sainthood Beckons for Priest Linked to Franco," *The Guardian*, October 4, 2002.

26. Hutchinson, *Their Kingdom Come*, 138.

27. Herbert L. Matthews, "What About After Franco," *Austin American*, December 1, 1965.

28. Letter from Escrivá to Franco, May 23, 1958, Opus Dei Awareness Network.

29. Elizabeth W. Green, "Opening the Doors of Opus Dei," *Harvard Crimson*, April 10, 2003.

CHAPTER NINE: THE NEW PRAETORIAN GUARD

1. David Montgomery, "Conquerors of the Court," *Washington Post*, January 2, 2019.

2. Jay Michaelson, "The Secrets of Leonard Leo, the Man Behind Trump's Supreme Court Pick," *Daily Beast*, July 24, 2018.

3. Sue Sturgis, "The Secret Money Behind the Push to Ban Abortion," *Common Dreams*, May 26, 2019.

4. Michael Walsh, *The Secret World of Opus Dei: An Investigation into the Controversial Sect at the Heart of the Roman Catholic Church* (Grafton, 1989), 170.

5. "Questionable Practices," Opus Dei Awareness Network.

6. Elizabeth W. Green, "Opening the Doors of Opus Dei," *Harvard Crimson*, April 10, 2003.

7. "Purpose of Opus Dei," *Real Catholic Online*.

8. Escrivá, *The Way*.

9. John L. Allen, Jr., *Opus Dei: An Objective Look Behind the Myths and Reality of the Most Controversial Force in the Catholic Church* (Doubleday Religion, 2005), 232.

10. "Index of Forbidden Books," Opus Dei Awareness Network.

11. Author's interview with Brian Finnerty.

12. "Secret by Statute: The Opus Dei Codes of Secrecy," Real Catholic Online.

13. "About CIC DC," Catholic Information Center.

14. Betty Clemont, "Opus Dei's Influence Is Felt in All of Washington's Corridors of Power," *Open Tabernacle,* January 22, 2019.

15. Michelle Boorstein, "Opus Dei Paid $977,000 to Settle Sexual Misconduct Claim Against Prominent Catholic Priest," *Washington Post,* January 7, 2019.

16. Joe Heim, "'Quite a Shock': The Priest Was a D.C. Luminary. Then He Had a Disturbing Fall from Grace," *Washington Post,* January 14, 2019.

17. Frederick Clarkson, "God Is My Co-Belligerent: Avatar Priests, Hijacked Theologians, and Other Figures of Right-Wing Revolt," *Religion Dispatches*, July 26, 2012.

18. Michaelson, "Secrets of Leonard Leo."

19. Michaelson, "Secrets of Leonard Leo."

CHAPTER TEN: THE COVER-UP GENERAL

1. David Rhode, "William Barr, Trump's Sword and Shield," *New Yorker*, January 20, 2020.

2. Marie Brenner, "'I Had No Problem Being Politically Different': Young William Barr Among the Manhattan Liberals," *Vanity Fair*, October 7, 2019.

3. "George H .W. Bush—the 11th Director of Central Intelligence," CIA News and Information, December 1, 2018.

4. George Packer, "The President Is Winning His War on American Institutions," *The Atlantic,* April 2020.

5. Frank Snepp, "Bill Barr: The 'Cover-Up General,'" *Village Voice*, October 27, 1992.

6. Murray S. Waas and Craig Unger, "In the Loop: Bush's Secret Mission," *New Yorker*, October 26, 1992.

7. "William P. Barr Oral History," University of Virginia Miller Center, April 5, 2001.

8. "William P. Barr Oral History," University of Virginia Miller Center.

9. Susan Hennessey, "The Disintegration of the American Presidency," *The Atlantic,* January 21, 2020.

10. William P. Barr, "Common Legislative Encroachments on Executive Branch Authority," July 27, 1989.

11. Rhode, "William Barr, Trump's Sword and Shield."

12. Frank Snepp, "Bill Barr: The Cover-Up General," *Village Voice*, October 27, 1992.

13. William Safire, "Essay; The Patsy Prosecutor," *New York Times*, October 19, 1992.

14. William Safire, "Essay: A Tale of Three Counsels," *New York Times*, December 28, 1992.

15. William Safire, "Essay; Justice Corrupts Justice," *New York Times*, August 31, 1992.

16. *Report of Special Counsel Nicholas J. Bua to the Attorney General of the United States Regarding the Allegations of INSLAW, Inc.,* March 1993; US Department of Justice, 1994 DOJ Report on INSLAW/PROMIS matter, released by the Department of Justice Office of Information Policy, September 30, 2013.

17. Thom Hartmann, "Has 'Cover-Up General' William Barr Struck Again?," *Common Dreams*, March 26, 2019.

18. David Johnston, "Bush Pardons 6 in Iran Affair, Aborting a Weinberger Trial; Prosecutor Assails 'Cover-Up,'" *New York Times*, December 25, 1992.

19. Mary Papenfuss, "William Barr's Partisan 'Authoritarian' Trump Defense Triggers Calls for His Impeachment," *Huffington Post*, November 17, 2019.

20. Author's interview with Brian Finnerty.

21. "Statement regarding U.S. Attorney General William Barr," Opus Dei, November 27, 2019.

22. Chris Mathews, "A Day in the Life of a Supernumerary," NBC News, May 17, 2006.
23. Email from Brian Finnerty to the author, February 28, 2020.
24. Author's interview with Frederick Clarkson.
25. John Spano, "Catholic Doctrine Is Cited in Priest Sex Abuse Cases; In Questioning Clergy, Some Lawyers Encounter the Principle of 'Mental Reservation,' Which Justifies Lying to Protect the Church," *Los Angeles Times*, March 26, 2007.
26. Charlotte Sector, "Ex-Opus Dei Members Decry Blind Obedience," ABC News, May 17, 2006.
27. Franco Ordoñez, "Trump Impeachment Trial Turns Spotlight on White House Lawyer Cipollone," *All Things Considered*, NPR, December 23, 2019.
28. Carol D. Leonnig and Rosalind S. Helderman, "Trump Has Chosen Washington Lawyer Pat Cipollone as Next White House Counsel, People Familiar with Decision Say," *Washington Post*, October 13, 2018.
29. "AG Nominee William Barr Must Repudiate Previous Statements Vilifying Secularism," Freedom from Religion Foundation news release, December 10, 2018.
30. William P. Barr, "Legal Issues in a New Political Order," *Catholic Lawyer*, January 1995.

CHAPTER ELEVEN: THE BOUNCING CZECH

1. Gordon Thomas and Martin Dillon, *Robert Maxwell, Israel's Superspy: The Life and Murder of a Media Mogul* (Carroll and Graf, 2002).
2. Ken Gross, "A Tycoon's Mysterious Death," *People*, November 18, 1991.
3. Tom Bower, *Maxwell: The Outsider* (Viking Penguin, January 1991), 477.
4. Thomas and Dillon, *Robert Maxwell, Israel's Superspy*, 298.
5. Nick Sommerlad, "Ghislaine Maxwell 'Ordered Shredding of Crooked Dad's Paperwork Hours After He Drowned,'" *The Mirror*, August 2, 2020.
6. "Soundbite," *The Observer*, February 23, 1997.
7. Kevin Cahill, "How They Killed Maxwell," *Sunday Age*, April 18, 1993.
8. Thomas and Dillon, *Robert Maxwell, Israel's Superspy*, 8.
9. Allan Sloan and Glenn Kessler, "U.S. Deals Weakened Empire," *Newsday*, November 7, 1991.
10. Gordon Thomas and Martin Dillon, "Robert Maxwell Was a Mossad Spy. He Asked Them for Pounds 400M. They Refused and Feared He Would Now Expose Them. So Three Israeli Agents Killed Him on His Boat; New Claim on Tycoon's Mystery Death," *Daily Mirror*, December 2, 2002.
11. "Maxwell, Colossus Even in Death, Laid to Rest on Mount of Olives," *Jewish Telegraphic Agency*, November 11, 1991.
12. Gordon Thomas, *Gideon's Spies: The Secret History of the Mossad* (Pan Books, 2000), 201.
13. Seumas Milne, *The Enemy Within: The Secret War Against the Minder* (Verso, 2004), 218.
14. Rob Evans and David Hencke, "Maxwell—the 'Red' the Feds Failed to Nail," *The Guardian*, October 13, 2000.
15. *Maxwell: The Downfall*, documentary directed by David Suchet, 2007.
16. Thomas and Dillon, *Robert Maxwell, Israel's Superspy*, 8.
17. Stephen Dorril, *MI6: Inside the Covert World of Her Majesty's Secret Intelligence Service* (Free Press, June 2000).
18. "Robert Maxwell Files (1923–1991)," FBI: The Vault.
19. "Robert Maxwell Files," FBI.

20. "Robert Maxwell Files," FBI.
21. Emily Hourican, "Robert Maxwell: Legacy of 'the Bouncing Czech,'" *The Independent*, October 17, 2016.
22. Evans and Hencke, "Maxwell."
23. Mark Burdman, "KGB Boss Says Robert Maxwell Was the Second Kissinger," *EIR*, August 12, 1994.
24. Author's interview with Yuri Shvets.
25. "On Their Toes," *St. Louis Post-Dispatch*, May 17, 1999.
26. Adam Lusher, "Adnan Khashoggi: The 'Whoremonger' Whose Arms Deals Funded a Playboy Life of Decadence and 'Pleasure Wives,'" *The Independent*, October 29, 2019.
27. Dylan Howard, with Melissa Cronin and James Robertson, *Epstein: Dead Men Tell No Tales* (Skyhorse, December 2019), Kindle location 365.
28. Dominick Dunne, "Khashoggi's Fall: A Crash in the Limo Lane," *Vanity Fair*, September 1989.
29. "Memorandum in Response to the March 1993 Report of Special Counsel Nicholas J. Bua to the Attorney General of the United States Responding to the Allegations of INSLAW, Inc.," July 29, 1993.
30. "Atlantic Southeast Airlines, Inc., Flight 2311, Uncontrolled Collision with Terrain, an Embraer EMB-120, N270AS, Brunswick, Georgia, April 5, 1991," National Transportation Safety Board, April 28, 1992.
31. Neil A. Lewis, "Reporter Is Buried Amid Questions over His Pursuit of Conspiracy Idea," *New York Times*, August 17, 1991.
32. "Writer's Death Raises Questions of Political Conspiracy: Casolaro Was Pursuing Alleged Reagan-Bush Scandals When He Died; Police Investigating," *Boston Globe*, August 14, 1991.
33. Jeffery A. Frank, "The Inslaw File," *Washington Post*, June 14, 1992.
34. Thomas and Dillon, *Robert Maxwell, Israel's Superspy*, 61.
35. Frank, "Inslaw File."
36. Anatoly S. Chernyaev, *The Diary of Anatoly S. Chernyaev*, ed. Svetlana Savranskaya and trans. Anna Melyakova, National Security Archive, 1991.
37. Chernyaev, *The Diary of Anatoly S. Chernyaev.*
38. Thomas and Dillon, *Robert Maxwell: Israel's Superspy*, 85.
39. Craig Unger, *House of Trump, House of Putin* (Dutton, 2018).
40. Thomas and Dillon, *Robert Maxwell, Israel's Superspy.*
41. Thomas and Dillon, *Robert Maxwell, Israel's Superspy*, 37.
42. Thomas and Dillon, *Robert Maxwell, Israel's Superspy.*
43. Thomas and Dillon, *Robert Maxwell, Israel's Superspy.*
44. "Debt Mountain Overhangs Sprawling Maxwell Empire," *Financial Post*, November 6, 1991.
45. Michael Kilian, "The 200-Foot Fetish," *Chicago Tribune*, July 26, 1989.
46. Thomas and Dillon, *Robert Maxwell, Israel's Superspy.*
47. Knut Royce, "FBI Tracked Alleged Russian Mob Ties of Giuliani Campaign Supporter," Center for Public Integrity, December 14, 1999.
48. Author's interview with Glenn Carle.
49. Author's interview with Glenn Carle.
50. David Johnston, "New Attorney General Shifts Department's Focus," *New York Times*, March 3, 1993.
51. Author's interview with Myron Fuller.

CHAPTER TWELVE: GHISLAINE AND JEFFREY

1. Lee A. Daniels, "Chronicle," *New York Times*, November 8, 1991.
2. "Inside New York," *Newsday*, November 22, 1991.
3. "Inside New York," *Newsday*.
4. Paul Farhi, "Maxwell Auditors Trace $1.2 Billion in Missing Money," *Washington Post,* December 9, 1991.
5. George Parker-Jervis and Peter Watson, "Banks Close In on Maxwell—Pressure Is Mounting for Kevin and Ian Maxwell, Who Must Satisfy Their Bankers This Week or Face Administration," *The Observer* (London), November 24, 1991.
6. David Hellier, "Maxwell's Time Bomb: A Fraud Investigation into Mysterious Events Surrounding a Loan of Just Pounds 60M Has Sent a Tremor Through the Complex Web of the Late Mogul's Empire," *The Independent* (UK), November 24, 1991.
7. Steven Prokesch, "Swiss Bank Is Demanding Maxwell Loan Repayment," *New York Times,* November 21, 1991.
8. "Misery in the Maxwell House," *The Scotsman*, November 16, 2001.
9. Associated Press, "Doc Denies Foul Play Call on Maxwell," *Daily News*, November 22, 1991.
10. Mick Brown and Harriet Alexander, "The Rise and Fall of Socialite Ghislaine Maxwell, Jeffrey Epstein's 'Best Friend,'" *Sydney Morning Herald*, January 31, 2020.
11. Michael Robotham, "The Mystery of Ghislaine Maxwell's Secret Love," *Mail on Sunday* (London), November 15, 1992.
12. Robotham, "Mystery of Ghislaine Maxwell's Secret Love."
13. Author's interview with Taki Theodoracopulos.
14. Vicky Ward, "Jeffrey and Ghislaine: Notes on New York's Oddest Alliance," *Vanity Fair*, March 8, 2011.
15. Author's interview with Christopher Mason.
16. Ezekiel Kweku, Matthew Schneier, Amy Larocca, Adam K. Raymond, Matt Stieb, James D. Walsh, Yinka Martins, Charlotte Klein, Kelsey Hurwitz, and Brock Colyar, "Who Was Jeffrey Epstein Calling?," *New York*, July 22, 2019.
17. Becky Ferreira, "Epstein Truthers Are Obsessed with a Sci-Fi Book About Child Sex Slavery Written by Bill Barr's Dad," *Vice*, August 16, 2019.
18. Mike Baker and Amy Julia Harris, "Jeffrey Epstein Taught at Dalton. His Behavior Was Noticed," *New York Times*, July 12, 2019.
19. Linda Robertson and Aron Brezel, "'Poor, Smart and Desperate to Be Rich': How Epstein Went from Teaching to Wall Street," *Miami Herald*, July 21, 2019.
20. Marc Fisher and Jonathan O'Connell, "Final Evasion: For 30 Years, Prosecutors and Victims Tried to Hold Jeffrey Epstein to Account. At Every Turn, He Slipped Away. Epstein's Apparent Suicide Is the Last in a Number of Escapes That Began with a Massive Fraud in the 1980s," *Washington Post* blogs, August 10, 2019.
21. Nelson D. Schwartz, "What 'the Bear' Means for the Street," *New York Times*, March 30, 2008.
22. Vicky Ward, "The Talented Mr. Epstein," *Vanity Fair*, June 27, 2011.
23. Emily Steel, Steve Eder, Sapna Maheshwari, and Matthew Goldstein, "How Jeffrey Epstein Used the Billionaire Behind Victoria's Secret for Wealth and Women," *New York Times*, July 25, 2019.
24. Khadeeja Safdar, Rebecca Davis O'Brien, Gregory Zuckerman, and Jenny Strasburg, "Jeffrey Epstein Burrowed into the Lives of the Rich and Made a Fortune," *Wall Street Journal*, July 25, 2019.

25. Caroline Hallemann, "Jeffrey Epstein Was Worth $577 Million When He Died," *Town & Country*, May 27, 2020.
26. Philip Weiss, "The Fantasist," *New York*, December 17, 2007.
27. Matthew Goldstein, Steve Eder, and David Enrich, "The Billionaire Who Stood by Jeffrey Epstein," *New York Times*, October 12, 2020.
28. Goldstein, Eder, and Enrich, "The Billionaire Who Stood by Jeffrey Epstein."
29. Edward Jay Epstein, "My Tea with Jeffrey Epstein," *Air Mail*, September 14, 2019.
30. Jesse Kornbluth, "I Was a Friend of Jeffrey Epstein; Here's What I Know," *Salon*, July 9, 2019.
31. Ben Schreckinger and Daniel Lippman, "Meet the Woman Who Ties Jeffrey Epstein to Trump and the Clintons," *Politico*, July 21, 2019.
32. Ward, "The Talented Mr. Epstein."
33. Fisher and O'Connell, "Final Evasion."
34. Gerber vs. Financial Trust Exhibit F.
35. Heather Timmons, "Jeffrey Epstein's Fortune Is Built on Fraud, a Former Mentor Says," *Quartz*, July 9, 2019.
36. Michael Wolff, *Fire and Fury* (Henry Holt, 2018).
37. Landon Thomas, Jr., "Jeffrey Epstein: International Moneyman of Mystery," *New York*, October 28, 2002.
38. Seymour M. Hersh, *The Samson Option* (Random House, 1991).
39. Steven Jude Hoffenberg, individually, and as Index No. constructive trustee of the Noteholders and Bondholders of Towers Financial Corporation, related actions: Case No. 94 CR 213 (RWS) Plaintiff, Case No. 95 CR 213 (RWS) v. Judge Robert W. Sweet; Jeffrey E. Epstein, individually, and as President and Chief Executive Officer of the Financial Trust Company, the Financial Trust Company, XYZ Corp. and ABC, Inc.
40. "Libya's Cyrenaica Hires Canada-Based Lobbyist to Help Sell Oil," Reuters, January 7, 2014.
41. Katherine Clarke, "Former Reported IDF Arms Dealer Lists Fifth Avenue Pad for Nearly $10M," *Real Deal*, April 4, 2012.
42. Craig Unger, "The Trouble with Ari," *Village Voice*, July 7, 1992.
43. Author's interview with Martin Dillon.

CHAPTER THIRTEEN: SEX, SPIES, AND VIDEOTAPE

1. Author's interview with Jesse Kornbluth.
2. Ward, "The Talented Mr. Epstein."
3. Emine Saner, "'She Was So Dangerous': Where in the World Is the Notorious Ghislaine Maxwell?," *The Guardian*, December 12, 2019.
4. Tom Bower, *Maxwell: The Final Verdict* (HarperCollins, 1995), 40.
5. Tom Bower, *Maxwell: The Outsider* (Viking Penguin, 1991).
6. Bower, *The Final Verdict*.
7. "Epstein Investigation Turns to Identifying Alleged Associates, Clients," NPR *Morning Edition*, August 13, 2019.
8. Bower, *The Final Verdict*.
9. "Deadline Arrives for *NY Post* Bidders," Associated Press, January 23, 1988.
10. Nick Davies, *Death of a Tycoon* (St. Martin's Press, 1993).
11. Gordon Thomas, *Gideon's Spies: The Secret History of the Mossad* (Pan Books, 2000).
12. Gordon Thomas and Martin Dillon, *Robert Maxwell, Israel's Superspy: The Life and Murder of a Media Mogul* (Carroll & Graf, 2003), 84.

13. Thomas and Dillon, *Robert Maxwell, Israel's Superspy.*

14. Eliza Relman, "The 25 Women Who Have Accused Trump of Sexual Misconduct," *Business Insider*, May 1, 2020.

15. Craig Unger, *House of Trump, House of Putin* (Dutton, 2018).

16. Annie Karni and Maggie Haberman, "Jeffrey Epstein Was a 'Terrific Guy,' Donald Trump Once Said. Now He's 'Not a Fan,'" *New York Times*, July 9, 2019.

17. Nicolas Kristof, "Donald Trump, Groper in Chief," *New York Times*, October 7, 2016.

18. Nanette Holland, "Reigning Miss Russia Finds New Friends, Fun in Florida," *Tampa Tribune*, April 8, 1995.

19. "Anna Alexandrovna Malova—Biography, Information, Personal Life," Stuki-Druki (Google Translate).

20. Holland, "Reigning Miss Russia Finds New Friends."

21. "Anna Alexandrovna Malova," Stuki-Druki.

22. Unger, *House of Trump.*

23. Tim Ryan, "Trinidadian Sings for Her Title," *Honolulu Star-Bulletin*, May 13, 1998.

24. Deborah Mitchell and Beth Landman, "The Race to Be Number Two," *New York*, June 15, 1998.

25. George Rush and Joanna Malloy, "Vow Wow! Book to Say JFK Was Wed Twice?," *Daily News*, October 31, 1997.

26. Mark Singer, "Trump Solo," *New Yorker*, May 19, 1997.

27. James Beal and Jenny Awford, "'I Was Corrupted,'" *The Sun*, August 27, 2019.

28. Ben Widdicombe, "Christina Oxenberg Is Related to Royalty and Hollywood Stars—and She Is Ready to Tell *All* Her Stories," *Town & Country*, December 19, 2019.

29. Widdicombe, "Christina Oxenberg Is Related to Royalty."

30. Christina Oxenberg, "Sunday Story: Epstein's Libido," *Patreon*, May 23, 2020.

31. Author's interview with Christina Oxenberg.

32. Author's interview with Christina Oxenberg.

33. Oxenberg, "Sunday Story: Epstein's Libido."

34. Sarah Blaskey, *The Grifter's Club: Trump, Mar-a-Lago, and the Selling of the Presidency* (PublicAffairs, 2020), Kindle location 18.

35. Sebastian Shakespeare, "Socialite Christina Oxenberg Tells All About Jeffrey Epstein and Ghislaine Maxwell to the FBI as She Says She Is 'Disgusted' by the 'Creepy' Pair and Calls a Hotline to Help," *Daily Mail*, February 20, 2020.

36. Saner, "'She Was So Dangerous.'"

37. Sharon Churcher, "Epstein's Girl Friday 'Fixer': Dead Tycoon's Daughter Ghislaine Maxwell and the Girls She Hired for Paedophile's Stable," *Daily Mail*, March 7, 2011.

38. Sharon Churcher and Polly Dunbar, "Teenage Girl Recruited by Paedophile Jeffrey Epstein Reveals How She Twice Met Bill Clinton," *Daily Mail*, March 5, 2011.

39. Jesse Kornbluth, "I Was a Friend of Jeffrey Epstein; Here's What I Know," *Salon*, July 9, 2019.

40. Karni and Haberman, "Jeffrey Epstein Was a 'Terrific Guy.'"

41. Julie K. Brown, "Even from Jail, Sex Abuser Manipulated the System. His Victims Were Kept in the Dark," *Miami Herald*, November 29, 2018.

42. *Dateline*, NBC, September 29, 2019.

43. Marc Fisher, "Jeffrey Epstein, Accused of Sexually Abusing Teenage Girls, Surrounded Himself with Influential Network of Defenders," *Washington Post*, July 9, 2019.

44. Loulla-Mae Eleftheriou-Smith, "Prince Andrew Sex Allegations: Jeffrey Epstein's Butler Alfredo Rodriguez, Who Stole Tell-All 'Black Book,' Dies Age 60," *Independent*, January 7, 2015.

45. Deposition of Christina J. Pryor, Florida Southern District Docket, Alfredo Rodriguez case, December 9, 2009.

46. Jon Swaine, "Jeffrey Epstein Scandal: Women with New Identities Run Firms from Epstein-Linked Property," *The Guardian*, January 7, 2015.

47. Michael Gross, *Model: The Ugly Business of Beautiful Women* (Dey Street Books, May 1995).

48. Conchita Sarnoff, "Jeffrey Epstein Pedophile Billionaire and His Sex Den," *Daily Beast*, July 22, 2010.

49. Gross, *Model*, 468.

50. Gross, *Model*, 467.

51. Lucy Osborne, Harry Davies, and Stephanie Kirschgaessner, "Teen Models, Powerful Men and Private Dinners: When Trump Hosted Look of the Year," *The Guardian*, March 14, 2020.

52. Emily Shugerman, "Models Say Jeffrey Epstein's Closest Pal Drugged, Raped Them," *Daily Beast*, September 16, 2019.

53. Kim Bhasin, Jordyn Holman, and Bloomberg, "Major Retailers Had 'Tremendous' Concerns About Fashion Model Scout's Ties to Jeffrey Epstein," *Fortune*, August 19, 2019.

54. Ben Graham, "Mystery over Jeffrey Epstein's Missing Mate Jean-Luc Brunel," *Australia's News*, December 14, 2019.

55. *Jeffrey Epstein v. Bradley J. Edwards et al.*, "Exhibits to Statements of Undisputed Facts."

56. *Jeffrey Epstein v. Bradley J. Edwards et al.*, "Exhibits to Statements of Undisputed Facts."

57. James West, "Former Models for Donald Trump's Agency Say They Violated Immigration Rules and Worked Illegally," *Mother Jones*, August 30, 2016.

58. Michael Gross, "Inside Donald Trump's One-Stop Parties: Attendees Recall Cocaine and Very Young Models," *Daily Beast*, June 25, 2020.

59. "Andy's Hush-Hush Visit," *New York Post*, April 21, 1999.

60. Thom Smith, "Society Snapshots," *Palm Beach Post*, February 20, 2000.

61. Karni and Haberman, "Jeffrey Epstein Was a 'Terrific Guy.'"

62. Wolff, *Siege*, 14.

63. Beth Reinhard, Rosalind S. Helderman, and Marc Fisher, "Donald Trump and Jeffrey Epstein Partied Together. Then an Oceanfront Palm Beach Mansion Came Between Them," *Washington Post*, July 31, 2019.

64. Wolff, *Siege*, 14.

65. Sarnaff, "Jeffrey Epstein Pedophile Billionaire."

66. Shugarman, "Models Say Jeffrey Epstein's Closest Pal."

67. Peter Pomerantsev, *Nothing Is True and Everything Is Possible: The Surreal Heart of the New Russia* (Public Affairs, November 2014).

68. Richard Johnson, "Jeffrey Epstein's East Side Mansion Houses Russian Playmates," *New York Post*, March 8, 2016.

69. Anna Nemtsova, "The Russian Sleazeball Peddling Girls to Billionaires," *Daily Beast*, July 29, 2019.

70. Alena Antonova, "Eva Hercegova Said Hello to Russian Businessmen," *Kommersant*, March 17, 2003.

71. Nemtsova, "The Russian Sleazeball."

72. "Interview Listerman: 'Profession—Introducing People.' Shaggy Gold Merchant," *Moscsp*, June 25, 2019.

73. Nemtsova, "The Russian Sleazeball."

74. Vladimir Kozlovsky, "Colorful Listerman," *Kstati*, September 25, 2019.

75. "The Fall of the Oligarchs," *Russian Press Digest*, September 16, 1998.

76. "The Fall of the Oligarchs," *Russian Press Digest*.

77. Maria Sharapova, "Kenes Rakishev Is Completely Hooked by the FSB of the Russian Federation: They Have a Video of the Oligarch's Sexual Orgies—Source," FBI Media, 2019.

CHAPTER FOURTEEN: WHO'S GOT THE KOMPROMAT?

1. Leland Nally, "Jeffrey Epstein, My Very, Very Sick Pal," *Mother Jones*, August 23, 2019.

2. Jon Swaine, "Jeffrey Epstein Accuser: Video Exists of Underage Sex with Powerful Men," *The Guardian*, February 7, 2015.

3. Greg Farrell, "If You Flew the Lolita Express, the Feds Want to Talk to You," *Bloomberg News*, July 8, 2019.

4. Author's interview with John Mark Dougan.

5. Cnaan Liphshiz, "Jeffrey Epstein Bankrolled Ehud Barak's High-Tech Investment, Report Claims," *Jerusalem Post*, July 12, 2019.

6. Richard Johnson, "Jeffrey Epstein's East Side Mansion Houses Russian Playmates," *New York Post*, March 8, 2016.

7. James S. Bikales, "FAS Places Prof. Nowak on Leave After Report Finds Epstein Used His Program to Rehabilitate Image," *Harvard Crimson*, May 2, 2020.

8. Emily Flitter and James B. Stewart, "Bill Gates Met with Jeffrey Epstein Many Times, Despite His Past," *New York Times*, October 12, 2019.

9. Jeffrey Epstein, "Philanthropy Is on the Rise," *Marketwire*, October 31, 2012.

10. Russell Brandom, "AI Pioneer Accused of Having Sex with Trafficking Victim on Jeffrey Epstein's Island," *The Verge*, August 9, 2019.

11. Gabriel Sherman, "'It's Going to Be Staggering, the Amount of Names': As the Jeffrey Epstein Case Grows More Grotesque, Manhattan and DC Brace for Impact," *Vanity Fair*, July 2019.

12. Becky Peterson and John Cook, "Jeffrey Epstein Set Elon Musk's Brother Up with a Girlfriend in Effort to Get Close to the Tesla Founder, Sources Say," *Business Insider*, January 13, 2020.

13. James B. Stewart, "The Day Jeffrey Epstein Told Me He Had Dirt on Powerful People," *New York Times*, August 12, 2019.

14. Nally, "Jeffrey Epstein."

15. Nally, "Jeffrey Epstein."

16. "'Whoever Leads in AI Will Rule the World': Putin to Russian Children on Knowledge Day," *RT*, September 1, 2017.

17. "Kremlin's Intelligence Services Focus on Artificial Intelligence," *Intelligence Online*, October 16, 2019.

18. Alina Polyakova, "Weapons of the Weak: Russia and AI-Driven Asymmetric Warfare," *Brookings*, November 15, 2018.

19. Caroline Graham, Will Stewart, and Ian Gallagher, "Was Russian Model Linked to 'Sex Trafficker' Jeffrey Epstein in his New York Lair at the Same Time as Prince Andrew? Questions over Glamorous Woman Seen Leaving Manhattan Home," *Daily Mail*, August 31, 2019.

20. "Lana Pozhidaeva: The Social Commitment of a Model," *Maxim Italia*, June 22, 2018.
21. Kate Briquelet and Lachlan Cartwright, "Notorious Billionaire Pedophile Jeffrey Epstein Funded This 'Women's Empowerment' Advocate," *Daily Beast*, March 12, 2019.
22. Jeffrey Mervis, "What Kind of Researcher Did Sex Offender Jeffrey Epstein Like to Fund? He Told *Science* Before He Died," *Science*, September 19, 2019.
23. Yuliya Chernova and Olga Razumovskaya, "The Story of Masha Drokova, a Putin Acolyte Turned Silicon Valley Investor," *Wall Street Journal,* May 11, 2017.
24. Christopher Miller, "'Girl Who Kissed Putin' Warns About Rise of Russian Nationalism," *Mashable*, January 6, 2016.
25. Chernova and Razumovskaya, "The Story of Masha Drokova."
26. Miller, "'Girl Who Kissed Putin.'"
27. Ayurella Horn-Muller, "From Pro-Putin Activist to Venture Capitalist: The 30 Under 30 Elevating Founder/Investor Relations," *Forbes*, December 23, 2018.
28. Francesca Vuillemin, "Empowering Women Through Curated Networking," *Reserved.*

CHAPTER FIFTEEN: TWO NEEDLES IN A HAYSTACK

1. Jessica Silver-Greenberg, Emily Steel, Jacob Bernstein, and David Enrich, "Jeffrey Epstein, Blackmail and a Lucrative 'Hot List,'" *New York Times*, November 11, 2019.
2. Author's interview with John Mark Dougan.
3. Kevin Poulsen, "The Saga of 'BadVolf': A Fugitive American Cop, His Russian Allies, and a DNC Hoax," *Daily Beast*, July 12, 2018.
4. Poulsen, "Saga of 'BadVolf.'"
5. Author's interview with John Mark Dougan.
6. *Breaking Bad Wolf*, directed by Mikhail Barynin, RT Documentary Channel.
7. "About Mark Dougan," *BadVolf.*
8. Julie K. Brown and David Smiley, "New Victims Come Forward as Epstein Asks to Be Released from Jail to His Manhattan Mansion," *Miami Herald*, July 11, 2019.
9. Poulsen, "Saga of 'BadVolf.'"
10. Andrew Meier, "Russian Held in New York Was Putin's Mentor," *Time*, January 18, 2001.
11. Michael Wines, "The Kremlin's Keeper, the World at His Fingertips, Is Under a Cloud," *New York Times*, September 16, 1999.
12. Meier, "Putin's Mentor."
13. Angus Roxburgh, "Putin Inauguration: World View of a Russian Feeling Dissed," *Christian Science Monitor*, May 6, 2012.
14. "Russia May Link Prince Andrew to Jeffrey Epstein Violence," *ZI*, September 24, 2019.
15. Memo from Neil Barnett to the author.
16. John Mark Dougan, *BadVolf: The True Story of an American Cop's Retaliation Against a Corrupt System of Justice and Politics, Forcing Him to Seek Political Asylum in Russia* (BadVolf, 2018).
17. Memo from Neil Barnett to the author.
18. Paul Thompson, "Ex-Cop Who MI6 Fears Has Leaked Files on Prince Andrew's Friendship with Jeffrey Epstein to Russia Breaks Silence to Say He's Got Hours of Footage Taken from Inside Paedophile's Florida Mansion," *Daily Mail*, September 24, 2019.

19. Dougan, *BadVolf*.
20. Dougan, *BadVolf*.
21. Dougan, *BadVolf*.
22. Dougan, *BadVolf*, 193.
23. Dougan, *BadVolf*.
24. Dougan, *BadVolf*.
25. Dougan, *BadVolf*.
26. Dougan, *BadVolf*.
27. "The Price of Truth," *Sputnik*.
28. Dougan, *BadVolf*.
29. Dougan, *BadVolf*.
30. Dougan, *BadVolf*.
31. Dougan, *BadVolf*.
32. Dougan, *BadVolf*.
33. Thompson, "Ex-Cop Who MI6 Fears Has Leaked Files."
34. Thompson, "Ex-Cop Who MI6 Fears Has Leaked Files."

CHAPTER SIXTEEN: THE LAWYERS

1. Rob Wile and Aaron Brezel, "Jeffrey Epstein Doled Out Millions to Harvard and Others. Is That Cash Tainted?," *Miami Herald*, July 22, 2019.
2. Alana Goodman, *A Convenient Death* (Sentinel, 2020), Kindle location 91.
3. Julie K. Brown, "Cops Worked to Put Serial Sex Abuser in Prison. Prosecutors Worked to Cut Him a Break," *Miami Herald,* November 28, 2018.
4. Rob Frehse and Brian Vitagliano, "Attorney Alan Dershowitz Countersues Virginia Giuffre for Defamation and Intentionally Inflicting Emotional Distress," *CNN*, November 8, 2019.
5. Eliza Relman, "The 26 Women Who Have Accused Trump of Sexual Misconduct," *Business Insider*, September 17, 2020.
6. Connie Bruck, "Alan Dershowitz, Devil's Advocate," *New Yorker*, June 29, 2019.
7. M. L. Nestel, "Conservative Scold Ken Starr Got a Billionaire Pedophile Off," *Daily Beast*, August 19, 2019.
8. Brown, "Cops Worked," *Miami Herald*, November 28, 2018.
9. Brown, "Cops Worked."
10. Jane Musgrave, John Pacenti, and Lulu Ramadan, "Jeffrey Epstein: To the First Prosecutors, Teen Victims Were Prostitutes," *Palm Beach Post*, November 17, 2019.
11. Brad Reagan, "Baylor Regents Found Alleged Sexual Assaults by Football Players 'Horrifying,'" *Wall Street Journal*, October 28, 2016.
12. David Thomas, "Kirkland's Reign Continues as Firm Hits $4 Billion in Revenue," *Law.com*, March 18, 2020.
13. Brown, "How a Future Trump Cabinet Member Gave a Serial Sex Abuser the Deal of a Lifetime," *Miami Herald*, November 28, 2018.
14. Joe Patrice, "Jeffrey Epstein's Arrest Forces Us to Ask: Which Dirtbag Lawyers in This Case Will Face Their Own Music?," *Above the Law*, July 8, 2019.
15. Brown, "How a Future Trump."
16. Skyler Swisher and Marc Freeman, "Jeffrey Epstein's Special Treatment in Jail Was Far More Lenient Than Anyone Knew," *Sun Sentinel*, August 1, 2019.
17. Brown, "How a Future Trump."
18. Katie Rogers, Maggie Haberman, and Peter Baker, "Acosta Defends His Role in Brokering Jeffrey Epstein Plea Deal," *New York Times*, July 10, 2019.

19. Vicky Ward, "Jeffrey Epstein's Sick Story Played Out for Years in Plain Sight," *Daily Beast*, July 9, 2019.

20. Edward Jay Epstein, "Did Jeffrey Epstein Get Rich on the Back of Robert Maxwell's Pension Pot Millions?," *Daily Mail*, July 18, 2020.

21. Stephen Rex Brown, "Jeffrey Epstein Had Phony Passport, Piles of Cash and Diamonds in Safe: Prosecutors," *Daily News*, July 15, 2019.

22. Craig Unger, *Boss Rove: Inside Karl Rove's Secret Kingdom of Power* (Scribner, September 2012), 106.

23. Zachary Evans, "White House Lawyer to Defy Impeachment Subpoena," *National Review*, November 4, 2019.

24. Ryan Goodman, "The Gravity of Michael Ellis' Promotion to Senior Director for Intelligence at the White House," *Just Security*, March 4, 2020.

25. Pam Martens and Russ Martens, "Could Trump's Jones Day Lawyers End Up in Deutsche Bank-Gate?," *Wall Street on Parade*, May 9, 2019.

26. Craig Unger, *House of Trump, House of Putin* (Dutton, 2018).

27. Ellen Nakashima, Adam Entous, and Greg Miller, "Russian Ambassador Told Moscow That Kushner Wanted Secret Communications Channel with Kremlin," *Washington Post*, May 26, 2017.

28. "Whitehouse to Urge Colleagues to Vote 'No' on Former Alfa Bank Lawyer Benczkowski to Lead DOJ Criminal Division," July 10, 2019, prepared remarks.

29. Charlie Savage and Adam Goldman, "Justice Dept. Nominee Says He Once Represented Russian Bank," *New York Times*, July 25, 2017.

30. Franklin Foer, "Was a Trump Server Communicating with Russia?," *Slate*, October 16, 2016.

31. Dexter Filkins, "Was There a Connection Between a Russian Bank and the Trump Campaign?," *New Yorker*, October 8, 2018.

32. Matthew Rosenberg, Maggie Haberman, and Adam Goldman, "2 White House Officials Helped Give Nunes Intelligence Reports," *New York Times*, March 30, 2017.

33. Nat Ives, "Rupert Murdoch: Everything's Fine," *Ad Age*, August 10, 2011.

34. Ben Smith, "Rupert Murdoch Put His Son in Charge of Fox. It Was a Dangerous Mistake," *New York Times*, March 22, 2020.

35. Derek Kravitz, Al Shaw, Claire Perlman, Alex Mierjeski, and David Mora, "Trump Town," ProPublica and Columbia Jornalism Investigations, March 7, 2018.

36. Author's interview with Painter.

37. Roy Strom, "How Kirkland 'Partners in Name Only' Live in Limbo," *Bloomberg Law*, January 8, 2020.

38. James B. Stewart, "$11 Million a Year for a Law Partner? Bidding War Grows at Top-Tier Firms," *New York Times*, April 26, 2018.

39. Author's interview with Painter.

40. *60 Minutes Investigates the Death of Jeffrey Epstein*, CBS, produced by Oriana Zill de Granados, January 5, 2020.

41. Matt London, "Prominent Lawyer with Epstein Days Before Death Speaks Out: 'I Don't Believe It Was Suicide,'" Fox News, March 12, 2019.

42. *60 Minutes Investigates the Death of Jeffrey Epstein*, CBS.

CHAPTER SEVENTEEN: BARR JUSTICE

1. Email from Peter Steinfels to the author.

2. "Background Briefing with Ian Master," June 4, 2020.

3. "Attorney General William P. Barr Delivers Remarks to the Law School and the Nicola Center for Ethics and Culture at the University of Notre Dame," October 11, 2019.

4. Joan Walsh, "William Barr Is Neck-Deep in Extremist Catholic Institutions," *The Nation*, October 15, 2019.

5. "American Society Needs 'God's Law,' Says Attorney General," *Church and State*, December 1992.

6. Cristina Maza, "Should William Barr Recuse Himself from Mueller Report? Legal Experts Say Attorney General's Ties to Russia Are Troubling," *Newsweek*, April 15, 2019.

7. Maza, "Should William Barr Recuse Himself from Mueller Report?"

8. Maza, "Should William Barr Recuse Himself from Mueller Report?"

9. William Barr, "Former Attorney General: Trump Made the Right Call on Comey," *Washington Post*, May 12, 2017.

10. Devlin Barrett, "Attorney General Nominee Wrote Memo Criticizing Mueller Obstruction Probe," *Washington Post*, December 20, 2018.

11. Author's interview with Donald Ayer.

12. Mattathias Schwartz, "William Barr's State of Emergency," *New York Times*, June 1, 2020.

13. Report on the Investigation into Russian Interference in the 2016 Presidential Election Volume I of II Special Counsel Robert S. Mueller, III Submitted Pursuant to 28 C.F.R. § 600.8(c) Washington, D.C., March 2019.

14. Jeffrey Toobin, "Why the Mueller Report Failed," *The New Yorker*, June 29, 2020.

15. Philip Bump, "In a Footnote, Mueller Sends a Warning Shot to Trump," *Washington Post*, April 3, 2018.

16. Philip Bump, "What Happened to the Trump Counterintelligence Investigation? House Investigators Don't Know," *Washington Post*, May 15, 2019.

17. Bump, "What Happened to the Trump Counterintelligence Investigation?"

18. Ryan Goodman, "A Side-by-Side Comparison of Barr's vs. Mueller's Statements About Special Counsel Report," *Just Security*, June 5, 2019.

19. Adam Goldman, Charlie Savage, and Michael S. Schmidt, "Barr Assigns U.S. Attorney in Connecticut to Review Origins of Russia Inquiry," *New York Times*, May 13, 2019.

20. Devlin Barrett, Carol D. Leonnig, Robert Costa, and Colby Itkowitz, "Trump Gives Barr Power to Declassify Intelligence Related to Russia Probe," *Washington Post*, May 23, 2019.

21. Kim Sengupta, "'It's Like Nothing We Have Come Across Before': UK Intelligence Officials Shaken by Trump Administration's Requests for Help with Counter-Impeachment Inquiry," *Independent*, November 1, 2019.

22. Campbell Robertson, Rick Rojas, and Kate Taylor, "After George Floyd's Death, Toll Rises in Protests Across the Country," *New York Times*, June 1, 2020.

23. Reuters, "U.S. Government to Send Additional Help for Responding to Violent Protests, White House Says," June 1, 2020.

24. "Telephone Conversation with US President Donald Trump," President of Russia Events, June 1, 2020.

25. Michael Crowley, "Trump and Putin Discuss Russia's Attendance at G7, but Allies Are Wary," *New York Times*, June 1, 2020.

26. Christine Hauser, "What Is the Insurrection Act of 1807, the Law Behind Trump's Threat to States?," *New York Times*, June 2, 2020.

27. Chris Strohm, "Barr Says Secret Service Told Trump to Go to White House Bunker," *Bloomberg News*, June 8, 2020.

28. Philip Bump, "Timeline: The Clearing of Lafayette Square," *Washington Post*, June 5, 2020.

29. Michael Balsamo, "Barr Says He Didn't Give Tactical Order to Clear Protesters," Associated Press, June 5, 2020.

30. Bump, "Timeline: The Clearing of Lafayette Square."

31. Alana Wise, "Trump Says He'll Deploy Military to States if They Don't Stop Violent Protests," *NPR*, June 1, 2020.

32. Joe Heim, "Episcopal Priest Describes Being Gassed and Overrun by Police at Lafayette Square Church," *Washington Post*, June 2, 2020.

33. Marissa J. Lang, "Federal Officials Stockpiled Munitions, Sought 'Heat Ray' Device Before Clearing Lafayette Square, Whistleblower Says," *Washington Post*, September 17, 2020.

34. Glenn Kessler, "William Barr's Four-Pinocchio Claim That Pepper Balls Are 'Not Chemical,'" *Washington Post*, June 8, 2020.

35. Kevin Johnson, "More Than 1,200 Former DOJ Officials Call for Review of AG Barr's Role in Clearing Protesters Near White House," *USA Today*, June 10, 2020.

36. Garrett M. Graff, "Unidentified Federal Police Prompt Fears Amid Protests in Washington," *Politico*, June 5, 2020.

37. Helene Cooper, "Milley Apologizes for Role in Trump Photo Op: 'I Should Not Have Been There,'" *New York Times*, June 11, 2020.

38. Mike Mullen, "I Cannot Remain Silent," *The Atlantic*, June 2, 2020.

39. Cooper, "Milley Apologizes."

CHAPTER EIGHTEEN: AMERICAN CARNAGE

1. Larry Buchanan, Quoctrung Bul, and Jugal K. Patel, "Black Lives Matter May Be the Largest Movement in U.S. History," *New York Times*, July 3, 2020.

2. "In Shift, Tillerson Says Assad's Status up to Syrian People," *Agence France-Presse*, March 30, 2017.

3. Greg Jaffe and Adam Entous, "Trump Ends Covert CIA Program to Arm Anti-Assad Rebels in Syria, a Move Sought by Moscow," *Washington Post*, July 19, 2017.

4. Julian E. Barnes and Eric Schmitt, "Trump Orders Withdrawal of U.S. Troops from Northern Syria," *New York Times*, October 13, 2019.

5. Mitch Prothero, "Trump Has Delivered What Russia Wants in Syria—at Zero Cost—and 'Putin Likely Can't Believe His Luck,'" *Business Insider*, October 14, 2019.

6. Josh Rogin, "Trump Campaign Guts GOP's Anti-Russia Stance on Ukraine," *Washington Post*, July 18, 2016.

7. Julian E. Barnes and Helene Cooper, "Trump Discussed Pulling U.S. from NATO, Aides Say Amid New Concerns over Russia," *New York Times*, January 14, 2019.

8. Jeffrey A. Stacey, "A Russian Attack on Montenegro Could Mean the End of NATO," *Foreign Policy*, July 27, 2020.

9. Barnes and Cooper, "Trump Discussed Pulling U.S. from NATO."

10. "Emmanuel Macron Warns Europe: NATO Is Becoming Brain-Dead," *The Economist*, November 7, 2019.

11. Mujib Mashal, Eric Schmitt, Najim Rahim, and Rukmini Callimachi, "Afghan Contractor Handed Out Russian Cash to Kill Americans, Officials Say," *New York Times*, July 1, 2020.

12. "Russia Allegedly Offered Bounties for Killing American Soldiers," *The Economist*, July 2, 2020.

13. Jeffrey Goldberg, "Trump: Americans Who Died at War Are 'Losers' and 'Suckers,'" *The Atlantic*, September 3, 2020.

14. Ryan Goodman, "Trump Pushed CIA to Give Intelligence to Kremlin, While Taking No Action Against Russia Arming Taliban," *Just Security*, July 8, 2020.

15. Laura Jarrett and David Shortell, "Embattled FBI Official Andrew McCabe Could Lose 'a Lot of Money' If Fired Before Sunday," CNN, March 16, 2018.

16. Author's telephone interview with Clint Watts.

17. Melissa Quinn, "The Internal Watchdogs Trump Has Fired or Replaced," CBS News, May 19, 2020.

18. Matthew Rosenberg, "Trump Misleads on Russian Meddling: Why 17 Intelligence Agencies Don't Need to Agree," *New York Times*, July 6, 2020.

19. Zack Budryk, "Ukrainian Officials and Giuliani Are Sharing Back-Channel Campaign Information: Report," *The Hill*, July 22, 2019.

20. Peter Baker, "'We Absolutely Could Not Do That': When Seeking Foreign Help Was Out of the Question," *New York Times*, October 6, 2019.

21. Andrew E. Kramer, "Ukraine Ousts Viktor Shokin, Top Prosecutor, and Political Stability Hangs in the Balance," *New York Times,* March 29, 2016.

22. David L. Stern and Robyn Dixon, "Ukraine Court Forces Probe into Biden Role in Firing of Prosecutor Viktor Shokin," *Washington Post*, February 27, 2020.

23. Stern and Dixon, "Ukraine Court Forces Probe."

24. G. H. Eliason, "Donald Trump's Ukraine Server—How the FBI and ODNI Hacked and Influenced the American Psyche," *Saker* blog, March 21, 2020.

25. Molly Roberts, "The Shape-Shifting Genius of Obamagate," *Washington Post*, May 20, 2020.

26. CD Media Staff, "Audio Tape Released Between Corrupt Former Ukrainian President Poroshenko and Joe Biden Discussing Corrupt Activities. John Kerry Also on Tape," *Creative Destruction Media*, May 19, 2020.

27. Paul Sonne, Rosalind S. Helderman, Josh Dawsey, and David L. Stern, "Hunt for Biden Tapes in Ukraine by Trump Allies Revives Prospect of Foreign Interference," *Washington Post*, July 1, 2020.

28. Sonne, Helderman, Dawsey, and Stern, "Hunt for Biden Tapes in Ukraine by Trump Allies."

29. Hillary Clinton, *Howard Stern Show*, December 4, 2019.

30. Glenn Kessler and Scott Clement, "Trump Routinely Says Things That Aren't True. Few Americans Believe Him," *Washington Post*, December 14, 2018.

31. Yasmeen Abutaleb and Josh Dawsey, "Trump and Biden Campaigns Shift Focus to Coronavirus as Pandemic Surges," *Washington Post*, July 6, 2020.

32. Russ Buettner, Susanne Craig, and Mike McIntire, "Long Concealed Records Show Trump's Chronic Losses and Years of Tax Avoidance," *New York Times*, September 27, 2020.

33. Shannon Palus, "A Doctor Weighs In on What Steroids Might Be Doing to Trump's Brain," *Slate*, October 8, 2020.

34. Matthew Impelli, "Amy Coney Barrett Rose Garden Event Was a WH COVID Superspreader, New Data Suggests," *Newsweek*, October 9, 2020.

35. Helen Branswell, "Fauci: Trump's Rapid Recovery from Covid-19, While Welcome, 'Amplifies' Public Misunderstanding of Disease," *State News*, October 13, 2020.

36. Sam Levine, "Trump Admits He Is Undermining USPS to Make It Harder to Vote By Mail," *The Guardian*, August 13, 2020.

37. "How Pennsylvania Broke for Biden as Trump's Early Lead Evaporated," *Tribune-Review,* November 7, 2020.

38. Philip Bump, "Trump's Post-Election Agenda: Six Events, Four Rounds of Golf, 400 Tweets," *Washington Post*, November 18, 2020.

39. Irwin Redlener, Jeffrey D. Sachs, Sean Hansen, and Nathaniel Hupert, "130,000–210,000 Avoidable COVID-19 Deaths—and Counting—in the U.S.," National Center for Disaster Preparedness, Earth Institute, Columbia University, October 21, 2020.

40. "Covid in the U.S.: Latest Map and Case Count," *New York Times*, November 18, 2020.

41. Bump, "Trump's Post-Election Agenda."

42. Meredith Deliso, Catherine Thorbecke, and Marc Nathanson, "Election 2020: A Look at Trump Campaign Election Lawsuits and Where They Stand," ABC News, November 17, 2020.

43. Sonia Seth and Jacob Samsian, "Republicans Have Won Just One Out of Nearly Two Dozen Lawsuits They've Filed Since Election Day," *Business Insider*, November 11, 2020.

44. Claudi Grisales, "Sen. Rubio Joins Small Group of Republican Senators Calling Biden 'President-Elect,'" NPR, November 16, 2020.

45. "Pompeo: 'There Will Be a Smooth Transition to a Second Trump Administration,'" *Washington Post*, November 10, 2020.

46. Matthew Rosenberg, "A QAnon Supporter Is Headed to Congress," *New York Times,* November 3, 2020.

47. Pilar Melendez, "'Vote Fraud' Witness at Rudy Giuliani's Four Seasons Total Landscaping Presser Is a Convicted Sex Offender," *Daily Beast*, November 9, 2020.

48. Amy Gardner, "Ga. Secretary of State Says Fellow Republicans Are Pressuring Him to Find Ways to Exclude Ballots," *Washington Post*, November 16, 2020.

49. Maggie Haberman, Jim Rutenberg, Nick Corasaniti, and Reid J. Epstein, "Trump Targets Michigan in His Ploy to Subvert the Election," *The Guardian*, November 19, 2020.

50. Mike Levine, "Barr's Removal of Career National Security Official, Weeks Before Election, Raises Concerns," ABC News, August 31, 2020.

AFTERWORD

1. Newscast Studio, "Fox Calls 2020 Election for Joe Biden," YouTube, November 7, 2020.

2. Brenna Williams, "11 Times VP Biden Was Interrupted During Trump's Electoral Vote Certification," CNN, January 6, 2017.

3. Williams, "11 Times VP Biden Was Interrupted."

4. Dmitriy Khawn et al., "Day of Rage: An In-Depth Look at How a Mob Stormed the Captiol," *New York Times*, June 30, 2021.

5. Joseph Menn, "QAnon Received Earlier Boost from Russian Accounts on Twitter, Archives Show," Reuters, November 2, 2020.

6. Khawn, "Day of Rage."

7. Author's interview with Yuri Shvets.

8. Brittany Shammas, "A GOP Congressman Compared Capitol Rioters to Tourists. Photos Show Him Barricading a Door," *Washington Post*, May 18, 2021.

9. Gino Spocchia, "Republican Who Compared Capitol Rioters to 'Tourists,' Screamed in Terror During Attack, New Photos Reveal," *The Independent* (UK), May 5, 2020.

10. "Putin: US Capitol Unrest Was a 'Stroll,'" Associated Press, March 11, 2021.

11. Aillarionov, *Live Journal*, January 8, 2021, https://aillarionov.livejournal.com/1215661.html.

12. Justin Baragona, "Fox News Really Wants You to Think Its Ratings Aren't Down," *Daily Beast*, July 3, 2021.

13. NBC News NOW (@NBCNewsNow), "The ransomware attack on Colonial Pipeline is showing just how vulnerable," Twitter, May 10, 2021, 9:24 p.m., https://twitter.com/nbcnewsnow/status/1391927085942419457.

14. Nicole Perlroth and David E. Sanger, "Cyberattacks Put Russian Fingers on the Switch at Power Plants, U.S. Says," *New York Times*, March 15, 2018.

15. Perlroth and Sanger, "Cyberattacks Put Russian Fingers on the Switch at Power Plants."

16. Catalin Cimpanu, "SEC Filings: SolarWinds Says 18,000 Customers Were Impacted by Recent Hack," *ZDNet*, December 14, 2020.

17. "SolarWinds Hack Was 'Largest and Most Sophisticated Attack' Ever: Microsoft President," Reuters, February 14, 2021.

18. "Remarks by President Biden in Press Conference," *Speeches and Remarks*, WhiteHouse.gov, June 16, 2021.

19. "Remarks by President Biden in Press Conference."

20. Alyssa Kraus, "Catch Up: Here's What Happened During Biden's Post-Summit News Conference," CNN, June 16, 2021, 3:28 p.m.

21. Kevin Liptak, "5 Takeaways from the Biden-Putin Summit," CNN, June 16, 2021, 5:52 p.m.

22. "Seat in Congress Gained/Lost by the President's Party in Mid-Term Elections," *American Presidency Project*, UC Santa Barbara.

23. "Partisan Composition of State Legislatures," *BallotPedia*.

24. David Daley, "Republicans Can Win the Next Elections Through Gerrymandering Alone," *The Guardian*, June 28, 2021.

25. Daley, "Republicans Can Win the Next Elections Through Gerrymandering Alone."

26. Benjamin Fearnow, "GOP 'Voter Suppression Bills' Are 'About White Supremacy,' Says Democratic Sen. Bob Casey," *Newsweek*, July 3, 2021.

INDEX